Marvelous Protestantism

Marvelous Protestantism

Monstrous Births in Post-Reformation England

Julie Crawford

The Johns Hopkins University Press
Baltimore

© 2005 The Johns Hopkins University Press
All rights reserved. Published 2005
Printed in the United States of America on acid-free paper

Johns Hopkins Paperback edition, 2012
9 8 7 6 5 4 3 2 1

The Johns Hopkins University Press
2715 North Charles Street
Baltimore, Maryland 21218-4363
www.press.jhu.edu

The Library of Congress has catalogued the hardcover edition of this book as follows:

Crawford, Julie, 1968–
    Marvelous Protestantism : monstrous births in post-Reformation
England / Julie Crawford.
        p.   cm.
    Includes bibliographical references and index.
    ISBN 0-8018-8112-9 (alk. paper)
    1. English literature—Early modern, 1500–1700—History and
criticism.   2. Body, Human, in literature.   3. English literature—
Protestant authors—History and criticism.   4. Protestantism and
literature—History—16th century.   5. Protestantism and literature—
History—17th century.   6. Protestants—England—Intellectual life.
7. Abnormalities, Human, in literature.   8. Marvelous, The, in
literature.   9. Childbirth in literature.   10. Punishment in literature.
11. Reformation—England.   12. Monsters in literature.   I. Title.
PR428.B63C73 2005
820.9'3561—dc22   2004026031

A catalog record for this book is available from the British Library.

ISBN-13: 978-1-4214-0586-5
ISBN-10: 1-4214-0586-5

Contents

Preface

This book focuses on accounts of monstrous births published between the 1560s and the 1660s, the period of most strenuous struggle for the direction of English Protestantism. Beginning with the popular texts of early Protestant reformers, whose stories of monstrous births testified to the errors of Catholicism, the first chapter traces the ways in which stories of monstrous births developed from being anti-papal and anti-monastic signs to being tools for disparate messages of social reform. I show how stories of monstrous births, particularly "fashion" monsters (monstrous births whose deformities resemble the excesses of contemporary fashion), reveal the ways in which superstitious and marvelous effects were put to use by Protestant reformers and how these ideas seeped into social reform, or what scholars have called the "reformation of manners," particularly as it pertained to women. The second chapter focuses on one such issue of social reform—the problem of disorderly or wandering women and their bastard offspring—and argues that while monstrous births were meant to register divine judgment for illegitimate reproduction, the stories in which they are told nonetheless highlight the recognizable, and often sympathetic, crises of the women involved.

Chapter 3 centers on a particular monstrous birth recorded in the parish church of Standish, Lancashire, in 1612, and looks at the uses to which it was put to by one godly minister in a particularly troublesome region and in the popular press. The monster, double-bodied and two-faced, is read both as a punishment for its bastard-bearing parents and as a sign of religious equivocation and dishonesty. In understanding the monstrous birth as a marvelously public exposure of these secret crimes, the minister-author's interpretations betray great fears about the invisibility—and therefore unpoliceability—of private beliefs and behaviors. The stories' references to James I, an arguably two-faced Protestant leader, also reveal the complex uses of the metaphor of the monstrous body politic at both the local and national levels.

The last two chapters focus on the period between the civil wars and the Restoration, when stories of monstrous births were produced in greater numbers than ever before. Chapter 4 examines the ways in which stories of headless monsters embodied the forms of religious dissent in the 1640s, a period that culminated with the beheading of the king. These monsters simultaneously registered the absence of a head, of either church or state, and their mothers' refusals to subject themselves, and their religious beliefs, to patriarchal and ecclesiastical authority. Chapter 5 focuses on the mid-seventeenth-century phenomenon of sectarian women who claimed to be pregnant with Christ by the Holy Ghost and on the story of one such woman's monstrous birth. Reflected through the famous story of the New England antinomians Anne Hutchinson and Mary Dyer—both of whom were accused of giving birth to monsters—as well as a range of equally notorious English cases, the pamphlet story of Mary Adams's monstrous birth addresses a very real religious threat. Yet as part of its publisher's larger agenda, the story also reveals the politically interested, even opportunistic nature of such seemingly incontrovertible tales of divine judgment.

The conclusion of *Marvelous Protestantism* explains the ultimate cultural effect of such revelations, beginning with the stories of prodigious births that accompanied the restoration of the monarchy. While royalist stories erased the mothers' part in producing marvelous births, claiming that they came directly from God to speak exclusively about the restoration of the king, religious dissenters' stories of prodigious births saw them as divine punishments for their parents' corrupt acquiescence to the restored Church of England. The popularity of the dissenters' prodigy tales instigated a concerted effort on the part of learned and Church of England authorities to deem accounts of monstrous births and other prodigies mere propaganda and to discredit the popular belief in prodigies as divine signs. They attempted to achieve this end by locating the belief in prodigies solely in the minds of the superstitious and impressionable: religious "Enthusiasts," especially women. Yet their agenda was not comprehensively achieved. Many later seventeenth-century English Protestants continued to see and deploy monstrous births not only as divine signs but as testament to the power and religious significance of their mother's beliefs, behaviors, and imaginations. Despite the rise of natural science and the persistent accusation of vulgar superstition, traces of this belief system persisted well into the period known as the Enlightenment.

Acknowledgments

In the far recesses of its memory, this book began life as a dissertation at the University of Pennsylvania. No part of this book—or of my career—would have been possible without the example, pedagogy, and support of the Renaissance faculty at Penn: Rebecca Bushnell, Margreta de Grazia, Maureen Quilligan, Peter Stallybrass, and, most substantively, the inimitable Phyllis Rackin. I could not have asked for better teachers. Thanks are also due to the reference librarians at Penn's Rare Book Room: Dan Traister, Michael Ryan, and, especially, John Pollock. Many of my graduate student colleagues at Penn have continued to provide both scholarly and personal support for me and for this project in the years since graduate school, and I am especially grateful to Giselle Anatol, Juliette Cherbuliez, and Rayna Kalas. They have been the best of friends.

Three NYC writing groups have provided invaluable help with conceptualizing and completing this book. I would like to thank Mary Bly, Mario DiGangi, Will Fisher, Bonnie Gordon, Gil Harris, and Natasha Korda; Pam Brown, Bianca Calabresi, Susan O'Malley, Tanya Pollard, Sasha Roberts, Nancy Selleck, and Cristine Varholy; and Rachel Adams, Christina Kiaer, Kristina Milnor, and Sandhya Shukla. I am also grateful for the support of my colleagues at Columbia University, especially Jonathan Arac, David Damrosch, Jenny Davidson, Ann Douglas, David Eng, David Kastan, Joel Kaye, Alice Kessler-Harris, Ed Mendelson, Christia Mercer, Roz Morris, Rob Nixon, Julie Peters, Jim Shapiro, and Paul Strohm; and of my wider community of scholars and friends, chief among them Christina Antonick, Crystal Bartolovich, Sara Beam, Andrew Botterell, Alison Chapman, Jon Connolly, the epically generous Fran Dolan, Leigh Edwards, Rhonda Frederick, Jonathan Grossman, Bill Heinzen, Nora Jaffary, Phil Joseph, Barbara Kigozi, Rue Landau, Debbie Lunny, Jean Lutes, Lily Milroy, Peter Parolin, Litty Paxton, Cindy Port, Julie Schutzman, and Gillian Silverman. I would also like to thank my research assistants John Bird, Tianhu Hao, Ari Friedlander, and Matt Zarnowiecki for their patient and often inventive assistance, and the English and IRWaG office staffs, especially Joy Hayton, Michael Mallick, Yulanda Denoon, the late Kathleen Savage, and Page Jackson. Finally, this book would not be what it is today without the intellectual encouragement, wisdom, and support of Rachel Adams and Jean Howard.

For help with both archival research and obtaining image reproductions and permissions for use in the final product, I thank the staffs of the Folger Shakespeare Library, especially Teresa Taylor; the British National Archives; the Union Theological Library; the British Library, especially Michael Woods; the College of Physicians of Philadelphia; the British Museum; and the county archives of Kent and Lancashire. In addition, I extend special thanks to Todd Lane at the Medical Library at Yale, John-Robert Durbin at the Huntington Library, and John Tofinelli and Sarah Witte at the Columbia University Library. This book owes an enormous debt of gratitude to the anonymous readers for the Johns Hopkins University Press; to the scrupulous copyeditor, Elizabeth Yoder; and to the entire Johns Hopkins staff, especially to its editor, Michael Lonegro, a model of efficiency and professionalism.

Finishing the research for this book entailed many visits to London, where I relied on the hospitality, friendship, and support of Jen Harvie and Deb Kilbride; Eliane Glaser; and, for many weeks over many years, Jane Hunter, Mark, Hugh and Annabel Walsh, who always made me feel like part of their family. My final thanks go to my siblings and their partners, Cindy Crawford, Brian Denega, Ian Crawford, Kate Wilson, Janet McLean, and especially Patrick Crawford, who has always expressed an interest in this book and has offered to cast the movie version; and to my parents, Pat and Bill Crawford, who have offered unflagging support of me and my (often curious) interests and projects over many years. My scholarly grandfather, Pearce Martin, was a big supporter of this book and would have loved to see it in print. For her unfaltering belief in this project, scrupulous scholarly integrity, patience, and all-round intellectual and editorial genius, this book, and everything else I have to offer, is dedicated to Liza Yukins, the greatest thing since pie. During the final stages of this book's production, Jonas was born, and he is perfect in every way.

Marvelous Protestantism

"Strange News" and the Reformation of England

Monsters show us the workes of Nature, not only turned arsiversie, misse-shapen and deformed, but (which is more) they do for the most part dis-cover unto us the secret judgement and scourge of the ire of God.

— E. FENTON, *Certaine Secrete wonders of Nature* (1569)

The ideal punishment would be transparent to the crime that it punishes.

— MICHEL FOUCAULT, *Discipline and Punish* (1977)

In his seventeenth-century diary, the Reverend Oliver Heywood records that when one S.K., the daughter of R. Kershaw of Wyke, was "in troubles of mind about 3 or 4 yeares agoe," he and another minister "spent a day in prayer for and with her." But when her father died, "she shakt off all such, was marryed, betook herself to sensual courses, and is reported to be of a bad carriage, bore a child which was strangly deformed, now at last she hath borne another March 1679, and was thought to be drunk wn she began travelling [travailing]." Alive when it was born, the child was monstrously deformed, with no real legs or arms but "5 things like fingers at the elbows, 5 things like toes at its knees, [and] a soft thing in the place of the head." Heywood ends his recounting with a half moan, half exhortation: "[O]h prodigious hand of God, little observed."[1] In this re-markable account, Heywood suggests that S.K.'s monstrous child is related to her sexual and alcoholic disorderliness, but perhaps more importantly, he un-derstands it as a divine punishment for her moral decline after the loss of her fa-ther and for her failure to be comprehensively comforted and catechized by the religious guidance of Heywood and his fellow preacher. It is S.K.'s "troubles in mind," Heywood implies, that lie behind both her behavior (her "sensual courses" and "bad carriage") and her monstrous birth.

Later in his diary Heywood, himself a nonconformist Protestant, records a disagreement between two other ministers, Dr. Hook and Mr. Lambert, about monsters: "Mr Lambert sd God had a special hand therin for punishing of some sin. Dr. [Hook] started up and cryed out, O blasphemy! wch begot further controversy, and they fell [. . .] into most grievous reproachful words at table before all the company in a very shameful manner." During their argument Hook threatens to "shed out [Lambert's] bowels."[2] Heywood decries their fighting ("oh dreadful, divisions, subdivisions"), but seconds Lambert's claim that deformed children are "rebukes" from God, divine punishment for human errors that proceed with "no magistrate to put them to shame."[3]

This book begins with the question of what it was about the possible religious meanings of monstrous births that caused two men of God to nearly come to blows in a discussion about them. What is the perceived relationship between divine punishment (God's "special hand") and the socioreligious police work, or lack thereof, of earthly ministers and magistrates? What, moreover, does Heywood believe to be the relationship between S.K.'s state of mind and behavior and the monstrous body of her child? And how do such questions about female order relate to questions of divine judgment and the work of the early modern ministry and magistracy? Answers to these questions lie in a genre of published stories about monstrous births that specifically read such births as messages from God, the causes behind their creation and the forms of their monstrosity often carefully adumbrated to the acts and beliefs of the women who produce them. (In such a story, for example, S.K.'s child's headlessness would be read as a sign of her willfulness as well as her failure to subject herself to the appropriate authorities.)

These stories of monstrous births are told, and often illustrated, in materials ranging from books of marvels, chronicles, and midwifery texts to the sermons, diaries, wills, and parish records of the men and women of early modern England. The primary texts I focus on are the numerous broadsheets, broadsheet ballads, and pamphlets published between the 1560s and the 1660s that tell stories of monstrous births and often of the women who produced them.[4] These texts are part of a literary genre that I call "marvelous Protestantism," Protestant fables of divine punishment that provide a rich source of information about, and creative reimaginings of, particular social and religious controversies, and in turn a new chapter in the history of the reading practices of early modern England.[5]

Ultimately, I argue that printed and illustrated stories about monstrous births, one of the most recognizable and popular genres of the early modern period, constitute a specific genre of popular texts, one singularly concerned with reading and interpretation. In these stories the monsters themselves are texts: their bodies are transparent to the crimes they punish, and they render the private beliefs and behaviors of early modern men and women spectacularly legible. The narrative accounts of their production and appearance, moreover, tell us why and how to read them. As the title of one monster pamphlet, *A wonder worth the reading* (1617), suggests, marvelous Protestant texts initiated an interpretive process; each text was a dialogic enterprise that first seduced readers and then provided them with answers to questions they might not even have known they had.[6]

While popular texts about monstrous births have been used as evidence in the history of science and identified as one example of the rise of "yellow journalism," here they are considered as a literary genre with specific conventions and uses.[7] While these materials and their uses have become less understood over time, the chapters that follow remind us how to read them, illuminate the diverse uses to which they were put, and explain their diverse cultural and ideological effects. In claiming that monstrous births "discover unto us the secret judgement and scourge of the ire of God," the authors who told their stories sought not only to claim this ire for their own ends but to help readers "discover" its targets as well.

Hugging Ephemera

In Shakespeare's *The Winter's Tale* (4.4), the chapman Autolycus's pack is full of ballads about strange births. According to the poet Abraham Holland, moreover, early modern readers "hugge[d]" ballads and pamphlets about "Monsters and deformed things" more fervently than the compositions of real poets.[8] John Stockwood similarly criticized buyers who "tarry & stand gasing like silly passengers, at an Anticke picture in a painters shoppe"; John Earle mocked country wenches who melt for "Stories of some men of Tiburne, or a strange monster"; and Sir John Davies satirized the story of "some new freak with two heads recently born in a remote shire of England."[9] Scholars have thus read such stories as low-culture rags, the necessary other to the formation of more serious literary texts.[10] The survival of such a "surprising" number of broadsheets and pamphlets about monsters is seen as a cautionary case against determining the reading patterns of former cultural periods: the survival of these texts is indebted merely to the texts' sensationalism and their woodcut illustrations or to the anachronistic whims of collectors.[11]

Yet to accept the judgment of their condemners—writers invested in promoting other kinds of texts—as the final word on the meaning and purchase of popular stories about monstrous births in early modern England is short-sighted. Such a reading suggests that the success of ephemera about "Monsters and deformed things" is testament, somehow, to its failure; that the stories' very popularity and appeal testifies to their insignificance.[12] In contrast, *Marvelous Protestantism* reads these texts' popularity as testament to their cultural significance. As the quotations above suggest, texts about monstrous births were widely disseminated, read, and talked about in early modern England; they were simultaneously condemned as vulgar and closely associated with the maintenance of social order; and they have survived in an interpretive chain from early modern reader to collector/antiquarian to "new new historicist" in the present day.[13] That readers "hugged" stories about monsters and peered in shop windows at "Anticke pictures" suggests not only that illustrated stories about monsters appealed to readers but also that writers and publishers might have deployed the monstrous story and picture to popularize their messages, reaching a wide audience through visual enticement and content at once sensational and pedagogical.

These messages were, as I have suggested, often religious. An early English translation of Erasmus used a woodcut of a headless monster from the Mandeville stories to present the state of the world "inespeciall of the spiritualite how farre they be from ye perfite trade and lyfe of Criste," intimating connections between deformed bodies and mutilated or imperfect Christianity (fig. I.1).[14] The ballad writer William Elderton published *The true fourme and shape of a monsterous Chyld* in 1565 as part of his ongoing castigation of papists (fig. I.2); William Barley, a printer with godly investments, drafted a monster story entitled *Strange newes out of Kent* (1609); William Jones, who published many tracts against the prelacy, published *A wonder worth the reading* in 1617; and William Leigh, a zealous Puritan reformer, published *Strange News of a Prodigious Monster* in 1613.[15]

Many of the writers and publishers of monster pamphlets were Protestant ministers or proselytizers, and they clearly saw the production and circulation of such marvelous stories as in keeping with their reforming mission. During Mary's reign, the printer of *The true description of two monsterous children borne at Herne in Kent* (1565) had been forced to turn over all copies of Cranmer's *Recantation*, which he had printed, to be burnt.[16] However, a number of the publishers had also been involved in printing wars over the dissemination of other

2ˡ

Here folowith a ſcorneful Image
oꝛ monſtꝛus ſhape of a maruelous
ſtꝛãge fygure called, Sileni alcibi
adis pꝛeſentyng ỹ ſtate ꝗ condiciõ
of this pꝛeſent woꝛld/ ꝗ ineſpeciall
of the Spirituallte how farre they
be from ỹ perfite trade and lyfe
of Cꝛiſte, wrytẽ in the laten
tonge/by that famous
clarke Eraſmus /
ꝗ lately tranſlated in to Englyſhe.

Figure I.1. Title page, Desiderius Erasmus, *Here folowith a scorneful image or monstrus shape of a maruelous stra[n]ge fygure called,* Sileni alcibiadis presentyng ye state [and] condicio[n] of this present world, [and] inespeciall of the spiritualite how farre they be from ye perfite trade and lyfe of Criste, wryte[n] in the laten tonge, by that famous clarke Erasmus, [and] lately translated in to Englyshe (Imprynted at London: By [N. Hill for?] me Iohn Goughe. Cum priuilegio regali. And also be for to sell in Flete-strete betwene the two temples, in the shoppe of Hary Smythe stacyoner, 1543), STC (2nd ed.) 10507[72], title page. Reproduced by permission of the Folger Shakespeare Library.

kinds of religious texts. John Wolf, for example, the publisher of *A Strange and Miraculous Accident happened in the Cittie of Purmerent* (1599), was imprisoned in 1582 for printing a privileged catechism.[17] More significantly, the author-publisher of *A wonder worth the reading* (1617), William Jones, had been imprisoned for publishing Puritan books that attacked the Church of England.[18] Thus, while stories about monstrous births carried educational or catechistical reli-

¶ The true fourme and shape of a monsterous Chyld/
Whiche was borne in Stony Stratforde,in North Hampton shire.
The yeare of our Lord,M.CCCCC.LXV.

¶ This is the fore parte.　　　　　¶ This is the backe parte.

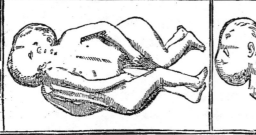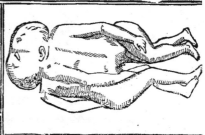

THis Childe was borne on Fryday,being the.xvi.daye of January, betwyxt.vi.and.vii.of the clocke in the morninge,and lyued two howres,and was christened by the Mydwyfe,and are both Women Chyldren, hauing two bodies,ioyning togither.With.iiii.armes, and.iiii.legges perfecte,& from the Nauell vpward one face, two Eyes, one Nose, and one Mouth, and three Eares,one beinge vpon the backe syde of the Head,a lytle aboue the nape of the Necke,hauing heare growinge vpon the Head. Whyche Chylde was borne out of Wedlocke. The fathers name is Rychard Sotherne,who is now fled And the Mother is yet lyuing in the same Towne. And this Childe was brought vp to London,wheare it was seene of dyuers worshipfull men and women of the Cytie.And also of the Countrey. To witnes that it is a Trouth and no Fable, But a warninge of God,to moue all people to amendment of lyfe.

YOu that do see this Childe disfigured here,
　Two Babes in one,disguised to beholde,
Thinke with your selues, when such thinges do appere
　All is not well,as wise heades may be bolde:
　But god that can in secretes shew the signe
　Can bringe much more to pas, by poure deuine.

¶ And we that lyue to see this wonder, howe
　The gase is geuen,to make this meruaile great,
Let one by one that this beholdeth nowe,
　Bewarned as the wonder giues conceate:
　To liue to mende the wonderous shape we see,
　Contrarie much, in all that ought to bee.

¶ For as we finde,this figure semeth straunge,
　Because it showes,proporsion not in vre,
So bare in minde,how time can choppe and chaunce,
　Disguising workes,in willes that be vnsure:
　From meane to more,from more to much excesse,
　Where Nature willes,desire should be lesse.

¶ Finis.　　W. Elderton.

¶ Imprinted at London in Fletestrete beneath the Conduit:at the signe of S. Iohn Euangelist,by Thomas Colwell.

Figure I.2. William Elderton, *The true fourme and shape of a monsterous chyld, whiche was borne in Stony Stratforde, in North Hampton shire* (Imprinted at London: In Fletestrete beneath the Conduit: at the signe of S. Iohn Euangelist, by Thomas Colwell, 1565), STC (2nd ed.) 7565. Reproduced by permission of the Henry E. Huntington Library.

gious messages, they were often resistant or alternative to those promoted by the established church.[19] They were, in other words, polemically casuistical in their intentions, and as such they testify to the battles of English Protestantism in its first generations.

The vast majority of these texts were vividly illustrated, and the "Antick pictures," or woodcut illustrations of monstrous births tell us a great deal about the role of visual imagery in Protestant proselytizing.[20] It has been a largely accepted scholarly commonplace to see early Protestant culture and its iconoclasm as leading to "enormous visual impoverishment."[21] Tessa Watt has complicated this picture of "visual anorexia" by pointing to the range of Christian imagery that did survive the Reformation, including the "idols in the frontispiece" of cheap printed texts.[22] As many scholars have noted, Catholic images were also replaced by the numerous woodcuts of Protestant martyrs featured in John Foxe's *Actes and Monuments of the Church* (1563), a text that brought a new visual vocabulary and focus for repentance and worship to the English populace. But for the most part, the role of the woodcut in the dissemination of Protestant ideas has been minimized. Although reformers made use of the woodcut for antipapal messages, the argument goes, they largely failed to exploit the potential of pictures as a productive way of disseminating Protestant ideas to a wide audience.[23]

Yet most scholars' attempts to retrieve the visual culture of Protestantism— in cheap print, wall paintings, or embroidered biblical scenes—have focused on "traditional Christian imagery."[24] In attempting to understand how the words and ideas of the Protestant religion were translated into visualized experience, scholars have paradoxically limited their focus to precisely those images that were the targets of iconoclastic reform. I argue instead that Protestantism was translated into visualized experience not only in the recognizably Christian (or Catholic) forms that iconoclasm made suspect and in Foxe's *Actes and Monuments*, but in stories and images of an entirely different kind. The broadsheets and pamphlets I focus on tell stories of God's wonder, but instead of featuring the "idols in the frontispiece" that good Protestants disallowed—God, Christ, the Virgin Mary, and the saints—they feature monsters (and occasionally bedridden women and surprised midwives). Indeed, John Day, the future publisher of Foxe's *Actes and Monuments* itself, printed one of the first illustrated broadsheets about monstrous births in 1552, clearly identifying it as a Protestant lesson (fig. I.3).[25]

While, as Watt argues, the godly "factotums" of men and women kneeling in

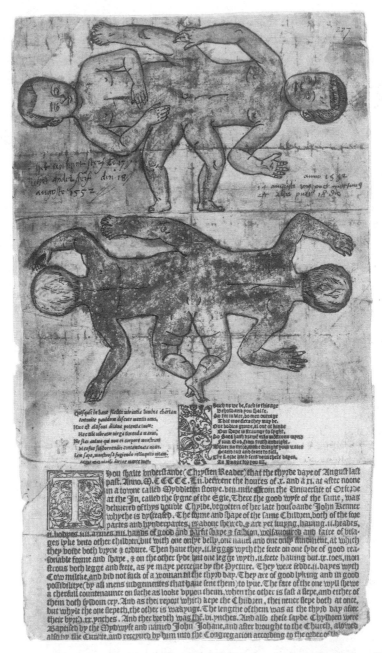

Figure I.3. Conjoined twins born in Middleton Stoney (Imprinted at London by Jhon [John] Day dwellinge over Aldersgate beneth S. Martyns, 1552). Reproduced by permission of the British Museum.

prayer served as familiar trademarks by which the buyer could recognize the religious ballad as a genre, woodcuts of monsters served a slightly more complex advertising purpose, attracting readers to the texts' godly content through the appeal of marvelous images.[26] Protestant fables of marvelous punishment have fascinating stories to tell, and it was in their woodcuts—their "monsters in the frontispiece"—that these messages were both signaled and emblematized.[27] Unlike many early modern woodcuts that were used and reused in a diverse array of texts, seemingly indifferent to the specific details of the images themselves, the woodcuts of monstrous births that I discuss in this book were, with only one exception, created uniquely for the texts they illustrated, suggesting a correlation between story and image integral to the texts' meaning.[28] More than a publishing quirk, the large number of cheap illustrated texts about monstrous births published in the first one hundred years of the English Protestant Reformation is testament to the continual vernacular deployment of stories of monstrous births as tools of Protestant struggle. These visual stories served as objects for Protestant education, reflection, and repentance, but they also made claims for the truth of specific, often controversial, Protestant doctrines and beliefs.

Archives in the Fiction

The arguments and readings in this book understand the Reformation and the spread of English Protestantism, not as a blanket imposition of a new religious order, but as a micropolitical process of reform enacted through local negotiations of belief and conformity. I argue that stories of monstrous births are specific to particular controversies as they were enacted at particular moments and in particular places. My methodologies in reading these stories are thus not only theoretical and theological but local. As studies of early modern social, religious, and cultural history are showing, there was no "English Protestant Culture." There were, instead, different negotiations and sites of religious belief and practice: one village's saints' days were another's popish crimes.[29]

The Book of Common Prayer was intended to create a uniform religious practice for the "whole Realm," but national legislation, whether religious or not, necessarily came into contact with local custom and local practitioners, and Protestant conformity was always a matter of negotiation.[30] Pamphlets with titles like *Strange Newes out of Kent,* and which focused on specific, very local controversies, were part of that negotiation. When one John Hilliard, "Preacher of the word of life in Sopley," published a pamphlet called *Fire from Heaven* about a monster born in his own town, he wrote: "Truly I am perswaded that in this Towne and the parts adioyning, where these Iudgements fell, ther is as much sinne raigning, as there is in a greater parte of the kingdome besides." Through comparisons to God's curse on Sodom and Gomorrah and "infinite other Cities that he hath iustlie plagued for their iniquities," Hilliard uses the monstrous birth as part of his work as Sopley's minister, reading it as punishment for the sins he wants to see reformed in the place in which it was born.

These stories thus attest to a kind of dialogue between the publishing center of London and the other regions of England. Like libels—the mocking rhymes, images, and stories that focused on local malefactors but sometimes made their way to the London press—stories of monstrous births brought county controversies to Fleet street.[31] While the primary audience for such stories may have been local, as Davies's indictment of the popular interest in "some new freak with two heads recently born in a remote shire of England" indicates, the interest in local stories of monstrous births was much broader. Davies's mockery may in fact attest to public interest in the events and beliefs of different counties, an interest informed by an awareness of and curiosity about regional difference and even dissent.[32]

I have discovered that not only were many of the writers of pamphlets about monstrous births ministers or Protestant activists themselves, but many of the mothers, midwives, justices, and witnesses featured in the pamphlets were based on real people involved in real controversies in real towns: godly minister versus recusant neighbor, Puritan versus conformist, sectarian versus Presbyterian. In *Fiction in the Archives* (1987), Natalie Zemon Davis has written on the fictional aspects of pardon tales, the ways in which people seeking pardons for crimes shaped their stories to contemporary explanatory and evaluative habits and narratives. While these fictional elements often stretched credulity, she argues that they served a moral and explanatory purpose that listeners could understand and accept. Stories of monstrous births were also familiar stories; they had an extensive history of warning, portending, and punishing with which readers were undoubtedly familiar. In fact, many monster pamphlets begin with a long list of precedents before they get to the one at hand. Yet stories of monstrous births could also be fitted to specific circumstances; and like pardon tales, they reveal the ways in which seemingly fictional or sensational tales nonetheless address topical issues.

There are, indeed, archives in the fictions of monstrous births: the stories refer to specific places and people, and address topical controversies, governmental legislation, and ecclesiastical laws. Using a methodology similar to Davis's, I look at the relationship between pamphlet stories of monstrous births and the "real" events to which they refer—not to get to "the truth" behind the story or to be what Leah Marcus calls an all-knowing "hunter and gatherer" of topical relevance,[33] but rather, to understand the ways in which tales of monstrous births were framed to substantiate the truth of controversial claims and to tell stories that sought to find not just curious readers but educable ones. Stories of monstrous births were deployed as a way of promulgating views that were not easily expressed elsewhere. Unlike sermons, which were usually subject to strict government control, popular stories often passed through the censors in much the same way as they have passed by some readers even today: as amusing and largely insignificant "strange news."[34]

Exemplary Tales

Long before Luther and Melanchthon established monstrous births as tools of Protestant polemic, monsters were popularly seen as religious signs.[35] The interpretation of monsters as divine comments on contemporary conditions or as divine revelations of or portents for the future had a long history in both the European and English imagination. According to Saint Augustine, monsters were signs of God's power over nature and his use of it for didactic ends.[36] Monsters were closely connected with Christian miracles and the marvelous and were frequently used in early Christian moral literature as objects for catechization and as allegorical images of virtue and vices.[37]

The divinely resonant stories of monstrous births discussed in this book also have their roots in medieval Catholic *exempla*, "pious fictions" of miraculous happenings and divine judgments that were inserted into sermons to confirm or illustrate the preacher's message.[38] In many *exempla*, as in the stories of monstrous births that emulate them, poetic justice is the reigning logic: a nun who eats without making the sign of the cross swallows a devil; the embraces of a drunken man cause the miscarriage of his wife; the dead body of a chaste but proud and talkative nun is burned black from the waist up, while the lower part is left intact.[39] In each story the punishment is, as Michel Foucault puts it, transparent to the crime it punishes, an illustration not only of the nature of the sin but also of its serious material effects. By engaging the imaginations of their listeners, *exempla* sought to teach the basic tenets of religious doctrine and practice, especially to those "vnlearnyd in the laten tonge."[40] "By redyng thys tale," one *exempla* concludes, "ye may lerne to knowe the x commaundementes and the vii dedely synnes,"[41] not as abstract concepts, but as lived realities.

Protestant stories of marvelous happenings similarly claimed pedagogical and catechistical aims. One seventeenth-century author claims that he uses his prodigies to "draw out instructions for learning, and information of the unlearned, and simpler sort," to make "some good use of them, to the benefit and good of our soules." [42] Yet as I suggested earlier, the lessons they taught were rarely as straightforward as the Ten Commandments; Protestant *exempla* often addressed the more controversial aspects or unresolved questions of reformed religion. In stories of monstrous births, these controversies—ranging from the form of marriage ceremonies to the nature of the indwelling of the Holy Ghost—are legible both in the monsters' bodies, which imaginatively and visually reflect the crimes they punish, and in the simultaneously moralistic and marvelous stories of their production.

The phrase "marvelous Protestantism" is thus only seemingly counterintuitive. It highlights the relationship between Protestantism and the marvels and miracles to which it was only ostensibly opposed.[43] Miracles were among the Catholic tenets and "superstitions" that Protestants rejected, claiming that "the age of miracles was over" and that everything God had wanted to reveal through miraculous revelation was already known.[44] Protestants thus decried the 1607 Catholic story of a miracle-working child as a "forged tale" and "a plain lie invented to win grace to the popish faction."[45] Yet despite Protestant efforts to discredit them, miracles were still understood by many to be revelations of divine will. Thus, many people who wanted to prove the divine truth of their doctrine or beliefs, including Protestants, claimed miraculous or marvelous signs as vindicating messages.[46] This is in many ways the argumentative dilemma in which the Reverend Oliver Heywood and his fellow ministers found themselves. Although the Reformation officially discredited Catholic miracles as superstition, Protestantism, as Keith Thomas pointed out years ago, nonetheless deployed many supernatural beliefs of its own.[47]

To alleviate this theological paradox, reformed theologians and philosophers endeavored to distinguish secular from sacred objects of wonder, differentiating between miracles (supernatural events "performed directly by God without mobilizing secondary causes") and marvels (preternatural or unusual occurrences).[48] Yet in actual practice, miracles and marvels were not so easily differentiated.[49] While monstrous births were technically marvels—unusual disruptions in natural processes—this did not preclude them from bearing divine significance.[50] As one monster pamphlet writer claimed, "[A]lthough Philoso-phers (and physitians) would attribute all these impeditions and alterations of Nature to secondary causes," they need to "look higher, and to take notice of the speciall hand of God, whose worke alone it is to sort and compound the activi-ties of secondary causes."[51] Thus, while monstrous births were category-defy-ing "wonders"—they made observers stand back and marvel at their singular-ity—they were also signs which required immediate investigation into their divine significance.[52]

Each monstrous birth thus pointed toward some larger significance; it de-manded, as *A wonder worth the reading* reminds us, to be read. Protestant writers and publishers who interpreted monstrous births as public and visible demon-strations of God's intentions took advantage of the interpretive confusion over the nature of marvels and miracles. Stories of monstrous births avoided contra-dicting the official Protestant doctrine that miracles had ceased, but they none-theless claimed to embody divine messages and to teach readers how to inter-pret them.[53] While these stories of marvelous Protestantism encouraged their readers to "look higher, and to take notice of the speciall hand of God," they were nonetheless always intimately concerned with what was happening down on earth.[54]

Morbid Symptoms and the Reproduction of Protestantism

In the period between the Elizabethan settlement and the restoration of the monarchy in 1660, the forms of English Protestantism were unstable, and threats to its establishment came less from Roman Catholicism than from within Protestantism itself. Antonio Gramsci has argued that during a period of crisis in authority, when "the old is dying and the new cannot be born," there appears "a great variety of morbid symptoms."[55] A central argument of this book is that for almost all early modern people the birth of a monster, a morbid symptom, signaled a crisis in the reproduction of religious and social norms and institu-tions. Monstrous births, which were usually dead at birth or died shortly there-after, were morbid symptoms in that they registered both disorder and death, but they also attested to a larger problem: the illnesses of which they were symp-tomatic.

The monster, moreover, represents a particular kind of crisis, intimately in-volved with bodies and their (re)productivity. As Lyndal Roper has pointed out, the term *crisis* is actually drawn from the pathology of the body: the moment of crisis in medicine is when the body either rallies from illness or succumbs to it.[56] The birth of a monster does not resolve the crisis it signals; instead, it points to the crisis's regenerative possibilities. Simultaneously a birth and a death, a monstrous birth attests to both the deadly seriousness of the illness and to the very real threat of its continued reproduction.[57] For while the monstrous body may succumb to the illness or disorder of which it is symptomatic, the body that produced it often rallies. Although monsters have often been discussed as signs or warnings from God, appearing directly to observation as if they came through no mediating body, the majority of the monstrous births I discuss in this book do not just appear; they are made, and understood to be made, in women's bodies. It is *women* whose acts and behaviors produce monsters. In stories of monstrous births, the crises of post-Reformation England occur, not in an abstract collective body politic, but in the disparate and gendered bodies of English believers.

The language of birth is of course a ubiquitous feature of Renaissance and Christian discourse, and the English Reformation itself is often presented in both early modern and modern critical thought as a birth. Patrick Collinson's *The Birthpangs of Protestant England* (1988) argues that Protestant England was born after Elizabeth ("Like the twins Esau and Jacob, whose contention began in the womb, the birthpangs of the English Reformation brought forth discordant triplets: Church, Dissent and Popery"), and Christopher Haigh's essay "The English Reformation: A Premature Birth, a Difficult Labour and a Sickly Child," interprets the Reformation through a metaphor of troubled reproduction.[58] Many early modern people understood the Reformation in similar terms: in his diaries, the Puritan Nehemiah Wallington states that the "poor church of God [. . .] is like a woman with child near her travail, which would fain bring forth and cannot"; and in his *Directions* (1658), Richard Baxter appeals to those already about the work of religious reformation that they "miscarry not in the birth."[59] Although scholars often assume that this language of reproduction and birth is metaphorical and gender neutral, I argue that it cannot be understood separately from the bodies of women.

All Christians necessarily understood birth as a reminder of Eve's fallibility and her responsibility for original sin. As Genesis 3:16 tells us: "Unto the woman he said, I will greatly multiply thy sorrow and thy conception; in sorrow thou shalt bring forth children, and thy desire *shall be* to thy husband, and he shall rule over thee." Divine punishment for women thus yoked the pain of childbirth to heterosexual desire and patriarchal order, and each birth was a citation of women's responsibility for original sin. As the speaker of Psalm 51.5 testifies, "Behold I was shapen in iniquity, and in sin did my mother conceive me."[60] Yet equally resonantly, it was through a woman, Mary, and a birth, the incarnation of Christ, that humanity was redeemed. While the Reformation displaced the Virgin Mary from her central role in Christian worship,[61] it nonetheless understood women's roles in marriage and the household as key to the implementation and establishment of the Protestant faith.[62] Reformation ideology—what Lyndal Roper has called a "theology of gender"[63]—identified motherhood as a simultaneous punishment and honor. (Luther famously stated that, unlike nuns, married women were sanctified by childbirth.)[64] Each human birth thus evoked both original sin and the promise of redemption, resulting in one of the great paradoxes of Christian life: because of Christ's incarnation, all human beings are, in the words of Julian of Norwich, a "marvelous mixture" of sin and grace.[65]

Stories about monstrous births take the premise of original sin—"Behold, I was shapen in iniquity"—to its logical conclusion: a monstrous birth *is* the shape of wickedness, not only the result of original sin but of more local and immediate forms as well. While a monstrous birth symbolized the triumph of sin (as one broadsheet put it, "A Monster oughly to beholde, conceyved was in syn"), it was never completely "unmixed" from God.[66] The monster's "wicked" shape also reveals the divine presence, exemplifying the intimate ways in which "the prodigious hand of God" works in human bodies.

While Protestants rejected the iconolatry of the Catholic monstrance—the vessel that held and displayed the host, or eucharistic body of Christ, during mass—they dedicated much attention to the divine presence in monstrous births. Both terms, *monstrance* and *monster*, derive from the Latin *monstrare*, "to show or reveal," and Protestant monsters thus shared with the Catholic host a representative schema of divine embodiment and revelation, albeit in punitive form.[67] Christ's incarnation was both the Word made flesh and, via the crucifixion, the means of "condemn[ing] sin in the flesh" (Romans 8:3). As a kind of divine monstrance, the monstrous birth serves a similar function: it is the divine(ly punitive) Word made flesh, condemning sin, quite literally, in human flesh.

The monstrous birth, among its other uses, thus testified that the human body was not completely divorced from the divine.[68] "A mediator between God and the human race," as Augustine puts it, "ought to have something in common with God and something in common with humanity" (*Confessions*, 219). Although Augustine is speaking of Christ, the logic applies equally well to mon-

strous births. In an age in which figurative representations of God were theologically suspect or disallowed, monsters were an ingenious way not only of
showing the divine presence in human life and in human bodies but of teaching,
in some incarnate form or another, the Word. Thus, while I have argued that
the language of birth and reproduction used so pervasively in discussing the Reformation cannot be separated from women's bodies, it also cannot be separated
from the central dilemma of Reformation theology: the question of the relationship between the human and divine. If the true church was going to be born,
it relied not only on God's directives but on human—and in particular, female—
bodies as well. Monstrous births, quite simply, signaled that something was
wrong with the way human beings were living the Word.

Reformist Physiognomy

Although Protestants rejected the Catholic belief that the human body in a
pure and uncorrupted state could reveal the sanctity of the saint, these kinds of
bodily determining questions did not disappear after the Reformation. As the
Puritan writer William Perkins suggested, the central question for Protestants
was "how a man may know whether he be the child of God or no?"[69] Despite
Calvin's insistence upon God's inscrutability and Perkins's own insistence that
"by the outward condition of any man, either in life or death, we are not to judge
of his estate before God," many Protestants did precisely this, searching their
lives and bodies for the outward signs or marks of election.[70] Robert Herrick's
poem "Upon a Scarre in a Virgins Face" plays with such ideas about the signs of
election when the speaker claims to his lover that while scars are "Heresie in others; In your face / That Scar's no schisme, but a signe of grace."[71]

Along with signs of election, certain predestinarian theories supplied the idea
of "markes" of reprobation by which God revealed to the marked "what judgement abideth for them."[72] Indeed, a great deal of providential literature, like *exempla*, illustrated God's judgments upon the transgressors of his commandments
in physical form.[73] Conventionally, diseases that marked the body, such as leprosy or syphilis, were seen as punitive visitations from God, often publicly out-
ing secret or shameful behaviors.[74] A 1496 woodcut by Sebastian Brandt, for example, features God smiting the body of the syphilitic who is "spotted with
whoredom" for all to see (fig. I.4).[75] For many Protestants as well, bodily sickness or disorder testified to a sickness of spirit and was seen as an admonitory
message from God.[76] Perhaps most famously, Shakespeare's Richard III views

¶ Tractatus de peftilentiali Scorra fiue mala de Franzos.
Originem. Remediaq3 eiufdem continens.copilatus a vene
rabili viro Magiftro Jofeph Grynpeck de Burckhaufen.
fup Carmina quedam Sebaftiani Brant vtriufq3 iuris pro
feſſozis.

Figure I.4. Sebastian Brandt woodcut, from Joseph Grunpeck, *Tractatus de Pestilentiali Scorra Sive Mala de Francos* (1496). Reproduced by permission of the Library of the College of Physicians of Philadelphia.

his monstrous physical deformity as a sign that he is not elect or "a man belov'd," and vows that he will instead "make [his] heaven to dream upon the crown."[77] I call this belief system "reformist physiognomy" because it suggests that one could determine from a given bodily form the state of the soul and that the body was transparent to the error, or righteousness, of its conscience.[78] For many Protestants, despite—or perhaps because of—the Protestant doctrinal focus on the inscrutability of God's ways and on the much-touted "inwardness" of post-Reformation belief, physiognomy took on a kind of predestinarian legibility.

Many believed that the effects of reformist physiognomy could carry over to the child, whose bodily form reflected not only its own state of salvation but also that of its mother.[79] Early modern women's prayers for pregnancy often presented childbirth as a joint project between the pregnant woman and God in which the human father is almost entirely absent. In one prayer, a woman asks God: "Wilt thou not bring foorth that which thou hast formed, that I may be delivered of that which I have conceived?"[80] Although the child, true to Protestant doctrine, is understood as God's "work" rather than the mother's—another woman's prayer describes God as a "worke-man," her womb as his "worke-house," and the child his "hand-worke"—the woman's conception and body are nonetheless constituent elements: it is she who "conceives" God's form. One woman's childbirth prayer pleads with God that her "woefull wombe" will bring forth a "sound and perfect creature after thine owne image," while another prays that Christ will let her "see this my dear child without any deformity, which sight is of the wonderful mercy of my God, far beyond my sins."[81] Contrary to Aristotelian dictum that woman provides the matter and man the form, these prayers suggest the extent to which a woman was responsible for "conceiving" her child, in both the biological and theological senses.[82] The child's body testifies to God's intentions and to the mother's ability to conceive of and reproduce those intentions.[83] According to this logic, God provides the perfect form, while the mother is responsible for any deformities or, quite literally, any misconception.

This perceived relationship between sin and deformity was indebted both to a belief in God's constant providential interventions into human life and to ideas about the formative powers of the maternal imagination.[84] Beliefs about the vulnerability and permeability of pregnant women suggested that both external events and the mother's own internal emotions, beliefs, and desires could directly imprint on the child, resulting in miscarriage, stillbirth, or monstrous deformity.[85] The natural philosopher John Baptista Porta explains the role of maternal influence in monstrous births with a literary example, Damascen's report that a certain young woman brought forth a child that was all hairy: "and searching out the reason thereof, he found the hairy image of *John Baptist* in her chamber, which she was wont to look upon." Porta explains the phenomenon thus: "The conceit of the mind, and the force of Imagination is great; but it is then most operative, when it is excessively bent upon any such thing as it cannot attain to. Women with child, when they long most vehemently and have their minds earnestly set upon any thing, do therby alter their inward spirits; the spirits move the blood, and so imprint the likenesse of the thing mused upon, in the tender substance of the child. And surely all children would have some such mark or other, by reason of their mothers longing, if this longing were not in some sort satisfied."[86]

Through altering her "inward spirits," a woman's illegitimate or inappropriate desires leave their traces on the body of her child in "the likeness of the thing mused upon." This theory of maternal imprinting enabled a fantasy of disciplinary access to women's secret longings in which her child's marked body literally revealed the nature of her desires. Thus, although the belief that women's imaginations could influence the outcome of a birth had positive implications— women could "bring forth fair and beautiful children" by placing "in the bedchambers of great men, the images of *Cupid*, *Adonis*, and *Ganymede*"—more often this putative ability was used to reprove them for their illegitimate desires and to curb their behavior.[87] In his book on childbirth, for example, the French gynecologist Jacques Guillemeau writes that "[d]iscreet women, and such as desire to have children, will not give eare unto lamentable and fearefull tales or storyes, nor cast their eyes upon pictures or persons which are uglie or deformed, least the imagination imprint on the child the similitude of the said person or picture."[88] Such formulations assume that women have powerful imaginations; that imagination is an active, largely unpoliceable agency; and that children (contrary to Aristotle) are (in)formed by their mothers' imaginative capacities. They also therefore suggest the importance of controlling the ideas to which women have access as well as the beliefs and desires that animate their imaginations.

Jane Sharp's *Midwives Book* (1671) similarly points out how a mother's "strengthe of mind" can affect the form of her child, but goes on to connect this effect with spiritual danger. Although the child in the mother's womb "hath a soul of its own," she writes, "yet it is a part of the mother untill she be delivered

[. . . and] whatsoever moves the faculties of the mothers soul may do the like in the child" (92–93). The forces that might move "the faculties of the mothers soul" ranged from illicit desires to ill-conceived doctrine or mistaken conscience, and these faculties could imprint the child, whose soul was only tenuously its own, with the physical signs of error. The state of the child's soul, in other words, hung in the balance between the mother's imagination and her spiritual righteousness.

This tenuous balance is the very problematic that reformist physiognomy, especially stories of monstrous births, claimed to bring to light. In *The sicke vvomans private looking-glasse* (1636), John Sadler notes that monsters are outcasts from God: "God himself commanded Moses not to receive [monsters] to offer sacrifice amongst his people . . . because the outward deformity of the body is often a signe of the pollution of the heart, as a curse layd upon the child for the parents incontinency" (136).[89] In this reading, monstrous births are the ultimate reprobates. Estranged from "God's image" and imprinted with their parents' errors, monsters are both outcasts from God and irrefutable testament to their parents' own spiritual reprobation.[90]

While the belief that the sins of the parents might be visited on the bodies of their children was widespread, it was the belief in *maternal* imprinting that was most often used to explain monstrous births. Contingently, stories of monstrous births claimed to bring women's secret desires and erroneous beliefs to public perception and thus condemnation. In many ways women were responsible for forming—with correct consciences and curbed imaginations—the bodies and souls of their children, and thus it was women who were responsible for the reproduction of Protestantism itself. The inverse, of course, was also true. The individual conscience, simultaneously the foundational buttressing and the troubled underground of Protestantism, met with imagination in the process of reproduction, and it was through this fraught process that children, or monsters, were made.[91] Thus the fantasy that one could read the state of the soul from that of the body—a fantasy that endeavored to give insight into God's intentions and render the secrets of the conscience (the inner citadel of Protestant belief) externally and materially legible—found its logical extreme in the monstrous birth. The monster's body was a demonstrable testament to error—sin condemned in the flesh—and the story of its production suggested the necessity of, and the divine sanction for, religious and behavioral conformity. The question of what that conformable Protestantism should look like, however, remained an ongoing and volatile debate for the duration of the sixteenth and seventeenth centuries.

Popular Casuistry

The conscience, what John Dod and Robert Cleaver called "an assises at home in our own soules," was considered by many to be an insufficient guarantor of individual conformity to divine will.[92] Casuistry was the science of applying general rules of conduct to particular cases of moral conscience, particularly in instances where the rules appeared to conflict or their application was unclear. Casuistical texts therefore intended to guide the individual conscience by explaining the law of God as it pertained to particular cases and providing models for readers to help them determine moral choices.[93] Scholars have argued that while Catholics had hundreds of volumes of casuistry to guide their moral theology, Protestant proselytizing relied largely on the "able ministers over the land, applying themselves in every case of conscience, as godly casuists unto all the distressed in mind."[94] (One thinks, for example, of an itinerant Oliver Heywood spending a day in prayer with a young woman experiencing "troubles of mind".) Protestant casuists, according to this argument, put the majority of their energy into sermons and private conferences rather than into print.[95]

Yet perhaps scholars have been looking for Protestant casuistry in the wrong *kinds* of print. Perhaps Protestant casuistry, especially of a more godly bent, was offered to lay people in popular stories that explained, with God's voice and in marvelous form, the answers to controversial matters of practical theology. Stories of monstrous births, I argue, were cases of conscience that intended to provide clear guidelines for religious and moral behavior through marvelously judgmental stories. The authors of these marvelous Protestant texts endeavored to provide readers with a moral theology remarkable both in its narrative and woodcut illustrations and in its message. Peopled as they are with recognizable and even sympathetic characters—resistant women, godly ministers, appalled witnesses, and wavering midwives—the texts address issues of real contention for early modern men and women. The cases of conscience wrestled with in broadsheet and pamphlet accounts of monstrous births involve many of the central religious and moral controversies of post-Reformation England: the religious and social significance of clothing; the legitimate forms of marriage and reproduction; the swearing of oaths and equivocation; conformity to the Book of Common Prayer; and the existence and nature of the signs of election and reprobation.[96] In each text the monstrous birth, through the narrative of its interpreter, testifies on one side of the debate, and its moral judgment is both spectacular and absolute.

In one exemplary pamphlet, entitled *A True and Certaine Relation of a Strange Birth which was borne at Stone-house in the Parish of Plinmouth, the 20 of October 1635*, the author-minister Thomas Bedford uses the monstrous birth to "touch upon a case of conscience, or two," including the necessity of churching women after childbirth, and reads the monster's specific deformities as signs of other doctrinal errors (fig. I.5).[97] Bedford explicitly identifies his text as a kind of popular casuistry (a story which "touch[es] upon a case of conscience or two"), and defends his interpretation against charges of "excesse in religious thoughts" or "overmuch curiositie."[98] For Bedford, as for Oliver Heywood after him, interpreting monsters is neither blasphemous nor an "excesse in religious thought"; it is a religious duty, and one particularly suited to the education of sinners and the guiding of the conscience. The monster, as the French prodigy-compiler Pierre Boaistuau put it in 1560, "hammers at the conscience," forcing each observer to reflect on his or her own sins.[99]

Broadsheets and pamphlets about monstrous births thus press providentialism into the service of claims to religious authority. Understood as a divine punishment, the monstrous birth either supplements extant ecclesiastical laws and punishments or, more often than not, serves as a vindication of those believed to be wrongfully absent. The monstrous birth promises that while earthly governors might ignore social and religious crimes, either through indifference or through commutations of existing sanctions, God will not. His punishment—a monstrous birth—will be both spectacular and noncommutable. In early modern England, punishment was meant not only to punish a crime but to illustrate it, to provide a lexicon for the immediate public perception of its nature and significance. Criminals thus were often forced to hold placards bearing, in illustrated or written form, the nature of their crimes.[100] Their bodies were mutilated with signs of infamy calibrated to reflect their crimes: dissenters' ears, tongues, and hands were cut off; shoulders, arms, and faces were branded with V for vagabond, SS for sower of sedition, and SL for slanderous libeler. Conditions and degrees of guilt could thus be seen at a glance, identifying the body's subjection to King, to God, to Law, and stamping the notion of authority—and, ideally, obedience—into the minds of all who beheld the marked and mutilated bodies.[101]

Figure I.5. Title page, Thomas Bedford, *A True and Certaine Relation of a Strange Birth which was borne at Stone-house in the Parish of Plinmouth, the 20 of October 1635. Together with the Notes of a Sermon, preached Octob. 22 1635 in the Church of Plinmouth, at the interring of the sayd Birth* (London: Printed by Anne Griffin for Anne Bowler dwelling at the Marigold in S. Pauls Church-yard, 1635), STC (2nd ed.) 1791, sig. A2v-A3. Reproduced by permission of the Henry E. Huntington Library.

Yet many crimes, such as adultery and bastardy, were difficult to discern and therefore to punish. Some reformers, like Philip Stubbes, prayed that such sinners "might be cauterized and seared with a hote yron on the cheeke, forehead, or some other parte of their bodye that might be seene, to the end the honest and chast Christians might be discerned from the adulterous Children of Sathan." "But (alas!)" he continued, the vice of adultery "wanteth such due punishement as God his Word doth commaunde to be executed theruppon."[102] Stubbes imagines a system of corporal punishment—branding on the forehead "or some other parte of their bodye that might be seene"—that redresses the failures of earthly magistrates and ministers to execute God's judgments. The pamphlets I discuss in the chapters that follow, articulate a penal system similar to the one fantasized by Stubbes. In these pamphlets, the deformed bodies of monstrous births reference a punitive system that marks the bodies of criminals with specific visible signs of their purported crimes: a limbless monster is a divine version of the earthly punishment for the blasphemer or heretic who was to be "torn limb from limb"; the headless monster a divine form of the earthly punishment reserved for traitors who defied their heads of state or church.[103] Yet monstrous births also provide the kind of policing of the secret or sexual crimes for which Stubbes longed, a visible "branding" executed only by God but vindicating the determinations of his self-appointed 'saints.'

Monstrous births thus combine divine punishment with earthly punishment, making publicly legible those crimes, particularly those by women, which were difficult to police. Monsters were a way of reckoning with the frighteningly invisible interiority of private conscience, but they were also punishments for controversial social crimes. In one pamphlet discussed in chapter 2, for example, the monstrous child of an unmarried woman is born with a deformed ring finger, a clear sign of its mother's sexual error. Such "crimes" as giving birth outside of church-sanctioned marriage were considered by some godly Protestants— whom one historian calls "moral entrepreneurs"—to be religious crimes, and as such inadequately prosecuted by the ecclesiastical authorities.[104] They were crimes that proceeded, in the Reverend Oliver Heywood's phrase "with no magistrate to put them to shame."

As Stuart Hall has noted, "The magistrate and the evangelical police have, or ought to have, a more 'honored' place in the history of popular culture than they have usually been accorded. Even more important than ban and proscription is that subtle and slippery customer—'reform.'"[105] In other words, unlike explicit legislation, popular cultural forms could promulgate reformist views with less didacticism and greater subtlety. Yet in the stories I discuss, the push for religious reform did not come primarily from those in power (the representatives of the Church of England or the king); it came from those who wished to see the Reformation carried further (Puritans, or the "godly"),[106] loosened for individual interpretation (sectarians), or pushed backward (recusants or papists). The monstrous births reported in Protestant texts thus do not simply combine Protestant and 'residual' Catholic belief systems; they deploy divine registers of punishment for ideological control, both by and against the extant, and oft-changing, political and ecclesiastical structures of post-Reformation England.

POPULAR TEXTS about monstrous births do not necessarily provide direct access to the beliefs of those who produced or read them, but they do tell a unique history of early modern England, one in which separations between Protestantism and marvels, between fact and fiction, and between patriarchal control and women's subjection are less clear-cut than they might seem if we only attend to high cultural or prescriptive literature.[107] While they understood themselves to be in competition with "the trifling tales of Gawin and Gargantua," which were "utterly without either grave precept or good example," stories about prodigies and monstrous births were not merely "iestes or fables"; they were something much more serious.[108] Yet although I have focused largely on the punitive and pedagogical aspects of stories of monstrous births, the stories of their production are neither simply admonitory nor morally definitive. The stories may have had reformist intentions, but when someone read or was read to, it was not, as Natalie Zemon Davis puts it, "the stamping of a message on a blank sheet."[109]

All stories are transformed in their reception, and while stories of monster-producing women were certainly judgmental, they were still marvelous stories with popular appeal. As Michel Foucault has written about the circulation of other popular texts about crime and punishment, "the interest of 'curiosity' is also a political interest."[110] That is, a story's appeal may lie as much in its recounted dissent as in its punishment. The reader may be interested in what Thomas Laqueur has called the "humanitarian narrative" of the people and events involved rather than in the moral lesson the pamphlet purports to offer.[111] In stories of monstrous births, the monster is described, pictured, witnessed, and judged. With the divine reprimand before them in such spectacular form, the magistrates and ministers, much as Oliver Heywood wished, put the crime to shame. Yet the stories' parameters and implications are not so easily fixed. Indeed, in a number of pamphlets the monstrous birth is left behind for the scrutiny of ministers and magistrates, but the mother gets away.

CHAPTER ONE

Protestant Reform and the Fashion Monster

In 1523 two of the most influential European Protestant reformers, Philip Melanchthon and Martin Luther, issued a pamphlet entitled *The Papal Ass of Rome and the Monk Calf of Freyberg* (*Deuttung der czwo grewlichen Figuren, Bapstesels czu Rom und Munchkalbs czu Freyerberg ijnn Meysszen funden*) that established stories of monstrous births and their accompanying woodcuts as central tools of Reformation religious polemic. The illustrated pamphlet was meant to serve as a divine indictment of the papal and monastic institutions against which Melanchthon and Luther were working. With his propagandistic use of the monk calf, Luther was conscious of breaking with the medieval chronicle tradition in which monsters and other prodigies foretold general misfortune and political upheaval.[1] "Instead of the general interpretation of monsters as signifying political change through war," he wrote in a 1523 letter, "I incline towards a particular interpretation which pertains to the monks."[2] In Luther's pamphlet the monk calf was not primarily a harbinger of doom or political disaster, but rather an admonitory sign directed toward Catholics and in particular toward the institution of monasticism. A monster warns (*monere*) and demonstrates (*monstrare*), but, Luther suggests, it is a remonstrance aimed at a particular abuse or vice, and it requires an act of interpretation.

While the monk calf was clearly anti-Catholic in its initial instantiation, its eye-catching woodcut and directed critique were immediately recognizable as useful propagandistic tools. It is Luther's shift to "particular interpretation[s]" of monstrous births—pointed readings that outline exactly what behaviors and beliefs a specific monstrous birth signals and reproves—that explains why popular printed stories about monstrous births played such a prevalent role in reforming Europe.[3] In the period following the monk calf's appearance, stories of monstrous births were increasingly deployed for other kinds of Protestant evangelizing, particularly what early Elizabethan Protestants called "preaching."

This chapter takes as its subject the complicated genealogy of the monk calf in the English popular press and imagination. In particular, it focuses on the ways in which related stories of monstrous births, especially monsters whose deformities resembled human fashion excesses, came to be deployed as basic lessons in Protestant doctrine and as tools of social discipline. I argue, moreover, that the success of these marvelous stories relied on the use of discredited Catholic beliefs, particularly in the relationship between the material and the divine, in the service of Protestant reform. Directed toward a populace recently deprived of many aspects of the old religion, these stories were frequently addressed to specific regions that were lacking sufficiently Protestant direction and, increasingly, to women. While the monk calf originally appears as an indictment of Catholicism, its most prevalent legacy lies in the history of the reformation of individual, often female, believers.

The Monk Calf

The monk calf was purportedly born with a large flap of skin on its back and a bald spot on its head, deformities resembling the cowl and tonsure of a monk. The story circulated throughout reforming Europe from the 1523 appearance of Luther's and Melanchthon's pamphlet, and an English translation prepared by an active translator of French Huguenot texts appeared in Elizabethan England in 1579 during a period of particular concern about the infiltration of Jesuits and secular Catholic priests into the country (the English College at Rome was founded in the same year).[4]

As does the original, the translation focuses on a reading of the symbolic meaning of each of the monster's deformities (fig. 1.1). Luther notes that by clothing a calf with a "religious habite, & with a Monkes coole [cowl]," God clearly reveals "that the Monkery is nothing els but a vaine appearance and shewe

HEERE FOLLOWETH THE POR·
trayture or Figure of the other, that is to wit, of a
𝔐oonkisℏ 𝔠alfe, calued after this fashion
in the Citie of Friberge in the countrey of Misne.
Anno. 1528.

Figure 1.1. Title page, *Of two Woonderful Popish Monsters, to wyt, Of a Popish Asse which was found at Rome in the river of Tyber, and of a Moonkish Calfe, calved at Friberge in Misne. Which are the very foreshewings and tokens of Gods wrath, against blinde, obstinate, and monstrous Papists. These bookes are to be sould in Powles Churchyard at the signe of the Parat* (Imprinted at London by Thomas East, dwelling by Paules Wharfe, 1579), STC 17797. Reproduced by permission of the Folger Shakespeare Library.

of godlynesse, and outward hipocrisie of a holy lyfe allowed by God" (14v). The monk calf's physical monstrosity symbolizes the vanity of the monk's claim to achieve holiness through the superficialities of dress (a "*shewe* of godlynesse"), and signals a divine condemnation of his attempts to make or fashion himself into a holy figure through purportedly sacred rituals and forms of dress. The deformed calf's "Moonkish apparaile rent full of holes about the thighes, feete, and belly" signifies that "in that solytarie religion and in those Ceremonies and observations ful of deceits, there is no agreeing that is perfect or whole," and the fact that the monk calf's cowl "was tyed and close behinde at the backe, and that towards the belly or before it appeared to be open or unsewed" (15), signifies monastic lecherousness as well as the incoherence of Catholic doctrine.[5]

The monk calf's central message is thus intimately concerned with clothing: because monks unnaturally attempt to fashion themselves as holy, God, through the divine manipulation of nature, steps in to reprove this presumption with the birth of a monster. In asserting that the monk's "coole" is merely a disguise, Luther asks, "[I]f in taking away the coole or frocke, the Calfe remaineth but a Calfe, what shall the Moonke remaine, when his frocke & coole shal be taken from him?" The question is a familiarly Protestant one, and wholly rhetorical: a monk is nothing but a man, with or without his monastic habit. In Luther's view, Catholic garments have no divinely supported material efficacy. Just as a priest cannot make a surplice holy—a Catholic belief vociferously discredited by Protestants—the assumption of holy garments, as consecrated and ritualized as the act may be, cannot make a monk a legitimate servant of God.

Yet the surprising aspect of the story is that Luther's monk calf does seem to suggest that Catholic garments have material efficacy, even if that efficacy is wholly negative. While Luther explicitly reads the monk calf as a critique of the superficiality of Catholic vestments and habits, the monk calf itself implicitly testifies to their constitutive power. It is the monkish apparel that (literally) makes the calf monstrous and thus makes it visible as a sign of Catholic error. In other words, it is precisely those discredited Catholic beliefs in the efficacy of holy objects—materials blessed by the priest and thus endowed with spiritual power in the Catholic view; "hallowed" by "sorcerers and coniurers" in a critic's view— that animate the monk calf as a critique of Catholicism.[6] Apparel does not make the monk holy, but it does make him monstrous; either way, the figure of the monk calf relies for its effect on the belief that clothing has the power to imprint the wearer. The monk calf is a divinely mandated and hyperbolic version of what Peter Stallybrass and Ann Rosalind Jones have shown to be a fundamental European cultural belief in the "transnaturing" material efficacy of clothing,[7] its significance heightened by traditional Catholic associations between clothing and ritually solicited supernatural power.

Although Luther firmly discredited the idea that priestly or monastic garments were sacred, he was still writing in what scholars have called a "sacralized" world.[8] For Luther, as for those Protestants who followed him, sacred power certainly intruded into the human world, but it came only from God and never at human—and certainly never at Catholic—behest.[9] While Protestants held that Catholics could not solicit or activate divine power through their rituals or consecrations, they did believe that divine power interfered in human lives in ways both mundane and marvelous. The monk calf was clearly a sign of such divine interference.

Both Melanchthon and Luther believed in "physical predictions [. . .] grounded by God in nature" and claimed that "scrutiny of them is in no way at variance with the law of God but contemplation of the divine work and order."[10] While Luther was careful to note that "there is a difference between natural signs and the signs instituted by God," he nonetheless claimed that "when God wills it, a comet glows as a sign of terror, just as when He wills it, the rainbow in the heavens flashes back His sign of grace."[11] Religious attention to natural signs was not, in other words, inimical to early Protestant belief. Yet as we have seen, the power of the monk calf's message also relied on traces of discredited "superstitious" Catholic beliefs in the efficacy of material things. The monk calf works both as a divine sign and as a cultural icon whose very material form embodies the Reformation controversy over the relationship between physical matter, in this case clothing, and divine potency. The story reveals the ways in which even the most theologically foundational Protestants deployed "superstitious" beliefs in their proselytizing efforts.

In the years following, the monk calf makes appearances in a wide range of sixteenth-century European texts, from gynecological treatises to books of wonder. In many of these later texts, however, the monk calf appears, not as a sign of monastic presumption, but as a sign of more secular kinds of fashion excess. In these representations the holes in the monk calf's monastic habit have become the fashionable slashes in doublets and hose; and even when the monk calf itself is not pictured, as in a woodcut of a monstrously deformed English horse, its punitive logic is certainly apparent (figs. 1.2 and 1.3).[12]

The monk calf became a particularly useful referent for English Protestants during the Elizabethan religious settlement of the 1560s. It is in this period that

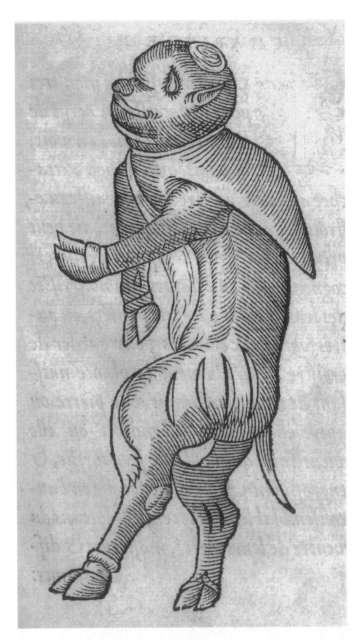

Figure 1.2. Woodcut from Ambroise Paré, *Deux livres de chirurgie I. De la generation de l'homme, & maniere d'extraire les enfans hors du ventre de la mere, ensemble ce qu'il faut faire pour la faire mieux, & plus tost accoucher, avec la cure de plusieurs maladies qui luy peuvent survenir. 2. Des monstres tant terrestres que marins, avec leurs portrais. Plus un petit traité Des plaies faites aux parties nerveuses* (Paris: André Wechel, 1573). Reproduced by permission of Yale University, Harvey Cushing/John Hay Whitney Medical Library.

Figure 1.3. Woodcut from Edward Fenton, *Certaine Secrete wonders of Nature, containing a description of sundry strange things, seming monstrous in our eyes and judgement, bicause we are not privie to the reasons of them. Gathered out of divers learned authors as well Greeke as Latine, sacred as prophane* (London, 1569), STC 10787. Reproduced by permission of the Henry E. Huntington Library.

the representational logic of Luther's monk calf transforms into what I term English "fashion monsters"—monstrous births whose deformities resemble human fashion excesses. Fashion monsters, both animal and human, appeared in such numbers and marvelous forms during the 1560s that they attracted the attention of everyone from a London merchant to the Queen herself. They also became the subject of numerous illustrated published accounts. While the monk calf is not explicitly mentioned in these accounts, they are nonetheless equally concerned with the nexus of issues that the monk calf's story solidified, deploying officially discredited beliefs in efficacious materiality in the service of Protestant reform and providing tools for individual religious contemplation in an era of ostensible visual and imaginative impoverishment. The cultural scene that sets the stage for this flush of stories is pre- and early-Elizabethan London, with its tense and, as I will argue, interrelated controversies over acceptable church vestments and appropriate secular fashions. In such conditions appeared the monk calf's first English afterlife—as a cat.

The Monk-Priest Cat

On April 8, 1554, during the second year of Queen Mary's reign, someone in London hanged a cat. Henry Machyn, merchant tailor of London, records the event in his diary: the cat was hanged on the gallows beside Cheapside Cross, with the crown of her head shaved, wearing a garment "like to that the priest wore that said mass," and holding in her forefeet "a piece of paper made round, representing the wafer."[13] The motivations behind the hanging were undoubtedly contempt for Catholic or popish garments and those who wore them, and the desire to make a spectacular comment on the contemporaneous controversy over the symbolic or mystical nature of the communion "wafer" (here rendered as a flat, inanimate piece of paper in clear representation of the cat killer's Protestant views).

The disfigured cat was clearly intended to mock Catholic beliefs in the power of specific garments and ceremonies. Yet in mocking the material religious symbols of the Catholic faith, the cat-murderer's actions nonetheless attest to the trenchant early modern belief in the power of material objects, particularly clothes, to make figures both recognizable and sources of cultural power. Cats, like calves, certainly had symbolic resonance on their own. While the monk calf accessed popular medieval symbolism of calves as figures of faith, often sacrificed upon altars, cats were more readily pejorative.[14] Known primarily as cunning killers of mice, cats' purported preditoriness was allegorized for many ends, including the condemnation of predatory Catholic and popish priests.[15] Cats were also popularly seen as the familiars or minions of witches and the devil, in much the same way that Protestants were encouraged to see Catholics and their priests.[16]

While the cat killers certainly meant to access these popular beliefs and associations, it was only by shearing the cat's head and dressing her in a surplice—the controversial garment that priests, including English priests, wore at the controversial ceremony called the mass—that the cat became a recognizable figure—a hybrid monk-priest—affording the tableau its power of mockery or, depending on the observer's own beliefs, sacrilege. When Machyn observes the investiture of a number of actual monks two years later—surely one of the last such public rituals in London—he explains how the men were "shorne in" to their identities as monks and notes their "prossessyon after the old fassyon in ther monkes' wede, in collys [cowls] of blake" (119). As we saw with the monk calf, a monk's two defining features were the shorn head and the cowl, and it was through the ritualized assumption of these fashions that ordinary men became (holy) monks. It was precisely these beliefs about clothes, both in their ordinary role of making social relations and public roles meaningful and legible, and in their contested function as sanctifying and efficacious holy objects, that made the hanging of an ordinary cat such an effective message.

After the accession of Elizabeth, church vestments became a central concern of the Elizabethan religious settlement.[17] Were garments such as the one "the priest wore that said mass," "old fassyon" (as Machyn describes the investiture of monks) and irredeemably Catholic and superstitious, or were they a necessary part of the Church of England's liturgy and order? The Thirtieth Elizabethan Injunction (1559) dictated that all of those in ecclesiastical vocation "shall use and weare such seemly habits, garments and such square caps as were most commonly and orderly received in the latter year of the reign of King Edward the Sixth, not therby meaning to attribute any holiness or special worthiness to the said garments, but as St Paul writeth: *Omnia decenter et secundum ordinem fiant* (I Co. 14:40). (Let all things be done decently and in order)."[18] While denying superstitious and Catholic beliefs that these garments held "any holiness or special worthiness," Elizabeth nonetheless supported their continued use as a way of upholding the status of the church and its clergy and, by extension, of herself. In a number of other publications, not to mention her negotiations with bishops, ministers, and critics, Elizabeth repeatedly insisted that ministers in the Church of England wear certain church vestments, in particular the surplice, "for decencie and comely order, uniformitie, and obedience to our Prince" (Avi).[19] In other words, the issue of priestly clothing was Erastian, a matter of Elizabeth's royal control over the church.

However, some Protestant reformers, many of whom would come to be called Puritans, resisted the Queen's insistence on using "the outwarde apparell and ministring garmentes of the popishe church" in their reformed church.[20] Many Protestant critiques of priestly vestments seemed contradictory, simultaneously claiming that vestments were *adiaphora*, or "things indifferent"—without scriptural buttressing, without substantive meaning or efficacy, and unnecessary for salvation—and that they were fundamentally "poisonous." The pollution of Catholic practices, as the Puritan Thomas Cartwright put it, "did stick to the things themselves" and "the wearing of them had power to pollute and make un-

clean the wearers."[21] Thus, while Protestants who refused to wear church vestments denied Catholic belief in the positive powers of vestments—that they
could make their wearers holy—they nonetheless believed that they held a negative or poisonous power.[22] The fact that critics fluctuated between dismissing
clothing as flatly indifferent and protesting against its alarmingly animating potential illustrates the core of the dilemma. Much like the debate over transub-
stantiation, that is, and much like the figure of the monk calf, the vestiarian controversy was intimately engaged with one of the central unresolved matters of
the Protestant reformation: the nature of the relationship between materiality
and divine potency. This debate continued, unresolved, for the duration of the
Elizabethan era.

While the first few years of Elizabeth's reign were deeply concerned with the
role of vestments in the reformed church, they were equally concerned with reg-
ulating secular apparel. During the 1560s, the most active period of the vestiarian controversy, Elizabeth published no fewer than seven proclamations on secular apparel, indicating that her concerns with "decency and order" extended to
all forms of dress. While the regulation of apparel was not new (Elizabeth recy-
cled statutes from the reigns of previous regents), it gained new urgency and resonance during her reign. Elizabeth's insistence that ministers in the Church of
England wear certain church vestments for order and "obedience to our Prince"
was matched by her desire to control the attire, and settle the social legibility
and order, of her other subjects. Conformity in dress was a necessary marker of
social order—as one edict put it, excess in apparel led "to the disorder and confusion of all the degrees of all states"—but most importantly, it was a matter of
the Queen's ultimate power to authorize and make her subjects and, in turn, a
sign of their obedience to her.[23] The seriousness with which Elizabethan authorities viewed matters of secular fashion was made emblematically clear in
another piece of punitive Cheapside street theater, also recorded by Henry
Machyn.

An apprentice, Machyn reports, was pilloried in Cheapside on July 9, 1561,
ostensibly for stealing money from his master but actually for his sartorial presumptions. Machyn records that the "nuw aparell" the apprentice had purchased
with the stolen money—"shurtt, dobelet, and hose, hat, purse, gurdyll, dager,
and butes, spurs, bitt-hose and a skarff"—"dyd hang up on the pelere" (262).
What is most telling in this description is that Machyn makes no reference to
the apprentice's body; only the clothing—the real "matter" of the apprentice's
illegitimate self-fashioning—is displayed upon the pillory. Just as the hanging of

the shorn cat on the gallows was simultaneously an indictment of Catholic beliefs in the power of clothes and a nod to their significance, so does the pillorying of the apprentice's clothes testify to their perceived power. As Jones and Stallybrass have shown, it was substantively through clothing, or fashion—a term derived from the Latin *facere*, 'to make'—that one was made into a subject in early modern Europe: servant or priest, monk or merchant.[24] As Elizabeth well knew, the constitutive agency of clothing was complex: through livery, people were made subject to authority, but through the rejection of livery, or by choosing, buying, or stealing their own attire, people could transform themselves into independent, even rebellious subjects.[25] While the thieving apprentice's actions clearly disrupted the firmly entrenched social legibility that clothing created, it was the widespread belief in the fundamentally transnaturing power of clothing that made his crime so serious and dictated that it was the clothes themselves—the real agents of identity-making—that were to be pilloried.

In Machyn's diary we see, within seven years of each other, two noted hangings—religious and secular spectacles linked via the punitive display of powerful forms of clothing. Indeed, I believe that the debates over the "holiness or special worthiness" of church vestments in the 1560s added a new element to the widespread European belief in the transnaturing power of clothes: their Catholic associations with sacred power and their related Protestant associations with pollution heightened beliefs in the (often dangerously) constitutive and animating power of clothes. At a moment of complex Protestant renegotiations over the efficacy of rituals and material objects, clothing of all kinds was imbued with great symbolic meaning and thus subjected to new scrutiny. The post-Reformation belief in, even obsession with, the transnaturing power of clothing was one of the ways in which the magical or superstitious ideas associated with Catholic belief and ritual were reconfigured in the Protestant era. As Luther deployed the superstitious resonance of material efficacy in his representation of the monk calf's monstrosity, English Protestant reformers in the early 1560s used similar beliefs to warn against secular fashion excesses. Along with human-made public comments on the dangers of clothing, such as the cat priest and the apprentice thief, the privileged figures of such reformist warnings were fashion monsters. The monk calf's second afterlife, the ruffed calf, was one of these.

The Ruffed Calf

A year after he wrote about the pillorying of an apprentice's clothes, Henry Machyn records in his diary that on April 11, 1562, someone brought to London "a pyde calff with a grett ruffe [about] ys neke, a token of grett ruff that bowth men and women [wear]" (280). Immediately following this entry, Machyn notes that the very next month brought "a proclamacion of the aht [act] of a-ray," which limited the wearing of "grett ruffes and grett brechys." For Machyn the ruffed monster is both a transparent indictment of human fashion excesses and a harbinger of a law intended for their reformation. He sees the relationship between the monstrous birth and the act of array as perfectly legible: God's signs inform the work of earthly magistrates, and it is through monstrous births that their labors are portended, if not solicited.

The next month—May 6, 1562, to be exact—did see the publication of *Articles for the due execution of the Statutes of Apparell, and for the reformation of the outrageous excesse therof.*[26] The publication, which insists on the dissemination of the statutes "to all partes and parties," orders "all Justices and officers to whom the reformation [of apparel] may pertayne," to "haue speciall regarde to the obseruation and execution, with all seueritie of the law," ensuring that abusers "shalbe duely punished for theyr offences." The act does, as Machyn accurately notes, refer specifically to ruffs, particularly "double Ruffes, either at the coller or sleves," and dictates that "Ruffes shall not be worne otherwise then single [. . .] as was orderly and comely used before the commynge in of the outrageous double Ruffes, which nowe of late are crept in."[27]

The conjunction between monstrous calf and statute on apparel was, for Machyn, utterly self-evident. As his straightforward account suggests, there was widespread belief in what Robert Scribner has called a "causal nexus" between human error and material consequences: the failure to observe divine and monarchal laws could lead to anything from crop failure and plague to the birth of monsters.[28] Indeed, Elizabethan legislators made specific use of this belief. A special grace "appointed to haue been said" at York upon the accession of Elizabeth in November 1558 wonders how Catholics and other sinners have not been warned by "these vncouth signes in the ayr, these frequent monsters, and these straunge, terrible, and hurtfull tempests whearby as Gods displeasure might be apparaunt vnto all men, euen so his wrathe to be feared of them chefely, as chefely deseruyng the same?"[29] A prayer from the early 1560s similarly focuses on "such fearful tokens of [God's] displeasure," including "horrible and monstrous shapes against nature [. . .] which do betoken to us none other thing, but thy plagues to come upon us for our degenerate and monstrous life and conversation."[30] Less idiosyncratic than ideological, Machyn's interpretation was thus in keeping with a state-supported belief system.

Indeed, Machyn was not the only Englishman who experienced 1562 as a year of monsters. The contemporary historian Sir John Hayward includes in his list of monstrous births born in that year a two-headed foal, a pig with hands, a double-bodied pig, and a whole series of calves and lambs "having collars of skinne growing about their necks, like the double ruffes that then were in use."[31] Many of these monstrous births were recorded in illustrated broadsheets and accompanied by moralizing verses.[32] (For broadside representations of two of the births mentioned by Hayward, the pig with hands and the double-bodied pig, see fig. 1.4.) While governmental and ecclesiastical disciplinary ordinances like the *Articles for the due execution of the Statutes of Apparell* were themselves often widely printed and disseminated, illustrated broadsheet accounts of divinely punitive natural disasters like monstrous births endeavored to both buttress and exemplify the laws' divine mandate.

Machyn's "pyde calff with a grett ruffe [about] ys neke" is one of two monstrous births reported in a broadsheet published by Thomas Marshe in April 1562.[33] According to the accompanying verses, the calf was born with a ruff-like ring of flesh "clapt about his chinne," a detail which should "drive doubtful seeres to prove by speache / Themselves not calves." In discrediting excessive fashion that goes "beyond nature's shape," nature produces, via the supernatural interference of God, a monster. Much like Luther's monk calf, the ruffed calf symbolizes material presumption and excess, but it reproves the "excesse" of secular rather than monastic fashion. The ruff supercedes the cowl as the sign of monstrous presumption, and like the monkish garments, it is credited with a kind of miraculous efficacy, an ability to imprint flesh with its deforming principle.

The publisher of the broadsheet, Thomas Marshe, was actively involved in the production and dissemination of anti-Catholic pamphlets and doctrinally pedagogical Protestant tracts about such issues as Protestant martyrs and priestly marriage.[34] He printed a text for magistrates on how to punish vice, a guideline for sermons on the Gospels, and, in 1566 and 1567, John Stow's *The summarie of Englishe chronicles*. The monster broadsheet seems to have made its way into Stow's text. In his entries for 1562—the same date as the publication of the

Figure 1.4. The Shape of ii. Monsters. MDLxii (Imprinted at London at the Long Shop in the Pultry by John Alde), STC 11485. Reproduced by permission of the British Library.

broadsheet and of Machyn's and Hayward's sighting of the ruffed calf—Stow records the births of many monsters, including "one calfe [which] had a coller of skinne growyng about the necke, lyke to a double ruffe, which to the beholders seemed strange and wonderfull").[35] For Marshe, who also published almanacs and prognostications of future events, the monstrous birth clearly served an effective pedagogical, even evangelizing function not radically distinct from the other Protestant texts he printed.[36]

In fact, many broadsheets, like Marshe's, used terms like "preaching" to describe the work of their monster texts. As scholars of Elizabethan Protestantism have pointed out, preaching was a matter of great concern to many Elizabethan reformers. Given the numbers of clergy deprived from their cures for refusing to sign the Elizabethan Oath of Allegiance, as well as the administrative difficulties of providing the realm with appropriately educated preaching ministers, many of even the most basic lessons of Protestant faith were only haphazardly communicated. Thus, just as Elizabeth wanted her statutes on apparel disseminated throughout the realm to "all partes and parties" both by print and legislation, many reformist writers and printers of popular texts hoped their texts would serve similar ideological or educational functions, either supporting or, with increasing frequency, supplementing Elizabethan legislation. As one broadsheet puts it, God uses monstrous births to call people "to repentaunce and correction of manners"; and still another, much like Henry Machyn, places its monstrous birth in the context of recent social legislation:

Good lawes of late renewde wee see,
Much sinne for to suppresse:
God graunt that they fulfilde maye bee,
To ouerthrow excesse.[37]

The Ruffed Child

Monstrous animals were not the only monsters born in 1562. On August 14, 1562, Bishop John Jewel of Salisbury wrote a letter to the Swiss reformer Heinrich Bullinger that he concluded with a description of the monsters born in England that year, including "infants with deformed bodies, some without heads, some with strange heads; some with trunks but without upper arms, lower arms, or legs; some of them composed of only bones, completely without any meat, just as the pictures of death are painted."[38] This final skeletal monster is also the subject of a ballad broadsheet entitled *A discription of a monstrous Chylde, borne at*

Chychester in Sussex (fig. 1.5).[39] The ballad verses insist that by reading similar stories "in scripture, and elles where," readers will see that "when suche thinges came out of kynde," they declare God's wrath:

> The scripture sayth, before the ende
> Of all thinges shall appeare
> God will wounders straunge thinges sende
> As some is sene this yeare.

While monstrous animals were certainly dire, the author suggests that a human monster, "Procedinge from a Christian brest," is an even more notable condemnation of human sin. The particular monster pictured in the broadsheet is said to demonstrate God's anger at the monstrous "abuse and vyce / That here in Englande now doeth rayne," including fashion excesses, and the author intends for its publication to serve as a focus for repentance for each beholder or reader:

> But here thou haste by Printing arte
> A signe therof to se
> Let eche man saye within his harte
> It preacheth now, to me.

The "Printing arte" provides an object, both visual and exegetical, for personal self-castigation and repentance. (Readers are encouraged, in a strategically ambiguous presentation of the doctrine of predestination, to "amend" their lives in order "To lyue therto, as we should doe / God gyue us all the grace"). The broadsheet offers a simple lesson, rather badly told. Yet its combination of arresting visual effect (the author calls it "A sight to make the[e] quake") and the attempt to give it a wider readerly context—"In scripture, and elles where"—makes the monstrous birth a particularly effective form of preaching.[40] While "reading stories" such as this one can and should lead people to the Scriptures in search of analogous tales, what the "Printing arte" can do is bring signs directly to individual people, encouraging them to read the monster as a personal message ("It preacheth now, to me") and thus as a personal encouragement to reform. As another broadsheet verse puts it, "All ye that dothe beholde and see, this monstrous sight so straunge, / Let it to you a preachyng be, from synfull lyfe to chaunge."[41]

While such popular texts as *A discription of a monstrous Chylde, borne at Chychester in Sussex* were meant to supplement the work of reformers, offering ba-

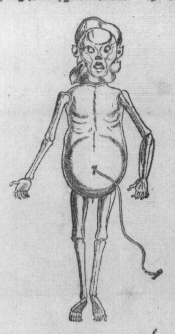

Figure 1.5. A discription of a monstrous Chylde, borne at Chychester in Sussex, the xxiiii. daye of May. This being the very length, and bygnes of the same. MCCCCCLXII. (Imprynted at London, by Leonard Orkin for Fraunces Godlys. In the yeare of oure Lorde, 1562), Huth 50 (33), STC 6177. Reproduced by permission of the British Library.

sic Protestant lessons in entertaining forms, they were also intended to supplement or replace the visual culture displaced or discredited by the iconoclasm of the Reformation. Avoiding the iconolatry of traditional Catholic devotional images such as the *agnus dei*, images of pity, and *arma Christi* (emblematic pictures of the five wounds of Christ), these texts nonetheless combined the visual, marvelous, and doctrinal for personal ends.[42] Rather than simply sensational or generically moralizing, the texts offered basic lessons in, and provided the material means for, individualized Protestant devotional practice. As Bishop Jewel himself suggests, the Chichester monster, especially as it is rendered by the broadsheet's self-consciously signaled "Printing arte," invokes the *memento mori* (it appears, in his words, "just as the pictures of death are painted") and serves a similar representational function: the monstrous birth is a reminder of human mortality and an object for personal repentance.[43] Indeed, contemporary readers certainly saw not just prodigious monsters, but the Chichester monster in particular, in such a light. Someone added a series of sketches of "Prodigies which, contrary to the course of nature, saw the light, Anno Domini 1562" to the will of Margaret Lane, probated and enrolled in March 1562, and the series includes accurate representations of monsters in contemporary broadsheets, including the skeletal monster described and pictured "completely without any meat, just as the pictures of death are painted" and almost identical to the woodcut in the broadsheet account (see fig. 1.6).[44] The compiler of Margaret Lane's will, for one, saw the broadsheet account of a monstrous birth as a kind of *memento mori*, inscribing it right next to the textual record of a woman's life and foreseen death.

Yet while the broadsheet insists that the monster is meant to serve as a focus of repentance for each individual reader, the fact that it explicitly identifies the specific location of the monster's birth—Chichester, Sussex—suggests another important aspect of the reformist intentions of popular stories about monstrous births. Many monstrous births were interpreted not only as the results of specific behaviors but as messages for specific regions, especially in regard to regional problems of social and ecclesiastical order. Chichester, Sussex, for example, was without consistent episcopal leadership between 1558 and 1570, and often without preaching ministers to implement the reforms that such leaders would have desired.[45] While the first decade of Elizabeth's reign was "dominated by a struggle for the parish," as Brian Manning puts it, many of the parish pulpits of Chichester, Sussex, were empty, and many of the people of Chichester retained their habitual, or Catholic, forms of piety.[46] They were not, that is, reformed. It is therefore my contention that such "preaching" broadsheets as *A discription of a monstrous Chylde, borne at Chychester in Sussex*, whose punitive sto-

Figure 1.6. "Prodigies which, contrary to the course of nature, saw the light, Anno Domini 1562" from the will of Margaret Lane. PRO PROB 11/45/fo. 58. Reproduced by permission of the Public Record Office, London.

ries were clearly located in places that needed them, served two related functions: they clarified the basic tenets of Protestant faith (laid out, of course, in greater depth in the Book of Common Prayer, to which readers were encouraged to turn), and they provided a kind of supernaturally vetted form of socioreligious discipline.

If it had become customary in the 1560s to associate monstrous births with the socioreligious discipline of sartorial presumption, the Chichester monster was no exception. John Hayward's interpretation of the monster points out that not only did the monstrous child resemble "an anatomye, without any flesh," but it had about its neck "a collar of fleshe and skinne, pleighted and foulded like a double ruffe, and rising up unto the eares, as if nature would upbraide our pride in artificiall braverie, by producing monsters in the same attires."[47] Indeed, the broadsheet's woodcut represents the monster with a kind of ruffed collar, and its verses allude to the deforming effects of fashion excess.

There were thus a number of "particular interpretations" of the Chichester monster. For the anonymous author of the broadsheet, the monster provided the occasion for a popular print sermon, meant to serve both as a private object for reflection and repentance ("Let eche man saye within his harte / It preacheth now, to me") and as a message to and about a specific region without an effective preaching ministry. For Bishop Jewel, it was a divinely sent *memento mori* reflective of the momentousness of early Elizabethan religious settlement. And for the compiler of Margaret Lane's will, it was a prodigious marker of the passage of an early Elizabethan life. Finally, much like his contemporary Henry Machyn, John Hayward relates the monster's particular deformity to current disciplinary judgments of "double ruffes," and sees it as an "upbraid[ing]" of human pride in "artificial braverie," an association undoubtedly informed by other popular stories of fashion monsters. While the "particular interpretations" of the Chichester monster varied somewhat, they nonetheless relied on popular belief in a causal nexus of punitive warning as well as a "superstitious" mixing of divine agency and human matter. The monster's "preaching," moreover, was clearly widely disseminated and widely effective. Much like the monk calf, it too had its afterlives.

A similar broadsheet entitled *The true discripcion of a Childe with Ruffes borne in the parish of Micheham in the Cou[n]tie of Surrey* records the June 1566 birth of a monstrous "woman childe" named Christian (fig. 1.7). According to the description accompanying the woodcut, the child's body was well proportioned

saving y it is as it were wunderfully clothed with such a fleshly skin as the like at no time hath ben seene. For it hath the saide fleshly skin behinde like unto a Neckerchef growing from the veines of the Back up unto the neck as it were with many Ruffes set one after another and beeing as it were something gathered, every Ruf about an inche brode, having here growing on the edges of the same, & soch Ruffes coming over y Shoulders and covering some part of y Armes proceding up unto the nape of the neck behinde and almost round about the necke, like as many womens Gownes be, not cloce to gither before: but that the throte beeing (with a faire white skin) bare betweene bothe the sides of the ruffes.

The author describes—and holds up for scrutiny—both the monster's "wunderfull" deformity and specific women's fashions: specifically elaborate trelissed ruffs, and gowns that are open at the front. The accompanying verse, "An Admonition to the Reader," refers, like other verses before it, to the great variety of monstrous births born in recent years:

> Our filthy lives in Piggs are shewd,
> our Pride this Childe doth bere:
> Our raggs and Ruffes that are so lewd,
> beholde her fleshe and here [hair].

> Our Beasts and *Cattel* plagued are,
> all monstrouse in their shape:
> And eke this Childe doth wel declare,
> the pride we use of late.

> Our curled here her here doth preche
> our ruffes and gises gaie:
> Our strange attire wherto we reche,
> our fleshe that plese we may.

Although the monster's disfigurements preach a lesson for all beholders to refrain from fleshly pride and fashion excess—"Our curled here her here doth preche"—the final stanza interprets it as a specific message for women:

> And ye O England whose womankinde,
> in ruffes doo walke too oft:
> Perswade them still to bere in minde,
> this Childe with ruffes so soft.

The monster's deformities resemble women's clothing, and it is thus read as an admonitory message specifically for "womankinde."

Like the monk calf, whose clothing does not close properly, signifying the monk's lecherousness ("the Coole was tyed and close behinde at the backe, and that towards the belly or before it appeared to be open or unsewed"), the mon-

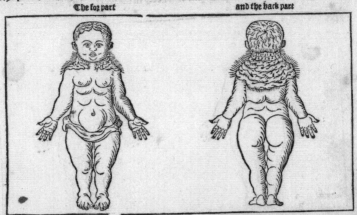

The true discripcion of a Childe with Ruffes borne in the parish of Micheham in the Countie of Surrey in the yeere of our Lord. M.D.LXVI.

The for part   and the back part

This preset yeere of our Lor M.D.Lxvi the .vii. day of June one Helene Iermin the wife of John Iermin Husbandman dwelling in the parishe of Micheham was deliuered of a Woman Childe named Christian beeing aft this maner & fourme following. That is to say, the face comly & of a cheerful countenance. The Armes and hands, Leggs and Feet of right shape, and the Body & all other members therunto appetteining, wel proporcioned in due fourme & order, sauing y it is as it were wunderfully clothed with suche a fleshy skin as the like at no time hath ben seene. For it hath the said fleshy skin behinde like vnto a Neckerchef growing from... verely of the Back vp vnto the neck as it were with many Ruffes set one after another and beeing as it were somthing gathered, euery Ruf about an inche brode hauig here growing on the edges of the same, & so w Ruffes cōming ouer y Shoulders and couering some part of y Armes proceding vp vnto the nape of the neck behinde and almoste round about the neck, like as many womens Gownes be, not close to gtther before: but that the throte beeing (with a faire white skin) bare betweene bothe the sides of the ruffes, the said ruffes about the neck beeing double and as it were thick gathered, muche like vnto the Ruffes that many do vse to weare about their necks.

This Childe beforesaid, the day of the date vnder written, was tobe seene in Glene Alley in Suthwark beeing aliue and v weeks olde and is i dayes not vnlikly to liue long.

An Admonition vnto the Reader,

This picture prest in paper white, our natures doth declare: whose fourme so straunge vp new may lerne vs to beware. (tures spite

By natures spite, what do I saye, doth nature rule the roste: Say god it is say wel I may: by whom nature is tost.

The face ful fair, the members all, in order stand and place: But yet so muche, by natures thrall, doth worke a great disgrace.

This ruffeling world in ruffes al rolde, doth God detest and hate: As we may lerne the tale wel tolde, of Childzen borne of late.

What meanes this childe by natures thus Ruffed for to bee: (wroth But by these Ruffes our natures spurh, we might be bolde and see.

Her squares our squaring both set out, this here our hertes doth cheke: This monstrouse monster out of dout, agreeth in eche respect.

Our filthy liues in Pigg? are shewd, our pride this Childe doth bere: Our ragg? and Ruffes that are so lewd, beholde her fleshe and pere.

Our Beast? and Cattel plagued are, all monstrouse in their shape: And eke this Childe doth wel declare, the pride we vse of late.

Our curled heere her here doth preche our ruffes and gises gate: Our straunge attire wherto we reche, our fleshe that plese we may.

The poet telleth how Daphnes was, transformd into a tre: And Io to a Cow did passe, a straunge thing for to se.

But poets tales may passe and go, as trifels and vntrueth: When ruffes of fleshe as I do troiwe, shall moue vs vnto ruthe.

Deformed are the things we wers, deformed is our hart: The Lord is wroth with all this gere, repent for fere of smarte.

Pray we the Lord our hart? to turn, whilest we haue time and space: Lest that our soules in hel do burn, for voiding of his grace.

And y O England whose womankinde, in ruffes do walke so oft: Parsw ade them stil to bere in minde, this Childe with ruffes so soft.

In fourme as they bothe nature so, a maid she is in deed: God graunt vs grace how euer we go, for to repent with spede.

FINIS. QVOD.

Imprinted at London by John Allde and Richarde Johnes and are to be solde at the Long Shop adioining vnto S. Mildreds Churche in the Pultrie and at the litle shop adioining to the Northwest doore of Paules Churche. Anno domini, M.D.Lxvi.the .xx.of August

Figure 1.7. The true discripcion of a Childe with Ruffes borne in the parish of Micheham in the Countie of Surrey in the yeere of our Lord. MDLXVI (Imprinted at London by *John Allde and Richarde Johnes* and are to be solde at the Long Shop adioining unto S. Mildreds Churche in the Pultrie and at the litle shop adjoining to the Northwest doore of Paules Churche. Anno domini. MDLXVI the xx. of August [1566]), STC 1033. Reproduced by permission of the British Library.

strous child has ruffs "almost round about the necke, like as many womens Gownes be, *not cloce to gother before:* but that the throte beeing (with a faire white skin) bare betweene bothe the sides of the ruffes." The monster is a figure of women's fashion excesses: it exposes them as they expose themselves, and the monstrous throat of the child hyperbolizes the allure of "white skin" provided by contemporary fashion. The idea that a woman's real body (her "faire white skin") can be glimpsed in the apertures of her gown is both highlighted and erased by "Christian's" body; the flesh-ruffs allow no such easy separation between fashion and flesh.

The ruffed child's merger of garment and flesh embodies the belief in the efficacious power of fashion, but it also testifies to the fact that gender identity is not a ground of absolute difference but something constructed through the accretion of material and behavioral details. The ruffed monster demonstrates, in other words, that the "transnaturing" power of clothing can be brought about, even made, by women themselves. The broadsheet thus does more than criticize women's fashions; it serves as an indictment of the fashioning work of women themselves.[48] Monsters, as we will see in the next chapter, are often the products of women, but they are also, as is the case here, figures for women. In encouraging women to "bere in mind" the divine admonition of the monstrous birth, the author of the broadsheet clearly intends the story to be a form of popular preaching specifically directed toward women. While many broadsheets about monstrous births direct all readers to study Scripture and repent for their sins, others, like *The true discripcion of a Childe with Ruffes*, direct their "particular interpretations" at women, identifying women as the causes of monstrous births, the targets of their judgments, and the recipients of their lessons.

In many ways *The true discripcion of a Childe with Ruffes* is a popular echo of the homily on apparel, a lesson most women would readily "bere in mind." From the time of its first appearance in 1563, the Elizabethan "Homilie Against Excess of Apparel" also preached specifically to women.[49] Like *The true discripcion of a Childe with Ruffes*, the homily includes a specific critique of women's apparel, including "fine linen" and "launes," and of "the proude and haughtie stomacks of the daughters of England" who wore them.[50] Rather than behaving "as becommeth Christians," showing subjection to the Heavenly Father (and, for women, their earthly husbands), English women and men "deforme" themselves "by [excessive] aray" (II.6.1–340–41; II.6.1–254). Because of such human failure to fear or obey either God or Queen, the homily intones, "wee needes looke for GODS fearefull vengeance from heaven, to ouerthrowe our presumption and pride" (II.6.1–169–70). *The true discripcion of a Childe with Ruffes* tells the story of a "Christian" female literally deformed by "aray" and provides an example of God's "fearefull vengeance" for the human presumption and pride the homily preaches against. Much like *exempla*, those fantastic tales that enlivened medieval sermons, the broadsheet story of the ruffed child teaches by marvelous example rather than homiletic proscription. Unlike the official Elizabethan publications of the acts of array that simply provided tables listing the appropriate and prohibited forms of Elizabethan fashion (see fig. 1.8), *The true discripcion of a Childe with ruffes* pictures these monstrous fashions as well as their abuse, providing a visual and exegetical synthesis of homily, legislative act, and marvelous tale.

During the 1560s, these broadsheet stories of fashion monsters deployed discredited marvelous and visual effects largely in the service of the Elizabethan settlement. During the years following, as many Protestant activists shifted their focus from reforming the church to reforming society and its behaviors—an enterprise in which they considered the established church insufficiently invested—fashion monsters appeared in slightly different guises.[51] Richard Jones's 1566 publication of *The true discripcion of a Childe with ruffes* was in keeping both with the flush of stories about monstrous births—recognized tools of castigation and reform—and with a trend for cheap printed popularizations of Reformation ideas. During the 1560s and 1570s Jones published popularizations of biblical stories (such as the story of *The destruction of Sodom and Gomorra*) to be sung to popular tunes,[52] anti-papal rhymes, defenses of the Queen against Catholic rebels, a defense of the Sabbath ("With a shorte admonishment to all popish priests and negligent ministers"), and, in 1570, a ballad entitled *A meruaylous straunge deformed swyne.*[53] Around 1580, the period in which Patrick Collinson sees Protestants turning away from the use of popular forms such as songs and ballads, Jones began publishing more recognizably Puritan texts directed towards the reformation of manners: conduct books and guides for Christian living. In 1579 he published Thomas Pritchard's *The schoole of honest and vertuous lyfe: profitable and necessary for all estates and degrees,* and in 1580 William Hergest's *The right rule of christian chastitie,* both of which paid particular attention to guiding the behavior of maids, widows, and "younge gentlewomen."[54] Jones's most successful publication, however, was Phillip Stubbes's *The Anatomie of Abuses* (1583), a text featuring the "most fearefull examples of Gods heauie iudgements inflicted vpon the wicked"—including the monstrous punishment of a proud and overdressed woman.

In his epistle to the reader, Stubbes famously seeks the "reformation of maners and amendement of lyfe," of his fellow Englishmen, and spends a great deal of time condemning "tripartite" pride: "the pryde of the hart, the pride of the mouth, & the pryde of apparell."[55] Stubbes claims that pride of apparel offends God the most: "For as the pride of the heart & mouth is not opposite to the eye, nor visible to the sight, and therefor intice not others to vanities & sin (notwithstanding they be greevous in the sight of God) so the pride of apparel, remaining in sight, *as an exemplarie of evill,* induceth the whole man to wickedness and sinne" (28). Given that pride of apparel is "an exemplarie of evill," it is not surprising that Stubbes, like others before him, relies on judgmental *exempla* to address its threat. Much attention has been paid to Stubbes's rehearsal of the class and gender inscriptions of fashion and its role in anti-theatrical discourse, but Stubbes's condemnation of fashion also has to do with a different kind of material effect. For Stubbes, pride of mouth is less insidious than pride of apparel. "[W]ords fly into the aire, not leaving any print or character behind them to offend the eyes," he writes, but "this sinne of excesse of Apparell remayneth as an Example of evyll before our eyes, and as a provocative to sinne" (30). Unlike words, which, in keeping with Protestant denunciation of Catholic belief in the miraculous and material efficacy of the spoken word, "flye into the aire, not leaving any print or character behind them," fashion, like a dangerous idol, imprints itself both on the eye of the beholder and on the body of the wearer. Stubbes claims to "put no religion" in attire as Papists do, "placing all their religion in hethen garments & Romish rags," as long as English people "observe a meane, and exceade not in pride" (38). Yet for Stubbes, there *is* "religion" in clothing: its association with the arrogant presumptions of Catholic belief has forever tainted fashion. Attire gives rise to pride, and its very material seduction is a form of efficacy.

The Anatomie of Abuses is famous for its enumeration of the fashions of the period: the "slashed, jagged, cut, carved, pincked and laced" doublets, and the "monsterous ruffes" which "stand a full quarter of a yarde (and more) from their [wearers'] necks, hanging over their shoulder pyntes, instead of a vaile" (51). But it is also famous for its almost hysterical belief in the transnaturing power of fashion: "new fangled fashions rather deforme us then adorne us [. . .] makyng us rather to resemble savadge Beastes and stearne Monsters, then continent, sober, and chaste Christians." Most of the fashions he attacks are those favored by women: ruffs made of linen that "will not chafe their tender skinnes, nor ulcerat their lyllie white bodyes," and other garments which "transnatureth them,

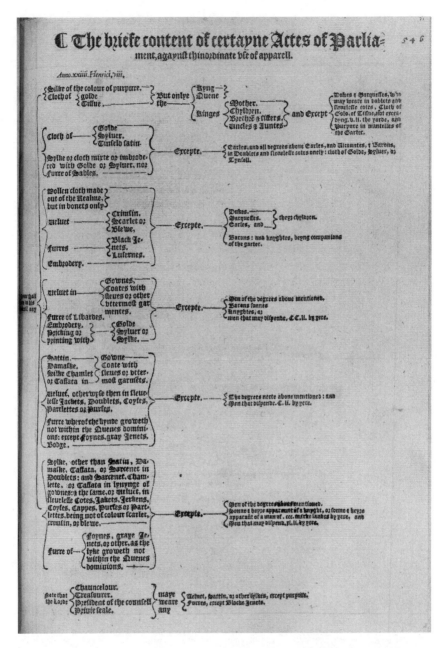

Figure 1.8. The breife content of certayne actes of Parliament, against thinordinate use of apparel (Imprinted at London: In Powles Churchywarde by Richard Iugge and Iohn Cawood, Printers to the Quenes Maiestie, 1562), STC 7952. Reproduced by permission of the Folger Shakespeare Library.

❡ The briefe content of certayne Actes of Parliament,
agaynst thinordinate vse of Apparell.

Anno. xxiiii. Henr. viii.

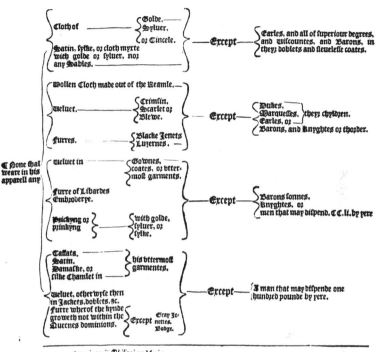

❡ None shal weare in his apparell any

Cloth of — Golde. — Syluer. — or Tincele. / Satin, sylke, or cloth myrte with golde or syluer, nor any Sables. — **Except** — Earles, and all of superiour degrees, and viscountes, and Barons, in theyr doblets and sleueless coates.

Wollen Cloth made out of the Reamle. — Veluet, — Crimsin. Scarlet or Blewe. / Furres. — Blacke Ienets Luzernes. — **Except** — Dukes. Marquesses. } theyr chyldren. Earles, or Barons, and Knyghtes or thorder.

Veluet in — Gownes, coates, or vtter most garments. / Furre of Libardes Embroderye. / Prickyng or prinkyng } with golde, syluer, or sylke. — **Except** — Barons sonnes, Knyghtes, or men that may dispend. C C. li. by yere.

Taffata. Satin. Damaske, or silke Chamlet in — his vttermost garmentes. — **Except** — A man that may dispende one hundred pounde by yere.

Veluet, otherwyse then in Jackets, doblets. &c. / Furre wherof the kynde groweth not within the Queenes dominions. — **Except** Gray Ie nettes. Badge.

Anno. i. & ii. Philippi & Mariæ.

❧ None shal weare anye sylke in

Hatte. Bonet. Nyghtcappe. Gyrdell. Scabarde. Hosen. Shoes. Spurre lethers. — **Except** — The sonne & heyre, or daughter of a knight, or the wyfe of the sayd sonne. A man that maye dispende .xx. li. by yere, or is worth two hundred poundes in goodes.

❡ These be the briefe contentes but of certayne partes of the lawes nowe remaynyng in force, to the obseruation whereof, her Maiestie thinketh best to induce her subiectes by this shorte memoriall, and yet neuertheless wysheth that all of inferior estates, shoulde not neglect the rest of the same lawes, lest if they shalbe founde to contemne these orders here mencioned, they may feele the payne of the rest.

Anno. M. D. LIX. Mense Octobris.

❡ There be certaine other exceptions in the statutes: As for such as haue licence by the Queenes Maiestie or such as shall runne in any Iustes, or shall serue in warre, or shall haue apparel geuen them to be worne by her Maiestie, and such lyke. All which are well to be considered by them that wyll clayme any priuilege therby, and that at theyr peryll.

❧ And where there is mencion made of values of yerely lyuelodes and goodes, the best accompt therof is to be made by the taxations of this last Subsedie, so as if any wyll be excused by pretence of his liuelode or substaunce, to offende, it is as meete that he aunswere to the Prince in Subsedye for that value, as seeke defence to breake any good lawe, wherof her Maiestie geueth to all men admonition.

makinge them weake, tender and infirme" and "deform[ing]" their souls (53, 54, 64). In fact, the range of fashions Stubbes singles out for attack, from the "lyllie white" skin to the particular style of ruffs ("three or foure degrees of minor ruffes, placed gradatine, step by step, one beneath another, and all under the Maister devil ruffe" [71]) are precisely those featured in the broadsheet of the deformed "woman childe," Christian, which Jones published seventeen years earlier.

For Stubbes, human clothing is a sign of the fall, and given that the fall was occasioned by a woman's pride, women's failure to treat clothing as a reminder of sin and mortality is particularly galling. He criticizes women who "weare Lattice cappes with three hornes, three corners I should saie, like the forked cappes of Popishe Priests," and women who metamorphose their hair, "a signe of subjection," into an ornament of pride (67–69). Many medieval *exempla* focused on the punishment of sartorially vain women, and women's monstrous headdresses were the subjects of sermons, satires, and even church *miseres*. While condemnations of proud fashions and their deforming power gained new resonance during the Reformation through their association with polluting Catholic vestments, Stubbes's linking of priest's forked caps and women's fashions suggests the extent to which these connections came to be associated specifically with women.[56]

Stubbes imagines a range of divine judgments for the "presumptuous audacitie" of those women who dared to change God's "woorkmanship" through fashion (64). Among them is the story of "the fearfull Iudgement of God shewed upon a gentlewomen" on May 27, 1582. The woman, the daughter of a rich Antwerp Merchant, prepared herself for a wedding by "plumyng of her self in gorgious arraie." She "curled her haire, she died her lockes, and laied them out after the best manner," but could not get anyone to starch her ruffs. After fighting with the laundress, the woman began "to sweare and teare, to curse and hanne, castyng the Ruffes under feete, and wishyng that the Devill might take her, when she weare any of those Neckerchers againe." The devil obediently transforms himself into a young man, comes to her house, and sets her ruffs so perfectly that the young woman falls in love with him. "This dooen the yong man kissed her, in the doyng whereof he writhe her necke in sonder, so she died miserably, her bodie beyng Metamorphosed into blacke and blewe colours, most ugglesome to beholde, and her face . . . became most deformed, and fearfull to looke upon." When it came time for her funeral, the men went to carry the woman's coffin and could not lift it. When they opened it, they found inside "A blacke Catte, verie leane and deformed, sittyng in the Coffin, setting of great Ruffes, and frizlyng of haire, to the greate feare and wonder of all the behold-ers." Stubbes's story is a version of the proverb "speak of the devil and he will appear" and a sermon-enlivening *exempla*, but it also deploys the now familiar tradition of fashion monsters.[57] Like the popishly attired cat hanged in London in 1554, the ruffed cat is a familiar of sorts, a domestic servant of the devil dressed in his attire. But as a "metamorphosed" version of a proud and blasphemous woman, it is also a material sign of the literally deforming power of fashion and of God's judgment of what Stubbes considers a singularly destructive form of human pride.

Although Stubbes declares his belief in the Elizabethan sumptuary "laws, sanctions and statuts" (44) discussed earlier, his vision of orderly fashion goes beyond Elizabeth's concern with marking degrees and maintaining "decencie." For Stubbes, Elizabeth's statutes were more interested in upholding her power as supreme maker than in producing the godly discipline necessary to reform "Ailgna" (Stubbes's pun on a morally "ailing" England) into an ideal Protestant commonwealth.[58] *The Anatomie of Abuses* is a sustained moral lesson in, and guidebook for, godly discipline. But it is still, like its broadsheet antecedents, an-imated by marvelous, even superstitious, stories. Despite his critique of the pa-pist belief that there is "religion" in clothes, Stubbes nonetheless sees clothes as a route to the supernatural. Like Luther's monk calf, and like the broadsheets that follow it, Stubbes's fashion monster corrals a range of beliefs and effects into the service of specific religious and social judgments. The monk calf's final pur-chase—and, indeed, the purchase of the majority of the subsequent popular texts about monstrous births—is firmly in the realm of behavioral discipline directed at women.

Fashioning Punishments

Fashion monsters were a particularly Elizabethan phenomenon, indebted to a state-buttressed popular belief in divine punishment and intimately concerned with the ambiguous relationship between materiality and divinity. While the sta-tus of holy communion was certainly the most theologically pressing example of Protestantism's renegotiated relationship between materiality and divinity, con-temporary concerns with clothing, and concomitant stories of fashion monsters, were also animated by these debates. My argument throughout has been that from the monk calf to the ruffed child, stories of fashion monsters exploited confusions about the relationship between the material and the divine as well as between individual human beings and their God, creatively rechanneling popular beliefs into the service of Protestant reform. Replacing discredited images of popular devotion and accessing the force of the admonition of the monk calf, broadsheet stories of monstrous births were posited as objects for repentance for all beholders. The genealogy of fashion monsters also indicates the ways in which stories of monstrous births came to be associated with women and interpreted as judgments not only of their behaviors but of their productive capacities. The relationship between disorderly women and the literal reproduction of monsters is the subject of the next chapter, and one final story of fashion monsters offers a preview of the Jacobean pamphlets I will be discussing.

A True Relation of the birth of three Monsters in the City of Namen in Flanders was published in 1609.[59] Like its broadsheet antecedents, the pamphlet focuses on a woodcut image, but it also includes an extensive narrative explaining the circumstances of the births and "the particular interpretation" of their punitive meaning. In this story, anxiety about women's reproductive power, biologically linked to the creation of monsters, is conjoined with concerns about women as makers in other material and social ways. The story focuses on the relationship between the wife of "a poore labouring man," a woman of a good birth "and reputed always vertuous in her living," and her rich sister, a woman both vicious and proud (A4). During her pregnancy, the poor woman sends her husband to seek help from her rich sister in the name of *"womanly Charity"* (A4). The rich woman, however, rejects her sister's appeal, calling her a whore and a bastard. Claiming that she has friends coming to her house "to make merry," she has her servants eject her sister's husband from her house, "saying, It was a fit reward for a begger, that will call a Gentlewoman sister" (A4r). In her attempt to fashion herself as a "Gentlewoman," the rich sister unjustly relegates her sister's family to the socially marginal categories of "begger," "whore," and "bastard," and in direct disobedience to the Book of Common Prayer's catechism ("My duty towards my neighbor is to love him as myself, and to do to all men as I would they should do unto me"), refuses them any form of charity. While their story is about the decline of kinship networks and the failure to achieve a godly commonwealth, it is also, perhaps not surprisingly, about clothes.[60]

When the husband tells his pregnant wife of her sister's unkindness, she falls

Figure 1.9. Title page, *A True Relation of the birth of three Monsters in the City of Namen in Flanders: As also Gods Judgement upon an unnaturall sister of the poore womans, mother of these abortive children, whose house was consumed with fire from heaven, and her selfe swallowed into the earth. All which hepned the 16. of December last. 1608.* STC 18347.5. Reproduced by permission of the Folger Shakespeare Library.

A Citizens wife

Figure 1.10. Images of "A Citizens wife" (*above*) and "A Gentle woman" (*facing*) from John Speed's *Theatrum Imperii Magnae Britanniae* (London, 1616), STC 23044. Reproduced by permission of the Folger Shakespeare Library.

A Gentle woman

immediately into labor and delivers "three Monsters, striking a terrour to those women imployed in that businesse." The monstrous births attest to the materially vulnerable state of women's minds and bodies during pregnancy: the pregnant woman's shock at her sister's behavior literally imprints itself on her children, and the children are transnatured into divine remonstrances for the wealthy sister's crimes. The "ill-proportioned children" are a son and two daughters. The son is born with "a strange misshapen head" and "the fashion of a death's head" upon the back of his right hand (fig. 1.9). His deformity, like that of the skeletal monster Bishop Jewell describes as being "like the pictures of death," is a *memento mori*, and indeed, he predicts death through the coming of a plague. While the daughters' deformities cite fashion excesses, the proximity to the "death's head" suggests the seriousness of their messages as well: human clothing, as both Genesis and Philip Stubbes insist, is a sign of humanity's fall and meant not to be the source of pride but to put us "in minde of mortality."[61] The first daughter "had such dressings, and attyre on the head, by nature of flesh, as women have made by art of Bonelaces, and such like, with a fleshy Wardingale about the middle of it, as if Nature, having forsaken her old fashions, had now devised new" (A4). [62] The second daughter had "about the necke, a Ruffe laced, and Cuffes about the wrests, like the Ruffe, all of flesh, so artificiall in nature, as if Nature in her first work had intreated Arte to help her." The author of the pamphlet draws attention to the inverted relationship between "Nature" and "Arte" in both daughters' deformities, and to the paradox of something being "artificiall in nature" (the very paradox, in fact, of the fashion-monster). One monstrous daughter foretells "that God would punish the world suddenly, for our manifold transgressions," and the other prays to the God that gave her this "forme & life" that he not let her "live here in this world of Pride, of Lust, of Murther, and all wickednesse." Although the monsters are identified as punishments for a wide range of sins, their deformities inscribe specific women's fashions: bonelaces, farthingales, and ruffed collars and cuffs. Like the "woman child" in *The true discripcion of a Childe with Ruffes*, the monstrous daughters in *A True Relation of the birth of three Monsters* are figures of women as well as reprimands for them.

In the pamphlet's woodcut, the monstrous girls are born with the exact same fashions that the rich sister wears. Although the text specifically indicts her behavior, not her attire, it is clear that her headdress and ruffs represent her selfish and presumptuous self-fashioning as a "Gentlewoman." As two images of women included in John Speed's *Theatrum Imperii Magnae Britanniae* (1616) illustrate, the rich sister's dress is the height of early Jacobean fashion, from the high wired coiffure associated with Queen Anne, to the elaborate wired collar and ruffs (fig. 1.10). The rich sister's fashion may visually mark her as a "Gentlewoman," but her pride has more pernicious effects. While the monsters' mother dies of grief, the real punishment is reserved for her "proud, rich, unnaturall sister." As she flees from her burning house, "the willing earth gaped wyde, and swallowed her quick [. . .] And her wealth and all her substance was quite consumed with that quenchlesse fire, till Gods judgement was executed" (Br). The sister, wearing the unnatural signs of her monstrous presumption, is literally returned to nature; the transnaturing power of her own clothes are no match, ultimately, against the supernatural vengeance of God.

Fashion monsters emblematized the troubling effects of the transnaturing power of clothing, the belief that one could make oneself into something (or someone) new by the wearing of clothes. They relied for their punitive force on still-animate, if officially decried, Catholic beliefs in the material efficacy of objects. Stories of fashion monsters, that is, were both residual and reformist. They disseminated Protestant messages in visually and narratively compelling forms, making God's judgment marvelously hyperbolic as a way of buttressing either royal "acts of array" or more puritan messages of social discipline. *A True Relation of the birth of three Monsters in the City of Namen in Flanders* indicates that the monk calf's warnings held true for generations: fashion did bring people to judgment. Whether this judgment was made manifest by a God-made monstrosity or by human "preaching," the story of the fashion monster successfully exhibited the cause, the cry, and the catalyst for reform.

CHAPTER TWO

"The mother of a monster, and not of an orderly birth"

Women and the Signs of Disorder

"If thou ech part wylt understand"

As the broadsheet accounts of fashion monsters attest, in many sixteenth-century tales about monstrous births, the monsters' deformities correspond to specific crimes. *The forme and shape of a Monstrous Child borne at Maydstone in Kent* (1568), for example, encourages its readers to understand the significance of each individual deformity, promising readers both interpretive and moral clarity if they "ech part wylt understand" (fig. 2.1).[1] The woodcut's accompanying verses begin by stating that the monster's "gaspyng mouth" "doth full well declare" human greed, and proceed to an analysis of the fact that

> The hands which have no fingers right
> But stumps fit for no use:
> Doth well set forth the idle plight,
> Which we in these daies chuse.

The monster is also, however, intimately tied to the woman who produced it: one Marget Mere "whoe being unmarried, played the naughty packe, and was gotten with childe."[2]

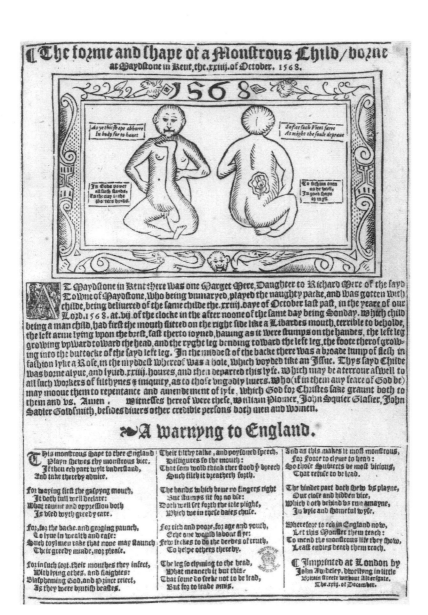

Figure 2.1. The forme and shape of a Monstrous Child borne at Maydstone in Kent, 1568. (Imprinted at London by John Awdeley, dwellyng in little Britain streete without Aldersgate, 1568), STC 17194. Reproduced by permission of the British Library.

Another broadsheet, *The true reporte of the forme and shape of a monstrous childe, borne at Muche Norkesleye* (1562), similarly identifies its monster as a result of a semi-illegitimate union, "begot[ten] out of matrimony" (fig. 2.2). While the monster's numerous "grossest faultes brast out in bodyes forme" are identified as the result of "want or to[o] much store / Of matter"—claims indebted to medical and teratological explanations of monstrous births as the result of insufficient or faulty reproductive matter and processes—the interpretation of the monstrous birth combines this explanatory framework with an analogy between physical deformity and sin. The author analogizes the monster's "want or to[o] much store / Of matter" to its parents' "want of honestye and excesse of sinne" and identifies its deformities as "Resemblyng sinnes." Assuming reader familiarity with monsters and the natural causes of their production, the author recasts this knowledge for specific moral ends: the child's absent limbs are "the shamefull marks / Of bastard sonne in bastard shape decryed" and testament to its parents' sins.

While many broadsheets provide similar interpretations, the monsters that appear in later pamphlets about monstrous births are accompanied by much more complicated narratives of blame for the people and crimes responsible for their production. Going beyond the broadsheets' focus on monsters' physical deformities and their corresponding sins, these narratives are more concerned with the women who produced them.[3] *A most straunge, and true discourse, of the wonderfull iudgement of God* (1600), for example, focuses on a Herefordshire woman who breaks her marriage contract, commits incest, and gives birth to a monster. Unlike some portentous monsters, such as the monk calf or the ruffed child, which seemingly come directly from God and through no notable intervening body, the monsters I discuss in this chapter are clearly identified as birth monsters; it is particular women who produce them. Rather than drawing correspondences between monstrous deformity (such as limblessness) and generic social ills (such as idleness), the stories draw correspondences between monstrosity and specific women's behaviors, particularly as they pertain to controversial post-Reformation debates over the legitimate forms of marriage and reproduction. Each pamphlet account provides a resonantly detailed social context for its monstrous birth, naming not only the place and circumstances of the birth but the identities of the mothers, midwives, ministers, and witnesses involved in each case. As I illuminate the ways in which these texts served as forms of case divinity, providing definitive judgments in controversial cases of behavior, I also argue that their very status as stories, particularly stories that understood them-

¶ The true reporte of the forme and

shape of a monstrous childe, borne at Muche Horkesleye, a village thre
myles from Colchester, in the Countye of Esser, the .xxi. daye
of Apryll in this yeare. 1562.

O, prayse ye God and
blesse his name

His mightye hande hath
wrought the same,

This monstrous world that monsters bredes as
As men tofore it bred by natiue kinde   (rise
By birthes that shewe corrupted natures strife
Declares what sinnes beset the secrete minde.

I meane not this as though deformed shape
were alwayes linkd with fraughted minde with vice
But that in nature god such draughtes doth shape
Resembling sinnes that so bin had in price,

So grossest faultes brast out in bodyes forme
And monster caused of want or to much store
Of matter, shewes the sea of sinne: whose storme
Oreflowes and whelmes vertues barren shore.

Faultye alike in ebbe and eke in flowd,
Like distaunt both from meane, both like extremes.
Yet greatst excesse the want of meane doth shrowde
And want of meane excesse from vertues meanes.

So contaryest extremes consent in sinne
which to bewray to blindest eyes by sight
Beholde a calfe hath clapt about his chinne
His chaunderne rest whence nature placed it right.

And rude dunes doutfull seers to proue by speache
Them selues not calues, and makes the fashion stale,
In him behold by excesse from meane our breache
And midds excesse yet want of natures shape.

To shewe our misse beholde a guiltlesse babe
Reft of his limmes (for such is vertues want)
Him selfe and parentes both infamous made
With sinful byrth: and yet a worldlyng scant.

Feares midwyfes route: bewrayeng his parentes faut
In want of honestye and creesse or sinne.
Made lawfull by all lawes of man, yet halt
Of limmes by God, seayd not the shamefull marke
Of bastard sonne in bastard shape destroyed.

Better farre better bugteen were his lyfe
Than geuen so. For nature iust enuyed
Her gyft to hym: and croyd wyth mayming knyfe
His limmes, to wreake her spyte on parentes sinne,

which, if she spare vnwares so many scapes
As wycked would to brede wil neuer linne
Theyr liues declare theyr maims saued frō theyr shapes
Scorchd in theyr mindes (o cruel prinye mayms
That festreth styll, o vnrecured sore)

Where thothers quiting wyth theyr bodyes shame
Theyr parentes guilt, oft linger not theyr lyues
In lothed shapes but naked flye to skyes.
As this may do whose soune tofore thine eyes
Though want thou seest, a monstrous vglye shape
whom frendly would to sinne doth terme a scape.

N Tupsday being the .xxi. day of Apryll, in this yeare of our Lorde God a
thousand fyue hundred thre score and two, there was borne a man childe
of this maymed forme at Muche Horkesley in Esser, a village about thre
myles from Colchester, betwene a naturall father and a naturall mother
hauing neyther hande, foote, legge, nor arme, but on the left sydei t hath a
Stumpe growynge out of the shoulder, and the ende thereof is rounde,
and not so long as it should go to the elbowe, and on the ryghte syde no
mencion of any thing where any arme should be, but a litel stumpe of one ynche in length, also on the left buttocke there is a stumpe comming out of the length of the thygh almost to the
knee, and round at the ende, and groweth something ouerthwart towardes the place where
the ryght legge should be, and where the ryghte legge should be , there is no mencion of any
legge or stumpe. Also it hath a Codde and stones but no yearde, but a lytell hole for the water
to issue out. Finallye it hath by estimation no tounge, by reason whereof it surketh not, but is
sucoured wyth liquide substaunce put into the mouth by droppes , and nowe begynneth to
fede wyth pappe beyng very well fauoured, and of good and chearefull face.

¶ The aforesayde Anthony Smyth of Much Horkesley husbandman and his wyfe, were
both maryed to other before, and haue had dyuers chyldren, but this deformed childe is the
fyrst that the sayd Anthony and his wyfe had betwene them two, it is a man chylde. This
chylde was begot out of matrimony, but borne in matrimonye. And at the makynge hereof
was liuing, and like to continue.

¶ Imprinted at London in Fletestrete nere to S. Dunstons church by Thomas Marshe.

selves as being in competition for readers, complicate their ultimate effects. While these pamphlets offer resoundingly punitive moral judgments of women's actions, that is, they also feature stories rich with mitigating circumstances—and ultimately, with sympathy.

Corporeal Punishment and "out rage in the flesh"

For many early modern people, monstrous births were public exposures of their mothers' hidden or as-yet-unpunished desires, disorders, and crimes. As such they were imaginatively correlative to the early modern punitive system that deployed physical markings as a way of making crimes and criminals legible. William Harrison's *The Description of England* (1587) spells out this early modern logic of counter-penalties in ways reminiscent of the broadsheets' readings of "Resemblyng sinnes." The offender guilty of manslaughter, for example, "hath his right hand commonlie stricken off," perjurers are "burned in the forhead with the letter *P,*" and those who utter seditious words against the magistrates "are punished by the cutting of one or both ears."[4] While those convicted of sexual infractions such as harlotry and adultery were also physically punished by carting, ducking, and wearing white penitential sheets in churches and markets, the punishments for sexual infractions, as Harrison points out with seeming nostalgia, used to be much more severe. While the adulterer "forfeited all his goods to the king, and his bodie to be at his pleasure," he writes, "the adulteresse was to lose hir eies or nose or both."[5]

This impulse to mark the bodies of sexually disorderly women was prevalent in both legal and popular opinion. In cases of sexual slander, to take one example, indicted slanderers often posited that women who had committed sexual indiscretions should be permanently marked by the signs of their crimes. They called sexually incontinent women "whore face" or "flat nosed whore," suggesting that unchastity could be detected in women's appearances, and threatened to provide these marks themselves by slitting the noses or scratching a "whores marke" into the faces of their targets.[6] This desire to mark those guilty of sexual crimes carried over into fantasies about reproduction. In 1608, a slanderer insulted a woman whom she considered "a nasty suttle queane" by imagining for her a liaison that would produce deformed offspring: "for halfe a crowne I will hire an Italian that shall gett nothing but jack an apes and munckes [monkeys] uppon thee."[7] According to this punitive fantasy, given an (in)appropriate sexual partner, the child of a sexually incontinent mother would bear the traces of

her mother's sinful character. Such beliefs in the necessity—and inevitability—
of punitive markings for sexual crimes have a special legacy in popular stories
about monstrous births. As the broadsheet "bastard sonne in bastard shape" suggests, the sexually incontinent woman may not lose her own nose, but her bastard child may well be born without one. Understanding "eche part" of a monster's deformity, then, entailed both an intimate knowledge of early modern
punishment and an attentive examination of its mother's lifestyle and behavior.

In *A most straunge, and true discourse, of the wonderfull iudgement of God* (1600),
the monstrous birth, identified as an "out rage in the flesh,"[8] resonates with the
corporeally punitive system discussed above. The monster's mother is identified
as a Herefordshire yeoman's daughter who ignores the marital contract to which
she had officially agreed, rejects "a man of competent wealth, and of a good name
and fame in the place where he dwelt," and enters into a life of elaborate sinfulness (2). The couple's betrothal, moreover, was well-known: the contract declared and "openly asked three times in the Church." As the author, identified
only by the initials I.R., explains, "[A]ll the people of those parts thought for
trueth, that a full match in marriage, should shortly after have been solemnized
betweene them" (B). When she rejects the man to whom she was contracted, the
young woman thus betrays her obligations not only to her family but to the entire community order ("all the people of those parts"). Women who refused to
"be ruled by their parentes and friends" or by any ecclesiastical rituals such as
the bans of matrimony violated what Annabel Gregory has called the politics of
"good neighbourhood," putting their own desires before those of the community.[9] For I.R., such women both admit and embody social disruption. The marginal note, "Note yee young maidens," next to this part of the story indicates his
desire that young women readers learn from the mistakes of one of their peers
and identifies the story as a lesson specifically for marriage-age women.

After breaking her marital contract, the young woman in the pamphlet travels to a different parish to work as a servant for an uncle with "three sonnes at
mans estate" and becomes sexually involved with one, or perhaps two, of them
(3).[10] The liaison between the young woman and her cousin(s) is unacceptable
"partly because hee was hir so neere kinsman: and partly for that she had
promised her selfe before to another man: and especially because their lust was
so hot" (3). Having ignored social taboos about incest and endogamy, violated
her marital contract, and felt excessive sexual desire, the woman is punished accordingly. God "(to shew his displeasure against mockerie with his holy institution of mariage, and his hatred of the sinnes of whoredome, adulterie, fornica-

tion, inceste, and all other uncleannesse) made this proud, this scornefull & unconstant wench, the mother of a monster, and not of an orderly birth" (3–4). The pamphlet's list of sexual crimes—"whoredome, adulterie, fornication, inceste, and all other uncleannesse"—is the exact list of sexual crimes warned against in the oft-repeated "Sermon agaynst whoredome and uncleanesse."[11] With the addition of the violation of marriage contracts (described by I.R. as "mockerie with [God's] holy institution of marriage"), they were also the sexual crimes that more godly Protestants, like I.R. and Philip Stubbes before him, believed the church courts did far too little to punish.

While I.R. labels the monster-producing woman in his pamphlet "disorderly," there was, of course, no consensus on what exactly comprised social order in early-seventeenth-century England.[12] Acts passed by the central government certainly attempted to define and codify social behavior, but they were not uniformly implemented.[13] Local, often parish-based officials such as churchwardens and justices of the peace were responsible for mediating between national legislation and local realities, and their focus was usually on good neighborliness rather than strict legislative conformity.[14] Any punishment of the Herefordshire yeoman's daughter would thus have depended less on the crimes she committed per se than on the community's feelings about her behavior. While there were certainly attempts in the period to harden public control over marriage entry as well as attitudes toward sexual immorality (including, for example, the idea that sexual relations were only licit after a church marriage), Puritan "moral entrepreneurs" like I.R. felt that it was their work to bring human behavior into line with what they saw as divine law.[15]

For the most part, prosecutions of sexual immorality relied on notorious cases. As Martin Ingram notes, "It often took a combination of questionable signs to create a [. . .] fame sufficient to stir churchwardens into action."[16] Sexually incontinent behavior, that is, had to be excessive enough—or marked by sufficiently "questionable signs"—to be talked about by the neighbors. While prosecutions for incest were comparatively rare in the period, convicted offenders of incest and other sexual crimes were forced to make public confessions in the church or marketplace, wearing a penitential white sheet or, on occasion, a placard marked "for incest" around their necks.[17] In many ways the monstrous child in *A most straunge, and true discourse* serves as a hyperbolically "questionable sign" of disorder. Like a placard marked "for incest," it publicly announces its mother's sexual crimes, providing the public exposure and police work that earthly officials were unable or unwilling to provide.[18] Although sexual crimes were largely unprosecuted in English parishes, I.R. suggests, the monster born in Herefordshire during the Feast of the Epiphany in the year 1600 testifies to the divinely mandated righteousness of Puritans' desire for their greater punishment.

The itemized list of the monster's deformities provides the reader of *A most straunge, and true discourse* with an entire range of "questionable signs": whores' marks notable for their divergence from a normative bodily standard. The deformities are excessive (the head is "longer than the heades of other children ordinarily are"); inverted or upside down ("the upper eye-lid upwards, and the lower eye-lidde downewards, the insides appeering outward"); and sexually indeterminate ("There appeared in this childe no evident signe of the sexe, either of man or woman") (5, 7). Yet while the monster's deformities as a whole give an impression of world-turned-upside-down disorder, I.R. singles out a specific deformity for attention. There was no "outward partition of fingers" in the monster's hands, he notes, and "[t]he finger of the left hand only (which in latine is called *digitus annularis*, and in english the ring finger) had a naile, and that finger towards the end was separated from the others" (6). Much like the 1568 broadsheet that identifies its monster's fingerless hands as signs of idleness ("stumps fit for no use"), I.R. identifies the monster's ring finger as a "Resemblyng sinne." By using the Latin term *digitus annularis* to describe the finger, I.R. further indicates the particular nature of its importance: Latin was the language of the church courts and thus the language used to police sexual morality. The monster's deformity has both legal and religious significance: what ought to be the symbol of legitimate, church-sanctioned matrimony—the ring finger—is in fact a sign of its monstrous infraction. In conjunction with the monster's other deformities, the ring finger reminds all beholders of the mother's incestuous and extramarital fornication, drawing particular attention to her broken marital contract.

Many of the story's details invoke deeply contentious debates over marriage in the post-Reformation period, from the freedom young women claimed in determining their marriages (often, as is the case here, in opposition to the will of their "family and friends") to the legitimate forms of matrimony. In a period in which marriage was no longer a sacrament and the application of both human and divine law unclear, broken and disputed marriage contracts were among the most prevalent cases of conscience.[19] It was precisely to facilitate proof in disputed cases that the church tried to insist that marital contracts or "handfastings" be adequately publicized, witnessed, and ultimately solemnized in church.

(In *A most straunge, and true discourse,* the fact that the contract between the young woman and her fiancé had been "published in the congregation" solidified the community's belief "that a full match in marriage should shortly after have been solemnized betweene them.")[20] Interpreted as a divinely sent, publicly legible punishment for a woman who breaks her marital contract, the monster is meant to show the legitimacy of spousal contracting, but it also suggests that the tenuousness of such contracts puts extra pressure on people's allegiance to their vows. The monstrous birth demonstrates both that contracts are insufficient guarantors of marital legitimization and that their violation, regardless of the adequate monitoring of churchwardens and their courts, will be punished. The monster's singled-out ring finger testifies to the binding status of its mother's marital contract, but it also invokes other controversies surrounding marriage in the post-Reformation church, particularly the use of the ring.

If, in the reformed Church of England, matrimony, which "had no visible sign or ceremony ordained of God," was no longer considered a sacrament, the Book of Common Prayer's "Form of Solemnization of Matrimony" insisted that the ring still play a role in the ceremony. (The man lays the ring "upon the book with the accustomed duty to the Priest and Clerk. And the Priest, taking the Ring, shall deliver it unto the Man, to put it on the fourth finger of the Woman's left hand.") The ring, however, was seen as a "token and pledge" of the marriage vow, and was imbued with no mysterious, efficacious binding properties of its own.[21] Yet for many godly Protestants, the use of the ring in marriage ceremonies suggested a too-fierce belief in the power of priests, words, and objects to effect unions; the ring was redolent, in other words, of popish superstition.[22] That I.R. seems to assume the magical efficacy of material objects when he identifies the deformed ring finger as a supernatural sign is less ironic than it might first seem; by claiming divine displeasure at its absence, he implicitly suggests the extent to which a ring makes a marriage. Like his godly predecessors, in other words, I.R. deployed superstitious ideas in the service of his reformist ends.

These ends, as I have already suggested, were disciplinary, and they become most clear in the description of the events following the birth. As soon as the three attending midwives see the monster, they send for the minister of Colwall ("[w]ithin whose charge [the monster] was borne") to christen it (B2v). The minister baptizes the monstrous child "What god will," a recognizably Puritan gesture mocked, for example, in Ben Jonson's *Bartholomew Fair* with the baptism of "Win-the-fight." In identifying the child as a sign of God's will, the minister designates it as a lesson in divine judgment for the entire community.

For I.R., earthly punishments should match the harsh judgment of God: "[A]ll magistrates, who have authoritie to punish [sexual and marital infractions] ought to be carefull, that too many offences of that kind be not redeemed by commutations: least it come to passe that there should be much more money payd to buy out sinne, then persons punished for sinne." If this happens, he continues, "we may say, as master Latymer said once in a sermon, that sin is good marchandise, in many Courts & Consistories."[23] In arguing that the church courts should be more invested in meting out punishment and pursuing reform than in making money, I.R. allies his work with that of the great Protestant bishop Hugh Latimer (who himself protested against the greed and corruption of the English church). In fact, I.R. goes on to defend "the preachers of the Gospell and their teaching [who] are slaundered and evill spoken of, by Papists, Brownists, and others, both abroade and at home." In his judgment, those who criticize the "preachers of the Gospell"—specifically the Puritan preaching ministers whom James I would come to consider the single greatest threat to his power—do "not rightly consider [. . .] that the multitude of the people breedeth sinne." For I.R., God's will is equally invested in punishing sinners and defending the work of godly ministers in their efforts to reform the "great multitude." In fact, the minister, identified by I.R. as "a zealous man, and a learned Preacher" and by the Hereford Call Books as Richard Barnard, did indeed baptize a deformed child as "Quod Deus Vult" in January 1600.[24]

A most straunge, and true discourse is thus both a resolution of a case of conscience, testifying to the divinely binding nature of marital contracts, and a broader statement of support for a specifically Puritan agenda. While the pamphlet's conclusion offers a brief sermon on the Decalogue (reprimanding people for their "failure to keep God's commandments"), it also offers a detailed program of Puritan behavior and reading. Bemoaning the popularity of theatres and the sins of "dalyance, sight, touching, talking lewdly of the actions of generation, writing of letters, making and reading of lewde and wanton bookes, ballads of love and pamphlets that tend that way," I.R. recommends instead that they keep "godly company" and attend divine services and sermons (10).[25] As alternative forms of entertainment, he suggests the Bible and other books that tell stories of monstrous births, and he ends by promoting a number of Puritan texts by name. Two of these books, William Hergest's *The Right Rule of Christian Chastitie* and Philip Stubbes's enormously popular *The Anatomie of Abuses* were, like *A most straunge, and true discourse*, published and sold by Richard Jones, the publisher whose long career of publishing godly texts is introduced in the first chapter. Such books, I.R. suggests, should be given both to the father and mother of the monstrous birth and to all "amorous yonkers, & lewd huswives" as guides for moral improvement and right living (9). The fact that these texts were all published by the same publisher, moreover, suggests Jones's desire to corner, if not create, a particular kind of market.

In the late sixteenth and early seventeenth centuries, writers and publishers like I.R. and Richard Jones created and promoted a new kind of literature: cheap pamphlet stories that competed with "lewde and wanton bookes, ballads of love and pamphlets that tend that way" for readers' leisure hours. As *A most straunge, and true discourse* testifies, many would-be reformers continued to use popular literary forms in their efforts at reform long after the Elizabethan settlement, and they certainly did not understand these texts as inimical to serious and weighty books like those of Stubbes and Hergest. By bringing "true life" stories from the counties (in this case, Colwell) to a wider public, these authors and publishers sought to capitalize on a new kind of literary culture. Stories of monstrous births undoubtedly made it to London presses because their associations with divine wrath made them singularly effective proselytizing material. But they also made it to the London presses because they were stories that focused on real-life dilemmas with which their readers wrestled, with varying degrees of anxiety, on a daily basis. Monsters promised stories with their morals, and they were stories that hit home precisely because they could have happened, and indeed did happen, in one's own backyard.

"A certain wandering yong woman"

A 1615 pamphlet entitled *Gods handy-worke in wonders* tells the story of "a poore wayfaring woman" who "beeing great with Child, but not neere her time, seeing the night approaching, stept into an old Barne to take up her lodging."[26] This lodging, we are told, is in a place near Feversham in Kent, at "a Farme called *Perre*." For the punishment of her sins, the story continues, God struck the woman with pains "more than women commonly suffer in such extremities." (The pain of giving birth to monsters "doubleth [the biblical] curse" of pain in childbirth.) The wayfaring woman gives birth to two children, one whole and female, the other hermaphroditic, headless, one-armed and with "no pappes, but prints and markes like them in their places" (Bv) (fig. 2.3). Like the monstrous birth in *A most straunge, and true discourse*, this monster is "not an orderly birth." It is characterized by confusion and faulty similitude: it has, among other deformities, only "the fashion of a mouth," and only "marks" resembling nipples.

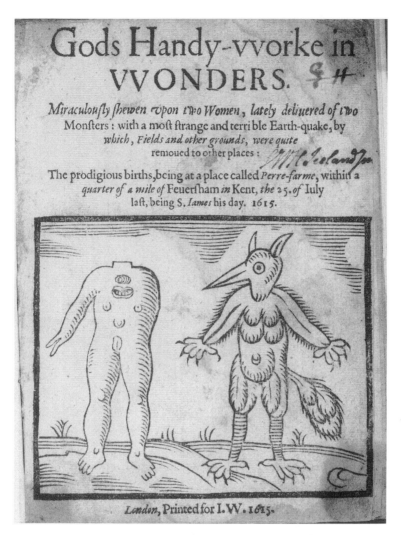

Figure 2.3. Title page, *Gods handy-vvorke in vvonders. Miraculously shewen vpon two women, lately deliuered of two monsters: with a most strange and terrible earth-quake, by which, fields and other grounds, were quite remoued to other places: the prodigious births, being at a place called Perre-farme, within a quarter of a mile of Feuersham in Kent, the 25. of Iuly last, being S. Iames his day. 1615* (London: Printed [by George Purslowe] for I. W[right], 1615), STC 11926. Reproduced by permission of the Henry E. Huntington Library.

The pamphlet's anonymous author acknowledges that while a pregnant woman "may by blowes or other misfortunes miscarry in [her] delivery, and bring Infants into the world maymed in limbes or deformed in countenance," when "Gods owne fingers shall crush the loynes in the wombe, and set his markes of feareful divine vengeance, on the brest of an unborne Babe, to turne it into a Monster, it is without all questions, a revenge and punishment for some extraordinary sinnes in the Parents." The author, that is, comes down on the same side of the debate on the significance of monstrous births as does Mr. Lambert in Oliver Heywood's diary entry: monstrous births are unequivocally God's punishments for their parents' "extraordinary sinnes." When an infant is born "dumbe, deafe or in a limbe mishapen," he writes, God has merely shaken his rod of anger, but when the birth is "prodigious and beyond Nature, the stripes are deep, for then he is angered indeede" (A3v).

The pamphlet identifies the monster's parents as Martha and Henry "Haydnot," an appropriate (and probably fictitious) name for the poor and homeless who wandered the English countryside in search of work. When examined by local officials about their place of dwelling, the Haydnots "reported it *had beene* in Chelmesford in Essex," the past tense duly noted. During the period in which *Gods handy-worke in wonders* was published, Kent, a maritime county, was indeed receiving a great deal of migration, and Kentish authorities were increasingly concerned with the problems of vagrancy and abandoned children. In fact, the "examination" of the Haydnots as to their parish of origin was a legislated procedure intended to facilitate the return of vagrants to their home parishes, thereby saving Kentish parishes the responsibility for their succor.

While the pamphlet certainly views the monstrous child as a sign both of its parents' "extraordinary sinnes" and of the necessity of policing vagrants, it also features a limited measure of human sympathy. After the Haydnots' deposition, the community succors the wayfaring woman by giving her money "out of Christian compassion" (Bv). Ultimately, however, the community legitimizes and entrenches its social order by burying the monstrous child and rejecting its criminal parents, who, quite simply, disappear from the narrative. While their disappearance testifies to the intractability of the social problems the pamphlet's judgments attempt to resolve, it also testifies to a wider social ambivalence about the plight of such wandering men and women.

As *Gods handy-worke in wonders* suggests, wandering pregnant women like Martha Haydnot (popularly considered a subset of vagrancy), were of concern to many early modern authorities. Although Martha Haydnot travels with the

father of her child, the pregnant wandering women who most solicited the attention of authorities were those who journeyed alone.[27] New national measures
to ensure the maintenance of bastard children and the punishment of guilty
mothers were passed in 1576 and 1610.[28] Moreover, the desire of some early
modern reformers to punish sexual offenders with severe physical sanctions followed an already well-established practice for the punishment of vagabonds.
Under subsequent Elizabethan and Jacobean acts, vagrants were branded either
with a V on the breast or with a Roman R,[29] and the 1598 Act for the Punishment of Rogues, Vagabonds, and Sturdy Beggars insisted that those arrested
"shall uppon their apprehension by th appoyntment of any Justice of the Peace,
Constable, Headborough or Tything man of the same County Hundred Parish
or Tything [. . .] be stripped naked from the middle upwardes and shall be openly
whipped untill his or her body be bloudye."[30] Much like a sexual offender, moreover, a convicted vagabond was also often forced to stand in public holding a
"picture of his own personage deformed in form and manner."[31] In theory, as
the earlier Elizabethan act proposed, such physical signs would make vagabonds'
"Roguish kind of life" manifest to all those who beheld them, wherever they
might be.[32] It was a theory of policing that attempted to render convicts' own
bodies the means of their control.

Despite these extant acts and punishments, wandering pregnant women were
nonetheless extremely difficult to locate and punish. Much as the monstrous
child in *A most straunge, and true discourse* serves as a hyperbolically "questionable sign" of its mother's marital and sexual disorder, the monstrous birth in *Gods
handy-worke in wonders* manifests its mother's "Roguish kind of life." A second-
generation, physically manifest version of the "picture of his own personage deformed in form and manner" that the vagabond was forced to hold in a public
place, the monster combines sought-after, publicly legible, and physical punishments for sexual offenders with those for vagabonds and other misplaced persons. In fact, the pamphlet's author understands the monstrous birth as a punishment analogous to the whipping of vagabonds "untill his or her body be
bloudye." When a birth is "prodigious and beyond Nature," he writes, God's
"stripes are deep, for then he is angered indeede, and at every such blowe hee
drawes bloud" (A3v). Once again, the monster pamphlet tells a marvelous story
of the public exposure and punishment of a disorderly woman.

The wandering woman's monstrous birth served another revelatory function
intimately connected to the complex contemporary understandings of unwanted
bastard births. Most unmarried women experienced pregnancy in secrecy and

with the fear of exposure and confrontation.[33] For understandable reasons, such women often claimed that stillborn or unwanted children were not fully children: one woman claimed that the child she miscarried after being raped "had no shape"; another claimed that she "had a miscarriage of *a mention of a child* not formed as it could be discerned whether it was a male or female"; another, that she had merely expelled a bit of "gristle."[34] In all likelihood these women diminished the human status of their births in response to the dehumanizing processes of impregnation and birth they had undergone. They were not children; they were terrible mistakes.

There was perhaps not such a big difference between these births and the purportedly monstrous births that solicited pamphlet retellings. In fact, I suspect that some original determinations of deformed and stillborn births as "monsters" were based on perceptions of their mother's sins rather than on the actual forms of the births themselves. Like the women's stories recounted above, pamphlet stories of monstrous births also diminish the human status of the births they recount—monsters are emphatically *not* images of God in man—but they do so by making them hyperbolically monstrous rather than barely human. In the pamphlets, it is the extreme remarkableness of the monstrous birth that exposes its mother's secrets and emblazons the nature of her sexual crimes. A monstrous birth reveals its mother's "want of virtue" and makes her secret or hidden shame inescapably public. Such fantasies of public exposure were perhaps a response to the unfixed nature of many wandering pregnant women, a way of pinning them down and making their bodies' products, if not their own bodies, subject to disciplinary attention.

As J. A. Sharpe points out, a number of factors would prevent a bastard birth being reported to secular authorities: local indifference; successfully concealed infanticide; the mother taking to the road; or the couple marrying to the satisfaction of their neighbors.[35] Yet sometimes, for reasons Sharpe does not take into account, revelation of paternity, not to mention marriage, was out of the question. Fathers of illegitimate children pressured the women they had impregnated to suppress information about their identities, and sex based on a promise of marriage was not the only cause of pregnancy.[36] Scholars discuss the abuse of such promises of marriage, but few discuss the possibility that women were raped or forced into sexual service by their masters or other members of their households. David Cressy states that the most common profile of a bastard-bearer was a single woman in her twenties, employed away from home as a domestic servant, who "succumbed to the pressures or promises of her master."[37] Based on the fact that a large proportion of mothers of illegitimate children were domestic servants, Sharpe writes that servants were "especially prone to sexual misdemeanors," while A. L. Beier locates the cause of pregnancy among servants in "illicit sexual unions."[38] Martin Ingram observes that some of the women accused of being impregnated by married men "may have been the victims of harassment and exploitation; but there are positive indications of this in only one case, and in that instance the woman seems to have resisted successfully. On the other hand, there is evidence that some of the married men encountered little or no resistance from the women they seduced."[39] Only Susan Amussen points out that such pregnancies might have been the result of rape or coercion.[40]

I dwell on this not only to point out scholarly blind spots (if not sexism), but to suggest that there were many mitigating circumstances behind bastard-bearing, and even infanticide, of which most early modern people, particularly women, would have been aware. For many women, geographical mobility was a matter of economic necessity (the "Haydnots" presumably travel from Essex to Kent in search of work), but it also enabled them to escape undesirable situations and bad reputations. As we saw in *A most straunge, and true discourse*, traveling to a different parish was one of the ways women could escape marital contracts, but it also enabled women to escape situations far more dire than unwanted marriages. The remarkable story of Agnes Bowker is illustrative. A servant from Leicestershire, Agnes became pregnant in 1568, took to wandering, tried to commit suicide, and finally placed herself in hands of a local midwife. She then gave birth to a "cat," fathered on her, she claimed, "by a diabolical shape-shifting beast."[41] David Cressy reads the story as a cover for infanticide in light of a recent act "to prevent the destroying and murthering of bastard children," and the connections he makes are certainly persuasive.[42] Yet there are many aspects of the story that remain unknown. Why, for example, was Agnes Bowker wandering? Why did she try to commit suicide? And why does she identify the father of her monstrous birth as "a diabolical shape-shifting beast"?

While it is impossible to answer all these questions, contemporaneous pamphlet stories about unknown wandering women who give birth to monsters illuminate some of the complex social issues around women's experiences of vagrancy and bastardy in early modern England. Pamphlet reimaginings of particular cases both cite and resist the legal and social strictures facing pregnant wandering women. While they certainly endeavor to teach lessons about common cases of domestic and social conduct—bastard-bearing, they insist, is wrong—their focus on the wider contexts surrounding these women and their pregnancies tells a more complex story about crime and its punishments. Decisions about the severity and enforcement of punishment for bastard-bearers were often—to the dismay of godly reformers—left to the judgment of local authorities. But they were also mitigated by popular indifference and sympathy. Homeless or wandering pregnant women, in other words, were not simply the objects of social and legal injunction. There are historical records of vagrant women who, after giving birth to their bastard children, disappear "unchurched and unpunished," a fact that suggests a failure to persecute, if not the traces of popular sympathy.[43]

The sight of vagrant pregnant women walking the highways of England was not uncommon, and it figured in the consciences of many early modern people. In 1645, for example, Thomas Peyton warned Henry Oxinden that his daughter Margaret Hobart, aged 18 and pregnant with her first child, was not being looked after properly. "There is a daughter of yours I heare towards lying in," he writes, "and her husband minds it as much as my cowes calving . . . shee is as unprovided [for] as one that walkes the highwaies."[44] Support for such wandering women was thus not only a burden but a matter of compassion. While the monstrous births in pamphlets about wandering women such as *Gods handy-worke in wonders* promise that women's crimes will not pass unnoticed, the pamphlets themselves offer stories as marked by compassion as by judgment. Much like contemporaneous stories of women who escape "unchurched and unpunished" after giving birth to their illegitimate children, some of these pamphlets feature social policing of an entirely different order.

"for womanhood sake"

A pamphlet authored and published by William Barley in 1609, *Strange newes out of Kent, of a monstrous and misshapen child, borne in Olde Sandwitch*, is, like those pamphlets discussed above, concerned with women's physical and social locations and the punishment for their crimes.[45] The story, like that told in *Gods handy-worke in wonders*, takes place in Kent, in the "principall Town" of Sandwich, a place "bordering upon the Sea, rich, and populous, and well stored with substantiall and welthy inhabitants." The first character we are introduced to is Goodwife Wattes, "a very honest poore old woman, wel-beloved of the country, and of an honest conversation amongst her neighbours, one that takes great paines for her living, and most willing to keepe her credit upright." In July 1609,

Barley reports, "there came unto this old pore womans house, a certaine wandering yong woman, as it seemd great with child, handsome, and decently apparelled" (Aiiii). Weeping, the wandering woman "requested for Gods sake that some Christian-like charitie might be shewed her, & houseroome for that night afforded her for womanhood sake" (B). Barley reports that the wandering woman's big belly "drew such pittie and womanly nature from this good old woman Mother Watts, that she not onely granted her houseroome and lodging for that night, but also sucker, helpe and furtherance, (if it so should happen) at the painefull hower of her deliverie."

Goodwife Watts's actions, no matter how "womanly," were, however, illegal. Church courts were expected to punish not only actual sexual offenders but also the "bawds, harbourers or receivers of such persons."[46] The county of Kent, moreover, had specific laws for "Keeping Potential Paupers out of the Town," including a 1579 decree against those who have "receaved and harbored within their houses diver persons for lucres sake" who "as bothe dailie are and in tyme to come will be verie chargeable and burdenous to this towne and the whole inhabitants thereof."[47] In Sandwich itself, innkeepers were instructed to inform the mayor of any foreigners arriving at their houses either in the daytime or at night.[48] It was thus no easy matter for an uncertified and pregnant wandering woman to find a place to give birth, let alone someone to "stand her friend in her misery."[49]

Those indicted for harboring sexual offenders often lived in market towns and other well-frequented locations, a detail reflected in the pamphlets. Goodwife Wattes is an upstanding citizen in a market town, and the woman who helps the wandering pregnant woman in a similar pamphlet, also published by William Barley, is "a Marchaunts wife of good accompt in the Citie."[50] Many of those who harbored such women did so, not for "lucres sake," but out of compassion. In fact, a number of harborers presented in the church courts defended their actions in the name of "Christian pitty."[51] In 1610, for example, Anne Frie of Broad Hinston told the church courts how she took in a "'walking woman . . . in travail of child in the open street" "for womanhood's sake."[52] The fact that harboring women in both the pamphlets and in the church court records use the same explanatory defense for their actions suggests not only the dialogue between court records and popular texts but also the prevalence of the ethos. As these stories indicate, not everyone believed that such female crimes as homelessness and bastard-bearing merited harsh punishments.

Strange newes out of Kent climaxes with the birth of a monster. Like the "wayfaring" woman in the previous pamphlet, "this bigge belly wandring yong woman [. . .] fel into a most strange labor" which

> much affrighted the old woman Mother Watts, and in her minde strook such a fear, that she immediately called in her neighbours, being women all of a willing forwardnes in such a busines: but through the inward laboring of the womans bodie, not any of them all knew how to shift in such a dangerous case, wherefore amazedly they looked one of another, til such time as one goodwife Hatch, the yonger, was sent for, being a Midwife of a milde nature, and of good experience, who at her comming thither, so cunningly shewed her skill, that with the helping hand of God, this distressed yong woman was speedily delivered (B).

The pamphlet describes a community of women that is neighborly, resourceful, and efficiently businesslike.[53] The midwife, Goodwife Hatch, serves as its cohering center. Midwives played singularly complex roles in early modern society: helpers of women, they were also meant to serve as their monitors (extracting the names of fathers from unmarried women in the throes of childbirth, searching for signs of adultery and witches' marks, policing the religious rites with which children were welcomed).[54] And while they served a womanly gender function, they were also economic agents with considerable power.[55] (The wandering woman's support of this female economy—in the midst of her own pains, she gives the midwife "vii. Shillings" for her "diligent paines"—illustrates her respect for their labors.) The independent and inter-reliant women pictured in this pamphlet are a potential threat not only to proper birth rituals and records but to Kentish social regulations as well. Depending on their response to the birth, they can either serve or disrupt community policing of vagrancy and bastardy.

The child borne by the unknown woman, described as a "miracle in nature, or rather Gods wonder," was "quite disfigured from humaine creation, as by the picture is rightly deciphered" (Bii) (fig. 2.4).[56] Like the monsters discussed above, it is "no childe rightly shapt," but is headless and with a double-face in the middle of its body: "The face, mouth, eyes, nose, and breast, being thus framed together like a deformed peece of flesh" (Bii). With its appearance, the monstrous birth "drove the Midwife goodwife Hatch and the rest of the company into a great fright, even readie all to sinke downe dead to the ground with feare." The monster punishes the wandering woman, but it also terrorizes the midwife and her neighbors, reminding them of the power of God, the fallibility of women, and the crucial role they play as the go-betweens between childbirth and the maintenance of social order.

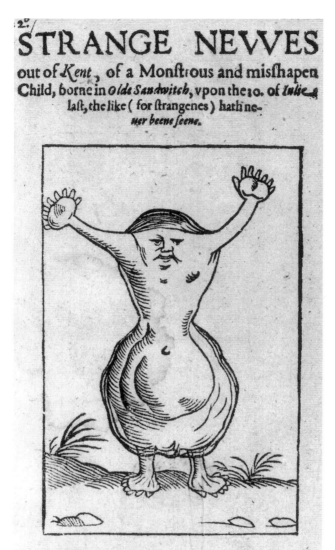

STRANGE NEVVES

out of *Kent*, of a Monſtrous and misſhapen
Child, borne in *Olde Sandwitch*, vpon the 10. of *Iulie*
laſt, the like (for ſtrangenes) hath ne-
uer beene ſeene.

Imprinted at London by **T. C.** for **W. Barley**, and are to be
ſold at his ſhop in Gratious-ſtreete. 1 6 0 9.

Figure 2.4. Title page, *Strange nevves out of Kent, of a monstrous and misshapen child, borne in Olde Sandwitch, vpon the 10. of Iulie, last, the like (for strangenes) hath neuer beene seene* (Imprinted at London, By T. C[reede]. for W. Barley, and are to be sold at his shop in Gratious-street, 1609), STC 14935. Reproduced by permission of the British Library.

Terrified as they are, the midwives at first do nothing whatsoever about the birth. On the following Sunday the young woman sends Mother Wattes to buy the necessaries for a "weake woman in child-bed." "But now," Barley tells his readers, "marke what in the meane time hapned, & *let all women in such a case consider what might be done*, & how strongly nature in this newe delivered woman prevailed" (Biii, emphasis added). Like I.R.'s marginal "Note yee young maidens," Barley's insistence that "all women" need to consider the significance of "what might be done" in "such a case" identifies the pamphlet's story as a case of conscience. Yet the sentence's confusing syntax reflects the complexities of the case Barley is presenting. Just as it is unclear whether the description of the woman's strong "nature" refers to her womanly fortitude or her monstrous, evil-disposed nature, it is unclear whether women readers are to mark the doings of the midwives or of the birth mother. How exactly *should* all women "in such a case consider what might be done"? What the woman does, in this case, is disappear, leaving behind eight more shillings for the burial of her deformed child.

When Wattes returns from the shops to find the wandering woman gone, she immediately calls in her neighbors, "where (making knowne unto them all these aforesaid proceedings) with a generall consent, they certified the same unto the Magistrates." The monster thus passes out of the hands of the women—by their "generall consent"—and into the hands of the official magistracy. The progression of the story suggests, finally, that the functioning of "good neighbourhood" works in conjunction with official legislation on bastardy and vagrancy and with those responsible for its administration: magistrates and the ministers. After Watts and her neighbors call them in, the magistrates "upon good consideration, togither with the advice of a reverend and learned Minister, of Saint Clements church in Sandwitche, one M. Simons," determine what to do. (Like the minister featured in *A most straunge, and true discourse*, Peter Symon was the actual minister of the parish church Sandwich in the first two decades of the seventeenth century.)[57] The pamphlet reports that Simons "verie charitably" buries the monster, "giving many godly admonitions to the people, concerning this most strange birth." Such "terrible examples of Gods wrath," his sermon intones, "may lead us out of the pathway of perdition [. . .] if wee be not graceless." As in the broadsheets discussed in chapter one, the pamphlet ends its lesson about appropriate behavior, with a cautionary reminder about the realities of predestination: if we avoid sin *and* if "we be not graceless," we will avoid divine wrath.

Yet as tidy as it is, Barley's predestinarian reminder is not the end of the story:

there are "[s]ome other things concerning this wonder [. . .] to be considered of." In particular, Barley refers to "one of the Seargeants wives of Sandwitch, that by the sight and corrupted smell proceeding from the child, received such a conceit, that to this day she is not scarce well, but sickly, and much decayed in health." In Sandwich, the sergeant was the officer meant to keep watch "for fear of fire, thieves or other evil disposed persons," and, if any "suspicious persons" were found, to confine them until morning.[58] He was also responsible for publishing the ordinances throughout the town and for making "proclamation audibly and distinctly in the market and the fourteen usual places [. . .] that every inhabitant, male and female, do conform to these ordinances to be proclaimed, on pain that shall follow."[59] Finally, the sergeant was the officer responsible for the maintenance of orphan and bastard children.[60] In having the sergeant's wife bear visceral witness to the monstrous disorder in her community's midst, Barley both reveals his intimate knowledge of the unique system of governance in Sandwich and illustrates the threat that vagrancy and bastard births pose to the community. The sergeant's wife's reaction, like the ultimate actions of the midwife and neighbor women, suggests that such monstrousness infects the whole community and that women are particularly susceptible to the influences of a bad nature. As the clearly identified property of both common legal jurisprudence and an individual man, the sergeant's wife is afflicted by the monstrous birth in a way that gives a sense not only of the contagion of misplaced women but also of the vulnerability of women who know and keep their place. It is these women who must be protected from the influence of the wandering women and their bastard births.

Yet despite the remarkable outcome of the wandering woman's story in *Strange newes out of Kent*, wandering and foreign women were not in fact unusual in Kent. While little is known about the wandering woman featured in the pamphlet, she is "supposed to be ones daughter in the Isle of Tennet." A great deal of the migrational pressure affecting Kent in the early seventeenth century did indeed come from the Isle of Thannet, which had no market town of its own. Many of the migrants to Kent, moreover, were women.[61] A pregnant serving girl named Mary Mont, for example, walked all the way from Thannet to Canterbury (the county's Cathedral town) in search of poor relief in 1580, a period during which Sandwich itself was "burdened with great numbers of children" for the poor rates.[62] The situation did not approve drastically in the intervening years. In 1609, the year *Strange newes out of Kent* appeared in print, the Sandwich corporation voted a grant of £25 for the settlement of local vagabonds in Virginia; some of those rounded up were doubtless bastard-bearing women and their children.[63] Yet while poor migrants may have helped to erode certain aspects of civic neighborliness in Kent, long-distance migration also resulted in what Peter Clark has identified as a form of "feminine emancipation." Many unrecorded women moved in and out of Kentish towns, handled petty trade, and generally fended for themselves.[64] Thus, the wandering woman's strange appearance in and disappearance from Sandwich was, unlike her birth, unremarkable. As the "shifting" and resourceful women surrounding and supporting her attest, the wandering woman was a figure both legislated against and intimately, even sympathetically, familiar.

Although the neighborhood women eventually turn the monstrous child over to the authorities in seeming obedience to the laws protecting Sandwich against vagrant women and their bastard children, by the time they do so, the child is already dead and its mother is long gone. Furthermore, the woman herself remains an unplaced variable:

> it could not be knowne by any meanes what she was, from whence she came, not whither she was going, nor as yet it is not knowne for a truth to what place she is travelled, but for a certaintie she was proved to be a wanderer, & supposed to be ones daughter in the Isle of Tennet, but of what life and conversations she hath bene, and is of, none can justly say as yet. (Biiiv)

The fact that the "wandering yong woman" pays for the women's labor, escapes from the jurisdiction of official punishment, and remains, "as yet," unknown and unlocated, suggests that such women continued to escape both legislation and the "entrepreneurial" moral efforts of godly reformers. Just as they haunted the imaginations of legislators, so did such women haunt the imaginations of popular texts and their readers; as the "as yet" indicates, popular curiosity did not cease with the woman's disappearance.

Readings

In his discussion of scaffold literature, Michel Foucault argues that "beneath the apparent morality of the example not to be followed," each story of a convicted felon's confession offered "a whole memory of struggles and confrontations."[65] While the printing and distribution of such explicitly admonitory texts was in principle subject to strict control, and the stories were expected to have the effect of ideological control, these stories of everyday history were received so avidly "because people found in them not only memories, but precedents."[66] Despite their official condemnatory tone, that is, the stories of condemned criminals so popular with readers were also narratives of social dissent, even resistance. While Foucault focuses on stories of condemned men, the pamphlets discussed in this chapter served similar functions. Even more dramatic than death by hanging, the women's punishments are physically correlative to their crimes: the monsters' deformed bodies bear the signs of their mothers' errors, making them spectacularly and publicly legible. Like the correlation between the woodcut images and their accompanying descriptions, the correlation between the women's crimes and their monstrous births may be fixed—the reader is told exactly what the monster punishes, and that the crime is serious—but the events and relationships in the stories are often much more ambiguous than the morals that seek to contain them.

A case of conscience is only a moral dilemma because of its mitigating circumstances, the fact that it involves a range of choices and values, and that it is not easy to resolve. Finely tuned to specific and local controversies, pamphlets about women who give birth to monsters were earmarked as remonstrances, but they were also compelling narratives replete with mysterious women, compassionate harborers, zealous—perhaps over-zealous—ministers, and by-the-book legal functionaries. As with all cases of conscience, readers were meant to apply these stories and judgments to their own consciences, to understand and internalize the lesson, and, if need be, to use them to guide their own actions. If they were godly readers, they would be able to read the cause and effect unambiguously and ally themselves not only with godly ministers but with God himself. If they "be not graceless," the stories might even help to save their souls. Yet although the lessons are clear, the stories nonetheless reveal that there are multiple options for the resolution of each case, that the rules are not clear, and that the laws—such as those against bastardy or infanticide, or harboring a pregnant and homeless woman—are often unfair. In presenting a range of issues surrounding such crimes and pointing out that others are "as yet" unknown, the stories force readers to examine their own consciences in order to determine what is right. In encouraging "all women in such a case [to] consider what might be done," there is, nonetheless, always the chance that they might do wrong.

Thomas Laqueur has argued that the eighteenth century saw the rise of the "humanitarian narrative," a story—novel, autopsy, social inquiry—in which the details of the suffering bodies of others engender compassion in the readers or hearers of these stories. Compassion, in turn, comes to necessitate ameliorative action.[67] In these humanitarian narratives, he claims, the individual body becomes "the common bond between those who suffer and those who would help."[68] I am not arguing that stories of monstrous births are humanitarian narratives; on the contrary, the bodies that receive the detailed attention are hideously deformed and dead, and the texts often specifically argue against compassion for the women involved. The explicit intent of these stories is not to solicit compassion, but rather to provide ethico-religious guidelines for dealing with controversial issues—what Barley, like his coreligionists, calls "cases." There are, as I.R., Richard Jones, and William Barley suggest, "right rules" of Christian chastity and legitimately godly behavior; and, equally importantly, there are "zealous and learned" preaching ministers to guide people in learning and obeying them.

The team responsible for *Strange newes out of Kent*, Thomas Creede and William Barley, printed other pamphlets of "strange things lately hapned" and true-life crimes, including the story of the "brideling, sadling and ryding, of a rich churle in Hampshire" by "a professed cunning woman" named Judeth Philips. (Philips was eventually sent to Newgate and whipped through the city in February 1594 in punishment for her crimes.)[69] Barley also published the 1592 version of Thomas Harman's famous text about vagabonds, *Caveat for commen cursetors vulgarely called vagabones*, which includes stories of the deceits of female vagabonds, or "doxies."[70] Harman, a justice of the peace in Kent, reputedly kept close records of the wayfarers who stopped at his door to beg, including the stories of one Bess Bottomly, who "hath murdered two children at the least," and a "walking Mort," or vagabond woman, who conspired with a local wife and her "loving gossips" to give birth to her bastard child in the privacy of the woman's barn.[71] Barley published texts that he claimed stood in distinction to "unlawful bookes of ribaldie, merry lyes and unprofitable stories to please fond phantasies, which doth derogat the glorie of God." Like I.R. and Richard Jones, he promoted a new genre of "good" books, "little exercised of many."[72]

Barley's "good" books, which dealt with topical issues and featured characters taken from real life, were in many ways the forerunners of realistic fiction. Along with older stories such as "Celestina the Faire," Barley and his peers offered stories with roots in local controversies that simultaneously sought to reform and entertain. While this was not a new tactic, what I am arguing here is that the casuistical nature of these texts—their attempts to render the moral ambiguities surrounding any given case in recognizable detail—afforded them a meaning, and thus a textual life, beyond their morals. Just as the woman in *A most straunge, and true discourse* slips the thrice-spoken marriage contract, and the wandering woman in *Strange newes out of Kent* pays her bill and escapes the magistrates, so do the pamphlet stories evade their authorized limits, allowing readers to determine their own readings.

CHAPTER THREE

Forms of Imperfect Union

On January 11, 1612, the following burial notation was made in the register of the parish church of Standish, Lancashire: *"Duobus [sic] puer: immaturat."*[1] The parish registers for the year include four baptisms and five burials of children identified as "illegitimate," two of whom were described as "immatura," but the child described, somewhat cryptically, as "duobus puer" is a special case. This "double child," only partially formed or still-born, was recorded by one William Leigh, rector of the parish, and has a popular textual life far beyond this brief notation.

Over the next year, William Leigh would tell the story of this birth in two different textual forms. In one form, an illustrated pamphlet, the monstrous birth is read as a punishment for local sinners, an example of a case of moral controversy resolved by a spectacular judgment from God. In the other form, a sermon, Leigh reads the monstrous birth as a Protestant portent, a warning on a national level of God's wrath against England and its religious equivocators. The monster thus has both a local and a national significance: it is a story about the people of Standish, Lancashire, and their parish minister, but it is also portent warning all Protestants to fit their inner beliefs to their outward vows of faith.

Each text thus renders the monster's story a case of conscience: in publicizing parishioners' secret sins, either sexual or religious, the monster attests to the errors of parishioners' consciences and seeks to guide their reformation. Like those that preceded it, the story of the Standish monster is a story about the spread of Protestant belief and the tools used to effect it, but it is also a story about the political implications of such tellings.

WELL BEFORE THE BIRTH of the monster, William Leigh had established himself as a reform-minded or Puritan minister, engaging in battles with both the episcopacy and his parishioners. In 1590 the "preaching ministers" of Manchester sent a letter to the Archbishop of York concerning issues raised in the latest visitation about "matters of conformitie" in their churches, and the second signatory of the letter was "W. Leygh, parson of Standish."[2] In their letter, the ministers claim that none of them had been presented (formally charged) during the visitation for refusing to use or preaching against "the co[mm]on boock in anie part thereof," nor for refusing to "were [wear] the surplice" (10). Having established their adherence to the basic articles of conformity, the ministers ask the Archbishop to take knowledge of "the obstinate papists and the zealous professors of religion" amongst whom they live. The one sort is too superstitious and "make everie ceremonie of our church, but especially that of the crosse, as an idoll of their church"; the other sort "so far caryed into scandall at those things which so greatly are drawen into abuse by the papists, that plainely many of them would in sundrie places, leave us and our ministracon, yf wee shold [use them]" (11). The ministers argue that in reclaiming parishioners from "papistrie" and in defending their parishes against its pressures, they have been forced to abandon certain ceremonial aspects of religious practice dictated by the Book of Common Prayer. The "zealous professors of religion," they argue (perhaps disingenuously), would leave the reformed church if its ministers used ceremonies tainted by popish abuse.[3] The ministers conclude their letter by stating their belief that when the Archbishop fully understands their situation, he will let them proceed as normal, promising as they do a greater "reformacon of our country from the grosse idolatry and heathnish prophanacons which yet continue with many amongst us, then yf a more strict course were taken in these smaller matters of inconformitie in the preachers" (13).

Yet as we have seen, matters of "inconformitie," particularly in the "smaller matters" of church-dictated ceremonial practice, were highly controversial. The *adiaphora*, or "things indifferent," that were determined by the Church of England to be, if not essential to salvation, signs of the church's ultimate control over matters religious, were often the material means by which more godly Protestants like Leigh resisted the dictates of the ecclesiastical authorities. The Archbishop points out in his letter of response to the ministers that, despite their protestations to the contrary, all the ministers who signed the letter had, in fact, been presented for not wearing the surplice and for speaking against the Book of Common Prayer (10).[4] He is also adamant about the importance of "smaller matters," noting in handwritten comments in the margins of the ministers' own letter that it is "[a] small comendacon for anie in auctoritie to winck at the busines of the church" (12) and that there are sufficient "ecclesiasticall censures and lawes for the [people's] reformacon" (11).[5] To the Archbishop, the idea that giving religious radicals a little liberty in "smaller matters" will keep them from "medl[ing] with state and govermt" is a dangerous one. "[O]f such litel sparckes," he writes ominously and with great prescience, "cometh often tymes great flames."[6]

Yet the Archbishop's claim that there are "ecclesiasticall censures and other lawes for [the people's] reformacon," was precisely the preachers' problem. In their opinion, the extant laws and censures were insufficient for the reformation they sought: ceremonies redolent with the stink of popery still tainted the reformed church, the "zealous" were threatening to leave it, and the papists were banging at the door. The preaching clergy saw themselves as battling against local justices, bailiffs, and commissioners who refused to enforce the anti-Catholic censures and laws that did exist and who allowed recusants "to shift out of the way and avoid being apprehended" ("A Letter sent from the Preachers," 79).

This epistolary dialogue between local parish ministers and archbishop reveals some of the central dilemmas of post-Reformation religious order: the disparate contexts in which ministers worked (Lancashire, the county in which the presented ministers worked, was, as they attest, largely recusant); the "things indifferent" around which much post-Reformation religious rancor centered; and the differences between ecclesiastical laws and the desires of local ministers, magistrates, and the parishioners themselves. The ministers' godly nonconformity rests on their appeal to the greater fear of popery and its "gross idolatry," but for the Archbishop, the threat to religious order comes less from popery than from zealous lawbreaking. The fact that the ministers identify themselves as "preachers" in their letter and that they have been presented for "inconformitie" testifies to their problematic status vis-à-vis the church. Like "praying," "preaching" was in fact often a "concealed weapon" of ministerial dissent, a threat not only to ecclesiastical hierarchy but to royal supremacy.[7] In the hands of "preaching" ministers, that is, "reform" often entailed criticism and, potentially, disloyalty to the church.[8] The contests between "preaching ministers" and ecclesiastical authorities exemplified in this 1590 exchange would escalate under the next monarchical regime. For James I, the "private spirit of Reformation," particularly the separation of one's personal beliefs from the dictates and outward ceremonies of the church, even in "smaller matters of inconformitie," was a much greater threat to religious stability than quiescent recusancy.[9]

William Leigh, who was rector of the Standish parish from 1586 until his death in 1639, understood his role to be that of a "preaching" minister, inscribing his pulpit with Paul's words from 1 Corinthians: "Necessity is laid upon me; yea, woe is unto me, if I preach not the gospel."[10] The parish of Standish was a particularly volatile one, divided between powerful Catholic families who resisted many of the changes of the Reformation, and a strong Puritan movement headed by Leigh.[11] As the letter to the Archbishop of York suggests, Leigh was notorious for presenting recusants to the authorities, and he sat as a justice at the trial of several recusants and priests.[12] After the accession of James I, Leigh preached at court and the king appointed him tutor to his eldest son, Prince Henry. Leigh quickly became a loyal supporter of the prince and remained so until Henry's death in 1612.[13] Yet as we have seen, Leigh's own relationship to the authorities was often resistant, and he seems to have fallen from favor with the king. In 1610 James, who was deeply concerned about "the humours of Puritanes, and rash-headed Preachers, that thinke it their honour to contend with Kings," took a property he had previously given to William Leigh away and gave it to another minister.[14] This sign of disfavor was likely the result of Leigh's Puritan views. The criticisms leveled at the episcopacy in the 1590 letter to the Archbishop of York continued to inform Leigh's religious practice, and his career continued to be somewhat more radical than the established church—and its head—liked. It is into this uneasy situation that the Standish monster was born, its doubled body held up by William Leigh as a sign of England's imperfect union with God, and its story wielded as a critique of the policies not only of the ecclesiastical authorities but of the official head of the church.

Bastards

The year in which Standish buried its five illegitimate children, including a conjoined monster, was part of a period in which reform-minded Lancastrians were concerned with bastardy as well as recusancy.[15] Yet as we saw in the previous chapter, bastard bearers had to be caught to be punished, and not everyone wanted to turn to either secular or ecclesiastical authorities for the management of their communities. (As John Crompton of the neighboring town of Bolton declared, "he cared not for the bisshope" and "had no king but God.")[16] While many Puritans had their own misgivings about the ecclesiastical establishment, they certainly saw moral and social policing as necessary for the reformation of the people. In 1613, for example, William Leigh preached a sermon before the authorities at the Lent Lancashire Assizes and dedicated its publication to the Lancashire Attorney General. As he wrote in his epistle: "[I]f you pleade not, and we preach not, neither state can long stand."[17] Despite their belief in the reforming power of preaching and prayer, Puritans still saw the need for juridical intervention and earthly punishment, and it is in the service of these ends that Leigh made one of his two polemical uses of Standish's "duobus puer."

ON JUNE 12, 1613, the publisher Samuel Man registered a pamphlet entitled *Strange Newes of a prodigious Monster, borne in the Township of Adlington in the Parish of Standish*, for which William Leigh was titularly identified as the chief informant.[18] The monster is described as having "a strange and wonderfull shape, with foure legges foure Armes, two bellyes, proportionably joyned to one back, one head two faces, like double-faced *Janus*, the one fore, the other behind" (A4v). The pamphlet's frontispiece features a woodcut of the conjoined monster, its two faces looking in opposite directions (fig. 3.1). Leigh initially interprets the monster as a Protestant portent for the nation as a whole, putting it in the context of other anti-Catholic monstrous births: a whale that appeared off the coast of Cornwall in 1588; a monster bearing the shape both of a man and a beast, which warned of "that fearefull yet memorable warre of *Tyrone*"; and a double-bodied monster "produced in Antwerpe in the yeare foregoing the beginning of those troubles of the low Countryes, which the matchlesse cruelty of *Rome* and *Spayne*, hath plagued with unspeakable miseries" (A4). Just as these monsters portended threats to international Protestantism (the Armada, the Irish rebellion, the wars in the lowlands), so does the local monster, born in recusant-hindered Standish, signify grave dangers to its English offshoot. England, he insists "has more monsters than anywhere else" (A3). Along with their history of forewarning popish threats from the outside, monstrous births are also warnings of the threat to Protestantism from inside England itself.

As Leigh writes, "It behooves us to looke about, when such examples beyond the order of Nature are brought forth to put us in minde of our iniquities, es-

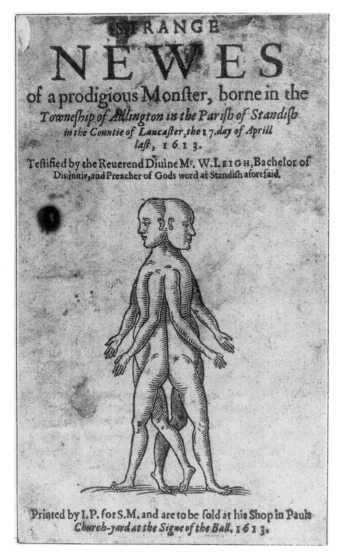

Figure 3.1. Title page, *Strange Newes of a prodigious Monster, borne in the Township of Adlington in the Parish of Standish in the Countie of Lancaster, the 17 day of Aprill last, 1613. Testified by the Reverend Divine Mr. W. Leigh, Bachelor of Divinitie, and Preacher of Gods word at Standish aforesaid.* (Printed by I. P. for S.M. and are to be sold at his Shop in Pauls Church-yard at the Signe of the Bull, 1613), STC 15428. Reproduced by permission of the Folger Shakespeare Library.

pecially the sinnes of Adultery and fornication" (A4v). As we have seen, monstrous births were often interpreted as the result of the parents', particularly the mothers', sins, and were frequently employed in early modern popular broadsheets and pamphlets as punishment for sexual crimes. Monsters, as one ballad puts it, are "bastard sinnes in bastard shapes decried," and Leigh similarly reads his monster as testament to the fact that "*Bastard slippes shall never take deepe roote*" (B).[19] Like the monstrous births in the broadsheets and pamphlets in chapter 2, the Standish monster makes "secret" sexual transgressions and histories materially legible, rendering the mores and actions of parishioners that were overlooked by the authorities fantastically public.[20]

Conjoined twins or deformed infants often served as figures of such illegitimate sexual unions. A 1566 ballad entitled *The true description of two monsterous children* includes a woodcut illustration of conjoined twins who are simultaneously strangling and embracing one another (fig. 3.2). The twins freeze in bodily form the prohibited sexual embrace of the parents, both demonstrating a prior deed and warning against its reproduction. Such births, as the ballad states, "forewarne *both man and wyfe:* / How *both estates* ought to bewayle, / their vile and wretched lyfe."[21] The figure of the Standish monster similarly evokes and inverts its parents' deed: the twins are forever separated, literally facing away from each other even in their conjunction. As popular emblems, conjoined twins were grotesque inversions of Plato's Androgyne and Ovid's Hermaphroditus, both of which were allegorized as Christian symbols of wedded concord. The comparison between the Standish monster and "double-faced *Janus*," the two-faced Roman God of peace and war, beginnings and endings, similarly lends the figure emblematic resonance. Renaissance emblematists often made Janus into a moral emblem encouraging the reformation of behavior. Geoffrey Whitney's 1586 version, for example, claims that "Janus bids us alter with the yeare / And make amendes, within the yeare begonne," encouraging readers to look backwards on their sins and forward to their reformation (fig. 3.3).[22]

Leigh's message of reform similarly focuses on the relationship between past acts and future effects. The father and mother of the child, he tells us, "were both *branded*"—the father "of lewd carriage and conditions"; the mother "with the *marke of Basterdy,* and from her Parents crimes in Adultery" (A4, emphasis added). The product of such marked parents, the monstrous birth is not only the "curse" that God "denounceth against Bastardy," but testament that the sins of adultery and fornication "are ever iustly punished by the righteous lawe and iustice of God, even upon the Childrens children unto the third and fourth gener-

Figure 3.2. John Mellys, *The true description of two monsterous children, laufully begotten between George Steuens and Margerie his wyfe, and borne in the parish of Swanburne in Buckingham shyre, the. iiii. of Aprill. anno Domini. 1566. the two children hauing both their belies fast ioyned together, and imbracyng one another with their armes: which children wer both a lyue by the space of half an hower, and wer baptized, and named the one John, and the other Joan.* (Imprinted at London: by Alexander Lacy, for William Lewes: dwellyng in Cow lane aboue Holborne cundit, ouer against the signe of the Plough, 1566), STC (2nd ed.), 17803. Reproduced by permission of the British Library.

Figure 3.3. Emblem from Geoffrey Whitney, *A Choice of Emblemes, and other Devises* (London, 1586), STC 25438, 108. Reproduced by permission of the Henry E. Huntington Library.

ation of them that hate him" (A4v). For Leigh, monsters are "punishments be-twixt the Justice of God, and the unrighteousness of Man" and serve as the puni-tive records of corrupt lineages (A2v). While punishment, according to Fou-cault, is "an art of effects," it also looks forward to the future: "One must punish exactly enough to prevent repetition."[23] Indeed, it is repetition that Leigh seeks to prevent, arguing that if people continue to sin, they will find "the continu-ance of punishment" (A2v). These "fatherly menaces," he warns, "will bee turned into causes of greater mournings" (B3).

According to Leigh, the conjoined monster's lesson in the "ougliness of sinne" (A3) was widely effective. When news of its birth came, he reports, "Cer-taine Gentlemen, and many of the common people [of Standish], that were then at Cockpit [. . .] left their sports and went to behold it with wonder and amazement." Even "the most impious of all could not but confesse, that [the monster] was a notable example of Gods fearefull wrath" (B). In turning away from their "sports," the people of Standish turned, at least momentarily, in accordance with Puritan desires. As the county most associated not only with recusancy but with popular festivities and sports, Lancashire experienced a great deal of Puritan interference about its ungodly entertainments. In fact, in 1591 the ever-vigilant Puritan ministers of Lancashire wrote a letter complaining explicitly about the prevalence of both bastardy and "cockfights and other unlawful games" in the county. Not only did these activities take place on Sundays, holidays, and during divine service, but they were attended by "justices of the peace and some Ecclesiastical Commissioners."[24] Those who should be policing such activities, in other words, were participating in their perpetuation. James I, however, famously defended "publicke spectacles of all honest games [. . .] for conveening of neighbours, and for entertaining friendship and heartliness." Sports, in his view, were politically useful: "[T]his forme of contenting the peoples mindes hath beene used in all well governed Republicks."[25] Published a few years after Leigh's pamphlet, James's dedication of his Book of Sport to the citizens of Lancashire was, among other things, a slap at the interfering hands of the county's Puritan ministers. In *Strange Newes*, Leigh imagines that God himself serves the role that secular and religious authorities refused: he leads people away from their sports to listen to his lessons.

As the authoritative witness both of the monster and of its divine significance, "Master William Leigh, Bachelour of Divinity, a very worthy and Reverend gentleman, Preacher of the Parish of Standish aforesaid" (Bv), signals his intimacy with God's designs and reminds readers of his divinely mandated role as a local enforcer of religious and social reform. When Leigh writes that he leaves the consideration of the monster's significance "to the godly disposed," he implicitly asks his readers to align themselves with a specific moral position. He invites his readers to position ("dispose") themselves in contrast not only to those ungodly "justices of the peace and some Ecclesiastical Commissioners" who attend cockfights and ignore the fornication in their midst, but to the policies of a king who allows that to happen. Although James I purportedly bemoaned the fact that "fornication is thought but a light and veniall sinne, by the most part of the world" and recommended that leaders "count every sinne and breach of Gods law, not according as the vaine world esteemeth of it, but as God the Iudge and maker of the lawe accounteth of the same," he also had a somewhat relaxed application of the law. Men, he argued, are prohibited "from any wayes invading or molesting their neighbours persons or bounds."[26] Laws, he continued, are rules for "vertuous and sociall living," not "snares to trap [. . .] good subjects."[27] James reserved punishments such as branding for those who most threatened social order; fornication before marriage, while a "venial sin," did not necessarily interfere with James' vision of "vertuous and sociall living."

But for godly ministers like Leigh, venial sins *did* stand in the way of virtuous living and thus in the way of the Reformation itself. The parents in *Strange Newes of a prodigious Monster,* Protestant juridical subjects whom Leigh imagines as "branded" and "marked" with the signs of sexual deviance, produce a monster that testifies not only to their crimes but to God's recognition and condemnation of them as such. "These monstrous and prodigious birthes," Leigh tells us, "are not greatly to be marvelled at, if we look but only into the causes of them, which for the most part are our sinnes." Leigh thus encourages popular marveling: in order to give "full satisfaction to some people that were incredulous of it, unless they might be made also eye witnesses," the monster's grave was opened, "and the body layde to the view" of over five hundred "beholders" (Bv). In encouraging people not only to behold it but to look into its causes, Leigh renders the monster proof of the divine condemnation of the sins of fornication and bastardy, acts which many did not, in their private consciences or relaxed interpretation of the law, consider sins at all. In figuratively "invading or molesting [. . .] neighbours persons or bounds," the monstrous birth attests to the need for juridical accordance with divine law. A monster is born, not just as a reminder of original sin, but as a demonstration against the specific sins Puritans sought to rectify.

A similar logic informs a 1617 pamphlet by the Puritan William Jones. Entitled *A wonder worth the reading,* the pamphlet's monstrous birth is interpreted as a warning for London and a punishment for the myriad sins of its citizens, including "great pride and excesse in apparel," "whoredome, luxurie, [and] drunkenesse."[28] Such sins, Jones continues, are committed daily "in the presence both of God and man, as though the Magistrate had no law to punishe them: nor the Minister courage to reprove them: for feare of offending a great man in his parish, or loosing part of his pension" (A4). Much like William Leigh's criticism of the Stuart failure to punish ungodly behaviors and buttress the work of preaching ministers, Jones's pamphlet is critical of the socially and politically compromising situation in which preaching ministers found themselves. While Leigh uses Standish's monstrous birth to seek implicit support for a Puritan agenda, Jones explicitly asks readers to consider the religious and social costs of the Stuart persecution and divestment of godly or preaching ministers: "the late silenced and deprived ministers in England."

Like Leigh's, William Jones's Puritanism led to various forms of silencing and deprivation.[29] In the first few years of James's reign, Jones secretly published pamphlets attacking, among other things, "the uniust usurpacon of the Prelats over his Maie's Subiects and the lawes and liberties of the land"; the rites and ceremonies in the Book of Common Prayer; and the deprivation of "Prechers" who refused the "Subscripcion and Ceremonyes urged" by the ecclesiastical authorities.[30] In July 1609 the Star Chamber court arrested him for publishing "scandalous, factious and seditious bookes and pamphletts" tending "to the breedinge and begettinge of schisme, errors and disorder in the Church and to the dissolvinge and frustratinge of [the King's] most religious and christian purposes and resolutions."[31] James himself took particular interest in Jones's punishment, calling him "that Puritan Printer" and ensuring his imprisonment.[32] In 1616 William Jones gained possession of a new printing press and continued to print radical godly texts, including the Puritan text that would lead directly to James's 1624 banning of "seditious books."[33] The year after securing this press, Jones published *A wonder worth the reading*, which couches his more actionable Puritan critiques in a genre that had become so prevalent as to seem, at least to some, "harmless."[34] Unlike the texts for which Jones was prosecuted, the pamphlet's title does not mention papists or Puritans, "things indifferent," or preaching ministers; but the story does take a clear Puritan position on such issues.

In Jones's pamphlet, the monster serves as remonstrance for those who profane the Sabbath by ignoring "preachings and prayings" and "conferences of instructions publickly taught." (Like Leigh, Jones castigates those who consider "Church assemblies, and the religious exercises therein, no better, then of common meetings for sports.")[35] While Puritans viewed these exact forms of public preaching as the basis for the reformation of society, James I saw them as a threat to his control: the potentially seditious work of "brainsick and heady preachers."[36] For Jones, on the other hand, social disorder is a direct result of the civil and ecclesiastical failure to support public "preachings and prayings." People behave "as though the Magistrate had no law to punishe them: nor the Minister courage to reprove them" precisely because magistrates and ministers are not doing their work. The godly ministers have been persecuted and deprived of their parishes, and the extant ministers are hampered in their work by such political considerations as the "feare of offending a great man in his parish, or loosing [sic] part of [their] pension" (A4). In a truly godly community, the minister's work would not be limited by the fear of offending anyone, even if that "great man" were the king himself. Jones suggests that through a combination of preaching the word and "conferences of instructions publickly taught," ministers and magistrates would be able to exert moral control over a society currently given over to common sports and pastimes and moral laxity; and, as in Leigh's pamphlet, the monstrous birth testifies to the divine sanction for his agenda.

Like his forebears, Jones sees his pamphlet as a form of popular casuistry. In much the same way as the 1562 broadsheet discussed in the first chapter asked each reader who beheld its monstrous birth to "saye within his harte / It preacheth now, to me," Jones asks "every honest heart, *to apply this to his owne conscience, and seriously to weigh and consider the sinnes of the land*" (A3v, emphasis added). While each beholder of the monster is told to apply the message of the monstrous birth to his or her "owne conscience," that individual conscience is aided by God, who has "dispersed the glorious light of his word, both in the publike Ministrie and private exercises thereof" (A4). Although the individual conscience was considered the grounds of the reformed religion, as Jones's instructions suggest, many reform-minded Protestants believed that the conscience required the guidance of both public and private instruction. As I suggested earlier, English Protestantism may have had relatively little official moral theology or "case divinity" to match the massive science of casuistry in the Catholic Church, but many Protestants nonetheless endeavored to provide answers to controversial cases of conscience, often in popular printed forms like *A wonder worth the reading*.

Puritans were not opposed to pamphlets in the way they opposed "lawful recreations" like sports: popular illustrated texts were a means not only of catechizing the people but of providing answers to matters of controversy and, ideally, of empowering the casuists who deployed them. When Leigh leaves the interpretive discrimination of the monster's significance to the "godly disposed," a catchword for Puritans, he signals that his pamphlet's religious message dissents from the status quo. When he puts a woodcut of a monstrous birth on the cover, he seeks readers who are disposed to curiosity. Both acts endeavor to disseminate a message about "vertuous living" in whatever way they can. Yet while Leigh's pamphlet was local in its origin and intent, he nonetheless saw the Standish monster as the opportunity to make a larger comment on English religious order. Like William Jones, Leigh was concerned with the guidance of the individual conscience, but he knew that the greatest cases of conscience did not have to do with domestic matters of sex or civil behavior but rather with the question of faith itself. One of the most serious problems facing Protestant reform was equivocation, the insincere or two-faced avowal of Protestant faith and allegiance. If the conscience was the grounds of the reformed faith, it was nonetheless the place in which many recusants (or other skeptics of the Church of England) located their own dissenting faith, outwardly vowing loyalty to the church and king of England, and privately disavowing their legitimacy. Even more than secret or unrecognized sins like fornication, the private nature of equivocation made it extremely difficult to police. It was thus to this end that Leigh next deployed the story of Standish's monstrous and two-faced birth.

Equivocators

"A double minded man is unstable in all his ways."   —JAMES I.8

On May 31, 1613, William Leigh published two of his sermons in a volume entitled *The drumme of devotion, striking out an allarum to prayer, by signes in heaven, and prodigies on earth*.[37] After giving a list of biblical prodigies, Leigh offers a familiar description of the monstrous birth born in his Standish parish: "a dead childe, base borne, of lewd parents, having four leggs, and foure armes, all out of the bulke of one bodie: with one plaine back without seame or division, it had but one head, and that of a reasonable proportion, with two faces, the one looking forward, and the other backward" (42). As in the pamphlet version, Leigh interprets the monster as remonstrance for the sins of its "lewd" parents, particularly the absence of "virginall and conjugall chastity," but he also reads the monster within a different register of meaning. A symbol of England's disordered body politic, the monster's "many legges and armes may tax our intollerable pride, and averise," and its "Two mouthes taking in, & two bellies casting out, taxe our insatiable desire of belly cheere & drunkennes." The deformed child's most distinguishing feature, however, is its two faces, which

> taxe the world of palpable hypocrisie, divelish deceit, & damned *equivocation*: First, in us Protestants whiles we say we beleeve, and yet do not live the life of the Gospel we professe: wherein we doe but Sophisticate with the Lord, & *equivocate* with his Saints: for what avayleth it, a tongue to speake well, with a mentall reservation to do evill? Next, it may seeme to taxe the damnable doctrine of our *Romish* equivocators, who are double-faced to deface all truth, and to destroy all commerse both with God and man (44–5, emphasis added).

Leigh reads the birth as an indictment of "double-faced" Catholic equivocators who vow one thing but believe another, but he also sees it as an indictment of Protestants who say they live by the gospel but "equivocate" with the Lord and "his Saints," Puritans' shorthand term for the godly elect. In this reading, those who refuse the bidding of the saints are no better than the papists in their "sophisticat[ion]," or duplicitous wranglings, with God. For Leigh, the monstrous birth both symbolizes the dangerous conjoining of Catholicism and Protestantism in the body of England and exposes the secret corruptions and "mentall reservations" of ostensibly conforming Protestants.

In viewing the monster as a symbol of a disordered body politic, Leigh not only deploys a dominant metaphor of statehood but uses the figure of the conjoined monster as a symbol of a mixed Catholic and Protestant state. In *A Comparative Discourse of the Bodies Natural and Politique* (1606), a text glorifying state sovereignty and claiming nearly unlimited power for the king, the royalist Edward Forset writes that like the individual human body "Britannia" must have only one head: "[I]t were utterly impossible, or unsufferablie mischevious, to admit any partnership in the regall dignitie. Let us imagine a bodie so monstrous, as whereunto two heads were at once affixed, shall not that bodie receive much damage by the division and confusion of those two heads? must not the bodie in that case either be divided by alotting of one side to the one, and the other side to the other head?"[38] Like Leigh, Forset figures a religiously divided country as a monstrous body: Catholic believers in a Protestant country set up two heads— one papal and one monarchical—to which the subjects, or body, might pay allegiance.[39] The idea of a single head to the body politic was of course central to the Reformation conflict between the papacy and the emerging national monarchies. In England it was famously exemplified by Henry VIII's famous "volte-face," or about face, in which he denied papal supremacy and proclaimed himself "Supreme Head of the Church of England," a position inherited, in turn, by James I.[40]

The figure of the two-headed monster had already been deployed at different troubled moments of English religio-political history. The Marian exile John Ponet, for example, interpreted a conjoined monster born in Oxford in 1552 as a sign forewarning the period following the death of Edward VI. In this era, he wrote, there will be "two headdes, diverse governours, and a towarde division of the people."[41] *Coopers Chronicle* similarly identifies the same conjoined monster as a sign of England's politically divided future and claims that the fact that the children were both female led people to believe that they signified "the two

Quenes that were proclaimed after Kyng Edwardes death," the Catholic Mary and the Protestant Elizabeth.[42] This monster, moreover, enjoyed a wide representative life; it appears in John Day's 1552 broadsheet, and it is featured, in a slightly different form, in Stephen Batman's *The Doome*, among other texts (fig. 3.4). Through the image of a two-headed monster, Forset, a man unequivocally

Figure 3.4. Woodcut from Stephen Batman, *The Doome Warning All Men to the Judgement* (1581), John R. McNair, ed. (Delmar, N.Y.: Scholars' Facsimiles and Reprints, 1984), 278. Reproduced by permission of the Henry E. Huntington Library.

loyal to James, makes it clear that English subjects must have allegiance to only one head: the King of England, not the Pope of Rome.

In his own discussion of a monstrous body politic, William Leigh is less concerned with two heads than he is with one head that is two-faced, or equivocating. Equivocation—what Leigh calls "mentall Reservation"—was predicated on the idea that it was acceptable to make a spoken assertion or oath of loyalty or conformity if silent mental correction accompanied it.[43] English priests and recusants used equivocation in order to swear vows of allegiance to their regent while simultaneously vowing secret allegiance to their religion and their pope.[44] Such "doublefaced" equivocation was thus explicitly associated with Catholic treason, and Leigh's references to the "doublefaced, doubleharted, and doublehanded [forces . . .] threatening our destruction" and to the whore of Babel's "Romish faith and faction [. . .] daily breed[ing] even in the bowels of the kingdom" directly allude to Catholic insurrections (44). The monstrous activity in the "bowels of the kingdom" cites the Gunpowder Plot of 1605 in which Catholic forces conspired to blow up Parliament from below. An "equivocating" Jesuit priest, Henry Garnet, was seen as the inspiring force behind the plan and was executed with exemplary spectacle the following year.

In 1606 William Leigh published a pamphlet about the Gunpowder Plot in which he called the event a "Romish Monster, and Popish prodigie" that "was strangled in the birth, ere it could be borne."[45] The Gunpowder Plot traitors themselves were often represented as monsters. One contemporaneous text claims that they were exhibited to the populace as "the rarest sorts of monsters; fools to laugh at them, women and children to wonder, and all the common to gaze,"[46] a line seemingly cited by Shakespeare's Macduff when he tells the traitor Macbeth that he will be "painted upon a pole" "as our rarer monsters are."[47] Macduff's allusion to representations of "rarer monsters" on poles refers to the displaying of broadsheet pictures and pamphlet frontispieces of monstrous births; of broadsheet portraits of traitors, often physiognomically inflected; and of pictorial libels of local malefactors, who were often represented as monstrously deformed.[48] Leigh's description of his "rare monster" in *The drumme of devotion* similarly collapses the rhetoric for popish traitors with that of monsters, but this monster is an actual rather than a metaphorical birth, a portent and sign from God attesting to the popish threat: "a monsterous birth and mishapend broode, of that whore of Babel."

Leigh's use of the Standish monster in this context was buttressed not only by a range of interrelated practices of monstrous representation but by a wider culture of prodigies surrounding the Gunpowder Plot. On November 25, 1606, the Archbishop of Canterbury called for his chief justice to arrest a man for spreading tales of miracles, including the story of a piece of straw on which, by Catholic report, Henry Garnet's blood had fallen and his crowned head had miraculously appeared, and the story of a miraculous child reputed to attest to the righteousness of the Catholic faith.[49] Robert Pricket's 1607 pamphlet, *The Jesuits Miracles, or new Popish Wonders. Containing the Straw, the Crowne, and the Wondrous Child, with the confutation of them and their follies*, deems both stories fraudulent, and claims that the straw was inscribed by "some Popish painter" (B3) (fig. 3.5).[50] "New strawes are painted now," he mocks,

As if thereon two faithlesse faces stood:
Rightly to paint the painter well knew how,
For Garnet had two faces in one hood:
Equivocation his double face did cloake,
Equivocating himselfe at last did choake.   (B3)

At the last line a contemporary reader notes in the margins of the text both "Equivocation of Garnett," and "two faces," attesting to his or her recognition of the apt iconography of Catholic duplicity. The (Protestant) painter's image of a two-faced head both mocks the "miraculous" vision of Garnet's crowned head and serves as a monstrous figure of equivocation.[51]

Such "miraculous" stories, Pricket tells us, are told to "begile" the "faithlesse weake." Miracles are now "fully seast [ceased]"; "We live in Christ salvations only meanes" (D2). Yet many Protestants, including Pricket himself, understood James's survival of the plots against his life, including the revelation of the "damned [Gunpowder] plot," as divine miracles: "These miracles their truth doth farre surpasse, / Those idle tales that papists cast at us, / Their lies, their child, their straw, their lying grasse."[52] Claims of divine revelation and deliverance were in fact a structuring ideology of James's rule. Yet as I have already suggested, one of the most trenchant religious dilemmas of post-Reformation England was less whether God continued to reveal his divine plans to his subjects than the ways in which his subjects revealed their own allegiance and beliefs to their king: the problem of "mentall reservation" so decried by Leigh. Papists, Pricket acknowledged, can steal the hearts of a king's subjects, making them "secret traytors" "[w]hose outward shew can their close thoughts conseale."[53]

The real threat of traitorous "monsters," then, was less their notable physiognomy than the fact that, at least from the outside, they were not remarkable

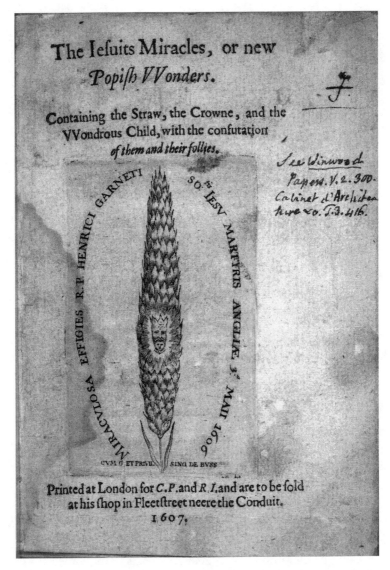

Figure 3.5. Title page, *The Jesuits Miracles, or new Popish Wonders. Containing the Straw, the Crowne, and the Wondrous Child, with the confutation of them and their follies* (Printed at London: [By Nicholas Okes] for C. P[urset] and R. I[ackson] and are to be sold at his shop in Fleetstreet neere the Conduit, 1607), STC 203401. Reproduced by permission of the Henry E. Huntington Library.

at all. The punishment and dismemberment of traitors' bodies was thus an important part of execution for treason: they and their bodies had to be rendered exemplary. One of the more famous prints of the executions of the gunpowder plotters shows the severed head of a traitor (presumably Garnet) and the traitor's heart as if they are parallel signs: the severed head a symbol of treason against the king, and the extracted heart—the inner citadel of Christian faith—a sign of the heresy of popery and the crime of equivocation. Beneath both lies the limbless, headless body (fig. 3.6). In the print, the executioners expose the traitor's heart as a revelatory document, a sign of the state's ability to police inner belief, to get into that inner sanctum of Englishmen that is only partially revealed by outward vows. If, in conventional Protestant iconography, the heart was the temple of true faith, in the representations of executed traitors it is an emblem of heresy. The traitor's heart bears no cross or other sign of sanctification the way a saint's might; his heart is not a martyr's relic but a symbol of betrayal. Yet despite the revelatory fantasies of such popular prints, no contemporary observer could ignore that such revelation and exposure could happen only *after* death. God may "miraculously" reveal the earthly plans of traitors, but before execution the heart and its secrets beat quietly inside each believer. From the outside, "rarer monsters" look only like men.

After the Gunpowder Plot, James passed an act that asked Catholics to take an Oath of Allegiance renouncing the pope's claims to be able to depose kings and release subjects from allegiance to their sovereign. James insisted that it was a civil oath and denied the pope only "temporal and not spiritual or ecclesiastical power."[54] It was to be signed by those "who although they were otherwise Popishly affected, *yet retained in their hearts the print of their naturall duetie to their Soveraigne.*" James insisted that he intended "no persecution against them for *conscience cause*, but onely desired to be secured of them for civill obedience."[55] In order to deal with Jesuitical equivocation, the Oath of Allegiance included the claim that the words were to be spoken "according to the plaine and common sense and understanding of the same words, *without any Equivocation*, or mentall evasion, or secret reservation whatsoever."[56] Yet the Oath itself had a built-in equivocation: it allowed Catholics to continue practicing their faith in their consciences and allowed for a separation of the spiritual from the civil. In some ways the Oath could thus be seen as a legalization of duplicity. For Protestants like Leigh, this separation—at least for Catholics—was simply untenable.

As the Gunpowder Plot and the execution of its perpetrators should have shown, the claim that subjects' hearts could simultaneously bear "the print of

Figure 3.6. The Execution of the Gunpowder Plotters (1606), BMC71. Reproduced by permission of the British Museum.

their naturall duetie to their Soverainge" and be "otherwise Popishly affected" was not only false but dangerous. In admitting a distance between outward attestation and inner belief, James admitted an enormous instability into the settlement of English religion. His claim that he meant "no persecution against them for conscience cause, but onely desired to be secured of them for civill obedience" challenged two basic tenets of religious order: the idea that "conscience" was about obeying God's handwriting within us—and *not* a matter of individual faith and interpretation—and the idea that the king's conscience was the conscience of the realm.[57] James certainly asserted that conscience was not the same thing as opinion and actively denied what he saw as the anarchic Puritan claim to personal conscience.[58] Elsewhere he wrote of the necessity for the prince to keep conformity "betwixt his outward behaviour and the virtuous qualities of his mind," and he even expressed his desire "that there were a Christall window in my brest, wherein all my people might see the secretest thoughts of my heart."[59]

In his writing, James fantasized an utter conformity between the inner citadels of his heart and his outward behavior; but in his Oath of Allegiance, he seemed to suggest a different model for the people of England. While he insisted on his subjects' vows of loyalty, he implied that their consciences and hearts need not be open to the state. In the opinion of Protestants like William Leigh, James thus produced a body politic that was monstrously two-faced.

In Leigh's sermon, the monstrous birth's doubled form embodies the duplicity of equivocation, and its two faces signify those English subjects who vow Protestant conformity but "sophisticate" with, or adulterate, its meanings. Yet the monster is also, as we have seen, a figure for a disordered body politic; and for Leigh the English body politic is disordered less by two heads—Catholic and Protestant—than by two *faces*. Like Forset, Leigh sees any association with, or allegiance to, Catholicism as threatening the sovereign's power. But unlike Forset, Leigh seems to suggest that the proximity of Catholicism to English Protestantism is partly the responsibility of the "head," or James I himself.

James was in fact already notorious among committed Protestants for admitting Catholics to his inner circle, for attempting to make alliances and peace with Catholic countries, and for offering toleration to English Catholics.[60] Like Leigh's two-faced monster, James did look both "forward" and "backward" in his dealings with Catholics and Protestants: he gave "audience and accesse to both sides," freed "Recusants of their ordinarie paiments," and refused to persecute Catholics who gave "an outward obedience to the law" by attending the services of the Church of England.[61] Many viewed James's dealings with Catholics as fundamentally equivocal. Anthony Weldon claimed that the king's familiar motto, *Beati pacifici* (Blessed are the peacemakers), was implicitly joined to another, *Qui nescit dissimulare, nescit regnare* (He who does not know how to dissimulate, does not know how to rule).[62] James's own politic "dissimulation" with Catholics had already made his Protestant conviction suspect in the minds of some of his subjects.

When Leigh wants to "proceed yet further and *make use of the prodigie*" in his sermon, he thus links its birth to a particular historical moment in English Protestantism. The monster was born in 1612, he tells us, right after the death of Prince Henry, James I's son and heir to the English throne. In place of this "[r]oyal & religious issue whereof [England is] unworthie," a Prince, "*so well fashioned in his life* [but] so soone forgotten in his death," the country is given a monster (47). If a king's true legitimacy was dynastic, the very birth of an heir was a judgment from God.[63] As James himself wrote, Henry was "not ours only as the child of a natural father, but as an heir apparent to our body politic in whom our state and kingdome are essentially interested."[64] Thus, Leigh's sermon suggests, the birth of the monster—an anti-heir—is also a judgment from God. Henry's death occasioned, or allowed for, the rebirth of the "monsterous birth and mishapend broode, of that whore of Babel," a monster who last attempted to see the light in the Gunpowder Plot. In linking the appearance of the double-faced monster to the death of Prince Henry, Leigh acknowledges Henry's centrality to radical Protestantism and his role as an alternative to James: a Head who would not give "accesse to bothe sides."

A fierce Protestant who did not believe, as James did, in peace-making with Catholics, Henry had, in fact, been seen by radical Protestants as an alternative to James.[65] Roy Strong suggests that *Love Restored*, the last masque Henry's commissioned, seems to criticize the king (the imposter Plutus) for "making friendships, contracts, marriages, and almost religion . . . *Tis he that pretends to tie kingdoms*."[66] As king, James endeavored "to tie kingdoms," not just through peace-making with Catholics, but through his own marriage—Queen Anne's purported Catholicism was a grave concern to many—and the marriages of his own children.[67] James even planned to marry Prince Henry to a Catholic bride, a proposal that caused much uproar, particularly among Puritan preachers, during the year in which Leigh published his sermon.[68] However, as Isaac Wake wrote shortly after Prince Henry's death, Henry himself was always firmly resolved that "two religions should never lie in *his* bed."[69] Henry, according to Wake, understood the analogical necessity of the Protestant family; he would never have married a Catholic and would certainly never have produced a bastard conjoined offspring.

As Leigh's sermon indicates, when Henry died, the cause of uncompromising Protestantism suffered a devastating blow, and James remained head of the nation and the church. Some even blamed James for Henry's death, and on November 5, 1612, "on the anniversary of a memorable deliverance" (the exposure of the Gunpowder Plot), the body of Henry, Prince of Wales, was "opened on account of vulgar rumours about his death."[70] Although his death "was proved to be from the hand of God,"[71] the opening of the Prince's body was in many ways a challenge to James's promise of a "crystal window" to his own heart. Some believed that the inside of Henry's body would reveal something about the contents of James's heart, show that the death of God's Protestant heir was at the hands of England's two-faced king. For Leigh, the timely coincidence of a monstrous birth and Henry's death was an occasion not only to foster anti-papal sentiment but to offer implicit criticism of, and warning for, James, as the head of both church and state, not to compromise the safety of England either through unions or equivocation with papists. The head of England cannot, as the monster does, have one face looking forward toward Protestantism, and one looking backward toward Catholicism. Equally importantly, and more subtly, Leigh suggests that the head should not sophisticate with the "Saints."

Godly Protestants' focus on the mental reservation and equivocation of papists did more than cast suspicion on their enemies; it also served to deflect attention away from their own participation in such practices. On November 25, 1612, for example, Gaspar Schoppius printed a treatise "to prove that Protestants profess equivocation as well as Jesuits."[72] Based on claims to conscience, some godly Protestants separated their inner faith—their membership in the invisible church of the elect—from their participation in the visible Church of England.[73] If the commands of lawful authority were against the law of God, they reasoned, these commands could be ignored, even actively resisted; and on such grounds Puritans could refuse to conform to the forms of worship dictated by the church and the Book of Common Prayer.[74] One such matter centered on the authority of "things indifferent," William Leigh's old problem. The means by which the ecclesiastical hierarchy could determine the conformity of ministers lay in external gestures: oaths, kneeling, wearing surplices, preaching from the Book of Common Prayer. A minister's refusal to participate in these "things indifferent" was necessarily schismatic, a choice of private conscience over public duty. It was precisely such a decision of "conscience"—the refusal to wear the surplice—that brought Leigh himself to the attention of the church authorities years earlier. Indeed, four years *after* the publication of his sermon against equivocators and two-faced monsters, one of Leigh's parishioners, Nicholas Assheton, recorded in his journal an after-dinner "argument abt Mr. Leigh's ministring ye Sacrament with[ou]t the Cirploise."[75] Assheton's father argued that Leigh's refusal to wear the surplice was a godly one; his neighbor, that it was unlawful. A few entries later, Assheton condemns the neighbor as "popish." Assheton's diary illustrates that some Protestants accepted certain forms of separation between private belief and outward conformity; equivocation, as Schoppius pointed out, was not solely the provenance of Catholics. Leigh's focus on papists as the practitioners of equivocation was intended not only to draw attention to James's two-faced dealings but to direct attention away from the secret (and not-so-secret) resistances of his Puritan co-religionists. The "Saints," he insists, should be left alone.

Yet while Leigh saw Catholicism (and anti-Puritanism) as the monster, James decried "another sort of Religion, besides a private Sect, *lurking within the bowels of this Nation.*" Using the same metaphorical language as Leigh (who warns that a "Romish faith and faction [. . .] doth daily breed even in the bowels of the kingdom"), James saw England's lurking threat as Puritans like Leigh who resisted James's desire for "a generall Christian union in Religion."[76] In addition to his criticism of "rash-headed Preachers, that thinke it their honour to contend with Kings," James criticized Puritans for setting themselves up as the elect, or the "Saints," and for calling themselves "the onely trew Church . . . and all the rest of the world to be *but abomination in the sight of God.*"[77] According to James, such believers, including those who reject the surplice and other signs of outward conformity, make "the scriptures to be ruled by their conscience, and not their conscience by the Scripture." They base their religion on "their owne dreams and revelations."[78] "I was ofttimes calumniated in their populare Sermons," James writes, and "I hate no man more then a proude Puritane."[79] It would be hard to call Leigh anything but a "proude Puritane," and while the Standish monster may not have been Leigh's "dream"—as we have seen, it had its origin in an actual birth—he certainly claimed the revelation of its significance as his prerogative, rendering his "populare Sermon" on prodigies a subtle critique of his anti-Puritan king.

As James's fulmination indicates—"I was ofttimes calumniated in their populare Sermons"—sermons did play a central role in the formation of popular opinion in seventeenth-century England. Although the crown tried to control preachers' words—both proscribing and prescribing topics for sermons—the pulpit was also the mouthpiece of Puritans and independent-thinking preachers like Leigh.[80] Many of those godly Protestants' sermons did, in fact, "calumniate" against the king, particularly in regard to his Spanish policy and his dealings with Catholics.[81] In the first decade of his reign, James imprisoned, legislated against, and executed preachers who inveighed against his policies, accused his Council of being traitorous papists, or even *planned* to preach "seditious sermons" about or before him.[82] (In 1612, the same year as Leigh's sermon, a Somerset rector was condemned to death upon the discovery of notes for a "seditious sermon").[83] Eventually, James passed a law aimed at "seditious Puritan" books that prohibited "the printing or importing of any work on religion, church government, or state unless approved by Archbishop or Chancellors."[84]

In this unsettled period before the passage of the law, Leigh's critique of Jacobean religious order in *The drumme of devotion* is biting, but it is also politic.

His sermon uses both the divinely revelatory polemic associated with the exposure of the Gunpowder Plot and conventional critiques—including those deployed by James himself—of the danger of a monstrously divided or two-headed body politic. Yet Leigh's sermon about a two-faced monster is also a carefully modulated critique of the ways in which the king, as head of the state, equivocates with papists, and the ways in which he has allowed his subjects to do the same. In its critique of mental reservation, Leigh's sermon also highlights the error of Protestants who "sophisticate," or disagree with, the Lord's "Saints" and their vision of Protestant reform. While Leigh's focus on such false Protestants deflects attention away from his own conscientious rejection of certain aspects of Jacobean religious order, his sermon and its revelatory monstrous birth lays claim to divine support for the resistant Puritan voice. It is the saints, after all, who can read God's signs and who can identify a "rare monster," no matter what its form, for what it really is.

For Leigh the story of the doubled child born in Standish, Lancashire, attests both to the dire nature of the sins of fornication and bastardy—matters "winked at" by many authorities—and to the absolute error of equivocation. If most cases of conscience in the seventeenth century dealt either with "domestic" matters, such as fornication, adultery, and bastardy, or with "religious" issues of allegiance and equivocation, this story shows the extent to which the domestic and religious were not separate spheres, particularly in the minds of godly reformers.[85] The "secret sins" of parishioners existed in the same sphere as their "inner faith": monstrous births were merely the extreme forms of the promise that private sins—particularly those sins ignored or protected by a faulty conscience—would be exposed. The conjoined monster served Leigh's own joint purposes of local moral reform and national reprimand—its body a sign of Protestant England's imperfect union, its story a vehicle of dissent.

CHAPTER FOUR

Heedless Women, Headless Monsters, and the Wars of Religion

After the often Puritan-authored and circulated broadsheets and pamphlets of the late sixteenth and early seventeenth centuries, the greatest number of popular illustrated stories about monstrous births were produced during the English civil wars and interregnum of the 1640s and 1650s, when questions of religious order and conformity were even more volatile than they had been in the earlier part of the century. In the earlier texts, monstrous births are considered both general warnings and sin-specific punishments, the stories of their production often finely attuned to particular social and religious issues, and frequently to the controversial behaviors of their mothers. The pamphlets published in the 1640s share many of these qualities. Printed, advertised, and circulated by publishers affiliated with a newly powerful Parliament, however, they primarily endeavored to promulgate parliamentarian views about religious and social order that were increasingly under pressure not only from more precise Protestants but from Nonconformists and sectarians of much more radical inclinations as well.

While the conjoined monsters discussed in the last chapter occasionally served as figures for a body politic now divided between royalist and parliamentary forces (e.g., fig. 4.1), the privileged figures of the 1640s were headless mon-

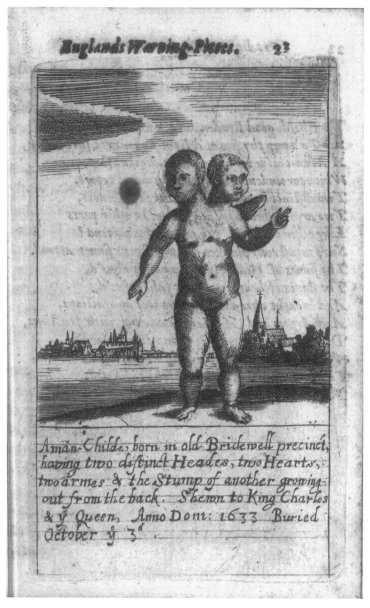

A man-Childe, born in old Bridewell precinct,
having two distinct Heades, two Hearts,
two armes & the Stump of another growing
out from the back. Shewn to King Charles
& y Queen, Anno Dom: 1633 Buried
October y 3.

Figure 4.1. Woodcut from John Vicars, *Prodigies & Apparitions or Englands Warning Pieces Being a Seasonable Description by lively figures & apt illustrations of many remarkable & prodigious fore-runners apparents Predictions of God Wrath against England, if not timely prevented by true Repentence* (1643), 22. Reproduced by permission of the Henry E. Huntington Library.

sters. The simplest explanation for this fact is that the period was marked by a series of beheadings, culminating in the beheading of the king, Charles I, in 1649. Thereafter, until the restoration of the monarchy in 1660, the country was ruled as a Commonwealth and Protectorate: a kingless, or "headless," body politic. Yet stories of headless monsters also invoked the proliferation of insurrections of all kinds—beheading was, after all, the punishment for treason—including those instigated by women. In the pamphlets, headless monsters are born to women who are themselves "headless": resistant not only to their husbands but also to the dominance of Parliament and its struggling ecclesiastical and ministerial systems. While headless monsters are seen as physical manifestations of their mothers' erroneous consciences—outward signs of monstrously disordered interiority—they are also seen as the products of their mothers' increasing participation in both private and public spheres as religious dissenters: recusant, anti-ecclesiastical, prophetic, sectarian. The women in these stories reproduce the religious disorder in the society around them, but they also produce it, giving it new and dangerous forms. The monsters' missing heads invoke familiar ideas of insufficiency of matter and excess of female imagination, but they also invoke a range of female desires, beliefs, public avowals, and activism specific to the religious and political turmoil of 1640s England.

Headless Women

The man is as the Head, and the woman as the body. . . . And as it is against the order of nature that the body should rule the head: so it is no lesse against the course of all good order, that the woman should usurpe authoritie to her selfe over her husband, her head.

> — THOMAS GATAKER, *Marriage Duties Briefly Couch'd Together* (1620)

I know of no true Divinity that teacheth men to be Lords over the Conscience.

> — KATHERINE CHIDLEY, *The Justification of the Independent Churches of Christ* (1641)

The image of the headless woman, a woman who either lacks or refuses the guidance of her husband, is one of the oldest tropes of gender relations. Emblem 16 of *The Theater of Fine Devices* (1614), for example, includes with its headless woman the motto: "Search for strange monsters farre or wide, / None like the woman wants her guide" (fig. 4.2).[1] In many popular pamphlets the logic of a

EMBLEME XVI.

Search for strange monsters farre or wide,
None like the woman wants her guide.

Great monsters mentioned are in stories found,
As was *Chymera* of a shape most wondrous,
Girion, Python, Cerb'rus that hel-hound,
Hydra, Medusa, with their heads most hideous,
Satyres and Centaures; all these same were found
In bodies strange, deformed and prodigious:
   Yet none more maruellous in stories read,
   Then is a woman if she want a head.

Figure 4.2. Emblem 16 of *The Theater of Fine Devices, containing an hundred morall Emblemes. First penned in French by Guillaume de la Perriere, and translated into English by Thomas Combe* (London, 1614), STC 15230. Reproduced by permission of the Henry E. Huntington Library.

woman's purported headlessness carries over to her offspring; the headless child is both a symbol and a product of its mother's lack of patriarchal guidance. In *Strange newes out of Kent, of a monstrous and misshapen child* (1609), for example, the headless child is the product of a seemingly husbandless "wandering young woman." In *A wonder worth the reading* (1617), the monster-child has only half a head, and two little horns "pricking up, behind each eare," deformities that combine the emblem of headlessness with the horns of cuckoldry. In both stories, the monstrous births attest to their mothers' failures to heed the appropriate authorities (figs. 4.3 and 4.4).

Similar ideas of headlessness and cuckoldry figure in a famous story told most memorably in a pamphlet entitled *A myraculous, and Monstrous, but yet most true, and certayne discourse, of a Woman . . . in the midst Of whose fore-head (by the wonderfull worke of God) there groweth out a crooked Horne* (1588).[2] The history of the woman's deformity is explained as follows:

> [S]ome affirme that in her youth shee was not so loyall to her husband as dutie ought, and that divers times there hath beene speeches tending to that purpose between her husband and her, wherupon hee suspecting lying same to be true, that shee was light of behaviour and charging her with it in these tearmes, that she had given him the horne, it is said, that shee not only denyed it, but wished of God that if shee had given her husband the horne, that shee might have one horne growing out of her owne forehead. (A2v)

As the pamphlet's frontispiece attests, a horn does indeed appear on her forehead (fig. 4.5). Margaret Owen's story suggests that visible signs will follow from private sins—what the author calls "secret offences"—providing a material signal for the public involvement in and punishment of private sexual behavior. After the appearance of her horn, Owen is purportedly "examined by the Justices of Peace of y said countrie," who inform "the councell of the Marches of Wales" and send her to London "to the end she might be seene of the Lords of the Queenes maiesties most honorable privie Councell" (A2v).[3] While Margaret Owen becomes a juridical subject through divine providence, her story is specifically identified as a warning for everyone "that they tempt not the lord God, in craving his vengeance to be seene upon them for their secret offences" (A3); her horn is an example of "the ancient assumption that sacrilege of any kind brought its own penalty."[4] Her private sins, that is, are exacerbated by her public lie, and it is precisely according to the terms of that lie—her wish "that if shee had given her husband the horne, that shee might have one horne growing out of her owne

Figure 4.3. Woodcut from *Strange nevves out of Kent, of a monstrous and misshapen child, borne in Olde Sandwitch, vpon the 10. of Iulie, last, the like (for strangenes) hath neuer beene seene* (Imprinted at London, By T. C[reede]. for W. Barley, and are to be sold at his shop in Gratious-street, 1609), STC 14935. Reproduced by permission of the British Library (see 2.4).

forehead"—that she is punished. Owen's story warns women not only against adultery but against lying about it, lest, in the words of another pamphlet that tells the same story, they "call vengeance on their heds."[5]

The relationship between women's untruthful or resistant public avowals and their appropriately correlative punishments is the animating logic of a number

Figure 4.4. Woodcut from *A wonder vvorth the reading, or, A true and faithfull relation of a woman, now dwelling in Kentstreet, who, vpon Thursday, being the 21 of August last, was deliuered of a prodigious and monstrous child* (London, Imprinted by William Jones, dwelling in Red-crosse-streete, 1617), STC 14935. Reproduced by permission of the British Library.

of later pamphlets about women who give birth to monsters. In these stories, however, the public vows that the women make are vows of religious dissent. In *A strange and lamentable accident that happened lately at Mears-Ashby in Northamptonshire 1642*, the author, who identifies himself as "John Locke, Cleric," begins his story by criticizing those who listen to the opinions of lay preachers and reject official religious ceremonies, "contemning and slighting Gods holy ordinances" (A2v).[6] Locke argues that the "pernicious and illiterate doctrines" of

Figure 4.5. Title page, *A myraculous, and Monstrous, but yet most true, and certayne discourse, of a Woman (now to be seene in London) of the age of threescore yeares, or there abouts, in the midst Of whose fore-head (by the wonderfull worke of God) there groweth out a crooked Horne* (1588), STC 69107. Reproduced by permission of the Henry E. Huntington Library.

these "over curious and nice zelots" have resulted in many examples of God's wrath and judgment.[7] "[T]hough thy intent in doing seeming good action be ever so good," he tells those who resist church ceremonies, "if thou have not warrant for not so doing, thou and thine action may happily perish together as the sequell of this story will declare" (A3v). The "warrant" for any action must come from clerics, Locke insists, not from believers' individual consciences.[8]

The primary case of conscience in Locke's pamphlet is that of Mary Wilmore, the pregnant wife of a rough mason who is "much perplext in minde, to think that her childe when it pleased God she should be delivered, should be baptized with the signe of the Crosse" (A3). The parish minister, however, "being a very honest and conformable man, not suiting with the vaine babling of erroneous Sycophants," tells her husband to "goe to Hardwicke, a Village neare adjoyning to one Master Bannard a reverend Divine, to know his opinion concerning the Cross in Baptisme" (A3). Bannard responds that although it is "no wayes necessary to salvation," the sign of the cross was "an ancient, laudable, and decent ceremony of the Church of England" (A3). While straightforwardly offered and backed up by the Book of Common Prayer—it is in fact a direct quotation from the baptismal ceremony—Bannard's verdict on the use of the cross was nonetheless highly controversial. Like the surplice, the use of the sign of the cross in baptism was considered one of the "things indifferent" of the reformed church: while not necessary for salvation, it had been written into church law at the Hampton court conference and was thus a church-sanctioned ceremony. Some, however, considered the sign of the cross a superstitious popish remnant that attributed too much efficacy to rituals—according to tradition, the sign of the cross made on the right hand and forehead signified that the baptized child was protected by God and that the destroyer could not touch her—and reaction against the new law was vociferous. William Bradshaw's *A Shorte Treatise of the crosse in Baptisme* (1604), to cite only one example, argued that the sign of the cross was "a humane ordinance," an idol, and that it "may not lawfully be used in the service of God."[9] Many godly or Puritan ministers and lay people thus resisted its use, and Mary Wilmore's parish minister was certainly aware that she was not alone in her concerns about the use of the sign of the cross.

With the increase of radical Protestantism and the decline of ministerial policing in the 1640s, obtaining conformity to what Reverend Bannard called the "ancient, laudable and decent ceremon[ies]" of the Church of England became an increasingly complex matter. By 1642, the year *A strange and lamentable accident* appeared in print, the Church of England was radically destabilized by parliamentary insurrection and civil war; the episcopal hierarchy, church courts, and most diocesan administrations had largely ceased to function. Moreover, the county in which Mary Wilmore lived, Northamptonshire, was known not only for its Puritanism but, increasingly, for its Independency and Congregationalism.[10] When the commissioner appointed by Archbishop Laud to report on nonconforming clergy and nonobservance of the Book of Common Prayer rubric visited Northamptonshire in 1635, he discovered widespread defiance of "indifferent" ceremonies, including the sign of the cross.[11] With the dominance of the Long Parliament in 1640, of course, both the scrutinizers and their focus changed: many members of Parliament were much more concerned with nonpreaching ministers than with nonconforming ones.[12] Yet as Parliament turned its energies toward the establishment of a Presbyterian system of ecclesiastical order, ministerial and parishioner resistance to ceremonies and rituals like the use of the cross in baptism was increasingly seen, not as a sign of Puritan godliness, but of sectarianism. In 1642, the year *A strange and lamentable accident* was published, Presbyterianism was on its way to being the established religion in Northamptonshire, but it faced much resistance from Baptists and Independents. Mary Wilmore's religious questioning aligns her with such sectarianism, and her story reflects the divide between Parliament's attempts to establish ecclesiastical order on a Presbyterian model, and the desires and beliefs of those who rejected it.

When the parish minister of Mears Ashby sends John Wilmore to a "reverend Divine" in a nearby village to inquire about the use of the cross in baptism, he echoes parliamentarian attempts to maintain ministerial control and parish conformity across large distances. In the absence of a coherent system of ecclesiastical policing, he seeks to maintain a chain of ministerial authority and ceremonial consistency in a county singularly threatened by radical sectarians.[13] As if to prove this point, Locke claims that Mary Wilmore's belief that "the Crosse in Baptisme [is] a pernicious, popish, and idolatrous ceremony" is the result of her "weaknesse, or too much confiding in the conventicling Sectaries" (A3). In sending a husband to seek ministerial resolution of his wife's case of ceremonial "conscience"—it is Mary Wilmore who is "perplexed," remember, not her husband—the minister thus attempts to return religious authority, both within the household and the parish, to conforming men. In fact, the "reverend divine" to whom Mary Wilmore's husband is sent was, like Locke himself, a Cambridge-educated deacon and priest who served Northamptonshire as a rector from 1608 until his death in 1644.[14]

If one of the most appealing ideas of Protestantism was the belief that the Lord "doth manifest himself to rule in the flesh of sons and daughters," promising all believers, men and women alike, a personal and unmediated relationship with God, this democratization of God nonetheless always threatened to replace the national church with the authority of the believers themselves.[15] In the 1640s, sectarianism was the most extreme manifestation of this threat. "If liberty be granted to sectaries," Thomas Case told the House of Commons in May 1647, "they may in good time come to know [. . .] that it is their birthright to be free from the power of Parliaments and [. . .] of kings, and to take up arms against both." "Liberty of conscience," he added, "may in good time improve itself into liberty of estate and liberty of houses and liberty of wives."[16]

The liberating effects of sectarianism on the consciences of "wives" is well documented. Many anti-sectarian attacks in fact focused on the involvement of women, punningly labeled "the weaker Sect."[17] In his 1647 heresiography, the Scottish Presbyterian Robert Baillie singles out the Anabaptists as the worst offenders because "many more of their women do venture to preach then of the other."[18] *A Discoverie of Six Women Preachers, in Middlesex, Kent, Cambridgshire, and Salisbury* (1641) includes the names of such women preachers and reminds readers of Paul's lines from 1 Corinthians: "Let your women keepe silence in the Churches [. . .] And if they will learne anything, let them aske their husbands at home."[19] In another pamphlet, *A Spirit Moving in the Women-Preachers* (1646), the women are seen as both ideological prey—"the Jesuites, Priests, and Separatists of our times and Church have made, and ever do make singular use of these female Creatures"—and as viragos who "wear [. . .] the breeches" and "draw and lead their husbands by the nose."[20] Like *A Discoverie of Six Women Preachers*, *A Spirit Moving in the Women-Preachers* repeats the line from Corinthians, referring women back to "their husbands at home," and defends churches as "the fittest and most decent places for preaching of the Word [. . .] though all sorts of Sectaries do now strive to discredit the same, by House-Preaching" (4–5).

The ambivalence about private homes expressed in *A Spirit Moving in the Women-Preachers* addresses a matter of concern intimately related to the extradomestic religious advice given to Mary Wilmore's husband in *A strange and lamentable accident.* Although a woman is supposed to ask her husband to teach her "at home," "House-Preaching," or preaching outside the church and without the sanctioned Book of Common Prayer service, was increasingly prevalent in the 1640s. As the Presbyterian heresiographer Thomas Edwards claims in his *Gangraena*, many sectaries move "to a new house every day the more to infect and possess the people."[21] The home was thus imagined both as a safe place in which women learned religious conformity under the guidance of their husbands, and as a potential site of often woman-led sectarian dissent. The fact that sectaries "use Houses in place of the Church" raised fears not only about the limited control of ecclesiastical jurisdiction but about individual female religious interpretation and resistance. Although we are not told where she meets with "conventiclers," it is clear that Mary Wilmore is not getting her ideas in church. And it is in her own home that Mary Wilmore makes her opinions about the sign of the cross known; she is singularly uninterested in the Pauline injunction about asking her husband to teach her about religion.

Although early Protestant propagandists celebrated women whose "consciences" encouraged them to resist the beliefs of their (Catholic) husbands and bishops—in John Foxe's *Actes and Monuments* (1563), to take one example, Joan Baker is praised for claiming that "[s]he could hear a better sermon at home in her house then any priest could make at Paules crosse"[22]—religious dissent was less celebrated when the resisted religion was that of the Church of England.[23] Women, moreover, were often in the forefront of such dissent, particularly during the period leading up to the civil war. In Calvinist Edinburgh in 1637, the resistance to Charles I's imposition of the Book of Common Prayer was reputedly opened by a crowd of "rascally serving women" at St. Giles' Church, who drowned out the Dean's reading, threw stools at the Bishop of Edinburgh, and, when evicted, stoned the doors and window.[24] In 1641 the women of Middlesex petitioned Parliament, proposing extempore prayer in preference to the Book of Common Prayer; and in another petition delivered the same year, a group of women claimed that, given the power of prelates "to exercise authority over the consciences of women, as well as men," they too should have a voice in public matters of religious settlement.[25] The freedom of conscience had, as Case feared, helped to liberate wives; and Mary Wilmore was, whether her parish minister liked it or not, one such wife.

Despite the fact that both her husband and the local ministers authorize the rite, Mary Wilmore persists in her dissent: "I had rather my childe should bee borne without a head," she tells them, "then to have a head to be signed with the signe of the Crosse" (A3). Her vehement resistance to the ceremony was shared by other women. Mrs. Dorothy Hazard harbored women about to give birth so that, being born in her husband's parish, they might "avoid the ceremonies of their churching, the cross, and other impositions that most of the parsons of other parishes did burden them withal."[26] Similarly, when a Newcastle minister attempted to make the sign of the cross on a child in June 1642, the child's mother "covered the child with the linen and kept it down with her hand," while another woman "laid hold of one of the curate's hands which was kept behind him by the father of the child."[27] Yet while Mary Wilmore's adamant rejection of the sign of the cross was neither unprecedented nor, in Northamptonshire, an extreme minority opinion, it was nonetheless made at great cost.

As was the case with Margaret Owens and her cuckold's horn, Mary Wilmore is punished according to the terms of her own wish: a month after her claim that she had rather her child "bee borne without a head, then to have a head to be signed with the signe of the Crosse," she was "accordingly delivered of a Monster, *Rudes indegestaque moles*, a child without a head" (A3v). The woodcut in the pamphlet's frontispiece represents a number of women around Mary Wilmore's childbed, including a midwife who is pictured from the back with her hands raised in a gesture of surprise (fig. 4.6). Although the role of midwives in monitoring social and religious legitimacy was anxiously buttressed by statutes—women "employed in the assistance and help of a woman in travail" were consistently reminded to "put far from [them] all superstitious conceits and idle fancies and to remember that God too was in the room"[28]—as the seventeenth century progressed, the fear was less of popish midwives welcoming infants with Catholic rites than of dissenting women conspiring to reject the rites determined by the present ecclesiastical order.[29]

While the emblematic surprise of the midwife in the woodcut can be read as the pamphlet's assurance that she is fully cognizant of the horrors that Mary Wilmore's dissent has produced, Locke is also undoubtedly aware of the threatening potential of the "lying-in." During the later seventeenth-century, childbed lyings-in, much like private homes, took on additional subversive valences. In *The Pleasures of Matrimony* (1688), for example, the author claims that the lying-in is "a time when women, like parliament men, have a privilege to talk petty treason against their husbands."[30] Such analogies between parliamentary and marital insurrection were not used merely to ridicule parliamentary rebellion: women *were* in fact committing "treason" against their husbands. Although Mary Wilmore's child is purportedly born headless, in the woodcut it appears as if its head has been severed from its body, a clear visual invocation of the iconography of the beheaded corpses of traitors (e.g., see fig. 4.7). The headless monster's visual similarity to the fate of traitors highlights the seriousness of Mary Wilmore's sectarian resistance to the will of her conforming husband: among her other crimes, she is a petty traitor.[31]

Figure 4.6. Title page, John Locke, *A strange and lamentable accident that happened lately at Mears-Ashby in Northamptonshire. 1642. Of one Mary Wilmore, wife to Iohn Wilmore rough mason, who was delivered of a childe without a head, and credibly reported to have a firme cross on the brest, as this ensuing story shall relate* (Printed at London: for Rich: Harper and Thomas Wine, and are to be sold at the Bible and Harpe in Smithfield, 1642), Thomason E.113[15]. Reproduced by permission of the British Library.

Figure 4.7. Title page woodcut, *The confession of Richard Brandon the hangman (upon his death bed) concerning his beheading his late Majesty, Charles the first, King of Great Brittain* (London: s.n.], Printed in the year year [sic], of the hang-mans down-fall, 1649), Wing (2nd ed., 1994), C5798A. Reproduced by permission of the Henry E. Huntington Library.

Locke tells us that the monster's headlessness was meant to arouse "the shame of the parents, in not having that part whereon it might have been markt with that token *whereof it should never after have beene ashamed*" (A3v, emphasis added). This divine vindication of the sign of the cross cites, once again, the Book of Common Prayer's baptismal ceremony. The ritual specifies that "the priest shall make a cross upon the child's forehead" while saying aloud, "We receive this child into the congregation of Christ's flock, and do sign him with the sign of the cross, *in token that hereafter he shall not be ashamed to confess the faith of Christ crucified.*"[32] It also states that although "the keeping or omitting of a ceremony, in itself considered, is a small thing [. . .] the willful and contemptuous transgression and breaking of a common order and discipline is no small offence before God."[33] The contradictory claim that the sign of the cross is simultaneously a "small thing" and its omission an "offense before God," allowed room, as we have seen, for individual judgment and personal conscience in matters of ceremony. Locke's citation of the ceremony indicates his prayer book conformity at the same time as it highlights the divine retribution for Mary Wilmore's failure to do so.

With her refusal of a "decent and laudable ceremony" of baptism, Mary Wilmore ensures that her child is neither regenerate nor "grafted into the body of Christ's Church."[34] The monstrous birth is a revelation of divine law, its headlessness an incontrovertible sign of the necessity of "indifferent" ceremonies as well as the treasonous nature of their omission. In teaching a story defending the central importance of a "small thing," Locke's pamphlet credits the sign of the cross—or more precisely, its omission—with a "crudely material efficacy."[35] If it was superstitious to believe that the sign of the cross could ward off evil spirits or make a child "come on better," was it not also superstitious to believe that its omission could monstrously deform a child? The Protestant deployment of superstitious beliefs was not, as we have seen, unusual. While ceremonial resisters often paradoxically accredited rituals they considered "popish" or illegitimate with a *negative* material efficacy—a 1643 newsbook, for example, reports the case of a nonconforming minister who claimed that ministers who "signed Children with the signe of the Crosse, did as much as in them lay to send such Children unto the Divell"—their conformist peers, like Locke, often saw their omission as having material results.[36] Although the pamphlet, like the Book of Common Prayer, insists that the sign of the cross "was no wayes necessary to salvation," it still raises the specter of material efficacy: without proper baptism, the story tells us, your child will be destroyed.

In the woodcut on the title page of the pamphlet, the church stamps its authority on Mary Wilmore's child by depriving it of a head. But although a cross is mentioned in the title—the child is "credibly reported to have a firme Crosse on the brest"—no cross appears in the woodcut (see fig. 4.6). At the same time as Locke establishes the church's authority by showing God's punishment for Mary Wilmore's resistance to the "laudable" ceremony, he (seemingly) capitulates to fears of charges of popish superstition and idolatry by visually omitting the sign of the cross. In the most famous of illustrated Protestant texts, *Actes and Monuments* (1610), John Foxe tells the story of a martyr who "desired of God some token to be given, whereby the people might knowe that they dyed in the ryghte." As he burned in the fire, Foxe reports, there appeared on this martyr's breast "a marvellous white crosse, as whyte as the paper, the breadth whereof extended from one shoulder to the other."[37] Shortly after *Actes and Monuments* appeared in print, Thomas Stapleton criticized Foxe's use of such miraculous stories: "Iff the Crosse of saint Oswalde semes a superstitious tale, how much more fonde and fabulous is the tale of one that suffred at Bramford, with a great white crosse appearing in his brest?"[38] Stapleton's critique of Foxe's "superstitious tale" seems to haunt Locke's own storytelling. Like Locke, Foxe included no actual images of crosses in his illustrations, but he understood the power of "superstitious" and "fabulous" tales in attracting and convincing Protestant believers.

The story of Mary Wilmore's monstrous birth thus both makes use of beliefs in the efficacy of controversial religious rites and attempts to erase their most obviously "superstitious" traces. The monster itself conjoins familiar ideas of the dangers of women's desires and imagination with the material dangers of questioning religious rites. In Locke's pamphlet, a woman's conscientious resistance to patriarchal and clerical control is punished by the birth of a monster. The monster reminds her not only that all children are born in sin—a belief that sectarians were said to deny—but also that the sign of the cross—and all the dictates of the official church and its "Reverend divines"—are necessary for their salvation. Locke ultimately argues not only for the preservation of an embattled rite of the English church, but for the superiority of that church's newest institutional incarnation to the sectarian resistance gaining such purchase in Northamptonshire and elsewhere. He ends his pamphlet with a final comment on the "strange judgements of God have wee seene [. . .] in the times of revolters," and with a plea that "as there is one Lord, one faith, *and one baptisme*," may the "Lord grant that wee may joyntly agree in love, and that there remaine amongst us a godly consent and loving concord" (A3v–A4).

A strange and lamentable accident was published in 1642, and in 1644 the newly established Presbyterian *Directory of Public Worship* omitted the sign of the cross as part of the ritual of baptism. The *Directory* also insisted, however, that baptism was "not to be administered in any case by any private person, but by a minister of Christ. . . . Nor is it to be administered in private places, or privately, but in the place of public worship, and in the face of the congregation."[39] Even without the sign of the cross, that is, baptism remained a point of contention between the established church and sectarians.[40] Locke's desire for "one baptism" thus referenced both the specific issue of the sign of the cross and the larger problem of Baptist and Anabaptist schism. These sectarians' restriction of baptism, the seal of entry into the church, to adult believers signaled their rejection of a comprehensive or compulsory ecclesiastical system and thus of Locke's "godly consent and loving concord."[41]

The Anabaptists are the subject of a pamphlet entitled *Bloody Newes from Dover, Being A True Relation of The great bloudy Murder, committed by Mary Champion (an Anabaptist) who cut off her Childs head, being 7 weekes old, and held it to her husband to baptize* (1647). Like John Locke, the author of *Bloody Newes from Dover* is critical of the "diversity of Opinions, which are now held and maintained by too many sorts of people within this Kingdome," and the system of religious government he defends is now firmly Presbyterian. The pamphlet begins with the story of a Yorkshire husband and wife "who were of two severall Religion, and having a little son of some yeares of maturity, the good man (being a Protestant) desired to have him put to Schoole and to be brought up in the Protestant Profession: but his wife denied the same, saying, shee would have him brought up in the Catholike Faith, or else he should be of no Religion at all." Indeed, the author continues, "it fell out so: For this bloudy woman watching her opportunity, murdered the Boy."[42]

Having drawn attention to the destructive "diversity of [religious] opinions" held by English women, the author moves to the pamphlet's central story, which centers on a Dover couple named John and Mary Champian and their young child. Although the father, an "honest Tradesman," wants to christen the child "according to the ancient Custome of the Kingdome," his wife "would by no meanes condiscend to it, which much perplexed her husband" (A2).[43] Like Mary Wilmore's husband, another "honest Tradesman," John Champian's attempts to correct his wife's misunderstanding are fruitless. Eventually, when her husband is away from home, the "wicked minded" Mary Champian cuts off their child's head. When her husband returns, she greets him with the surprise: "Behold husband, thy sweet Babe without a head, now go and baptize it; if you will, you must christen the head without a body: *for here they lye separated*" (A2, emphasis added). When the husband shouts at her, "some of the Neighbors hearing him immediately came in, and seeing this foul misdeed, sent for the Officers of the Towne." Mary's murder of her child is an act of petty treason, but the means of the murder, beheading, cites the punishment for high treason. In the woodcut, the father, labeled "Presbyterian" for easy identification, throws up his hands in surprise, while the mother, Mary, labeled "Anabaptist," holds the child's bloody head in one hand and throws the headless body behind her (fig. 4.8).[44] Mary's is the same posture used by victorious executors: the new authority taking charge of the head of the usurped. But here it is not a tyrant who is usurped, but her husband and the authority of the Presbyterian Church.[45] Mary Champian's story echoes Locke's account of a headless woman "producing" a headless child, and her act of beheading—as she tells her husband, the head and the body "*lye separated*"—echoes the various separations being enacted in England at the time: a brutal (sectarian) division in the body of Christ.

Mary is apprehended and sent to prison "untill the next Assize, where by justice she must bee tryed according to the Lawes of this Realm." In prison, she feels penitent and sees strange visions: "[S]hee can no wayes fixe her eyes upon any thing, but presently [she conceived] the poore Babe to appear before her without a head" (A2v). Mary's vision explicitly invokes the language and visionary experiences of sectarian women prophets. When her grandson died, Lady Eleanor Davies, the most famous of the women prophets active during the civil war period, wrote to her daughter about a dream she had of a child beheaded for treason in which a group of women tried to quiet the bodiless head "which would not stop crying."[46] Such visions were explicitly related to the separation not only between the sects and the "body of Christ," but between king and parliament. Grace Cary, who saw an apparition of "a king's head and face without a body, which looked very pale and wan: it had a crown upon it and the crown was all bloody," interpreted it as a symbol of treason and death and translated it into a public plea for a reconciliation between king and parliament.[47] Some women sectarians also interpreted—or were said to interpret—their children's deaths as the result of their erroneous beliefs. Susanna Parr, for example, decided to break away from her Independent congregation after the death of her child: "When my bowels were yearning towards my child, I called to remembrance the Lord's tender bowels towards his children . . . when I considered the breach that the Lord had made in my family, I beheld how terrible it was to make a breach in

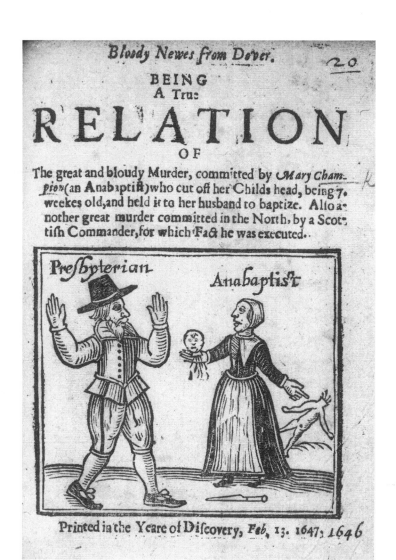

Figure 4.8. Title page, *Bloody Newes from Dover, Being A True Relation of The great bloudy Murder, committed by Mary Champion (an Anabaptist) who cut off her Childs head, being 7 weekes old, and held it to her husband to baptize* (1647), Thomason E.375[20]. Reproduced by permission of the British Library.

his family . . . then the work I was engaged in, the sin of separation, appeared nakedly unto me to be no other then a wounding of Christ's body."[48]

Like Susanna Parr's, Mary Champian's dissent is both "a wounding of Christ's body" and a threat to the entire body politic: once a breach in obedience is "laid open to the publique view," the author writes, "the whole body will endeavor to creep in after" (A2v). Her beheading of her own child thus serves as an emblem of the Anabaptist threat to the body of England. The pamphlet ends with an announcement of "the Ordinance for observing the Tenth Day of March next, a Day of Humiliation against the spreading of Heresies and Schismes," which was ordered "to be carried downe into the respective Counties of this Kingdome by the Sheriffes, and [. . .] published by the Ministers of every Parish [. . .] in their Church or Chappels" (A3v). In appending it to the sensational story of Mary Champian's murder of her child, the authors of the ordinance seek to give it the same comprehensive path of dissemination as popular ballads and pamphlets. Whether or not those who published and imagined the circulation of the pamphlet saw it as an effective means of maintaining ecclesiastical conformity over large distances, they certainly saw it as a way to disseminate their message in a singularly memorable way.

Roundheads

A similarly wonderful story is told in *A declaration of a strange and wonderfull monster: born in Kirkham parish in Lancashire* (1646).[49] According to the pamphlet, in 1646 one Mrs. Haughton, a "popish gentlewomen" and resident of Kirkham, Lancashire, gave birth to a still-born and monstrously deformed child and secretly buried it in the churchyard. After the burial, "some (in Gentlemen's habit) were seen to go in; supposed to be Popish Priests and Fryars" (4). The two secrecies here—the clandestine burial of a stillborn monster and the secret meeting of recusant Catholics—combine to create an atmosphere of pervasive corruption. Mrs. Haughton, we are told, has a Catholic genealogy herself: her mother also called "honest men Roundheads and many gentlemen did much use her house, which were suspected to be popish priests." Both women, in short, were harborers of priests, and their homes secret cabals of recusant organizing. The pamphlet reports that Mrs. Haughton owned "many popish pictures, and Crucifixes, and other popish trumpery wherein she much delighted" (5). While the private houses of sectarians were a source of great anxiety in the 1640s, recusant households had long been the subject of ecclesiastical concern. The Act of Uniformity's injunctions that sought to empty churches of idolatrous images also insisted that ministers "exhort all their parishioners to do the like within their several houses." And the visitation articles sought to police the insides of peoples' houses as well as the insides of their churches. Despite this history, many recusants did keep "popish trumpery" in their private homes, and in the actively anti-idolatrous 1640s, the keeping of such items was considered evidence not only of recusancy but of rebellious, anti-parliamentary intentions.[50] From the beginning of her story, Mrs. Haughton is identified as such a threat.

Much like sectarianism, the conspiratorial secrecy of recusancy was often explicitly associated with women. A 1641 pamphlet, *The Seven Women Confessors*, tells the story of a number of "popish" women who, "perceiving that *Jesuits, Priests*, nor *Fryers did not dare publickly to shew their faces*, impudently resolved to supply their places, and privatly proclaimed themselves Confessors."[51] The pamphlet, perhaps unsurprisingly, reveals the women to be whores, not confessors, thus sexualizing recusant women's activities and dealing with the difficulties of monitoring or policing the religious activity that goes on in private houses by rendering those houses "public" houses of ill-repute. Because of limits on the mobility and activities of Catholic men (given that they could be drawn and quartered if caught), women were often the heads of recusant households. The secret skulking of "Fryars and priests" around the Haughton house in *A declaration of a strange and wonderfull monster* and their intimate association with the secret burial of Mrs. Haughton's monstrous child suggest that the illegitimate activities of Mrs. Haughton's recusant household were more than merely devotional.[52]

Recusant women were in many ways a more serious threat to Protestant dominance than undercover friars and priests. Many of the recusant households full of "church stuff" in which the liturgical cycle was secretly celebrated were headed by women; men would often provide conformist cover for the household by going to Church of England services and celebrating mass at home with their wives.[53] Furthermore, although unmarried recusant women and widows were deemed responsible for their own actions and could be indicted, fined, and even imprisoned, married women could not. Even if indicted, the ultimate penalty for refusing to appear in court was outlawry, a charge that could not be imposed in the case of a married woman. Under laws of *coverture* a wife had no civil rights and could only be "waived."[54] Given that it was almost impossible to punish them, it was thus extremely difficult for Protestant activists to obtain the conformity of recusant married women like Mrs. Haughton.[55]

During the period in which *A declaration of a strange and wonderfull monster* appeared, the parish of Kirkham was dominated by recusant families, and the name "Haughton" had, as the pamphlet suggests, long been associated with the cause of obstinate recusancy in Lancashire. In the late sixteenth century a range of Haughtons were "detected for receipting of priests [and] seminaries" in their homes.[56] According to the pamphlet's anonymous author, although Kirkham was also home to "good Ministers, and some godly people," such people were in the minority and, much like William Leigh before them, "have suffered very much under [the papists'] reproaches and wicked malice" (4). As we saw in the previous chapter, Lancashire was already famous for its resistance to Protestant reform; the author of *A declaration* writes that no part in England was "fuller of Papists, and they were the chiefe Instruments in seeking to have that wicked *Book of Allowance for Sports on the Lords Day* to be published." (James I's notorious Book of Sports, republished by Charles I under the appeal of Lancastrians in 1633, continued to be a thorn in reformers' sides). Kirkham's recusant problem was pervasive, and in *A declaration of a strange and wonderfull monster* it centers on a particularly threatening recusant woman.

One of the pamphlet's chief concerns is with the relationship between Mrs. Haughton's recusancy and its (imagined) threat to the community. When the author focuses on Mrs. Haughton's "speeches" (3) in telling her story, the comment is not the typical injunction for women to be chaste, silent, and obedient, but rather an indictment of particular forms of seditious political and religious speech. Mrs. Haughton was said to often "hold a notable discourse with her neighbours about her religion," and "if she were at any time reproved for the superstitious fooleries she so affected, she would speak much in defence thereof [. . . and] expresse much invection against those godly protestants and others that reproved her" (5). She "hath been often heard to curse against Mr. *Prinn*, Mr. *Burton*, and Doctor *Bastwick*, and the Roundheads," and to "say that shee thought that the King and the Bishops were the righter part of us." Yet her activities as neighbor and citizen were for the most part sociable. Although she spent a lot of time in "popish devotion" and was "very zealous amongst papists," we are told, she was "friendly amongst neighbours," both "gentlewomen and Farmers wives." It was "onely when her Religion was touched [that] she expressed much passion" (5). Thus Mrs. Haughton is a threat to the community of Kirkham precisely *because* she is a good neighbor, someone who can maintain, for the most part, the "politics of good neighbourhood."[57] The author of the pamphlet attempts to disrupt the widely accepted notion that recusant Catholics

could make good neighbors by encouraging a separation between the godly citizens of Kirkham and their recusant—and thus secretly dangerous—neighbors.[58]

In order to achieve this end, the pamphlet focuses on one particular speech
that Mrs. Haughton made, a speech that was "most notorious, and hath rested
in the memory of some Gentlewomen, and others that heard her when she spake
it." The neighbors, "being in company with her [. . .] fell to discourse of the present miseries of the Kingdome, by these warres; and some spoke against the *Cavaliers*, and the *Papists* in the Kings Army" (6). Unlike the other women, Mrs.
Haughton criticized the Roundheads, and one of the women wished "if it pleased
God, that [Mrs. Haughton] had her eyes opened and was such a Roundhead."
In response, Mrs. Haughton replied, "I had rather have no head, nor life: nor
any of mine, I hope will ever be such . . . *I pray God, that rather than I shall be a
Roundhead or bear a Roundhead, I may bring forth a Childe without a head*" (6, emphasis added). Such open criticism of Parliament was not, of course, unheard of,
and parliamentarian officials occasionally succeeded in punishing it. On July 1,
1644, for example, one Mrs. Dorothy Crowch was called before the civil authorities in Lancashire and bound over to the next Sessions of the Peace for allowing her son and her guests "to singe reproachfull songs in her [ale-] howse
against the Parliament."[59] Yet although Mrs. Haughton is as guilty as Mrs.
Crowch, it is not the civil authorities who rebuke her. Her comment rather "pro-
voke[d] God to shew such a testimony of his displeasure against her," that he
caused her "to bring forth this Monster, whose Picture is in the Title-page of
this Book" (6) (fig. 4.9).

The frontispiece woodcut to which the reader is referred features the monstrous birth in the foreground and the interior of the recusant household in the
background. Like the illustration in *A strange and lamentable accident*, the pamphlet's woodcut is a story rather than an iconic image, a "single-setting narrative" that provides a visual tableau of recusancy.[60] The woodcut depicts a series
of scenes illustrating the main narrative elements of the pamphlet: a woman cutting her cat's ears (a story I will discuss shortly); the conversation or disputation
between a priest holding a rosary (undoubtedly one of the priests or "fryers" who
frequent Mrs. Haughton's household) and one brandishing the Bible (a representation of the debate between purveyors of popish superstition and godly ministers of "the Word"); the popishly-decorated interior of Mrs. Haughton's house;
and her childbed. This final scene features Mrs. Haughton in bed, with a midwife at the foot of the bed and a priest standing just behind her. The priest holds

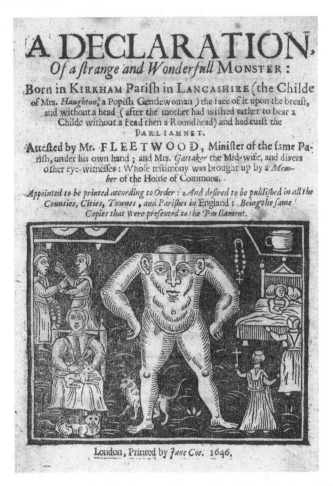

Figure 4.9. Title page, *A declaration of a strange and wonderfull monster: born in Kirkham parish in Lancashire* (London, Printed by Jane Coe, 1646), Thomason 53:E 325[20]. Reproduced by permission of the Henry E. Huntington Library.

a cross aloft in Catholic benediction, and the midwife's arms are raised in surprise (the identical place and posture of the attendant midwife in the frontispiece to *A strange and lamentable accident* [fig. 4.6]). The wall above Mrs. Haughton's head bears an image of an urn (an emblem of pregnancy) and a rosary. The proximity of superstitious imagery (the "popish trumpery" of crosses and rosaries), reproductive symbolism (the urn), and monstrous child suggests the deforming effects of idolatry and emblematically evokes beliefs in the ability of the maternal imagination to imprint the mother's monstrous desires on the body of her child. If gazing on images of Ganymede in their bedchambers could enable women to produce beautiful children, attention to, and contemplation of, priests and rosaries—the ideology and imagery of Catholicism—could certainly assist women in the production of monsters. Yet it is not primarily the act of *looking on* and worshipping idolatrous images that causes Mrs. Haughton's monstrous birth; it her public declaration of her popish beliefs and her desire that the body of her child testify to the passion of her beliefs: "I would rather bear a child without a head then a roundhead." Instead of bearing the physical badge of Puritanism—the definitive haircut that marks a "roundhead"—the child has no head at all. Its formative influences are deforming, and its headless body the monstrous product of popish resistance to Parliamentarian ascendancy.

Yet by publishing a woodcut that represents outlawed superstitious icons, the pamphleteer is in the strange position of policing recusancy via the representation of idolatrous images. *A declaration of a strange and wonderful monster* bears "idols in the frontispiece," the very crosses and rosaries for which people like Mrs. Haughton were arrested. Even though they are represented in a negative light, the icons are still credited with a kind of supernatural material efficacy— an ability, like the sign of the cross in baptism, to affect the child. As in *a Strange and lamentable accident*, the pamphlet also uses superstitious ideas of the material efficacy of words—in this case, Mrs. Haughton's claim that "she would rather bear a child without a head then a roundhead"—and miraculous revelation in order to discredit Catholic beliefs. Divine intervention not only sides with godly parliamentarianism, it exposes the threat of recusancy and locates that threat in the bodies and minds of women as well as in their homes.

The Haughton home had a long history of recusant activism. Years before the birth of the monster, we are told, Mrs. Haughton's own Catholic mother had declared that her cat "must be made a roundhead like *Burton, Prinne* and *Bastwicke*, and causing the eares to be cut off; called her cat Prynn (instead of Pusse)" (5).[61] Henry Burton, John Bastwick, and William Prynne were Puritan radicals who earned great notoriety for their resistance to Laudian episcopacy. Burton and Bastwick both had their ears cut off, and Prynne had his ears clipped twice and was branded on the cheek with *SL* for "seditious libeler" (he himself called the marks "Stigmata Laudis," after his arch-enemy Archbishop Laud).[62] For Puritans, the mutilated bodies of Prynne, Burton, and Bastwick were valorized as symbols of the sufferings of the godly, and the men were considered demimartyrs. In mutilating her cat, Mrs. Browne thus mocked the suffering of Puritanism's "idols," the heroic resisters of episcopal ("popish") tyranny. Reportedly, she "often said, that she hoped to see the Church flourish againe (meaning the Popish Church) and all Roundheads subdued"—a desire emblematized in her mutilation of her feline "Prynn."

It is perhaps not surprising to learn that the story of Mrs. Haughton's mother has its origin in a text written by William Prynne himself. In his 1641 description of the "Prelates Tyranny" over Burton, Bastwick, and himself, Prynne relates a 1637 story in which the Bishop of Chester, another of his sworn enemies, failed to punish the irreverent actions of "One *Mrs Hauton* of *Grimsor* in Lancashire, a Popish recusant."[63] After hearing of the punishments of the three men, Prynne tells us, this Mrs. Hauton set her three cats on "a kind of Pillory, where she cut off all their eares, and seared one of them in the cheekes, and then called them by the names of *Bastwick, Burton* and *Prynne*." Although "a grave minister" brought the story to the Bishop and asked him to order "the questioning and punishing [of] this audacious Recusant," the Bishop instead "checked the informer for a busie fellow, and in lieu of reformation falls to imitation of this Papist, hee and his servants ordinary calling a crop-eared Horse by the name of *Prynne*."[64] Clearly, the fact that the Bishop refused to punish the "audacious Recusant" Mrs. Hauton was an affront to Prynne, who bears, as he continually points out, *his* punishment on his body.

In a slightly later record of the "impudent obloquies and slanders of all pestilent and pernicious Anti-Parliamentarians," Prynne's friend John Vicars includes the story of "one Mistress *Haughton* wife to Master *William Haughton* of *Prickmarsh* within the parish of *Kirkham* in *Lefield* in *Lancashier*," who, on the 20th day of June, 1643, "was delivered of a childe still-borne, which had no head."[65] According to Vicars, the "Mistris Haughton" who gives birth to the monster is the granddaughter of the "Mrs. Hauton of Grimsor" who pilloried and de-eared her cats and whose tale was told by Prynne.[66] Vicars constructs a monstrous matriarchal legacy, combining one Mrs. Haughton's anti-Puritan street theatre with a second Mrs. Haughton's monstrous birth. In this genealogy, the second Mrs. Haughton receives the just—and emblematically physical—punishment that her (grand)mother did not receive.

During his petition to Parliament in April 1641, when Puritans were in a much better position than they had been 1637, Prynne argued that the loss of one's ears, an "infallible mark of [. . .] evill doing," was a great deformity. "The face of a man is that part wherein the *Image and majesty of God doth principally shine forth in our humane bodies*," he writes, and "the defacing and stigmatizing thereof is an high violation of the very Image of God himself engraven there-in."[67] Only God or Parliament, he argues, has the right to stigmatize a human face; any such act by popish prelates is a monstrous violation. In *A declaration of a strange and wonderfull monster*, Mrs. Haughton's headless monster, its face in its breast, is thus the perfect punishment, a "great reproach and indignity" for the views and actions of both Mrs. Haughton and her (grand)mother. In much the same way as her views mutilated God's true message, her child bears no "Image of God" in its face, and no "majesty of God" shines forth from its deformed hu-man body. Her monstrous birth is a divine judgment of Catholic error, and a vin-dication of Prynne's followers.

After Mrs. Haughton gives birth to her monster, we are told that the attend-ing midwife, a "godly" woman named Gattaker, "discharged her conscience" to Mr. Fleetwood, the minister of Kirkham, describing the monstrous birth and de-claring that "she verily believed that it was the hand of God upon [Mrs. Haughton], for those impreccations she wished upon her self" (7). Here the mid-wife's conscience does not lead her to resist the authorities but rather to seek them out, bringing Mrs. Haughton's recusant claims to the minister and thus to judgment. Fleetwood reports the story of the monstrous birth to "some of the Committee of the County," and it is passed on to "Collonel *More* an honest godly Gentleman, a Member of the House of Commons" (7). Through the interven-tion of More, the spheres of Kirkham, Lancashire, and London parliament and press intersect. As the pamphlet's title proclaims, Mrs. Haughton's crimes were brought from midwife to minister to House of Commons and finally "published in all the Counties, Cities, Townes, and Parishes" of England.

Indeed, the midwife, whom Kirkham parish records reveal to be one Mrs. Greenacre, widow of the former vicar, and the current minister, Edward Fleet-wood, did in fact sign such a certificate in 1645.[68] In 1642, three years before the publication of the pamphlet, the godly people of Lancashire, including Fleet-wood, had written to Parliament, asking for the suppression of papists and for more "preaching ministers."[69] Fleetwood, much like his countryman William Leigh, was already famous in Kirkham for his refusal to wear the surplice and his battles with local recusant families; in 1637 he was reprimanded for his dis-obedience to the dictates of the Church of England by none other than Prynne's enemy, the Bishop of Chester, who called him a "sillie and wilful man."[70] The relationship between Fleetwood the minister and More the parliamentarian thus enacts a fantasy in which Parliament and Puritanism hold sway even in Lan-cashire, a county notorious for its recusants and royalists: "The Certificate [of the monster] was shewed before divers of the Committee, and by Collonel *More* a Member of the House of Commons, brought up to *London*, and shewed to divers of the House" (7). Ultimately, Parliament is shown to work in seamless concert with local magistrates and ministers, and, much like *A strange and lamentable accident* and *Bloody Newes from Dover*, *A declaration of a strange and wonderfull monster* is used as a form of propaganda: the "Commons commanded it to be printed, that so all the Kingdome might see the hand of God herein" (7). With the circulation of such pamphlets, Parliament sought to promulgate a fantasy of religious and political control and coherence throughout the country. In the story of Mrs. Haughton's monstrous birth, divine punishment also serves juridical purposes. *A declaration of a strange and wonderfull monster* makes the secret realms of recusants and royalists permeable by (parliamentarian) men, and much like *A strange and lamentable accident*, imagines an omniscient ministry and magistracy headed by God himself, but administered by Parliament and its loyal ministers.

Yet while my reading thus far offers some sense of the juridical purposes of this pamphlet, there was a great deal more going on in Kirkham, Lancashire, when *A declaration of a strange and wonderfull monster* appeared on March 3, 1645.[71] Like Mrs. Haughton, many Lancastrians were supporters of the king and his ecclesiastical policy, and Lancashire was a royalist stronghold during the civil wars.[72] Parliamentary troops quartered in Kirkham during this period despoiled county churches of "popish trumpery," "removing the Books of Common Praier, Surplisses, Fonts, and breaking down of Organs where they found any."[73] Private recusant households were also singled out for parliamentary attack. Alexander Rigby, the leader of the local parliamentary forces, appointed captains to raise armies in Kirkham and, beginning in 1643, assigned the sequestered estates of papists to raise money to furnish them.[74] Rigby's colleague, Colonel John More, the MP who brings Mrs. Haughton to justice in *A declaration of a strange and wonderfull monster* and who later earned the honor of being the sole Lancashire regicide, came to the area himself and "made some fortifications with gates and barres."[75] Private recusant estates were also targeted to pay for these efforts.

Among these estates was the property of Sir Gilbert Hoghton of Hoghton, a prominent Lancashire royalist who was said to be "familiar with papists" and known for insulting Roundheads.[76] (True to the division within families that characterized the civil war, however, Hoghton's eldest son, Richard, was a parliamentarian, and his daughter Mary married none other than the parliamentarian leader mentioned above, Alexander Rigby).[77] Another targeted recusant estate was that of the foremost family in Lancashire: the Derbys. Lathom House, the Derby household, was the longest-lasting royalist stronghold in Lancashire, and like Mrs. Haughton's household, it was headed by a woman.[78] Much like Mrs. Haughton, Lady Derby, a woman whom parliamentarians explicitly compared to the Whore of Babylon, was notorious for her "speeches" against Parliament.[79] During her defense of Lathom, she reportedly called the parliamentarian leader Colonel Rigby an "insolent rebel" and swore that "when our strength and provision is spent, we shall die in a fire more merciful than Rigby, and then if the providence of God prevent it not my goods and house shall burn in his sight; myself, children and soldiers rather than fall into his hands, will seal our religion and loyalty in the same flame."[80] Apparently Lady Derby's wishes did not come true, for a few months before the appearance of *A declaration of a strange and wonderfull monster*, a parliamentary journal called *Perfect Occurrences* recorded the taking of the "goods and house" of Lathom. In addition to the list of those captured and killed, the newsbook records that the winners found within its walls "1 suppose[d] Popish priest" and "divers Popish bookes, beades, and crucifixes."[81] The secret contents of Lady Derby's house are much like those lurking inside Mrs. Haughton's: renegade priests, "popish trumpery," and anti-parliamentarian rebellion.

It thus seems likely that Mrs. Haughton's story was intended to counter the heroic effects of powerful recusant women like Lady Derby. In the spring of 1646 when the pamphlet appeared, Lancashire was at the center of the civil war: the king was marching north and parliament feared that if the king could enter Lancashire, royalist forces would gain many new troops.[82] Furthermore, the sequestration of royalist property in Lancashire, which was meant to fund the parliamentary war effort, was not proceeding as planned. Lancashire Commissioners admitted in July 1645 that the Ordinance of Sequestrations can only be successful "when the people are well-affected." "In Colonel Rigby's division," however, "most of the people were sequestrable but few sequestered because the condition of the county would not admit it in safety."[83] In other words, it was difficult to sequester the homes of delinquents because the largely recusant and neighborly "condition of the county" meant that neighbors would not turn against neighbors. Not even pro-parliamentarian or Puritan neighbors were guaranteed to sequester their recusant neighbors' property; Colonel Rigby, to take only one example, was married to the royalist Sir Gilbert Hoghton's daughter Mary.

When a royalist estate was sequestered, its revenue was no longer paid to the royalist owner but to the sequestrations official appointed by the county committee, and the royalist's wife and children were allowed only a fifth of his income. Sequestration would clearly effect not only Rigby's own in-laws, but the properties and livelihoods of other neighbors besides the Hoghtons and Derbys, particularly those of women. Royalism was still a force to be reckoned with in Lancashire in 1645 and 1646, and parliamentarians were using any means they could to render recusant royalists, particularly royalist women, the enemy, and to reduce the sympathy that people might have for their anti-parliamentarian neighbors. These means included popular pamphlets like *A declaration of a strange and wonderfull monster*, a story that built on an already notorious history of recusant female cruelty against the Puritan heroes Burton, Bastwick, and Prynne, as well as on recent local history. While *A declaration* points out that Mrs. Haughton was for the most part a good neighbor, it goes to greater lengths to cast suspicion—and finally judgment—on her only-seemingly harmless recusant activities. If royalist women were exposed as dangerous papists and threats to the entire community, their neighbors might not feel so badly about ransacking or sequestering their houses, full as they were not only of "popish trumpery" but of more monstrous threats as well.[84]

EACH OF THE pamphlets discussed in this chapter claims to have been "commanded into print by the Commons," and indeed their publishers were officially affiliated with Parliament. Richard Harper, the publisher of *A strange and lamentable accident*, published the records of parliamentary proceedings, as well as a Puritan history of God's "miraculous protection of his church and people," a text with clear affinities to the monster pamphlet.[85] The printer-publisher of *A declaration of a strange and wonderfull monster*, Jane Coe, also printed parliamentary proceedings and newsbooks "published according to Order of Parliament." One of these newsbooks, *Perfect Occurences*, was in fact the one that reported on the popish contents of Lathom House, a detail that further suggests connections between Lathom House and the recusant household pictured in such lively detail in *A declaration of a strange and wonderfull monster*.[86] Coe also printed the writings of Puritan ministers; a "list of the popish vicker-generalls, Jesuites, priests and fryers, in England, and their names and places to them assigned"; and a list of the "religions, held and maintained by the Cavaliers," a document which pays special attention to the beliefs of "Shee-Cavaliers."[87] Like *A declaration of a strange and wonderfull monster*, that is, Coe's other texts were concerned with locating "priests and fryers" and exposing the threat of "Shee-Cavaliers" like Lady Derby and Mrs. Haughton.

For both Richard Harper and Jane Coe, the publication of illustrated pamphlets of monstrous births was an integrated part of a political, religious, and professional agenda. Harper and Coe served Parliament by publishing parliamentary proceedings and thereby revealing to the population the nature of Parliament's processes, acts, and ordinances. But they also served the parliamentary cause by publishing marvelous and topical texts that highlighted the particular disciplinary protocols—including specific ordinances—that Parliament hoped to inculcate. In telling the stories of sectarian and recusant women, those figures popularly deemed most threatening to parliamentarian religious and political control, these texts sought both to police women's consciences and behaviors and to suggest the extent to which parliamentarian ordinances were coterminous with the will of God. Like the pamphlets that preceded them, that is, they sought to provide marvelous answers to topical cases of conscience that conformed to a specific vision of social and religious order.

CHAPTER FIVE

The ranters monster and the "Children of God"

> The Spirit itself beareth witness with our spirit, that we are the children of God. —ROMANS 8.16

> What? know ye not that your body is the temple of the Holy Ghost *which* is in you, which ye have of God, and ye are not your own?
> —I CORINTHIANS 6.19

> Trust not to that private spirit or Holy Ghost which our Puritans glory in, for then a little fiery zeal will make thee turn separatist.
> —JAMES I, *A Meditation upon the Lords Prayer* (1619)

One of the most famous illustrated stories in John Foxe's *Actes and Monuments* is a woodcut of three women martyrs being burned at the stake. The abdomen of one of the women is open, the wound and exposed viscera resembling both the reproductive pictures in anatomy texts and the disembowelment often enacted on traitors and heretics (or martyrs).[1] Out of this woman's belly leaps a child, perfectly formed, whose miraculous flight from the murderous fires of Catholicism is a sign of the resilient life force and truth of the Protestant faith (fig. 5.1).[2] In Foxe's story, the female martyr, whose name is Perotine Massey, is assured of her justification, and her miraculous child serves as a sign of Christ's dwelling within her.

For Protestants, while God was sovereign, his desires were understood through the individual conscience: as Thomas Goodwin put it many years later, the Holy Spirit "writes first all graces in us, and then teaches our consciences to read his handwriting."[3] The effects of the belief in the supremacy—and sanctity—of the conscience's intimacy with the Holy Spirit was seen as particularly liberating for women: Foxe's *Actes and Monuments* is full of stories of Protestant women who defended their righteousness or rebellion by claiming to have the

Figure 5.1. Image from John Foxe, *Actes and monuments* (London: John Daye, 1576), STC 11224, 1850. Reproduced by permission of the Henry E. Huntington Library.

Holy Spirit within. For example, when Anne Askew's interrogator asked her if she had the Spirit of God in her, she answered that if she had not, she was "but a reprobate and cast away."[4] The story of Perotine Massey and her miraculous child suggests that she, unlike her persecutors, had read God's handwriting correctly and was by no means reprobate and cast away. Despite the purported Protestant separation of human flesh from divinity, martyrs' bodies were understood as sites of just such a conjoining: examples of Christ's living word come in the flesh. In Foxe's story, Perotine Massey's child is not just a citation of the incarnation of Christ; it also testifies to the special role that women's bodies and consciences played in the incarnation and reproduction of the Protestant faith.

Yet the marvelous birth that is the centerpiece of this chapter features not a perfect Protestant child but a monstrous one, the child of one Mary Adams, a nonconforming woman who claimed to be pregnant with Christ by the Holy Spirit and instead gave birth to a monster. Mary Adams's story, told in a 1652 pamphlet entitled *The ranters monster,* suggests the extent to which many of the central beliefs of Protestantism—inner faith, the conscience, and the determination of election or reprobation—were understood in gendered terms and the extent to which they could go terribly awry.[5] As we have already seen, Protestant reform resulted in no comprehensive internalization of belief or conformity among English believers. While the individual conscience was the foundation of the Protestant faith, it could also be mistaken; the imagination—equally private and invisible—could usurp its function, inscribing human error rather than divine truth. To further complicate matters, "conception," both biological and theological, was a profoundly destabilizing undertaking, and as we saw in the introduction, beliefs in the permeability of pregnant women suggested that external events and internal disturbances could imprint on the child, resulting in miscarriage, stillbirth, even monstrous deformity.[6]

Reproduction was understood as an intermediary passage between divine intention and human flesh, and mothers' sins, beliefs, and even their thoughts were understood to have the ability to mar God's image. Each birth, then, testified to its mother's conscience or her imagination; it revealed either the perfection of God's image in human form or the presence of human error.[7] This particular logic of reformist physiognomy was related to what Edmund Morgan has called the "morphology of conversion," the belief that believers could determine their status as children of God through reading external, even physical, signs.[8] The very moment of birth testified to both the state of the mother's soul and that of her child's; the individual body's status as a temple of the Holy Spirit was immediately apparent to all.

Yet by going beyond the claim of an assured conscience to claim the literal indwelling of the Holy Ghost and the literal embodiment of Christ, Mary Adams's story invoked one of the most volatile religious controversies of civil war and interregnum England: the nature of the indwelling of the Holy Spirit.[9] While Puritans on both sides of the Atlantic worked to establish a rule of "visible saints"—Christians whose outward godly lives reflected and testified to their election—others insisted that assurance was invisible and provided directly by God to his chosen children only through the private witnessing of the Holy Spirit. These believers claimed that all externals—church, ministry, even Holy Scripture—were secondary to this private revelation. It was a period in which James's belief that the "fiery zeal" of trusting in a "private spirit" could make believers turn separatist came true. If these "invisible" saints, with their private witnessing and living Christ were to be discredited, it was through their claims of embodiment and the heresies they suggested. They would be discredited, to be more precise, through stories of women who claimed not only to bear Christ within them, but to have the power to bring him to others.

Spiritual and Monstrous Births

The Reformation brought with it a newfound interest in the Holy Spirit. Because of the early Protestant reformers' encouragement of private judgment and resistance to ecclesiastical (Catholic) authority, the Holy Spirit, as Anne Askew's claim suggests, came to serve as a radical witnessing force. Yet there remained, as Geoffrey Nuttall has pointed out, a persistent theological and imaginative vagueness about the concept.[10] Was the Holy Spirit a person, as the Creed suggested, and therefore like the Father and the Son, or was it a more abstract phenomenon? The term *spirit* was also open to a range of interpretations: perhaps the "spirit" that inspired the Reformers, as their critics pointed out, was actually the spirit of folly or of error. The question of how believers could know it was God's spirit and not their own imagination was thus both a very real question for Protestants and the grounds for hostile condemnation of some of their more radical beliefs.[11]

The belief in the determining power of conscience in matters of religion was further complicated by the more radical Protestant belief in the indwelling of the Holy Spirit, the belief that at the moment of conversion or election, the Holy Ghost comes into the body of the believer and thereafter guides their actions. Many believers thus sought to know by what "[i]nfallible tokens they might know assuredly the Inspiration of the Holy Spirit," and Richard Baxter, a Puritan with a desire for clear answers, listed ten marks "how it may be known whether we have Christ's Spirit or no."[12] Yet Baxter also warned that "all sober Christians should be the more cautious of *being deceived by their own imaginations*, because certain experience telleth us, that most in our age that have pretended to prophecy, or to inspirations, or revelations, have been melancholy, crackbrained persons [. . .] No person is more fit for a Quaker, a Papist, or any sectary to work upon than a troubled mind."[13] In Baxter's formulation, the imagination is the Holy Spirit's monstrous double, and the troubled mind that is unable to differentiate between the two will always be prey to the fiery zeal of godless separatism.

Mary Adams was one such troubled mind. Once "a great frequenter of the Church, and a most excellent pattern of true Holiness," she became, in turn, a follower of Anabaptism, of Familism, and finally, of Ranterism, believing ultimately that her body was, quite literally, the temple of the Holy Ghost and that he had impregnated her with Christ (4).[14] By the early 1650s, the Ranters were the most notorious of the antinomian sects. In *A Survey of the Spirituall Antichrist, Opening the Secrets of Familisime and Antinomianisme* (1648), the Presbyterian Samuel Rutherford cites one particularly dangerous sectarian tenet: the belief that in the conversion of a sinner "the faculties and workings of the soule on things pertaining to God, are destroyed and instead of them the holy Ghost comes in and taketh place." "As Christ was God manifested in the flesh," such sectarians were said to believe, "so is he incarnate and made flesh in every Saint."[15] Theologically, antinomianism was the belief that the moral or "carnal" law was not binding upon those Christians who were elect or under the law of grace, but it was antinomian claims to divine embodiment that would provide the movement's most notorious and contentious cases. In the eyes of those seeking Protestant conformity in 1640s and 1650s England—a desire imagined differently by Presbyterians like Rutherford and Oliver Cromwell's Independents—the purported antinomian beliefs that the Holy Spirit guided their actions and that their justification exempted them both from sin and from the need to do good works smacked of religious anarchy.[16] Antinomians, after all, obeyed the direct dictates of the Holy Spirit, not those of his self-appointed earthly exegetes. There was already a widely known history of divine punishment for antinomian error in mid-seventeenth-century England, however, and it had come in the form of monstrous births.

The Holy Spirit in the New World

"What hath God the father done for you? Children are taught to answer, He hath created me [. . .] And when the 2d Question is asked, What hath God the Son done for you? They are taught to answer, He hath redeemed me [. . .] And when a 3d question is asked; What hath the Holy Ghost done for you? They are taught to answer, He sanctifieth and comforteth me."

— JOHN COTTON, *Mr. Cottons Rejoynder to the Elders* (1637)

In New England, the antinomian controversy of the late 1630s centered on the opposition between the saving grace communicated by the Holy Spirit—Cotton's comforting witness—and the individual's obedience to moral law—his or her "works." The church fathers insisted that sanctification, or the outward living of a good life, could be a sign of justification, or saving faith, but the antinomians insisted that there was no connection between human righteousness and God's grace.[17] Justification, that is, was invisible and known only to the elect themselves. It was the antinomians' insistence on their direct access to Christ—his indwelling—that particularly riled the authorities. As Governor John Winthrop insisted, it was an error to believe that Christ resided in individual believers: "Christ was once made flesh *Joh 1.14* no other incarnation is recorded and therefore not to be believed."[18]

For John Cotton, whose preaching inspired the antinomians' most famous proselyte, Anne Hutchinson, Hutchinson ultimately took the belief in election, particularly her own, too far. As he told her during her 1637 examination for heresy, "I have often feared the highth of your Spirit, being puft up with your own parts."[19] Rather than being based on divine assurance, he claimed, her faith had been prostituted to her "owne Inventions."[20] Yet Hutchinson insisted that, much like Anne Askew, she had been informed of her views "By the voice of [God's] spirit to my soul," and that while the earthly authorities may have power over her body, "the Lord Jesus hath power over my body and soul."[21] Hutchinson claimed her conscience as the bulwark of her righteousness and God as her only guide. "If you do condemn me for speaking what in my conscience I know to be truth," she told Cotton, "I must commit myself unto the Lord."[22]

Under direct and sustained theological scrutiny, Hutchinson eventually admitted the error of her expression, if not her beliefs. Yet as Deputy Governor Thomas Dudley pointed out, while her repentance was on paper, it was "*not in her Countenance,* none can see it thear I thinke."[23] In other words, Hutchinson's inscrutable countenance testified that her body was subordinate, not to the church fathers, but to her conscience and its guiding faith. Without a visible sign of repentance, the ministers' claim that she "never had any trew Grace in her hart," that other invisible bastion of faith, was, according to their own logic, merely conjectural.[24] Although they repeatedly mention Hutchinson's "hardened heart," imagining it not as assured but as stubbornly and mistakenly unyielding to repentance or an admission of error, they effectually demanded that her body provide them with the evidence they required.

While the elders excommunicated Anne Hutchinson because of the dangerous implications of her claim to direct spiritual revelation—for "being above reason and Scripture," they pointed out, such claims "are not subject to controll"—it was her purported monstrous births that vindicated their judgment.[25] Shortly after her excommunication, Hutchinson reportedly delivered a series of monstrous births. John Winthrop summarized the appropriateness of Hutchinson's punishment thus: "[S]ee how the wisdom of God fitted this judgement to her sinne every way, for looke as she had vented misshapen opinions, so she must bring forth deformed monsters; and as about 30. Opinions in number, so many monsters."[26] The long history of monsters and deformed bodies being denied a place in a Christian commonwealth—their well-established status as reprobate "cast aways"—thus vindicated Hutchinson's excommunication and attested to the elders' righteousness in ejecting her from their church. The monstrous births reveal that Hutchinson had indeed been "puft up" with her own inventions, her conscience aligned, not with Christ, but with the more familiar and discreditable power of the maternal imagination. The Lord did, as Hutchinson claimed, have power over her body and soul, but it was not the assuring kind she claimed.

Given that one of Anne Hutchinson's greatest threats to ministerial control was her insistence on the *invisibility* of election (her claim that election was announced through a private revelation unaccompanied by any external visible signs), her monstrous births served a singularly illuminating function. In denying the church fathers their belief in a legible system of sanctification, Hutchinson denied them their role as interpreters of God's word and will. As visible signs of her reprobation, Hutchinson's monstrous births thus implicitly validated the fathers' claim that visible or external signs accompanied election. By showing its inverse—visible heresy—the story of the monstrous births attested to the truth of the Puritans' belief in "visible saints." Hutchinson's monstrous births thus both punished her crimes and re-elevated the fathers as the legitimate interpreters of God's will. While her followers might ignore the ministers—whom Hutchinson purportedly called "Nobodies"—no one dared to "sleight so manifest a signe from Heaven."[27]

Yet while the monstrous births were read as evidence of Hutchinson's reprobation, it is not true that they denied her power.[28] According to the fathers' interpretation, the monstrous births proved that the condition of the soul is shown in visible issue, but they also revealed, in spectacular form, the fundamentally determining power of the maternal psyche, that fraught realm of conscience and imagination. The monstrous births were understood both as signs from heaven—God's creations and signs of his wrath—and as the products of Hutchinson's own monstrous opinions. The power of the inscrutable realm of the conscience is particularly palpable in its error. The fathers were troubled both by Hutchinson's unredoubtable defense of the sanctity and assurance of her own conscience—a realm she submitted only to God—and by her acknowledged power over the consciences of the people, particularly the women and children, of the Massachusetts Bay Colony.

From its beginnings, the antinomian controversy was scripted as a battle over the family. Both Winthrop and Cotton understood children as the basis of the godly commonwealth: Winthrop had a vivid dream in which he visualized the election of his own children, and Cotton refused to baptize his child that had been born at sea until the family was part of a land-based godly common-wealth.[29] Yet both men were well aware of the extent to which women were the guarantors of children's spiritual states, from conception and birth into the "dif-fused mothering" that underwrote the Puritan nation.[30] They thus presented Hutchinson as a poisonous midwife infecting the consciences and bodies of women and children, a "breeder and nourisher" of error who broke the Fifth Commandment by dishonoring the "Fathers of the Commonwealth."[31] Though Hutchinson's gifts made her "fit to instruct [her] Children and Servants to be helpful to her Husband in the Government of the famely," Cotton claimed, she overstepped herself by providing religious education that differed from that of the church fathers.[32] If, as Jane Sharp suggests, the child's soul was contingent upon the mother's until the moment of birth, its formation under her tutelage was ongoing. Years later, Cotton Mather summarized the controversy: "[A] poyson does never insinuate so quickly, nor operate so strongly, as when women's milk is the vehicle therin its given."[33] It was thus especially important to the church fathers that Anne Hutchinson's children be made to renounce, or sever, the determining power of the maternal conscience by allowing their own con-sciences to be swayed by the ministers' entreaties. Throughout her trial the church fathers repeatedly called Hutchinson's children to the stand, asking them to disavow their mother and her views.[34] And without exception, they refused.

Although her children were important to the trial, Hutchinson's main body of support lay in the women of the colony whom she had served as both midwife and preacher. "[B]eing a woman very helpful in the times of child-birth, and other occasions of bodily infirmities," Winthrop wrote, she had "insinuated her-self" into the affections of women, discrediting sanctification and convincing them of "immediate revelation" signifying "the in-dwelling of the person of the Holy Ghost, and of union with Christ."[35] Through her own intermediary func-tion, Hutchinson thus both limited the influence of other intermediary religious forces and claimed that women's own consciences were the most important realm of religious truth. In addition to being "puft up with her own parts," that is, Hutchinson attempted to "[l]eaven the hartes of younge Weomen with [. . .]

unsound and dayngerous principles."[36] Cotton thus worried about Hutchinson's effect on other women and warned them to take heed that they "reaceve nothing for Truth which hath not the stamp of the Word of God from it."[37] It was thus doubly illustrative that while Hutchinson's own monstrous births were central to her conviction of heresy, one of the key factors in Hutchinson's actual trial was the monstrous birth of another woman, Mary Dyer, one of Hutchinson's most devoted acolytes.

Mary Dyer reportedly gave birth to and buried her monster in October 1637, and its existence was "providentially" revealed on the eve of Hutchinson's own trial for heresy.[38] To prepare for their case against Hutchinson, Winthrop and John Cotton "went to the place of [the Dyer monster's] buryall & commanded to digg it up to [behold] it, & they sawe it, a most hideous creature, a woman, a fish, a bird, & a beast all woven together."[39] The monster was also, according to Winthrop's account, a woman child born "without a head," a familiar figure of female lawlessness and sectarianism. Although Cotton was credited with playing a role in the burial (he "justified his having advised the women to bury the corpse quickly and quietly on the ground that God intended such monstrous births *only for the private instruction* of the parents and witnesses"), the burial was secretly performed by the women themselves: Anne Hutchinson, the midwife Jane Hawkins, and three other women.[40] The privacy of the birth room and the privacy of Hutchinson's women-only religious meetings were threateningly impenetrable by male eyes, and their danger was both emblematized by this private burial—an illegitimate usurpation of one of the most public functions of the godly commonwealth—and revealed by its exposure. Like Anne Hutchinson's monstrous births, Mary Dyer's birth was not merely a "private instruction": it was a public reprimand. As Winthrop put it, both monstrous births "were publike, and not in a corner mentioned, so this is now come to be knowne and famous all over these Churches, and a great part of the world."[41] The controversy and its monstrous births made the largely inscrutable female conscience and its diffuse social effects legible in a way that no condemnatory edict could.

While scholars have focused on the gendering of antinomianism, pointing to the ways in which Hutchinson's body became the nominalizing sign of a whole complex theological controversy, they have largely failed to acknowledge the extent to which the determining power of the conscience was a gendered issue.[42] Hutchinson's threat was so great not only because she denied the need for ministerial intermediation between Christ and the individual soul but because she highlighted the fact that women—their bodies and minds—were, from the moment of conception, the sole true intermediaries between God and humankind. Thus, while the official story of the antinomian controversy ended with the triumph of male interpretation, the dark and powerful underside of the story was the utter necessity, and power, of the female conscience.

News of the antinomian controversy circulated largely through the sensational story of Hutchinson's and Dyer's monsters and was widely disseminated in England, especially in London, during the 1640s.[43] It became a tool in the battle over religious toleration during the Cromwellian Protectorate and was deployed by Presbyterians seeking to discredit Congregational or Independent systems by suggesting that such loosely organized forms of worship inevitably fostered or led to sectarian error like that of the antinomians.[44] As one polemicist wrote with more hope than truth, the Hutchinson case brought the people of New England "closer to a system of Presbyterian rule."[45] The antinomian controversy rendered the female body a synecdoche for sectarianism and identified the female conscience as the most most important battleground of faith. These tropes found new purchase during England's own antinomian controversy, when the claims of female bodies and spiritual witnessing were even more extreme and the dream of Presbyterian rule—or indeed of any comprehensive public ministry at all—was tenuous at best.

England's Spiritists

While the Hutchinson and Dyer monsters certainly inform the story of Mary Adams's monstrous birth, Adams's specific claim of being pregnant with Christ by the Holy Ghost was something neither Anne Hutchinson nor Mary Dyer ever claimed. This particular aspect of Adams's claim is thus further contextualized by a series of related antinomian heresies rife in early 1650s England: what one historian has loosely grouped together as the "Free Spirit" movement.[46] Lodowick Muggleton and John Reeve, for example, claimed to have been chosen "Witnesses of the Spirit" in 1651, receiving direct contact from "an invisible Spiritual, yet personal God" which "the World knows nothing of."[47] While Muggleton and Reeve were both imprisoned for "Blasphemy and Execrable Opinions," their claims of invisible Spirit-witnessing paled in comparison to those who proclaimed a more literal spiritual embodiment.[48]

Mary Adams's claim to be pregnant with Christ by the Holy Ghost was in fact part of a wider mid-seventeenth-century phenomenon of English men and women claiming either to be Christ or to be pregnant with Christ. It was easy to read such claims as misinterpretations of the idea that the Holy Ghost resides in and guides the actions of individual believers, bringing them the living word of Christ.[49] As the Fifth Monarchist prophet Hannah Trapnel wrote, "some poor creatures call themselves Christ because of this oneness with Christ, they will have no distinguishing."[50] Some insisted, however, as the Presbyterian Samuel Rutherford feared, that "this oneness" was not a confusion: Christ really *did* reside in his saints. In *A Man-Child Born, or God Manifest in Flesh* (1654), the Ranter Richard Coppin told his followers that "Christ being born of the Virgin Mary in a corporeal substance of flesh and bones, was but a sign or shadow of his being born in you in spirit and glory."[51] While childbirth had long been "the archetypal metaphor for the agony of spiritual transformation," it was given new purchase in the 1650s.[52]

The two most notorious cases of couples who claimed divinity in the early 1650s involved "Ranters," the sect with whom Mary Adams ultimately allied. John Robins and his wife—who is identified in different accounts as Joan, Eve, and Mary—were arrested, along with a number of their followers, in May 1651. Robins was prosecuted for claiming that he had received "many Revelations from the Holy Ghost" and that he was God; his wife, for identifying herself as the Virgin Mary and claiming to be pregnant with "the onely and true *Christ*" (one writer wryly noted that she was indeed "very big").[53] While the Robinses were prosecuted at the Westminster Quarter Sessions in June 1651 and imprisoned in New Bridewell (where they reportedly disputed with visitors, including Muggleton and Reeve), their story had its greatest impact in the hands of the parliamentarian press, appearing in a range of different publications in May and June of 1651 as an exemplary case of sectarian error (fig. 5.2).[54]

The sensationalism of the Robins' story was surpassed only by that of William Franklin and Mary Gadbury, a couple tried at Winchester in January 1650 who identified themselves as the reincarnation of Jesus Christ and his spouse. Their story was memorably told by the Winton minister Humphrey Ellis in his *Pseudochristus* (1650).[55] According to Ellis's account, Mary Gadbury not only claimed to be the spouse of Christ but, speaking from her childbed (which reportedly shook with the fervor of her belief), told each convert that "she would *pretend her travail* to be for such a one [about to be] reborn in Mary" (21–22, emphasis added). Mary Gadbury, in other words, enacted the spiritual birth that others spoke of only metaphorically. Gadbury's most radical contemporary deployers of the metaphorical language of childbirth were sectarian women prophets. Elizabeth Poole described the onset of a prophetic trance with the

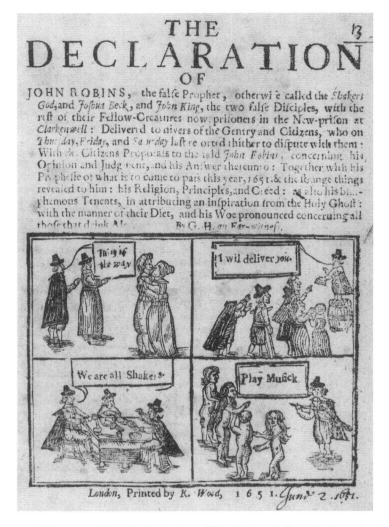

Figure 5.2. Title page, G.H., *The Declaration of John Robins, the False Prophet, otherwise called the Shakers God* (London, Printed by R. Wood, 1651), Thomason E.629 [13]. Reproduced by permission of the British Library.

claim that "the pangs of a travelling woman were upon [her]," and Jane Lead said that she must await the "travelling hour" as a sign that the "ghostly birth" was forming in her.[56] Gadbury's claim was thus readily associated with an increasingly prevalent and often subversive form of female spiritual agency.

Ellis's account of the nature of Mary Gadbury's "travail" was based on the examination of a woman named Margaret Woodward, who was present when Gadbury delivered her "birth." Although Woodward testified that Gadbury "was one night one hour in strong travel, and brought forth a spiritual birth," Ellis writes that "it was suspected that she was delivered of a childe, and had destroyed it, the Justices were very earnest with her to know the true father, and told her, *they did beleeve there was substance in that birth*, and that it was not altogether spiritual" (39–40, emphasis added). Indeed, he refers to a report "carried about the Countrey" that she had been "delivered of a Serpent, or some monstrous birth" (22). While both Gadbury and Franklin refused to admit that they had had a "fleshly" child, insisting that they were "wholly spiritual" and had "no name, no habitation, according to the Flesh," it was Mary Gadbury who bore the burden of the judicial authorities' scrutiny (40). Already concerned that Gadbury was with a man to whom she was not married—when she claimed that she accompanied Franklin not "as a carnal, but as a spiritual man," the judge replied, "So might any whore say the like"[57]—the authorities chose to believe that there was material "substance" in her birth and that she had killed her child. Her spiritual crimes, in other words, are rendered crimes of the flesh: adultery, whoredom, and infanticide.[58]

Two laws passed in 1650 clearly had an impact on the Franklin and Gadbury case: the Blasphemy Act ("for the Punishment of Atheistical, Blasphemous and Execrable Opinions"), which included a special report on Ranters and suggested harsh punishments for those who declared themselves to be God; and the Adultery Act, which made adultery a felony for women. It is telling that Gadbury is punished under the latter law.[59] Both Franklin and Gadbury were initially imprisoned in the Common gaol, where Franklin was fettered until the time of the Assizes; but Gadbury, having "so accompanied with another womans husband, and besides the Charge of that suspected Felony and Adultery, refusing to declare her name or condition, [declared] a lewd woman, & rogue in law," was sent to Bridewell, "the House of Correction" (44). Franklin agreed to retract his beliefs and repent, and was discharged on April 22, 1650 (53). But Mary Gadbury, who was reportedly "not so sensible of the danger she should expose her self unto"—although after having "tasted somewhat of the smart of the whip" at Bridewell, "the height of her spirit [began] to be somewhat abated" [41, 44]— was held until the next Quarter Sessions (51).[60]

Although the struggling Parliamentarian Council sought to establish governance over sexuality and spirituality as cornerstones of order, the fact that the policing of Mary Gadbury descended on her body and her purported "fleshly" crimes attests to the difficulty Puritans had in determining the criminality of any fellow believer's spiritual claim. Even John Cotton, who arguably turned on Anne Hutchinson in order to save his own place in the Massachusetts Bay community, admitted that neither he nor any other human observer could ever really know whether Hutchinson had "the spirit" or not.[61] In choosing to read Gadbury's crime as a crime of the flesh committed "under *the cloak* of Religion" (51), the authorities endeavored to return the spirited woman and her threatening regenerative promises to the policeable realm of the female body. If, as Anne Hutchinson insisted, only the human body was truly subject to earthly authority (the soul being the purview of Christ), persecution could most readily focus on a bodily crime.

Perhaps because of the sensational newsworthiness of such cases, anti-sectarian critics almost uniformly associated Ranterism with the liberty and sexual license of women. The royalist newsbook *Mercurius Fumigosis* (16–23 August 1654), to take one example, reports on the case of "she-Ranters" who went naked in the streets. Upon "being demanded if they had Husbands," the women replied that *"Their Husbands were within them, which was God." The Faithful Scout* of 1654 similarly records the activities of "Petticoat Preachers" at Cambridge, who, when asked where their husbands were, answered that *"they had no husband but Jesus Christ."*[62] Just as Trapnel explained people's Christ complexes as a misunderstanding of the orthodox belief in "oneness with Christ," so too did these women translate that oneness into a renegotiated vision of the marital union. And in much the same way as Anne Hutchinson claimed devotion to her divine Father over the church fathers, many women radicals purportedly chose a divine husband over an earthly one. It was, as we saw in Mary Gadbury's case, a short step to associating this liberation, not with spiritual freedom, but with sexual licentiousness.

It thus became a convention for anti-sectarian polemicists to see women's independent beliefs merely as a cover for sexual licentiousness. John Bunyan, for example, writes that he heard a man "'in Oliver [Cromwell]'s days' advise a girl whom he was tempting 'to commit uncleanness with him' to say, 'when you come before the judge, that you are with child by the Holy Ghost.'"[63] In other stories Ranter women are presented, like Mary Gadbury, as whores, their spiritual messages no more than disorderly erotic or reproductive urges. In Samuel Shepherd's *The jovial crew, or The devill turn'd Ranter* (1651), for example, a Ranter woman offers an open-ended sexual invitation: "Come some man or other / And make me a mother."[64] In a strangely literal reading, an author claiming to be the Digger Gerrard Winstanley asserted that "this excesse of Feminine society [among the Ranters] hinders the pure and natural Generation of man, and spills the seed in vaine." "[I]instead of a healthful gro[w]th of mankind," he continues, "it produces weaknesse and much infirmnesse" (G2), the child proving "either not long lived or a fool or else a sickly weakly thing that is a burden to himself" (G2v).[65] According to the author of this account, both the literal and figurative offspring of Ranters were insubstantial and deformed. Given the sectarians' lack of substantive doctrine, sectarian reproduction is configured as an eugenicist mathematics of insufficient form and carelessly managed matter, the offspring devoid not only of divinity but of humanity. The period in fact saw a surge of reformist physiognomical texts focusing particularly on this kind of childbirth, a phenomenon indebted, I would argue, not only to the popularly circulating story of the deformed offspring of Hutchinson and Dyer and the sexualization of sectarianism, but to the increasing threat of "invisible" saints.

Identified by such titles as *The Picture of a Puritane* (1605), *The Picture of a Papist* (1606), and *Brownisme turned The In-side out-ward* (1613), the texts I am identifying as reformist physiognomy claimed to expose or reveal the nonconforming Christian.[66] While the genre reached peak popularity during the civil war and interregnum with such (often illustrated) texts as *The Picture of a Roundhead and a Rattlehead* (1648), it found its ideal target in those "invisible" sectarian Christians who resisted or ignored outward and public forms of religion. One of the most successful and interesting of these texts was entitled *Rules to get children by vvith handsome-faces*.[67] The author, the pseudonymous George Spinola, claims that in his study of the physiognomies of men, he has found the most "non-conformities of parts in the Faces and Limbs" in those who are "familiarly called the Sectaries and Separatists" (A2). Spinola directs his discourse of face-mending to "invisible Christians" (particularly Brownists) so that their children may avoid the hideousness of their parents, who are "ill physiognomied" for denying that "they had any originall sinne at all" (27).

Not surprisingly, Spinola makes use of the belief in the power of the maternal imagination in his satire. Some of his "best Rules of Face-mending," he points out, "worke primarily by the strength and force of imagination, in which kind of imagination [sectarians] are known to have a greater share then [*sic*] of Reason, and a cleare intellectual mind" (A2). People, he reminds us, "do impresse into the thing begot that very affection which prevails and presides in them in or about the time of Generation" (A2v). If the "affection" at the time of generation is sectarian, the impression will be not only monstrous but adumbrated to the particular sectarian belief. In other words, it will expose the "invisible" Christian's beliefs for the errors that they are. Spinola warns sectaries that if they want children "with handsome Faces, and Symmetrical Limbs," they should abandon "those high speculations [. . .] concerning the immobility of Divine praedestination, and reprobation" because they make the Spirit weak and so "attenuated into single threds" that the resulting child must have "a long, thin, and narrow Face" (A4v). Excessive speculation about predestination or reprobation—the very thing for which many Puritans sought signs—literally deforms the children of sectarians, making their parents' religious errors physically manifest. Spinola warns that "[i]f these Precepts already given do not mend their *Faces* and *behaviours,* I beeleeve our *Honourable Patriots of the high Councell* will become such natural magicians as *Jacob* was, and lay Rods on 'em in their most private *Watring-troughs*" (A4v).

Spinola's satire deals in a singularly imaginative way with the issue of "invisible Christians" whose very threat lay in the fact that they could not be visibly or publicly identified. Invisible Christians swore, as we have seen, that the signs of election were not made visible and were known only to the believer by private witness of the Holy Spirit. By playing with ideas both of maternal impression and the signs of reprobation, Spinola imagines that sectarian offspring are in fact marked with the signs of their parents' errors. His allusion to Laban's sheep evokes not only the phenomenon of maternal impression but also the logic of marking one's property: through physical markings, sectarians are made subject not only to God (something they themselves desired) but to government and ecclesiastical forces as well. Spinola's threat that the "Patriots" of the High Council will find the Nonconformists in their private watering troughs—the private and often home-bound "conventicles" where they gather to worship—and mark them, certainly invokes Stuart practices of punitive marking. But it also imagines a means by which the forces of religious order could still police and punish the beliefs and practices of disparate sects, even in a time of political and ecclesiastical insecurity. Only by abandoning their deforming beliefs can sectarian parents avoid producing monstrous offspring. True invisibility—that is, normalcy—comes only with conformity.

Like the "ill-physiognomied" brethren exposed in Spinola's *Rules to get children by,* Mary Adams's monstrous birth does more than expose her errors; it vindicates the attention the religious authorities pay to her heretical views. In addition to claiming to be the Virgin Mary and impregnated by the Holy Ghost, Mary Adams also claims that "that which was within her [. . .] was the true Messiah; for she obstinately and very impiously affirmed, *that Christ was not yet come in the flesh*" (A2). This final claim was a Ranter view particularly decried by the heresiographers and singled out for attention in the aforementioned Blasphemy Act. In accordance with that act, the pamphlet tells us, the minister of Tillingham, Essex, one Mr. Hadley, arrested and imprisoned the pregnant Mary Adams. At the time of her delivery, midwives and other "good women of the Parish" came to her aid, but although they did their best "to bring her to a safe deliverance," the child was born dead (4). Immediately after its birth the women "*buried it with speed*, for it was so loathsome to behold, that the women's hearts trembled to look upon it; for it had neither hands nor feet, but claws like a Toad in the place where the hands should have been, and every part was odious to behold" (4, emphasis added).[68] Much like the monstrous birth that testified to Mary Dyer's heresy—there are specific parallels in the physical descriptions—Mary Adams's monstrous birth attests to the severity of her blasphemous claim.

According to the Scriptures, blasphemy against the Holy Spirit was the one unforgivable sin.[69] The ultimate punishment for blasphemy lay with God. For example, Daniel 3.29 declares that anyone who blasphemes God shall be "cut in pieces," and Leviticus 24:15 says, "Whosoever curses his God shall bear his sin." But the punishment of blasphemy was also the responsibility of the earthly governor. Leviticus continues: "He that blasphemes the name of the LORD, he shall surely be put to death; and all the congregation shall certainly stone him" (v. 16). In the punitive imagination of those who sought religious conformity, the visible signs of infamy imposed on the bodies of lawbreakers mimicked divine punishments: religious heretics, for example, were drawn and quartered—literally "cut in pieces." Earthly punishments endeavored to show the nature of the blasphemy: sowers of sedition were branded with SS, and the hands and tongues of blasphemers were removed.

Mary Adams's punishment for blasphemy against the Holy Ghost certainly had exemplary intent: her child's monstrously deformed flesh is the direct antithesis to her claim of bringing Christ in the flesh. As Leviticus claimed she would, Adams literally "bears" her sin, both in her child and in her own body. After the birth, she herself "rotted and consumed as she lay, being from the head to the foot as full of botches, blains, boils, & stinking scabs" (4). Yet while her body putrefied, Mary's "*heart was so hardened in wickednesse, that she had no power to repent.*" As in Anne Hutchinson's case, the author of *The ranters monster* shifts the focus from Mary Adams's spiritual claim and assured conscience to her "hardened heart." And as with Hutchinson, Adams's body bears the final judgment: when finally left alone, she "ript up her bowels" with a knife (4). Her disembowelment is an appropriate and poetic punishment for her crime, a self-inflicted version of the divine and state-sanctioned punishment for blasphemy and, as we saw in chapter 3, for treason. Adams's most blasphemous claim was that her body was uniquely a temple of the Holy Spirit. In opening her body for all to see, her final act reveals instead its evacuation.

Yet despite the drama of her self-evisceration, Adams's monstrous birth provides the most compelling evidence of her crime. Although the midwives had buried the monstrous birth "with speed," the minister with equal alacrity orders it to be dug up and shown publicly as an "example for all Christians." It is possible to read Hadley's decision as both a citation of John Cotton's disinterment of Mary Dyer's monstrous child and as a rebuttal to Cotton's belief in female spiritual witnessing and "private" lessons that led him to conceal the birth in the first place. But the disinterment also provides, I would argue, a fantasized excavation of the products and effects of women like Mary Gadbury, whose refusal of fleshly existence and defense of the sanctity of her beliefs so frustrated her earthly governors. Mary Adams's birth provides the "substance" the authorities looked for in Mary Gadbury's case in monstrous form, an incontrovertible affirmation of her error. Yet unlike Gadbury, Adams utters her blasphemy under supervision and gives birth in prison; the horrifying, if repressed, material evidence is exhumed and witnessed by all the authorities entrusted with policing religious conformity in the period: minister, church-wardens, constable, collectors, and headboroughs.[70] Just as Spinola's text imagines that invisible Christians will be found at their watering troughs, Adams—and, by extension, her sect—is "found" within the disciplinary purviews of prison, the bed scenes of sectarian promise made subject to a comprehensive system of punishment.

With their exhumation of the products of heresy, the minister of Tillingham, Essex, and his Christian magistrates provide an indictment of the sectarian heresies that they feared religious toleration would increase. When, three years before the publication of *The ranters monster,* the army's *Agreement of the People* called for toleration for all those who "profess faith in God by Jesus Christ however differing in judgement from the doctrine, worship and discipline publicly held forth as aforesaid," many of the ministers of Essex questioned the Agreement's vague definition of "Christianity."[71] "They know little," the ministers insisted, "that do not know that all the errors and sects that are or have been in the church of Christ since the Apostles days do all lay claim to the title of Christian religion [. . .] we care for the instructing of people in a publike way, and for the confutation of heresie and error."[72] Without the leadership of "the Christian magistrate," they argued, men will "crucifie the Son of God afresh, and put him to open shame."[73] Mary Adams's claim to bringing Christ in the flesh, while not historically unprecedented, was certainly a distinctive way of putting him to shame. And as the story shows, it necessitated the ordering presence of Christian magistrates.

If the antinomian controversy and its monster-bearing women came to serve as the case study for debates over toleration in the 1640s, by the 1650s spirit-witnessing and spirit-bearing women had usurped the role. *The ranters monster*'s implicit allusions to both the Dyer and Hutchinson and the Robins and Gadbury cases suggest the imaginative and representational economy of the phenomenon. Yet the pamphlet also cites another monster-producing woman. After a brief list of other blasphemers and their equally appropriate punishments, the author mentions, as if as an afterthought, the following "remarkable" detail: "That when the aforesaid Mary Adams was in prison, she used many Imprecations against the *Independents*; saying, *That rather then she would bring forth the Holy Ghost, to be a Round-head, or Independent, she desired that he might have no head at all*" (8). It is, as we know from the previous chapter, an old story, deployed in 1646 against an anti-parliamentarian recusant named Mrs. Haughton. The mother's audacious claim vindicates, as it did in the source text, the Roundheads, or Puritans, but its inclusion of the Independents—in 1652 the strongest force in both Cromwell's army and in London and its surrounding counties—suggests a more specific political motivation.

The relationship between Roundheads and Independents was in fact never entirely clear; Independents were Puritans of a particular ilk, whose rallying cry was freedom of conscience and freedom of assembly.[74] Much like Anne Hutchinson's, Mary Adams's story places the blasphemous sectarian woman in threatening contrast to the masculine order of Independency, illustrated, in this case, by the disciplinary Christian magistracy of the minister Hadley and his functionaries. Contrary to Presbyterian fears, the parish system of Tillingham, Essex—at least as it is represented in the pamphlet—was one that worked. While *The ranters monster* says little about public worship—the model preferred by Presbyterians and by those Essex ministers who petitioned against the vague Christianity of the *Agreement of the People*—it does instruct people "in a publike way," providing a singularly memorable "confutation of heresie and error."

Although the content of *The ranters monster* is utterly topical—Hadley was indeed the minister of Tillingham, Essex, in 1652, and Essex was home to many

Ranters—the woodcut is not. Yet while *The ranters monster* uses the same wood-cut as *A declaration of a strange and wonderfull monster* (1646), it is a poor repro-duction. Although many of the details of the original story are present—the monster, the bedridden woman, the audience around the bed, and the surprised midwife—the "popish trumpery" (crosses and rosary) is not (fig. 5.3). It is diffi-cult to determine whether this change is a result of the age of the woodcut or of intentional blocking, but it does suggest the publisher's consciousness of a sim-ilarity between the two texts and thus between threats of recusant and sectarian nonconformity. The reuse of both woodcut and central claim (the rebellious woman's desire to bear a child with "no head at all" rather than a Roundhead) also suggests that the story had a certain recognition factor. Although the figure of the woman in bed was not new, it did have new connotations in the 1652 con-text of Adams's story. Many sectarian women prophets delivered their visions and prophecies from their beds: both Mary Gadbury and the prophet Hannah Trapnel, for example, spoke to their followers from bed.[75] While the woodcut's first use exposed the threat of recusancy—the private goings on and activities inside an anti-parliamentarian woman's home and conscience—its second use attempts to expose the private, or, more threateningly, the publicly critical scenes of women sectarians who promised, in one form or another, to bring Christ in the flesh.

In the 1650s Independency was the "middle way" between Presbyterianism and the separatist sects.[76] If the Independents were insisting—as they would for-mally in 1658—that Christ was the only legitimate head of the church, they nonetheless had to defend themselves and their version of toleration against sec-tarians who claimed to make this presence of Christ immediate and not subject to any form of ecclesiastical mediation.[77] Cromwell, himself an Independent, asked for conformity "as far as conscience will permit and from brethren, in things of the mind we look for no compulsion but that of light and reason."[78] Independents thus walked a fine line between religious toleration and state se-curity, giving magistrates the power to bind bodies but not consciences.[79] (In fact, one of the things the New England elders were accused of in their handling of the antinomian heresy was of treating matters of conscience as civil crimes.)[80] Yet as the Hutchinson case made clear, it was not bodies or civil crimes that pro-vided the greatest threat to state security, it was the conscience. The persecution of Mary Gadbury attempted to circumvent the problem by reading her crime not as a matter of conscience but as a crime of the flesh, yet the imprisonment of Gadbury did little to address her true threat: her spiritual assurance and her

THE
RANTERS
MONSTER:

Being a true Relation of one MARY ADAMS, living at *Tillingham* in *Essex*, who named her self the Virgin *Mary*, blasphemously affirming, That she was conceived with child by the Holy Ghost; that from her should spring forth the Savior of the world; and that all those that did not believe in him were damn'd: With the manner how she was deliver'd of the ugliest ill-shapen *Monster* that ever eyes beheld, and afterwards rotted away in prison: *To the great admiration of all those that shall read the ensuing subject; the like never before heard of.*

London, Printed for *George Horton*, 1652. March 30

Figure 5.3. Title page, *The ranters monster: being a true relation of one Mary Adams, living at Tillingham in Essex, who named her self the Virgin Mary, blasphemously affirming, that she was conceived with child by the Holy Ghost; that from her should spring forth the savior of the world; and that all those that did not believe in him were damn'd: with the manner how she was deliver'd of the ugliest ill-shapen monster that ever eyes beheld, and afterwards rotted away in prison: to the great admiration of all those that shall read the ensuing subject; the like never before heard of.* (London, printed for Geoge [sic] Horton, 1652), Thomason E.658[6]. Reproduced by permission of the British Library.

purported ability to provide the same to others. Mary Adams's story endeavors to bring both the material regimes of civil discipline—prison and punishment—and the more providentialist beliefs fostered by Cromwell himself to bear on the problem. Adams's "oneness with Christ" is seen as the result of an erroneous maternal imagination, and her assured conscience as merely a hardened heart. According to *The ranters monster*, the bed scenes of sectarian promise are no more than the birthplaces of monstrosity.

Fables

"For we have not followed cunningly devised fables, when we made known unto you the power and coming of our Lord Jesus Christ, but were eyewitnesses of his majesty."   — 2 PETER 1.16

Mary Adams's story haunts the scholarship of early modern literary and historical scholars, many of whom treat it as a historical event.[81] Yet the entire public record of her story lies in the illustrated pamphlet discussed above, in two notices in parliamentarian newsbooks produced by the same publisher, and in a brief synopsis in a 1654 broadsheet entitled *A List of some of the Grand Blasphemers and Blasphemies, Which was given in to The Committee for Religion* (fig. 5.4).[82] Many of the story's details are historically accurate, but there is, as far as I have been able to determine, no historical record of the arrest or imprisonment of a woman named Mary Adams. Although the Adams story is certainly historically related to the notorious women of the antinomian and Holy Spirit controversies, it is less descriptive than it is symbolic, a hyperbolic version—and fantasized punishment—of widely known cases of sectarian disruption. In all likelihood the very name "Mary Adams" referred both to the originary story of Christianity that sectarians liked to invoke—Mary bringing forth the "new Adam" in Christ—and the contemporary spate of women prophets claiming divine pregnancies. The fact that the two most famous cases involved women named (or renamed by their followers or critics) "Mary" attests to the ongoing fascination with the figure of Mary as the mother of Christ, especially for those who believed in his living spirit. In fact, the 1654 edition of Pagitt's *Heresiography* suggests that sectarians, particularly Ranters, shared with papists a too-keen belief in the figure of the Virgin Mary and in its inevitable associations with, and reverence for, the power of women.[83]

The publisher of *The ranters monster*, George Horton, was a parliamentarian

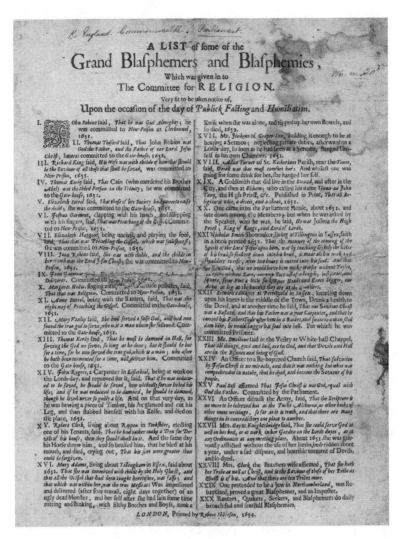

Figure 5.4. *A List of some of the Grand Blasphemers and Blasphemies, Which was given in to The Committee for Religion. Very fit to be taken notice of, Upon the occasion of the day of Publicke Fasting and Humiliation* (London, Printed by Robert Ibbitson, 1654). Reproduced by permission of the British Library.

printer who specialized in marvelous stories of witches, prodigies, apparitions, and other marvelous events.[84] Horton actively exploited the providential culture of Cromwellian England, arguing that contemporary signs and wonders were equal parts divine punishment for England's "Tyrannical Lordlyness" and "profane, sacriligious, mercinary and Prelatical hands," and vindication of the "Peoples Freedoms" and the "precious Saints."[85] Yet while claiming that the "visible Signals" of God were "clear to the Spirits" of those precious Saints, Horton was aware that he had to distinguish between the Saints' "Spirits" and those of the radicals. In addition to publishing defenses of the Independents and the army, Horton published a number of pamphlets on various sects (including the Ranters, who were, as the title of one pamphlet claims, "A Scourge to Englands Rebellion") that mocked their beliefs as superstitious.[86] His publication of an illustrated version of the John and Mary Robins story (see fig. 5.2), and then of *The ranters monster*, suggests that he had an eye for topical sectarian controversies and their exploitation.[87] As the Quakers advanced toward London from the North, Horton turned his attention to them, calling them a "Generation of Enthusiasts" who "attribute all their lewd and bold speakings and doings to the Spirit" and "leave no Art unassayed to dissuade and delude the people from entering into our publicke and Church Assemblies."[88] Those arts included, as would become famous, falling to the ground "quaking" with the force of the Holy Spirit and claiming "the pangs of the New birth." Yet the Quakers, who would prove to be the most long-lived of the antinomian sects, fought back. In 1655 the "Children of Light (who are by the world scornfully called Quakers)" responded to the "false reports, scandals and lyes" published about them in "several news Books and Pamphlets, put forth by, among others, *George Horton*, whose lyes and slanders shall not pass for truth." The Children of the Light reminded their critics of the Doctrine of the Apostles "to avoid prophane and vain Fables."[89] Horton's stories, in other words, were identified as propaganda: "vain Fables" with an intent to harm.

BLASPHEMERS WERE OFTEN identified by their claims that the gospel itself was "mere foolishness, a story of men, or rather a mere fable."[90] Sectarians were similarly accused of declaring the stories of the Scripture fables or allegories. In one pamphlet a Ranter is said to have proclaimed that the Bible was "a meer Romance," a series of tales designed "to keep People in subjection" which "had as much truth in it as the history of Tom Thumb."[91] In Michel Foucault's imagination of the ultimate lesson of the "hundreds of tiny theaters of punishment" of the punitive city, he argues that "each punishment should be a fable."[92] Each punishment, that is, should have a memorable moral legibility, perhaps even a claim to supernatural resonance.[93] This juxtaposition of "fables" is not simply playful: despite their derision of sectarian comparisons of the Gospels to fables, anti-sectarian polemicists nonetheless employed fables themselves, using exemplary stories with popular readerly appeal to both warn against and illustrate sectarian heresies. It is the very creativity of these punishments—their lively theaters—that provides their appeal.

As they increasingly became recognized as fables, stories of monstrous births, like the religious "truths" they were said to hail, came to be understood as politicized—and deeply interested—entities. What had begun, at the very beginning of the Reformation, as a simultaneously publicity-seeking and serious system of legible warning and error had become, in a period of religious dissent fought in texts as well as battlefields, merely topical, the stories' divine portentousness belied by their propagandist intent.[94] If everyone claimed wonders, that is, each story was itself sectarian. The genre of marvelous Protestantism would have its resurrection at the Restoration, as we will see shortly, but the recognizably partisan topicality of wondrous stories had lessened their force as Protestant truths. Monsters were becoming symbols in the modern sense: less divinely resonant than poetically just.

While stories of monstrous births were increasingly recognized as sectarian, however, they did not necessarily lose their efficacy as popular casuistry. As the author of *Teratologia: Or, A Discovery of Gods Wonders* wrote of his own stories in 1650, "Now whether these relations be stories, or fables, truthes or tales, I have not to say, but sure I am, that a good use may be made of them by anyone that is willing to be reformed and instructed."[95] Whether "truthes or tales," stories of monstrous births were increasingly "lessons and scholyngs" that relied less on claims to divine truth than on the press and the power either to censor it or to enter its public ministry. While still a story about the monstrous product of a rebellious mother, *The ranters monster* was most clearly the product of religious and political volatility, the tool of a publisher hoping with his "strange stories" and "wonderful admonitions" to keep a public reading and buying.[96]

The Signs of the Times

"Can ye not discern the Signes of the Times?"
— MATTHEW 6.3, CITED ON TITLE PAGE
OF *Mirabilis Annus* (1661)

"We must now believe without a sign."
— JOHN SPENCER, *A Discourse Concerning Prodigies* (1663)

In 1660 England was reborn. Again. This particular rebirth—the restoration of the monarchy—was accompanied by a wide range of prodigious signs, including strange births. For royalists, the Restoration was a sign of divine favor, and Charles II's return akin to the second coming of Christ. His return had been prophesied, they claimed, by prodigious infants crying "A King" from their cradles and even from within their mothers' wombs. For those who suffered under the Restoration, however, particularly those Puritans newly identified as "Nonconformists" by the restored Church of England, the Restoration was prodigious in an entirely different way, accompanied, not by signs of divine favor, but by what John Spencer would soon call "prodigies penal," punishments delivered by God upon the bodies of those who oppressed his "saints." This politically interested system of divine and punitive prodigies was not, of course, new. What was new was the condemnation, in print, of the propagandistic intentions of the deployment of prodigies, and a concerted effort on the part of learned and newly restored Church of England interests to associate the belief in, and the dissemination of, prodigy stories with ignorance, superstition, and fanaticism.

The decline in stories of prodigies in the later seventeenth century was not, then, solely the result of greater scientific knowledge; it was also the result of focused efforts to minimize the considerable political and cultural efficacy of such stories. These efforts involved discrediting the belief in an intimately providential God—a God concerned with the daily lives of individuals—and discrediting the belief that prodigies were divine signs. Such beliefs were deemed the provenance of the vulgar.[1] While this paradigm is in many ways familiar to scholars of seventeenth-century Europe—Peter Burke and Natalie Zemon Davis, for example, have brilliantly illustrated the attempts to distinguish learned from popular or "vulgar" culture in the period[2]—what has been less remarked upon is the way these efforts were particularly concerned with the female imagination.

As the proximate other to the conscience, the imagination was, as we have seen, a central concern of Protestant order, and the imagination had always been gendered: a potentially dangerous, materially efficacious force in the literal and metaphorical reproduction of human life and society. In the history of Protestant polemics traced throughout this book, the female imagination was also seen as a private realm about which God took particular care, often publishing its errors with monstrous births. While the female imagination was still considered potent in the later seventeenth century, the controversy over prodigies in the early 1660s concerned itself with minimizing its religious force and significance. Increasing attention was paid to the biological instability inherent in women's imaginations, particularly in terms of hysteria and melancholia, but the female imagination was also increasingly identified as being singularly vulnerable to superstition and to the religious delusion that was to characterize religious polemic for the next century under the term "Enthusiasm." As part of their effort to minimize the political effectiveness of dissenters' prodigy tales, Restoration apologists associated the belief in prodigies with those who were deemed to be biologically unstable, seized by superstition, fanatically enthusiastic. They endeavored, that is, to cast those with "impressionable" imaginations, especially women, as the sole believers of a belief system whose political potency they wanted to defuse. This strategy was based, at least in part, on the Church of England's pressing need to delegitimate both political and religious radicalism and the roles that women played in those movements. By severing the connection between the female mind and God, and by discrediting its central importance to religious truth and order, those dissenting women who prophesied the downfall of the monarchy or the coming of the Quaker God could be rendered "Fanaticks," and their attempts to read—let alone produce—the "Signs of the Times" rejected as mere nonsense. Stories of prodigious events were not only deemed superstitious propaganda; they were characterized as the purview of enthusiastic or irrational women. While prodigious monsters continued to be the seen as the "products" of women in the later seventeenth century, they were no longer associated with God, even in his punitive guise: they were the stuff, not of flesh, but of delusion.

Prodigious Births and The Reincarnation of the King

"Out of the mouth of babes and sucklings hast thou ordained strength because of thine enemies, that thou mightest still the enemy and the avenger."

— PSALM 8.2

"This mighty, though small, Champion."   — *The Age of Wonder* (1660)

A few months after the execution of Charles I, a pamphlet entitled *Vox Infantis, or the Prophetical Child* appeared in London. It proclaimed that a miraculous child, discovered by mowers in a Herfordshire field, had proclaimed that after three more years of war, the second King Charles would "win the field" and restore the land to its former glory.[3] After the coronation of Charles II, such royalist stories of king-prophesying infants proliferated. While they proclaimed, with divine and univocal clarity, the legitimacy of monarchical rule, these stories were also concerned with its enemies, both old and new. One pamphlet indicts Oliver Cromwell for trying "to extirpate the Royal Progeny."[4] "I may be so bold to say," the author writes, that if "an innocent Babe had been born with *Vive le Roy* in his mouth, he must have been food for his Sword, as well as the first-born were for Herod's" (A2). The persecution of the monarchy's loyal children, in other words, was analogous to the persecution of Christ. During Cromwell's reign, it was a crime "To say *God save the King*," the author continues, and the people were oppressed "like so many Mutes [. . .] not daring to mention the least dislike" (A2). As if to make up for such royalist muteness, *The true and most miraculous narrative, of a child born with two tongues* (1659) tells the story of an East-Smithfield child who "*three dayes after his Birth, was heard plainly, and expresly to cry out, A King, a King, a King.*"[5] The child's two tongues attest to the dual saving force of prayer and prophecy—"*whosoever calleth on his Name shall be saved*" (2)—and to the promise that in the last days "the Lord will poure out his Spirit on all flesh, and their Sons and their Daughters shall prophecy" (3).[6] The pamphlet intentionally conflates divine and royal authority: the "Name" of England's returning ruler is simultaneously "God" and "King."

The infant's proclamation of the return of the king was certainly portentous, but it also entailed the silencing of other voices. While the author admits that the Lord pours his spirit on daughters and "Hand-maids" (3), he also uses the story of the double-tongued child to make a joke about women: "I have heard many a man to say, that his own Wife, or his next Neighbours Wife, hath a thousand Tongues" (4). Women may talk a lot, the author points out, but "*now they are no sooner heard, then [sic] disregarded*" (4, emphasis added). This seemingly gratuitous and familiarly misogynist insult serves a more serious political purpose than first appears. Punishments used to silence women, such as branks and "Gossips bridles," focused on the physical and symbolic depression of the tongue and were used not only for women who were guilty of "gossiping" but also for women accused of blasphemy, heresy, and sectarianism.[7] In 1655, for example, the Quakers Dorothy Waugh and Anne Robinson of Cumberland were "led through the Street with each an Iron Instrument of Torture call'd a Bridle on their Heads to prevent their speaking the Truth to the People."[8] More than an anti-feminist commonplace, the association between women and unruly tongues in the pamphlet is a pointed response to the voices of dissenting women. Women were voluble, even occasionally solicited speakers during the commonwealth and interregnum periods. At least three women prophets, Elizabeth Poole, Grace Cary, and Eleanor Davies, spoke before the army or Parliament during the 1640s and 50s, often at the request of Cromwell himself.[9] Yet with the restoration of the monarchy, the author of *The true and most miraculous narrative* seems to suggest, such women "*are no sooner heard, then [sic] disregarded.*" While women may continue to speak, in other words, their views are now without political purchase.

In the course of the narrative it is revealed that when the two-tongued child first began to cry out "*A King, A King, A King,*" the midwife and attendant neighborhood women "entred into Councel," and concluded that as "the Name and the Authority of a King had been abolished by the Parliament," it was not fit that the prophecy "should be divulged" (6). The women's "Councel" mocks the audacious decision making of Parliament and invokes the *Parliament of Women* satires, but it also criticizes women's participation in, and support of, parliamentarian rule.[10] Much like Parliament's attempt to deny the divine right of kings, however, the women's efforts to muffle the child's message of monarchical legitimacy fail. Once the prophecy is divulged, the child becomes a cause célèbre among the London gentry—gentlewomen even send their coaches for it—and a barometer of royalist loyalty: upon meeting strangers the child cries, "*A King, a King, a King* [. . .]" and if there were any company about it that it did not like, it will put forth its hand and cry *Away, away*" (6). The story is recounted in a contemporaneous edition of the royalist newsbook, *The Loyall Scout*, in which the child's cries of *A King, A King, A King* and *Away Away* appear in black letter type, the lettering used in official government documents.[11] In this text, the voice of the prodigious royalist birth has the status of an authoritative state proclamation; divine providence and royalist press speak as one.

   The Age of Wonder, or Miracles are not Ceased (1660) tells a similar story of three "mighty, though small Champion[s]" which "have made audible & wonderful revelations in order to the restoring of Monarchy into this wretched Kingdom," by crying "A King" long before they could naturally attain language.[12] One of the stories is a retelling of the story discussed above, an account of a boy child "born with Teeth in his mouth, with two tongues in his mouth, and three Crowns upon his head," who not only spoke "A King," but was "overjoyed" if any one spoke the word "King" in his presence (4). In this account, the two-tongued boy is even taken to "the Commons House of Parliament, where, in his deportment and expressions, he foretold their declining," a decidedly apposite message to those of women prophets like Elizabeth Poole. The three miraculous children testify to the divine right of kings, revealing that God "is willing to make a won-derful Revelation of his Essential and Personal presence with Kings, who are his Chosen and Annointed Servants" (5). God "hath given Supernatural Power to Babes and Sucklings," the author continues, in order "to reveal his Mistery to them who are Babes in Grace, that they may become Babes of Grace by their obedience to his Ordination" (6). Contra Puritan belief, *The Age of Wonder* sug-gests that saving grace is contingent on submission to the monarch; the only true "Babes of Grace" are those who submit to the king's "politic Magistracy" (6).

   Yet despite their numbers and their backing by the king's press, royalist prodi-gies were not the only ones that accompanied Charles II's return to the throne. In 1661–62 dissenters published three collections of anti-royalist, anti–Church of England prodigies under the title *Mirabilis Annus*. Complaining that "so many *hundreds*, if not *thousands* of our able, godly *preaching Ministers* [had been] *removed into corners*" by the restored Church of England (indeed, by 1662 more than two thousand godly ministers had been ejected from their pulpits and forced into of-ten involuntary silence or nonconformity), the authors nonetheless claim that "the defect of their Ministry hath been *eminently* supplied by the Lords imme-diate preaching to us from *Heaven*, in the great and wonderful works of his Prov-idence."[13] (For the prodigy-filled frontispiece illustration to the first collection, see fig. C.1). Citing the opinions of learned men like Luther and examples from

Figure C.1. Image from *Eniaytos terastios. Mirabilis annus, or The year of prodigies and won-ders* (1661), Wing E3127. Reproduced by permission of the Folger Shakespeare Library.

Foxe's *Actes and Monuments*, the authors insist that "[p]rodigies and signs are *especially* for the sakes of wicked and ungodly men," and while they bode misery to the wicked, they prognosticate "much good to the *Sober* and *Religious* part of the World" (74, 80).

Although most of the prodigies in the *Mirabilis Annus* collections feature the poetically just deaths of those who preached against or persecuted Noncon-formists, such as mouth cancer or conflagration,[14] they also include a number of stories of monstrous births. One monster is born to a woman who attended the "Jovial Meetings" of a Sussex minister who had turned out the rightful godly minister for nonconformity; one to a woman whose husband persecuted Non-conformists; and another, born dead and "all over as black as Ink," to a woman who swore falsely against a godly minister, thus leading to his ejection from his parish.[15] A particularly hideous monster was born to a woman who had con-sorted with a "Runagado Priest" and "New conformist" (a former Puritan who had conformed to the restored church after the Restoration). The monster was born with its heart on the outside of its body, hanging "in a long piece of flesh which was about the neck of the Child, like the Ribbon of a Knight of the Garter in which his George hangs."[16] In the monster's body, the heart, the private bastion of Protestant faith, is rendered a public badge of prostituted service to the state. As the parents chose to serve conformist and monarchical interests rather than those of the true religion—literally trading their hearts for worldly and material favor—so their child bears the emblem of their hypocrisy.

The stories of monstrous births included in *Mirabilis Annus* are stories of individuals' participation in religious and political movements and thus stories of the ways that men and, in particular, women "reproduce" belief, even in its mutilated forms. As such, they complicate the univocal message of those state-sanctioned and circulated prodigy tales that attempted to align divine authority and prodigious witnessing solely behind the figure of "A King." Prodigious births, that is, told many different stories, and attested to a wide range of voices. While royalists claimed that two-tongued babes heralded the divine monarchy, their enemies claimed that monstrously deformed births signified God's anger at those who oppressed his true servants. Prodigies were political weapons used not only by those in charge of the government and the press but by those who wanted to undermine them. Among those who were arrested for circulating the *Mirabilis Annus* stories—what one Sergeant called the "Feminine part of every rebellion"—were three women, one of whom who was caught smuggling a copy beneath her coat.[17]

The *Mirabilis Annus* texts were indeed incredibly popular, circulating from secret warehouses and via underground routes as far as Bristol and Leicestershire.[18] By the time they published their second collection, the authors were defending their tales of punitive prodigies against charges of sedition, arguing that they sought not "Treason against man, but Loyalty and Subjection to Jesus Christ the King of Kings" (even this, of course, was a not-so-subtle critique of the earthly king).[19] The "watchful eye" of the press, as the authors themselves pointed out, was continually upon them (54). The newly established government considered the *Mirabilis Annus* tracts a serious threat, and both Sir Edward Nicholas, Charles II's secretary of state, and Sir Roger L'Estrange, his surveyor of printing presses, attempted to suppress them. L'Estrange believed that they aimed "to overthrow the Government by King and bishops [. . .] by the influence of the pretended signs from Heaven upon the people's minds."[20] Another critic called a related collection of anti-conformist prodigious events, *The Lords Loud Call to England* (1660), a "Nest of Sedition," the stories designed "to infatuate mens minds, and set their brains once more a madding, that they may be the more apt to kindle into a combustions, and break forth into another horrid Rebellion."[21] Prodigy tales were not just propaganda; they were the "Fanaticks'" call to war.[22]

The Ungoverned Imagination

John Spencer's 1663 *A Discourse Concerning Prodigies* was in many ways a direct response to the *Lords Loud Call* and *Mirabilis Annus* tracts, referring in its Preface to those "three or four several impressions of Books" which claim that "*England* is grown *Africa* and presents us every year (since the Return of his Majesty) with a new Scene of Monstrous and strange sights."[23] For Spencer, the dissenters' deployment of prodigies not only was politically motivated, but it undermined the very nature of authority: "How mean a value and regard shall the issues of the severest debates, and the commands of Authority, find, if every pitifull Prodigy-monger have credit enough with the People to blast them, by telling them that heaven frowns upon them, and that God writes his displeasure against them, in black and visible characters, when some sad Accident befalls the compilers with them?" (A4v). According to Spencer, not only is the age of miracles over, but the divine miracles recorded in the Scriptures were majestic and momentous, not the embarrassingly petty punishments imagined by dissenters. Would the God who moved oceans, he asks, "now ask us to a devout observation of the familiar miscarriages of Nature" or "to debase our selves to the bondage of some blinde and confused fears of his vengeance, upon the news of a monster?" (35).

Spencer is particularly skeptical of "prodigies penal" ("judgments upon Persons or Nations of a dreadfull and unusual figure") because when men's minds are "disturbed with love or hatred (as it falls out in religious differences) each party superstitiously interprets all accidents in favour of itself" and against its enemies (7).[24] Men, especially those Puritans who would have "the entailing of salvation solely upon their own people," should not believe that God's judgments have no greater design than "the service of their little passions and animosities" (96).[25] For Spencer, the interpretation of prodigies is a matter of authoritative interpretation; even if God does write messages in prodigies, "there is none on earth found able to read the writing, and (with any certainty) to make known the interpretation thereof" (6).[26] God and his ways are beyond the ken of mere mortals. Even if monsters do carry messages, that is, they are certainly not "lessons and scholynges for us all."

For Spencer it is ignorance, superstition, fear, and religious enthusiasm that lead people to receive prodigies as proclamations of God's judgments, and each of these qualities is gendered female. Ignorance of natural causes leads "(in more soft and impressive minds, especially) to superstition," and superstition is "a servile flattery of God, and an observance of him in little, weak, feminine instances of devotion" (103). The fear of prodigies reduces "the spirits of men to some cold and little observances, pale and feminine fears," and prophecies "carry the form of a *Woman,* as being delivered generally by that Sex, but constantly by persons extremely ignorant, credulous, talkative, and impotent both in mind and body." While the delivering of prophecies and the belief in prodigies were the provenance of "*Madmen, Persons transported by the heats of a feaver, Star-gazers, Fortune-tellers, and Women,*" the God of Scripture conferred the gift of divination "(generally) upon men, and those of a pious and learned education" (84). In what was to become a common refrain, Reason stood in contrast to Enthusiasm and superstition, and religious belief required the guidance of reason and learning: while God used to address himself, in the "non–Age of the Church," to the "lower faculties of the Soul (Phancy and Imagination)," since the coming of Christ, "all things are to be managed in a more sedate, cool, and silent manner" (11)—and needless to say, they were to be managed most effectively by "pious and learned" men.

In a companion text, *A Discourse Concerning Vulgar Prophecies,* Spencer is particularly contemptuous of the "Enthusiastic" belief discussed at length in the previous chapter: "that the Minds of Holy Men should conceive (like the Virgin Mary) by the sole overshadowings of the Holy Ghost, without any Assistances from Man or Humane Literature."[27] The cause of such beliefs was a "natural fervor and pregnancy of spirit in some more refined, and an heated Melancholy in other grosser Enthusiasts" (A3v). The Quakers, particularly Quaker women, were particular prey to these sorts of "Prophetic Frenzies" (A3v). Indeed, the Quaker leader George Fox believed that there were a thousand women who were "beyond the wisdom of the world," and that "the power of God hath wrought miracles among them."[28] As if in response to such claims, John Gadbury singled out the "silly Quakers conceited Revelation[s]" in his *Natura Prodigiorum, or A Discourse Concerning the Nature of Prodigies* (1660), and claimed that "for any man to credit, or give heed to vain, idle, and addle-headed women, and to esteem their Predictions or twarling stories, as prophecies, or Oracles, Is the greatest Argument of Imbecility or weakness that can be" (190).[29] Similarly, the case that inspired Meric Casaubon's 1655 *A Treatise Concerning Enthusiasm* was that of a woman who mistook her "strange raptures and enthusiasms" for divine rather than "melancholick" signs. He thus posited that women were more susceptible to enthusiasm, being "naturally weaker of brain, and easiest to be infatuated and deluded."[30] Henry More's *Enthusiasmus Triumphatus* (1656), to cite one final example, also sees enthusiasm as a physiological disease, analogous to what happens to women in "Hysterick Fitts, arising from the strength of their Fancies and Passions."[31]

If it was "Enthusiasm"—a strange blend of biological and intellectual vulnerability and religious delusion—that led people to have visions or prophecies, it was also enthusiasm that led the same people to see prodigious events, such as monstrous births, as divine signs that they themselves were capable of interpreting. Thus, in his efforts to discredit the political and manipulative uses of such prodigious events, Spencer banishes those things in which people take a "natural delight," such as "the pictures of Anticks, and Monsters," to a strangely ahistorical and ignorant past, stripping them of any religious or political import. Stories of prodigies "may perhaps serve to deceive the tedium of a Winter night," Spencer writes, but when they advance "from the chimney corner to the Church, and are adopted the measures of a religious faith or fear [. . .] 'tis time to throw contempt upon them."[32] Unlike the author of *Teratologia*, who suggests that whether or not they are "truthes or tales," good use can be made of prodigious stories, Spencer insists that "[a] lie never did, never could serve the interest of truth" (A4). Stories of monstrous births—deployed by royalist men of God only two years before, and indeed, for some hundred years, as matters adamantly *not* of the chimney corner but of the church—are relegated to a mythical and ignorant past: among the superstitious beliefs of the preliterate and prerational vulgar are stories of "births seal'd with the odd figures of an ungovern'd imagination, and many more (too mouldy with age to set before the Reader)" (24).[33] Stories of prodigies and monsters are "the recreations and entertainments of children," the provenance of those "troubled with the fits of the first Mother (curiosity and pride)," the "Pregnant arguments of a soft, vain, and unfurnished minde" (103, 104, 64).

Spencer's strategic—and false—history of a preliterate and superstitious belief in prodigies and portents would become a prevalent one. The seventeenth-century writer John Aubrey seems to cite Spencer's version of history when he refers, with nostalgia, to the "Old Wives Tales" and "Fables" that were lost with the coming of education and the popularization of the printing press.[34] Along with a range of other fables and beliefs, the portentous monstrous birth, once considered the joint product of an imaginatively potent mother and a punitive God, came to be seen as the product of women in another way: the imaginary or delusional offspring of their impressionable and untutored minds. The prodigy story, that is, became an Old Wives' Tale. If women's beliefs had once been held responsible for *producing* monsters, they were now held responsible for keeping such a false and even blasphemous belief system alive. Stories of monstrous births were thus relegated to the historical shelf of quaint and vaguely ridiculous superstitions, a "history" that would find a more benign, if no less patronizing, reclamation in the work of nineteenth-century antiquarians and folklorists.[35]

Monster Redux

While the story I have outlined above offers one history of what happened to the religious resonances of stories of prodigious and monstrous births in the later seventeenth century, there is another, perhaps more prominent history against which we need to balance it. This history proposes that their decline was due to the rise of Baconian science and the work of the Royal Society, enterprises that read monstrous births, not as divine signs or as punishments for mothers, but as rarities in nature. (Indeed, this history is evident throughout both Spencer's and Gadbury's texts.)[36] According to this narrative, as monstrous births became the subjects of scientific inquiry, their religious significance was increasingly accredited to no more—and no less—than the all-encompassing wonder-working of God.[37]

After the prodigy controversy of the early 1660s, stories about monstrous births continued to make their way into print, but the majority were, as scholars of natural science would predict, substantively different from their pre–Royal Society cousins. While monstrous births were still identified as "strange" and "wonderful," few monster pamphlets published in the last decades of the seventeenth century either indicted the mothers or made claims for the monsters' status as punitive or divine messengers. A 1687 pamphlet entitled *The Wonder of this present Age* removes any divine or maternal role in the birth whatsoever, claim-

ing that the monster was "Brought into the World by the great Skill and Experience of the most Famous Doctor *Hugh Chamberlain*" and, after its immediate
death, "preserved and made fit for Publick View, by Mr. *John Green*, Preserver
of Dead Bodies."[38] The monstrous child, in other words, was the pathologized
product of doctors, both "brought into" and ushered out of the world via the
hands of science.

As things "rare in Nature," monsters continued to be the subject of fascination for both empirical observers—one broadsheet claims that the parents of
monstrous twins were "offered a great Sum of Money for them to be carried
about"—and readers, but the interpretation of their causes was left largely to
"Doctors and Chyrurgeons" or, as the author of *A True Relation of Two Prodigious
Births* puts it, "to the judicious to contemplate."[39] While William Leigh leaves
the consideration of his monster's significance "to the godly disposed," identifying it not only as a case of conscience but as a means of Puritan interpellation,
the author of *A True Relation of Two Prodigious Births* simply, if somewhat cau-
tiously, signals that its monster is worthy of judicious contemplation. What
man, as Spencer put it some years earlier, "that hath any great thoughts of the
Majestie of heaven can once imagine [God] ever intended any base and deformed
monsters, the interpreters of any of his great counsels and purposes?"[40] What
man indeed. The age of marvelous Protestantism, with its small texts and their
intimately providentialist punishments, seems to have come to an end.

No historical shift, however, is thorough in its effects.[41] A 1668 pamphlet entitled *The strange monster or, true news from Nottingham-shire* concludes its story
of a monstrous birth with the plea that "The Reader will not look with the same
eyes (as the Fanaticks do) upon such monstrous births, accounting them Prodigies, and certain Foretellers of great mischiefs infallibly to ensue, since we see
that all ages have produced the like or more strange births" (6).[42] Yet although
the author seems to suggest that the history of monstrous births is one of factual
record rather than prodigious import, he is not willing to ignore the uses to which
the *other* monsters he cites—including the ruffed and conjoined monsters discussed in previous chapters—were put to use. "[L]et every one labour to break
off his own sins by repentance," he writes, "and then we shall not need to hear
any calamity which such prodigious births may seem to signifie" (6). Reform
and repent, he suggests, and save us the burden of interpretation. His advice is
not, in fact, so far removed from that offered in the 1562 monster broadsheet
discussed in chapter 1—"Let it to you a preachying be"—and navigates between

the (putatively) dominant beliefs that monsters were wonders of nature and that God's ways were inscrutable.[43] Even if it is not specifically identified or narratively rendered as a case of conscience, the monster pamphlet is still imagined as a personal object for reflection and repentance. It is the presumption of interpretation that is handled differently. As Foucault argues in *The Order of Things*, the function proper to knowledge is not seeing, but interpretation.[44] Thus, while often subject, in their material forms, to much empirical scrutiny and ocular proof, monstrous births nonetheless still implicitly solicited interpretation, both of their causes and of their intentions. Even anti-prodigy writers refused to claim that prodigies had no divine resonance whatsoever. John Spencer himself insisted that just as we must not lose "Philosophy in Religion, by a total neglect of second causes, and turning Superstitious; so neither must we loose [*sic*] our Religion in Philosophy by dwelling on second causes till we quite forget the First and become profane."[45]

Such hedging over the significance and interpretation of monsters brings us back to the debate over the monstrous births recorded by the nonconforming minister Oliver Heywood in the late seventeenth century, discussed at the beginning of this book. For both Heywood and his peer, Mr. Lambert, monstrous births reveal God's "special hand" in the "punishing of some sin"; they are "rebukes" from God for human, particularly maternal, errors that proceed with "no magistrate to put them to shame."[46] But for their rival, the conforming Presbyterian minister Dr. Hook, monstrous births are not divine signs; such beliefs are blasphemous and worthy of passionate reproach.[47] Whether Hook was reacting to Heywood and Lambert's unorthodox religious interpretations in general or to the specific issue of monstrous births is lost to history, as is the voice of "S.K.," the woman whose monstrous births were taken as signs not only of her own sins but of God's directives for human behavior. The Heywood debate does, however, illustrate that the controversy over the causes and meanings of monsters was ongoing and passionately polemical throughout the seventeenth century. At least for those who had less official power to affect the laws governing social and religious order, the divine and punitive qualities of monstrous births were still vibrant and, equally important, still useful.

A 1715 pamphlet, *The Miracle of Miracles*, tells the story of one Sarah Smith of Darken Parish in Essex who gave birth to a monster with six heads which, quite understandably, "[s]urprised many [of the] Thousand People that came there to see it." Magistrates eventually kill it, surgeons dissect it, and the local

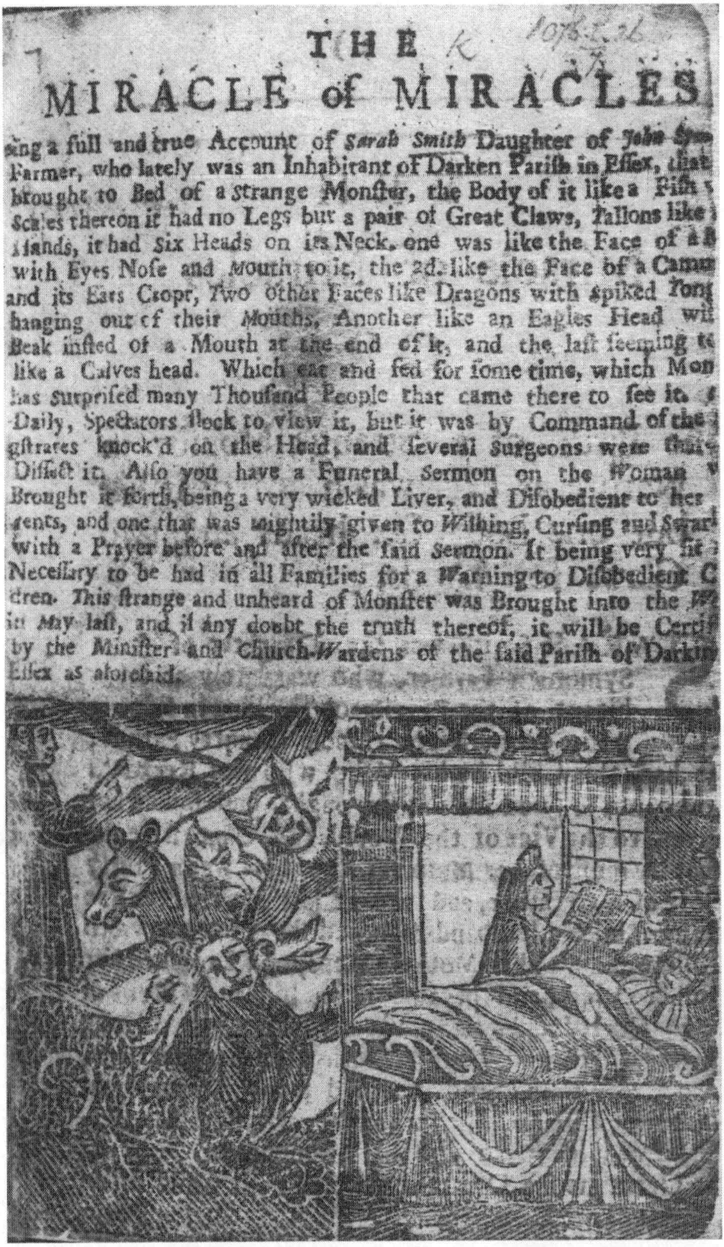
THE
MIRACLE of MIRACLES
[Be]ing a full and true Account of *Sarah Smith* Daughter of *John Sym*...
Farmer, who lately was an Inhabitant of Darken Parish in Essex, that
brought to Bed of a strange Monster, the Body of it like a Fish ...
Scales thereon it had no Legs but a pair of Great Claws, Tallons like ...
Hands, it had Six Heads on its Neck, one was like the Face of a ...
with Eyes Nose and Mouth to it, the 2d. like the Face of a Cam...
and its Ears Cropt, Two other Faces like Dragons with spiked Tong...
hanging out of their Mouths, Another like an Eagles Head wi...
Beak insted of a Mouth at the end of it, and the last seeming to ...
like a Calves head. Which eat and fed for some time, which Mon...
has surprised many Thousand People that came there to see it. ...
Daily, Spectators flock to view it, but it was by Command of the ...
gistrates knock'd on the Head, and several Surgeons were ...
Dissect it. Also you have a Funeral Sermon on the Woman ...
Brought it forth, being a very wicked Liver, and Disobedient to her ...
rents, and one that was mightily given to *Withing*, Cursing and Swear...
with a Prayer before and after the said Sermon. It being very fit ...
Necessary to be had in all Families for a *Warning* to Disobedient C...
dren. *This* strange and unheard of Monster was Brought into the W...
in *May* last, and if any doubt the truth thereof, it will be Certif...
by the Minister and Church-*Wardens* of the said Parish of Darkin...
Essex as aforesaid.

Figure C.2. Title page, *The Miracle of Miracles Being a full and true account of Sarah Smith who lately was an inhabitant of Darken Parish in Essex, that brought to bed of a strange monster* (London?, 1715). Reproduced by permission of the British Library.

minister offers a funeral sermon that interprets the monstrous birth as punishment for its (dead) mother, who was, among other things, disobedient to her parents and a "grievous Curser and Swearer, a Gamester" (6). John Spencer would certainly have considered this "miracle" entirely "vain and ludicrous," but he understood, perhaps as well as the majority of his countrymen, the efficacy of such stories and their fabulous illustrations (fig. C.2). Most people, he knew, neglect books and stories that are not "Somewhat antick and extraordinary."[48]

Notes

Introduction

1. Heywood, *The Rev. Oliver Heywood, 1630–1702. His Autobiography, Diaries, Anecdotes and Event Books*, 2:259.

2. While Leviticus claimed that deformity was "a curse layd upon the child for the parents incontinency," John 9 suggested, through questioning whether a blind man's disability was the result of his or his parents' sin, that it was no such thing: "Jesus answered, Neither hath this man sinned, nor his parents: but that the work of God should be made manifest in him" (John 9:1–3). Thus, the interpretation of the divine significance of human deformities, disabilities, and monstrous births was always open to dispute. In the fight between Hook and Lambert, Hook, presumably basing his interpretation on John, claims it is blasphemous to blame a monstrous birth on the parents' crimes. Lambert, like Heywood, clearly believes that the monster is a sign of God's displeasure at the mother's lifestyle. In another pamphlet about a monstrous birth, Thomas Bedford deals with John 9 in great depth, arguing that Christ's claim that the man's blindness was neither his nor his parents' fault was not meant to imply that any deformity was blameless. Many were, indeed, judgments from God. See Bedford, *A True and Certaine Relation of a Strange Birth*, 13.

3. Heywood, 2:278. Oliver Heywood was a Nonconformist divine. After a series of battles with Richard Hook, the new vicar of Halifax, and within a month after the Uniformity Act took effect (August 24, 1662), Heywood was excommunicated. Although a "silenced" minister, Heywood held conventicles at the houses of the Presbyterian gentry and farmers in open defiance of the act of 1664. On the passing of the Five Mile Act (1665), he left his residence to become an itinerant evangelist throughout the northern counties. His meetinghouse was licensed under the Toleration Act on July 18, 1689 (DNB).

4. The thirty broadsheets and pamphlets I examine are listed by name under "Primary Texts" in the bibliography. In *Travesties and Transgression in Tudor and Stuart England*, David Cressy similarly identifies more than two dozen publications describing monstrous births (31–32). "Whether this was news for people to use, and whether it reflected the anxieties of a troubled and divided culture," he comments, "is a subject for continuing research" (50).

5. There are other, related genres of "marvelous Protestantism," chief among them murder pamphlets and pamphlets about strange events (from fires to storms). These texts share many qualities: the combination of "Catholic" and "Protestant" belief systems that Peter Lake sees as the guiding logic of murder pamphlets; the providentialism outlined by Alexandra Walsham; and the standard "moralizing" that Sandra Clark sees as a defin-

ing feature of most early modern pamphlets. Yet popular stories of monstrous births told a particular kind of story intimately related not only to a long Christian history of inter-pretive meaning but to a specifically Protestant movement. Small texts about monstrous births were seen by contemporaries as a discrete phenomenon: they were singled out, and indeed sometimes bound together, as a readily identifiable genre. While numerous mon-sters of all kinds appear in other kinds of literary texts, from John Marston's "To Perfec-tion: A Sonnet," to Shakespeare's Richard III and his Caliban in *The Tempest,* I focus here on a specific figure—the monstrous birth—and genre—printed broadsheets and bal-lads—in order to illuminate a particular kind of reading and interpretive practice.

6. The full title is *A wonder worth the reading, or, A true and faithfull relation of a woman, now dwelling in Kentstreet, who, vpon Thursday, being the 21 of August last, was deliuered of a prodigious and monstrous child, in the presence of diuers honest, and religious women to their won-derfull feare and astonishment* (London: Imprinted by William Jones, dwelling in Red-crosse-streete, 1617), STC 14935. Monsters earned their status as signs and portents, "not from their ontology but their utility" (Bynum, *Metamorphosis and Identity,* 71). They pointed beyond themselves to meaning.

7. For the former, see Daston and Park, *Wonders and the Order of Nature,* chap. 5; and for the latter, see Shaaber, *Some Forerunners of the Newspaper in England.*

8. Holland, *Continu'd just inquisition of . . . paper-persecutors,* printed as part of Sir John Davies' *A Scourge for paper-persecutors* (London, 1625), A2v. The verse reads: "A generall Folly reigneth, and harsh Fate / Hath made the World it selfe insatiate: / It hugges these Monsters and deformed things, / Better than what *Iohnson* or Drayton *sings.*" According to Holland, readers hold popular texts about such subjects as monsters and hangings at Tyburne as "worke[s] divine" and "for their Bible take [them]."

9. John Stockwood, *A Bartholomew Fairing for parents, to bestow upon their sonnes and daughters* (London, 1589); John Earle, *Micro-cosmographie, Or, A peece of the world discov-ered: in essayes and characters* (London: Edward Blunt, 1628), sig. Fiv; and Davies, *A Scourge for paper-persecutors,* 55.

10. See, for example, Achinstein, "Audiences and Authors."

11. In his *Analytical Index to the Ballad Entries in the Stationers' Register,* Rollins points out that from 1557, when licensing began, to the end of the sixteenth century, over 2,000 broadside ballads had been recorded (he suggests, moreover, that again as many were *not* registered). Of these, only 260 survive from the whole century. And of these, according to my own and Carole Rose Livingston's calculations, 10 of them are about monstrous births (Livingston, *British Broadside Ballads of the Sixteenth Century,* passim). The numbers for the seventeenth century and for pamphlets are much more complex, but my point here is less about exact numbers than about the prevalence, survival, and popularity of cheap texts about monstrous births.

12. The term "ephemera" is equally suspect. As Cyprian Blagden notes, popular texts "may be 'ephemeral' now, but I doubt if they were so regarded in the seventeenth cen-tury by the purchasers for whom they were printed. 'O sister,' says Coke to Mistress Overdo in *Bartholomew Faire,* 'doe you remember the ballads over the Nursery-chimney at home o' my owne pasting up?'" (Blagden, "Notes on the Ballad Market," 164).

13. I am indebted for this term to Jonathan Gil Harris, who uses the term to discuss the "new" new historicist interest in antiquarianism, material objects, and strange stories in "The New New Historicism's Wunderkammer of Objects," *European Journal of English Studies* 4, no. 2 (2000 August): 111–23.

14. Desiderius Erasmus, *Here folowith a scorneful image or monstrus shape of a maruelous stra[n]ge fygure called, Sileni alcibiadis presentyng ye state [and] condicio[n] of this present world, [and] inespeciall of the spiritualite how farre they be from ye perfite trade and lyfe of Criste, wryte[n] in the laten tonge, by that famous clarke Erasmus, [and] lately translated in to Englyshe* (Imprynted at London: By [N. Hill for?] me Iohn Goughe. Cum priuilegio regali. And also be for to sell in Flete-strete betwene the two temples, in the shoppe of Hary Smythe stacyoner, 1543), STC 10507[72].

15. For information about the authors and publishers, see Rollins, "William Elderton: Elizabethan Actor and Ballad-Writer"; Lievsay, "William Barley, Elizabethan Printer and Bookseller"; and Curtis, "William Jones, Puritan Printer and Propagandist." The specific pamphlets will be discussed in detail in subsequent chapters.

16. He was bound over on March 12, 1556–7 (Duff, *A Century of the English Book Trade*).

17. The book John Wolf printed was John Day's *ABC and Little Catechisme*. When Christopher Baker, the Queen's printer, remonstrated with him, Wolf retorted that the Queen had no right to grant privileges and that just as Luther had reformed religion, so he, Wolf, would reform the government of the printing and bookselling trades. He was imprisoned in 1582. See McKerrow, *A Dictionary of Printers and Booksellers* (297). In May 1583 Wolf was declared to have "iij presses and ij more since found in a secret vault" (Arber, *A Transcript of the Registers*, 1:248). The wondrous birth in *A Strange and Miraculous Accident* was witnessed by a man identified as "a brother of the reformed Church of Jesus Christ," suggesting a resistant reformist message. *A Strange and Miraculous Accident happened in the Cittie of Purmerent, on New-yeeres even last past 1599. Of a yong child which was heard to cry in the Mothers wombe before it was borne, and about fourteene dayes of age, spake certaine sencible words, to the wonder of every body.* (Imprinted at London By John Wolfe, and are to be solde at his shop in Popes head Alley, neer unto the Exchange, 1599).

18. In 1636 William Jones, prisoner in the Gatehouse, petitioned Archbishop Laud for release, claiming that he regretted having printed books against the church and state. He was released in May (Greg et al., *A Companion to Arber*, 8).

19. In her brilliant study of cheap print and popular piety, Tessa Watt argues that much Protestant proselytizing was done through popular texts: "Religious treatises could be read aloud to the unlettered, but could never speak through the countryside as effectively as a broadside ballad could" (*Cheap Print and Popular Piety*, 69). Yet Watt defines a pamphlet as religious only according to whether its title contains one of several key terms: God, religion, the pope, or papists. Natascha Würzbach also assumes that religious ballads are different from "ballads of crimes and marvels" (see *The Rise of the English Street Ballad*, 67). Alexandra Walsham has complicated this division by drawing attention to the presence of Christian providentialism in popular texts about murders, natural disasters, and prodigies. Her work, however, focuses less on "reading" the pamphlets or their accompanying woodcuts than on pointing to their existence as evidence of a widespread belief in the intervening hand of God in early modern England (*Providence in Early Modern England*). As I argue in the last two chapters of this book, the story shifts somewhat when Parliament takes control of the press in the early 1640s and the "resistant" voices become dominant.

20. Many pamphlets included two illustrations—a separable title page woodcut, to be posted elsewhere, perhaps as advertisement, and another in the pamphlet itself, often accompanying the description of the birth.

21. Aston, *England's Iconoclasts*, 7. Images of Christ's sufferings, of the Virgin Mary and the saints, for example, had been central to the Catholic faith, serving pedagogical, commemorative, inspirational, and devotional purposes. But based on the second commandment: "Thou shalt not make unto thee any graven image, or any likeness of any thing that is in heaven above, or that is in the earth beneath, or that it in the water under the earth" (Exodus 20:4), Protestant reformers reacted against the role of the visual and sensual in religious practice and perception, arguing that holy images inspired dangerous ideas about the right way to see or conceive of God and were thus potentially idolatrous (see Holtgen, "The Reformation of Images," 120). According to a dominant historical reading, while Protestants initially employed older cultural formats such as ballads, songs, and visual imagery as reformist propaganda, by around 1580 they abandoned the use of visual and fictional cultural forms as "vain imaginings" (Collinson, *The Elizabethan Puritan Movement*, 82).

22. There was still a demand for religious figure subjects, Watt argues, but saints were replaced by Old Testament scenes, then by Apocrypha and parables, then by allegorical and classical figures (*Cheap Print and Popular Piety*, 135). Others have pointed to the rise of portraiture, particularly royal portraiture, and to the rise of the cult of the Virgin Queen as a replacement for the cult of the Virgin Mary. In this cult, Elizabeth was celebrated as Queen of Heaven and Earth, the *Virgo potens* "who bore Christ in her heart as a womb" (Holtgen, "Reformation of Images," 143). See also Strong, *Portraits of Queen Elizabeth*.

23. Watt, *Cheap Print and Popular Piety*, 132.

24. Ibid., 137. Watt focuses much of her attention on images "left over" from Catholicism.

25. *Conjoined twins born in Middleton Stoney* (Imprinted at London by Jhon Daye dwellinge over Aldersgate beneth S. Martyns, 1552).

26. Watt, *Cheap Print and Popular Piety*, 149. Watt suggests that images of monstrous births "may have satisfied some of the demand for the supernatural and miraculous in the absence of religious prints," but she argues that "it would be crude to think of monstrous creatures directly 'replacing' saints and pietas; indeed, in France the canards existed side by side with devotional images" (165). What I argue here is less that stories of monsters replaced stories of saints than that they told religious stories in increasingly inventive and polemical ways.

27. My term cites the common Protestant invective against the "idols in the frontispiece," the crude little woodcuts—often of God in his heaven—that ran along the top of ballad broadsheets. "Idols in the Frontispiece" is also the title of a chapter in Watt's book. Robert Scribner (*For the Sake of Simple Folk*) has shown us how German woodcut artists turned the Catholic iconographic tradition to the service of the Lutheran Reformation.

28. On the reuse of woodcuts, see Livingston, *British Broadside Ballads*, 42, 522.

29. As Michael Marrus says of France's religious wars, "Villages, in a certain sense, were sovereign" ("Folklore as an Ethnographic Source," 113).

30. The Book of Common Prayer endeavored to deal with local variations in church practice ("some following *Salisbury* Use, some *Hereford* Use, [..] some of *York*, some of *Lincoln*") by offering one model for the "whole Realm" (Book of Common Prayer, 10). Yet, as the authors of the Book of Common Prayer itself admitted, "the minds of men are so diverse, that some think it a great matter of conscience to depart from a piece of the least of their ceremonies" (12). On the negotiation between national edicts and local practice, see Wrightson, "Two Concepts of Order," 21–46, esp. p. 22.

31. As Adam Fox has argued, "What started out as a short ditty extemporized by amateurs in a locality could end up as a fully developed broadside, printed and perhaps dispersed nation-wide" ("Ballads, Libels and Popular Ridicule in Jacobean England," 71). Other texts also had their roots in local events. In 1586, for example, Nicholas Colman of Norwich published a broadside ballad by Thomas Deloney concerning a calamitous fire at nearby Beccles; the anticipated audience was presumably mostly local. See Eric A. Clough, *A Short-Title Catalogue arranged geographically of books printed and distributed by printers, publishers, and booksellers in the eight provincial towns and in Schotland and Ireland up to and including the year 1700* (London: Library Association 1969).

32. On the circulation of news to and from localities, see Cust, "News and Politics in Early Seventeenth-Century England," *Past and Present* 112 (1986): 60–90.

33. Marcus, *Puzzling Shakespeare*, 32.

34. The dismissal has been perpetuated by twentieth-century critics as well. Texts about crimes or monstrous births have often been called "sensational news pamphlets" and have been seen as "less serious, less considerable than moral or religious pamphlets, more frivolous, more ephemeral" (Clark, *The Elizabethan Pamphleteers*, 35, 34); Rollins calls them "frankly journalistic" ("The Black-Letter Broadside Ballad," 265).

35. Monsters invoked a long history of Protestant propagandizing. In 1523 Luther and Melanchthon issued a pamphlet entitled *The Papal Ass of Rome and the Monk Calf of Freyberg* that assured the success of monsters as a tool of religious polemic. See Andersson, "Popular Imagery in German Reformation Broadsheets," 120–50, and Scribner, *For the Sake of Simple Folk*, 136. The deployment of monstrous births by early English reformers will be discussed in chapter 1.

36. The roots of the belief in monstrous births as divine signs are ancient (Aristotle and Cicero, among others, wrote at length on their portentous significance). I am interested here in their Christian uses and the ways in which ancient divinatory procedures were modified by Christianity, and further by the Reformation. For a thorough summary of the classical and early Christian traditions, see Céard, *La Nature et les prodiges*, 3–30.

37. See Vieira, "Emblematic Monsters in Portuguese Pamphlets," 91.

38. On *exempla*, see Owst, *Literature and Pulpit in Medieval England*; Duffy, *The Stripping of the Altars*, 29; and Ward, *Miracles and the Medieval Mind*, 205. *Exempla* asserted divine approval for ecclesiastical or secular politics and could be fitted to topical or local circumstances and issues (Ward, 208). As Jacques de Vitry wrote, "Many will be stirred by examples who will not be moved by precepts," (cited in Ward, 28).

39. *The Exempla or Illustrative Stories from the Sermones Vulgares of Jacques de Vitry*, 222, 225, 252.

40. Ibid., 211.

41. Ibid., 213.

42. J. S., "To the Reader," *Teratologia: Or, A Discovery of Gods Wonders*, 2.

43. For a succinct critique of this (false) opposition, see Scribner, "The Reformation, Popular Magic and the 'Disenchantment of the World.'" My title also references a wider scholarly interest in the wonderful and marvelous. See Bynum, *Metamorphosis and Identity*, 38–39 for a survey of the field. The texts she mentions are Greenblatt, *Marvelous Possessions*; Kenseth, ed., *The Age of the Marvelous*; and Daston and Park, *Wonders and the Order of Nature* (chapter 5). A recent addition is Zakiya Hanafi's *The Monster in the Machine* (2000), which "attempts to track the ways human beings were defined in contrast to supernatural and demonic creatures during the period of the Scientific Revolution" (viii).

44. See Daston, "Marvelous Facts and Miraculous Evidence in Early Modern Eu-

rope," 95; and Eire, *The War Against the Idols*, 221–24. The question was endlessly debated, as the deep-thinker Lafeu puts it in *All's Well That Ends Well:* "They say miracles are past, and we have our philosophical persons to make modern and familiar, things supernatural and causeless. Hence is it that we make trifles of terrors, ensconcing ourselves into seeming knowledge when we should submit ourselves to an unknown fear" (2.3.5–6). Despite many competing explanations, in a broadly theological sense prodigious signs were popularly seen as the products of "the very hand of heaven."

45. For the first criticism, see Pricket, *The Iesuits Miracles, or new Popish Wonders;* and for the second, the *Diary of Walter Yonge*, 13. Miracles, under new Protestant scrutiny, required witnesses, and Yonge's witness, as a conforming Protestant, deems the popish child a false miracle.

46. Daston, "Marvelous Facts," 114.

47. Keith Thomas, *Religion and the Decline of Magic*, 77. See also Scribner, "Reformation, Popular Magic." Like Thomas, Scribner resists the argument that Reformation removed the "magical elements from Christianity" (475). The "Reformation was part of a great divine intervention in the world, part of God's ultimate plan for creation and humanity. It was the Enlightenment that first interpreted the Reformation as part of a long-term process of rationalization and secularization," and this view has been canonized in historiography (492).

48. Daston and Park, *Wonders and the Order of Nature*, 121.

49. On the difficulty of separating these two kinds of wonders in the dominant Christian culture, see Daston and Park, 16; and Walsham, *Providence in Early Modern England*, 230. Bynum similarly points out that wonder adhered to both marvels and miracles (*Metamorphosis and Identity*, 50).

50. Lorraine Daston argues that as part of sweeping changes in natural philosophy and theology in the mid-seventeenth century, prodigies changed from being signs, or portents signifying God's will and things to come, "to non-signifying facts" ("Marvelous Facts and Miraculous Evidence," 95). Daston and Park modified this view in *Wonders and the Order of Nature:* "Monsters had a kind of twilight status. They were not really miracles (or Protestants who claimed that miracles had ceased would not have made so much of them); nor were they natural events. . . . Instead they provided a paradigm for the cooperation of primary and secondary causes" (49, 192).

51. Bedford, *A True and Certaine Relation of a Strange Birth*, 14.

52. Wonder, according to Stephen Greenblatt, is an "emotional and intellectual experience in the presence of radical difference"; the marvelous a "departure, displacement or surpassing of the normal or the probable" (*Marvelous Possessions*, 14, 76). Bynum similarly argues that wonder (*admiratio*) was more than a physiological response, it "was a recognition of the singularity and significance of the thing encountered" (*Metamorphosis and Identity*, 39).

53. Marvels may have taken the place of miracles, as Greenblatt argues, but they certainly did not avoid "the theological and evidentiary problems inherent in directly asserting a miracle" (*Marvelous Possessions*, 79); as the accounts discussed in this book illustrate, marvels also required witnesses and interpretation.

54. In Bedford's formulation "the speciall hand of God" works alone "to sort and compound the activities of secondary causes." Those secondary causes were both biological and behavioral. Historically, the causes of monstrosities were classified in three categories: supernatural causes, which included God, the devil, and the stars; physical causes,

which included alterations in the male semen, the mixing of different semen, menstrual influences, and alterations in the womb; and mental, or maternal, influence. See Ballantyne, *Teratogenesis*, 5; and Paré, *On Monsters and Marvels*, 38.

55. Gramsci, *Selections from the Prison notebooks*, 276.

56. Lyndal Roper (*Oedipus and the Devil*, 38) argues that it is precisely the physicality of the concept of crisis, anchoring gender relations in the flesh, that makes the notion useful to feminist historians. It reminds us that gender is not just a social construct but one which involves the body.

57. In "The Promises of Monsters," Donna Haraway argues for displacing the terminology of reproduction with that of generation, particularly "the generation of novel forms": "Very rarely does anything really get reproduced; what's going on is much more polymorphous than that" (299). What monsters thus suggest is that each act of reproduction creates something new and that each "novel form" has a story to tell that is full of both dissent and regenerative possibility. I argue that although monsters were meant to moralize and naturalize institutions and behaviors, they just as often revealed the instability inherent in any type of reproduction.

58. Collinson, *The Birthpangs of Protestant England*, 155; and Haigh, "The English Reformation," 449–59.

59. Seaver, *Wallington's World*, 9–10; Keeble, *Richard Baxter: Puritan Man of Letters*, 74–76.

60. The Protestant service of Commination, or absolution from sin, ended with the recitation of this psalm. See the Book of Common Prayer, 23. Quotations from the Bible throughout are from *Authorized King James Version*.

61. For Protestant attacks on the cult of the Virgin Mary and other "richly symbolic feminine aspects" of Catholic belief, see Freedberg, *The Power of Images*, 387. As Huston Diehl has argued, the iconoclastic attack on images of adoration as seductive women often carried over into misogynist attacks on women themselves (*Staging Reform*, 164).

62. Lyndal Roper has argued that the Protestant clergy "had to develop a literature about marriage and womanhood which did more than align women with Eve and sexual temptation" (*The Holy Household*, 18). Yet while the "positive evaluation of marriage and of women as wives, and the doctrine of the priesthood of all believers have been adduced to argue that women's status improved," the sixteenth-century crisis in gender relations was also said to result in a more securely patriarchal ordering of the relations between the sexes (1). (See, for example, Stephen Ozment, *When Fathers Ruled: Family Life in Reformation Europe* [Cambridge, MA and London, 1983]). Yet, as Roper insists, "There was no 'golden era' of patriarchal relations. The 'crisis' was never resolved" (38).

63. Roper, *The Holy Household*, 1.

64. On Luther, see Rublack, "Pregnancy, Childbirth and the Female Body," 92.

65. Her actual expression is "medle so mervelous" (cited in Bynum, *Metamorphosis and Identity*, 71). An unmarked birth was considered an act of grace. As Thomas Bedford puts it, "We acknowledge it a speciall favour to the Soule (as it is reason wee should) that God doth exempt any from that common damnation, which is due to all by Adams transgression: And is it not to be confessed a Mercie to the body?" (*A True and Certaine Relation*, C3).

66. John Barker, *The true description of a monsterous Chylde Borne in the Ile of Wight*.

67. According to Bynum, the monstrance framed the moment of the revelation of the consecrated Host; it was a wonder, "the divine installed in food (or flesh or matter) in the

twinkling of an eye" (*Metamorphosis and Identity*, 62). In Latin, *monstrare* means "To show . . . demonstrate . . . expound, [and] reveal" and a *monstrum* is a "portent, prodigy, [or] sign" (*Oxford Latin Dictionary*, 2:1130–31).

68. The question of the body and the boundary between human and divine lay at the very heart of the Reformation (Roper, *Oedipus and the Devil*, 23). In Catholicism, the body was a vehicle of miracles; it was closer to God if kept chaste; it could reveal, in its uncorrupted state, the sanctity of a saint. But in the Reformation, the body became another "indifferent matter" (*ibid.* 42). Similarly, while Christ had once come in the flesh, he was now, according to Protestant iconoclasts like John Vicars, "only to be seen and considered after a spirituall manner" (*The Sinfulness and Unlawfulness of having or Making the Picture of Christ's Humanity*, 6). According to Vicars, Christ could be seen "spiritually" in the sacraments or the Scripture, or "in his living poore members, afflicted, persecuted, or in povertie" (59–60).

69. William Perkins, *The Workes*, i, sig. 004. In the 1590 introduction to her translation of John Taffin's *Of the markes of the children of God*, Anne Prowse writes that it order to "knowe assuredlie," "if wee be the children of God in some sort and measure[,] a tri- all must come" (London: Printed by Thomas Orwin for Thomas Man, 1590).

70. Seaver, *Wallington's World*, 3.

71. *The Complete Poems of Robert Herrick*, ed. J. Max Patrick (New York: New York UP, 1963).

72. Calvin, *Institutes of Christian Religion*, 3.21.7.

73. Some providentialist texts are: Zachary Bogan, *A View of the Threats and Punishments recorded in the Scriptures, alphabetically composed* (1653); S. Hammond, *Gods Judgements upon Drunkards, Swearers and Sabbath-breakers, in a Collection of most Remarkable Examples* (1659); Thomas Beard, *The Theatre of Gods Judgements* (1597); and Edmund Rudierd, *The Thunderbolt of God Wrath against Hard-heared and Stiff-Necked Sinners* (1618). Alexandra Walsham's *Providence in Early Modern England* is the authoritative study of Protestant providential literature.

74. Davenport-Hines, *Sex, Death and Punishment*, 27.

75. William Pusey, *The History and Epidemiology of Syphilis* (Springfield, IL: C.C. Thomas, 1933), 10. See also Saul S. Brody, *The Disease of the Soul: Leprosy in Medieval Literature* (Ithaca, NY: Cornell University Press, 1974).

76. Wear, "Puritan Perceptions of Illness in Seventeenth Century England."

77. *Henry VI, Part III* 3.2.163, 168. Margaret says that Richard is "like a foul misshapen stigmatic / Mark'd by the destinies to be avoided" (2.2.36–37), and Anne calls him a "lump of foul deformity" (1.2.57). On readings of Richard's monstrosity, see Charnes, *Notorious Identity*, 20–69, and Torrey, "'The plain devil and dissembling looks.'".

78. For a discussion of early modern physiognomy, see Juliana Schiesari, "The Face of Domestication: Physiognomy, Gender Politics, and Humanism's Others." The text she focuses on is Giovan Battista Della Porta's *Della fisionomia dell'uomo* (On the Physiognomy of Man) published in 1610.

79. For Calvin's claim that "we may rest assured that God would never have suffered any infants to be slain except those who were already damned and predestined for eternal death," see Harkness, *John Calvin*, 109.

80. Charlotte F. Otten, "Women's Prayers in Childbirth in Sixteenth Century England," 19. Otten's source texts are the prayers included in *The Monument of Matrones*

(1582). Women's abilities to call on supernatural support during childbirth were radically curtailed during the Reformation. One of the areas that Reformers attacked as superstitious were the practices associated with pregnancy and childbirth: the girdles and other relics which were sent to women in travail; the pictures of Madonna that were believed to protect the woman from danger of death in childbirth; the women saints to whom women prayed to for assistance in childbirth. See Duffy, *Stripping of the Altars*, 384–85; and Keith Thomas, *Religion and the Decline of Magic*, 73. After 1552 midwives were prohibited from invoking the names of saints or Mary as encouragement during childbirth (Duffy, 472). Childbirth was, of course, a perilous process: women in seventeenth-century England had a 6 to 7 percent chance of dying in childbed, and the death rates of children were high (see Crawford, "The Construction and Experience of Maternity in Seventeenth-century England.") Furthermore, the period saw increasing legislation around the deaths of children, particularly concerning infanticide, and thus increasing scrutiny of mothers (see Jackson, *New-born Child Murder*).

81. Otten, "Women's Prayers in Childbirth," 20; Elizabeth, Countess of Bridgewater, cited in Crawford and Gowing, eds., *Women's Worlds in Seventeenth-Century England*, 20. In her devotional diary, Mary Roberts of East Sussex similarly wrote of her conviction that the death of her child was the result of her sins: "He began to shake on a sabbath day morning for I desired to walk earlier on that morning." She has no doubt that the form of her child's death correlated directly with the form of her sin, in this case, even considering abuse of the sabbath. Similarly, when Elizabeth Turner miscarried in October 1662, she wrote: "I know not what ocationed But am jealous least it may be a punishment of some particular sin" (Crawford and Gowing, 198).

82. Aristotle's famous dictum in *Generation of Animals* that "the physical part, the body, comes from the female, and the Soul from the male" was used to naturalize theories of social difference as physiological difference. See Paster, *The Body Embarrassed*, 167. While the fantasy that the child bore the imprint of the father was widespread (in Shakespeare's *Richard III*, for example, Buckingham declares Richard's lineaments "the right idea of your father / Both in your form and nobleness of mind" [3.6.13–14]), the monstrous birth cast aspersions primarily on the mother's character. In the same play, Queen Margaret calls the future Richard III (the rare monster who lived), "Thou slander of thy heavy mother's womb!" (2.2.124–24). The fear that the mother's feelings could imprint her child are also prominent in the story of Richard III. In *Henry VI, Part III*, Queen Elizabeth "bridle[s] her] passion" "For love of Edward's offspring in my womb," "Lest with my sighs or tears I blast or drown / King Edward's fruit, true heir to th' English crown" (2.2.135–37).

83. Authors of monster pamphlets recognized the importance of conception in the production of monsters. As Thomas Bedford writes, "Strange births wee call them: more properly wee might terme them strange Conceptions" (*A True and Certaine Relation*, 12).

84. For the former, see Walsham, *Providence in Early Modern England*; and for the latter, Marie-Hélène Huet, "Living Images: Monstrosity and Representation," and *The Monstrous Imagination*. See also Maclean, *The Renaissance Notion of Woman*, 41.

85. Rublack, "Pregnancy, Childbirth, and the Female Body," 86.

86. John Baptista Porta, *Natural Magick*, 51.

87. Ibid., 53. In Huet's formulation, "As the visible manifestation of an unspoken and unspeakable desire, or an unchecked passion, the monster stands as a public rebuke to any violent aberration on the mother's part" ("Living Images," 73).

88. Jacques Guillemeau, *Child-birth, or The Happy Deliverie of Women* (London, 1612), 26; cited in Paster, *The Body Embarrassed*, 181.

89. In one of her sonnets, Lady Mary Wroth cites this idea as a commonplace when she claims that the child of love "ought like a monster borne / Bee from the court of Love, and reason torne" (*The Poems of Lady Mary Wroth*, ed. Josephine A. Roberts [Baton Rouge: Louisiana UP, 1983], P85, 132.)

90. Hildegard of Bingen (1098–1179) wrote (in the voice of Christ) that "parents who have sinned against Me, return to Me crucified in their children." In other words, the parents' sins were visited upon the bodies of their children. Cited in Walton, Fineman, and Walton, "Of Monsters and Prodigies," 9.

91. In many ways "conception," a woman's ability to conceive God's (human) form, was analogous to the conscience, the divine script within each believer that she or he simply had to read correctly in order to conform to God's will. Both referred to an intimate, and fallible, relationship between internal human agency and divine will.

92. John Dod and Robert Cleaver, *Seuen godlie and fruitful sermons*, G2v James I similarly called the conscience "the light of knowledge that God hath planted in man." *Basilicon Doron*, ed. Sommerville, 17.

93. See Gallagher, *Medusa's Gaze*; and Keith Thomas, "Cases of Conscience in Seventeenth-Century England," 32.

94. W. Loe, *Vox clamatis* (1621), 30, cited in Thomas, "Cases of Conscience," 37.

95. There were, however, divines like William Perkins who wrote on conscience and practical divinity (see Louis B. Wright, "William Perkins"). Published in the 1650s, Richard Baxter's *Directions* also presented answers to disputed questions of morality and religion (see Wood, *English Casuistical Divinity During the Seventeenth Century*). There were also numerous texts, like Thomas Sparke's *A short treatise very comfortable for all those Christians that be troubled and disquieted in theyre consciences with the sight of their owne infirmities* (London, 1580), which encouraged Protestants to examine their own consciences. As Thomas Newton puts it in another text, each Protestant should look "into his conscience . . . and most plainely behold his spiritual deformity by nature." *The True tryall and Examination of a Man's own self* (London, 1587).

96. On religious controversies, see Milward, *Religious Controversies of the Jacobean Age*; and on their relationship to social controversies, see Ingram, *Church Courts, Sex and Marriage in England, 1570–1640*; and Wrightson, *English Society, 1580–1680*.

97. Bedford, 13. Not coincidentally, Bedford also wrote "serious" tracts on church doctrine, including *A treatise of the sacraments according to the doctrine of the Church of England touching that argument. Collected out of the articles of religion, the publique catechism, the liturgie, and the book of homilies.* (London, 1638), and *Some sacramentall instructions; or, An explication of the principles of religion. Containing the sum of what all such persons as shall be admitted to the sacrament of the Lords-Supper ought to know* (London, 1649).

98. Bedford's full defense reads: "Let no man therefore taxe me of any excesse in religious thoughts, or count it overmuch curiositie, if I propound to you an observation or two" (Cv). In this claim, Bedford attempts to mitigate the contention exemplified by Hook and Lambert in their debate about the significance of monstrous births.

99. Boaistuau, dedicatory epistle in *Histoires prodigieuses* (1560): "frapper au marteau de notre conscience," cited in Jean Céard, "The Crisis of the Science of Monsters," 197.

100. Muchembled, *Popular Culture and Elite Culture in France 1400–1750*, 200–201.

See also Foucault, *Discipline and Punish;* and, for a firsthand account of criminal punishment in England, see Harrison, *A Description of England,* 187–94.

101. Muchembled, *Popular Culture,* 208.

102. Philip Stubbes, *The Anatomie of Abuses* (1583), 99.

103. There was particular concern that blasphemy or unorthodox religious opinion not "go withoute exemplarye punishmente" (Nokes, *A History of the Crime of Blasphemy,* 11).

104. Wrightson, "Two Concepts of Order," 23. Among other things, persecutions were rare because of the localized nature of government, and the unwillingness of churchwardens and justices of the peace to persecute their neighbors.

105. Stuart Hall, "Notes on Deconstructing 'the Popular,'" 443.

106. "Puritan" is used here to refer to Protestants who wanted to see the Reformation carried further but who were not necessarily Nonconformists. See Lake, "Defining Puritanism—again?" 3–29. For Lake, "Puritan" is a "polemical maneuver rather than a reference to any very stable or coherent Puritan position," and there is no simple dichotomy between "Anglican mainstream" and "Puritan opposition" (6, 9). For a summary of recent historical discussions of the term, see John Morgan's chapter on "The Problem of Definition" in his *Godly Learning,* 9–22.

107. Like other "popular" stories and texts in early modern Europe, stories about monstrous births have been disparately conceived of as sensational and topical "yellow journalism," as reflections of naïve belief or the means by which "the common folk found a means of self-expression," or as part of an endeavor on the part of the authorities to "tranquilize" or obtain ideological hegemony and control over their readers. The status of such texts and stories about monstrous births as "popular" addresses some important issues about early modern reading and belief. The term "popular" is both descriptive (belonging to, affecting, concerning, or open to all or any of the people; of lowly birth; low, vulgar) and directive: something is popular if it is "intended for or suited to ordinary people," or "studious of, or designed to gain, the favour of the common people" (*OED*). On the problems of the term "popular," see Natalie Zemon Davis, "The Historian and Popular Culture," 9–16. On the identification of marvelous pamphlets as "yellow journalism," see Shaaber, *Some Forerunners of the Newspaper;* Rollins, "Black-Letter," 273; and Sandra Clark, *Elizabethan Pamphleteers,* 35; as self-expression, see Louis B. Wright, *Middle-Class Culture in Elizabethan England;* and as tranquilization, see Muchembled, *Popular Culture,* 292.

108. Fenton, *Certaine Secrete wonders of Nature,* 13v.

109. Davis, "Printing and the People," in *Society and Culture in Early Modern France,* 192. As Davis points out, people do not necessarily agree with the books they read, and "without independent evidence can we be sure of how a rural audience took its tales of marvels . . . when a peasant read or was read to, it was not the stamping of a message on a blank sheet." Oral culture was still so dominant that it transformed everything it touched (192, 209). While some scholars have focused on the socially controlling aspects of "popular" cultures, others have focused on the interaction between elite and popular cultures, and on appropriation, resistance, and transformation, arguing that texts are "carriers of relationships" and part of sociability as well as education. See Chartier, "Leisure and Sociability: Reading Aloud in Early Modern Europe,", 103–20.

110. Foucault, *Discipline and Punish,* 67.

111. Laqueur, "Bodies, Details and the Humanitarian Narrative," 113. Other scholars have talked about how pamphlet stories, like cases of conscience, provided the ground for the moral dilemmas at the center of the novelistic tradition. See, for example, Starr, *Defoe and Casuistry;* and Lennard Davis, *Factual Fictions.*

O N E : Protestant Reform and the Fashion Monster

1. Daston and Parks, "Unnatural Conceptions," 26.

2. Luther to Wenzeslaus Link, January 16, 1523, in Luther, *Werke: Briefwechsel* (Weimar, 1930–70), 3:17, cited in and translated by Daston and Parks, n. 16. See also Andersson, "Popular Imagery in German Reformation Broadsheets." On the circulation of the story of the monk calf both before and by Luther and Melanchthon, see Scribner, *For the Sake of Simple Folk,* 127–29; on translations of the story into other languages, see 132, n. 57. See also Céard, *La Nature et les prodiges,* and Ewinkel, *De monstris: Deutung und Funktion von Wundergeburten,* 39–42. Calvin himself wrote a letter dated November 15, 1549, to the French translation of the pamphlet: *De deux monstres prodigieux, a savoir, d'un Ane-Pape . . . et d'un Veau-Moine* (Genève: Jean Crespin, 1557).

3. For the uses of such stories in German and Italy, see Scribner, Céard, and Ewinkel, and Niccoli, *Prophecy and People in Renaissance Italy.*

4. I am using here a 1579 English translation by John Brooke, *Of two Woonderful Popish Monsters, to wyt, Of a Popish Asse which was found at Rome in the river of Tyber, and of a Moonkish Calfe, calved at Friberge in Misne. Which are the very foreshewings and tokens of Gods wrath, against blinde, obstinate, and monstrous Papists. These bookes are to be sould in Powles Churchyard at the signe of the Parat* (Imprinted at London by Thomas East, dwelling by Paules Wharfe, 1579), STC 17797. All subsequent references to the text will be cited parenthetically. Brooke also translated the work of the radical Protestant Huguenots, Jean Crespin, Guy de Bres (STC 12476), and Jean Garnier (STC 11565). Significantly, Crespin had been responsible for the earlier French translation of the monk calf story, *De deux monstres prodigieux* (Genève, 1557). See Céard, *La Nature et les prodiges,* 81, on this translation. The translation suggests both the pan-European nature of sixteenth-century English reform—a German pamphlet translated by an English translator of the works of French radical Protestants—and the continuing relevance and efficacy of the monk calf story fifty years after its first appearance in print.

5. According to Luther, the pieces of the clothing signify sects: "[M]onkes knew very well to forge, invent & finde out so many differences of sectes and opinions, as there is of divers apparayle among them" (15).

6. Robert Crowley, *A briefe discourse against the outwarde apparell and ministring garmentes of the popishe church* [Emden: Printed by Egidius van der Erve, 1566], STC (2nd ed.) 6079, Bviii.

7. Jones and Stallybrass, *Renaissance Clothing and the Materials of Memory.*

8. Scribner, "Reformation, Popular Magic."

9. "All sacred action flowed one way, from the divine to the human" (ibid., 482).

10. Melanchthon, *Initia doctrinae physicae* (1549), cited by Maxwell-Stuart, ed., *The Occult in Early Modern Europe,* 6; Luther, *In primum librum Mose enarrationes* (1535–36), cited in ibid., 7.

11. The two quotations are from the "Marburg Colloquy" and "Lectures on Genesis," *Luther's Works,* 2:134, 147.

12. In Ambroise Paré's *Des monstres et prodiges*, the monk calf appears in the section on "Monstres qui se font par imagination" and is described thus: "Figure d'un Monstre fort hideux, ayant les mains et pieds de boeuf, et autres choses fort monstrueuscs" (36). The monk calf also appears with slashed breeches in Jacob Rueff, *De Conceptu, et Generation Hominis* (44). Slashing, a style in which the fabric of breeches and doublets was slashed in order to reveal the underclothing, originated among the Swiss, then moved to the French court, and became popular in England at the beginning of the sixteenth century. In *The Anatomie of Abuses*, Philip Stubbes complains of "dublets" which "disproportion the body of a man [. . .] wt great bellies hanging down beneath their *Pudenda* (as I have said) & stuffed with foure, fiue or six pound of Bombast at the least: I say nothing of what their Dublets be made [. . .] *slashed, jagged, cut, carued, pincked and laced* with all kinde of costly lace of diuers and sundry colours" (1583, fo. Eiir-Eiiv). In *Certain Secrete wonders of Nature* (1569), Edward Fenton includes a woodcut of a monstrously deformed horse purportedly born in 1555. The horse "according to hys portraict had all his skinne chequered and devided into great panes, after the order of the Dutchemens hose" (142). Stephen Batman records, but does not give an accompanying woodcut of, the same monster: "a monstrous Colt, having the skinne gagged every where, hanging breeches and a dublet cut, like to the fashion of the Launceknightes" (*The Doome Warning All Men to the Judgement*, 360).

13. *The Diary of Henry Machyn*, 59. Susan Brigden briefly refers to the story in her *London and the Reformation* (550), noting that despite the offer of a huge reward—£6.13s.4d.—the offenders were never found. Subsequent references to Machyn's diary will be cited parenthetically in the text.

14. On calves, see *Bestiary. Being an English Version of the Bodleian Library Oxford M.S. Bodley 764 with all the original miniatures reproduced in Facsimile*, translated and introduced by Richard Barber (Woodbridge: Boydell Press, 1993), 93. The monk calf also clearly referenced the golden calf of idolatry.

15. *Bestiary*, 109.

16. There was also a popular European convention that a cat appeared at the feet of Judas and was thus a figure for the traitor. It was shown at the feet of the pope in a volume entitled *Les Crimes des Papes* to signify perfidy and hypocrisy. For both examples, see Sillar and Meylower, *Cats: Ancient and Modern*, 42.

17. On the vestiarian or vestments controversy, see Haugaard, *Elizabeth and the English Reformation*, esp. 183–223; and Milward, *Religious Controversies of the Elizabethan Age*.

18. Bray, ed. *Documents of the English Reformation*, 343.

19. *Advertisements partly for due order in the publique administration of common prayer and usinge the holy Sacramentes, and partly for the apparell of all persons ecclesiasticall, by vertue of the Queenes maiesties letters commanding the same, the xxv. day of January 1566*, STC 10026.

20. Crowley (see note 6 above).

21. Thomas Cartwright's 1564 reply to Whitgift, cited in John Strype, *Annals of the Reformation*, 1:126.

22. Jones and Stallybrass briefly touch on this paradox: radicals who saw clothing as a form of transnaturing "agreed with those whom they opposed on the animating and constitutive power of clothes" (*Renaissance Clothing*, 4).

23. *By the Queene. The Queenes Maiestie consideryng to what extremities a great number of her subiectes are growen, by excesse in apparell, both contrary to the lawes of the realme, and to the disorder and confusion of the degrees of all states* (Imprinted at London: In Powles Church-

yarde, by Rycharde Iugge and Iohn Cawood: Printers to the Queenes Maiestie, 1566), STC (2nd ed.) 7995. Elizabeth published many proclamations, articles, and advertisements on the "inordinate vse of apparell" and "the reformation of the outragious excesse therof." *A decree of the priuye counsell at vvestminster. Anno.1.5.5.9.xx. October by England and Wales* (Imprinted at London: In Povvles Churchyarde, bi Richarde Iugge, and Iohn Cavvood, printers to the Quenes Maiestie, 1559), STC 7903. See, for example, STC (2nd ed.) 7905.5, 7954.5, 7948, 7946, 7949, 7950, 7952, 9339.5.

24. Jones and Stallybrass, *Renaissance Clothing*, 5.

25. Ibid., 5–6.

26. *Articles for the due execution of the Statutes of Apparell, and for the reformation of the outrageous excesse therof, growen of late tyme within the Realme. Devysed upon the Quenes Maiesties commaundement by advice of her Counsayle, the vi. of Maye. Anno. M.D.lxii* (Imprinted at London: In Powles Church yarde by Richard Iugge and Iohn Cawood, Printers to the Quenes Maiestie, 1562), STC 7946.

27. Ruffs were particular objects of debate in the period, and Elizabethan legislation limited the wearing of ruffs in a number of ways. Certain classes were restricted as to the sizes of ruffs they were permitted to wear, and other classes were prohibited from wearing them at all; thus, the wearing of ruffs was often an act of class transgression. Ruffs were also seen as signs of national betrayal and dissolution (they were both foreign and frivolous), and signs of male effeminacy and female extravagance. On this fashion, see Baldwin, *Sumptuary Legislation and Personal Regulation in England*; Jardine, *Still Harping on Daughters*; and Karen Newman, *Fashioning Femininity and English Renaissance Drama*. See also Jones and Stallybrass, *Renaissance Clothing*, 59–86. One ruff, "a full quarter of a yearde deepe and 12 Lengths," was in fact commonly known as "the English Monster," an appellation that undoubtedly contributed to the rash of stories about monstrous births described as having "collers of skinne growing about their neckes, liketo the double ruffes of shirtes and nekercheffes then used." See Edward Howes, *Addition to Stowe's Annals of England* (1615), 869; and John Stow, *The Chronicles of England*. Similar stories are recorded in Batman, *The Doome, Warning All Men to the Judgement* (1581), 390; and T. I., *A World of Wonders* (1595), Ev.

28. Scribner, "Reformation, Popular Magic," 486.

29. *A speciall grace*, 32.

30. Bull, *Christian Prayers and Holy Meditations*, 84. The prayer continues: "Woe and alas to these our days, that neither preaching by word most comfortable, nor preaching by fire most terrible, nor preaching by monsters most strange and ugly, neither yet by plagues and pestilence most horrible will stir up our stony hearts and awake us from our sins!" (85).

31. Hayward, *Annals of the first four years of the Reign of Queen Elizabeth*, 242.

32. Hyder E. Rollins was the first scholar to consider these texts seriously: "The value of ballads for the study of history is really so great that from extant printed copies, supplemented by entries in the Stationer's Registers of non-extant ballads and by manuscript collections, one could compile a history of Tudor and Stuart England that would be of extreme importance and of surpassing interest" ("Black-Letter Broadside Ballad," 272–73).

33. *The true reporte of the forme and shape of a monstrous childe, borne at Muche Norkesleye* (1562). Like the author of the Marshe broadsheet, Machyn identifies the monster's birthplace: "be-syde Colchester at a town callyd [blank]" (281).

34. In 1562, Marshe also printed a treatise on the burning of the Protestant martyrs Bucer and Phagius and a defense of the marriages of priests. See *A briefe treatise concerning the burnynge of Bucer and Phagius, at Cambrydge, in the tyme of Quene Mary, with theyr restitution in the time of our moste gracious souerayne lady that nowe is. Translated into Englyshe by Arthur Goldyng. Anno. 1562. Read and iudge indifferently according to the rule of Gods worde* [Imprinted at London: In Flete-strete nere to saynct Dunstons Churche by Thomas Marshe, [1562]), STC 3966; and John Véron, *A stronge defence of the maryage of pryestes, agaynste the Pope Eustachians, and Tatanites of our time, made dialogue wise by Iohn Veron, betwixte Robin Papyste, and the true Christian* (Imprynted at London: In Fletestrete nere to Sainct Dunstons Churche by Thomas Marshe, [1562?]), STC 24687. He also printed works by Thomas Becon and Laurence Humphrey, both writers with Puritan tendencies, and a text concerned with the "reformation of manners": *A myrrour for magistrates. Wherein maye be seen by example of other, with howe greuous plages vices are punished: and howe frayle and vnstable worldly prosperity is founde, even of those whom fortune seemeth most highly to fauour.* (Imprinted at London: In Fletestrete nere to Saynct Dunstans Churche by Thomas Marshe, [1563]), STC 1248.

35. John Stow, *A summarie of our Englysh chronicles. Diligently collected by Iohn Stowe, citizen of London, in the yeare of oure Lorde, 1566. The contentes wherof on the other syde appeareth. Perused and allowed accordyng to the Quenes Maiesties iniunctions* (Imprinted at London: in Flete-strete, nere to S. Dunstons Church, by Thomas Marshe [1566]), STC (2nd ed.), 23319.5, fol. 242. He also printed another edition in 1567, STC (2nd ed.), 23325.5.

36. See Oronce Fine, *The rules and ryghte ample documentes, touching the vse and practise of the common almanackes which are named ephemerides* [Imprynted at London in Fletestrete nere to S. Dunstons church by Thomas Marshe, 1558. STC (2nd ed.) / 10878.5; Lewes Vaughan, *A new almanacke and prognostication, collected for the yeare of our Lord God. M.D.L.IX.* [Imprinted at London in Fletestrete nere to Saincte Dunstones Churche, by Thomas Marshe, 1559. STC (2nd ed.) / 520; and Thomas Hill, *A necessary almanack . . . for 1560 . . . seruing wel for these thre next yeares* (London: T. Marshe, 1560).

37. The first quotation is from *The true discription of two monsterous chyldren borne at Herne in Kent;* the second is from *The Shape of ii. Monsters. MDLxii.*

38. Jewel also listed similar births among pigs, horses, cows, and chickens. The section of the letter, written in Latin, reads as follows: "Ex hac contagione nata sunt monstra: infantes foedum in modum deformatis corporibus, alii prorsus sine capitibus, alii capitibus alienis; alii trunci sine brachiis, sine tibiis, sine cruribus; alii ossibus solis cohaerentes, prorsus sine ullis carnibus, quales fere imagines mortis pingi solent. Similar alia complura nata sunt e porcis, ex equabus, e vaccis e gallinis" (*Zurich Letters*, Epistle L). Jewell was one of the leading figures in the early-Elizabethan Church of England and, during the period in which he wrote this letter, was engaged in a number of battles, including the vestiarian controversy, over the form and direction of the English church (see W. M. Southgate, *John Jewel and the Problem of Doctrinal Authority*, Cambridge University Press, 1985). This final monster was so remarkable that, according to Machyn, it was brought from Chichester "to the cowrte [court] in a box." The day after she saw the monster, which she perhaps considered an ill omen, Queen Elizabeth left Westminster for Greenwich (284).

39. John D., *A discription of a monstrous Chylde, borne at Chychester in Sussex.*

40. Helaine Razovsky ("Popular Hermeneutics: Monstrous Children in English Renaissance Broadside Ballads") argues that these broadsides encouraged the extension of

Protestant hermeneutics, which she defines as "a science or system of biblical interpretation," to extra-biblical texts," thereby encouraging individual reading and interpretation. While I certainly agree with her central claim, I also see these texts as having topical, polemical, and extra-religious purposes as well.

41. Barker, *The true description of a monsterous Chylde Borne in the Ile of Wight.*

42. On the attacks on, and decline of, such images, see Duffy, *Stripping of the Altars,* esp. 68–88; Aston, *English Iconoclasts;* and Watt, *Cheap Print and Popular Piety,* esp. 131–40.

43. See Llewellyn, *The Art of Death: Visual Culture in the English Death Ritual.*

44. PRO PROB 11/45/fo.58. I am indebted for this reference to Norman Jones, *The Birth of the Elizabethan Age,* 42.

45. Manning, *Religion and Society in Elizabethan Sussex,* 58. In the 1560s the episcopal administration in the diocese of Chichester was in a "state of chaos"; one-sixth of the clergy of the diocese of Chichester had been deprived of their cures for refusing to sign the oath of supremacy and would not be replaced with an educated "preaching ministry" until the 1570s (ibid., 34–36).

46. Ibid., 34. In the words of Matthew Parker, Sussex in the 1560s was "full of Papists & Popism" and desperate for men of "learning & Piety" (quoted in ibid., 69).

47. Hayward, *Annals of the first four years of the Reign of Queen Elizabeth,* 242v.

48. As Stephen Gosson puts it in *Pleasant quippes for upstart newfangled gentlewomen* (1595), a text also published by Richard Jones, women with painted faces, periwigs, ruffs, and "naked paps" do not have time "to carde and spinne / to brue or bake," or for any kind of "thriftie worke"). On the relationship between fashion excess and female misbehavior, see also such works as a 1615 pamphlet entitled *The picture of a wanton: Her lewdness discovered,* which includes a woodcut of an overdressed woman; and Richard Brathwait's 1631 *The English gentlewoman drawne out to the full body.*

49. The second volume of homilies appeared on August 1, 1563, and contributed twenty new homilies, including "An Homilie Against Excess of Apparel." The queen's printers, R. Jugge and J. Cawood, printed ten editions of the second volume in 1563 alone. See Ian Lancashire, "A Brief History of the Homilies," at www.library.utoronto.ca/utel/ret/homilies/elizhom3.html.

50. "An Homilie Against Excess of Apparel," in *Certaine Sermons or Homilies appointed to be read in Churches.* The cited lines are II.6.1–137 and II.6.1–141–42. All subsequent references to the homily will be cited parenthetically in the text.

51. Collinson, *The Elizabethan Puritan Movement,* 273, 102. On the reformation of manners, see Ingram, "The Reformation of Manners in Early Modern England," 47–88. This effort focused, not on the "inward state of mind, but on the externals of behaviour, and shading off into usages more nearly equivalent to what we mean by 'habits' or 'customs'" (ibid., 52–53). See also Spufford, "Puritanism and Social Control?"

52. *The destruction of Sodom and Gomorra, To the tune of the nine Muses* (Imprinted at London: by Richard Iohnes for Henrie Kyrkham, dwelling at the signe of the blacke Boy: at the middle north dore of Paules church, [1570]). He also published John Symon's *A pleasant posie, or sweete nosegay of fragrant smellyng flowers: gathered in the garden of heaunely pleasure, the holy and blessed bible. To the tune of the black Almayne* (Imprinted at London: by Richard Iohnes: dwellyng in the vpper end of Fleetlane, 1572), and John Phillips's *A balad intituled, A cold pye for the papistes, wherin is contayned: the trust of true subiectes for suppressyng*

of sedicious papistrie and rebellion: to the maintenance of the Gospell, and the publique peace of Englande. Made to be songe to Lassiamiza noate (Imprinted at London: By William How, for Richard Iohnes and are to be solde, at his shop ioyning to the southwest doore of Paules Church, [1570?]). As Tessa Watt points out, "The language of conflict between Protestant culture and popular culture was by no means the universal discourse of early Elizabethan reformers. From the 1550s to 1570s, the writers of metrical psalms and 'moralized' ballads borrowed the tunes of secular song as their route to the people's hearts" (*Cheap Print and Popular Piety*, 40).

53. William Kirkham, *Ioyfull newes for true subiectes, to God and the Crovvne: the rebelles are cooled, their bragges be put downe* (Imprinted at London: in Fleetstreete, by Wyllyam How: for Richard Iohnes [1570]); Humphrey Roberts, *An earnest complaint of diuers vain, wicked and abused exercises, practised on the Saboth day: which tende to the hinderance of the Gospel, and increase of many abhominable vices* (Imprinted at London: in the vpper ende of fleete lane, by Richard Iohnes: and are to be sold at his shop, ioyning to the southwest dore of Saint Pau[l's] Churche, 1572); and I. P. [John Philips, fl. 1570–91?], *A meruaylous straunge deformed swyne* (Imprinted at London: by William How, for Richard Iohnes: and are to be solde at his shop ioyning to the southwest doore of Paules Churche, [1570?]).

54. Thomas Pritchard, *The schoole of honest and vertuous lyfe* (Imprinted at London: by [William How for] Richard Iohnes, and are to be solde at his shop ouer against S. Sepulchers Church without Newgate, [1579]), and William Hergest, *The right rule of Christian chastitie: profitable to bee read of all godly and vertuous youthes of both sexe, bee they gentlemen or gentlewomen, or of inferiour state, whatsoeuer* (Imprinted at London: By [W. How for] Richard Iohnes, and are to bee solde at his shop ouer against S. Sepulchers Church without Newgate, [1580]).

55. Phillip Stubbes, *The Anatomie of Abuses* (Printed at London by Richard Jones, 1583), viii. All subsequent references will be cited parenthetically in the text.

56. On *exempla* about women's fashion, see Owst, *Literature and Pulpit in Medieval England*, passim; on the *miseres*, see Wright, *A History of Caricature and Grotesque in Literature and Art*, 101–2.

57. Years later, the Puritan John Vicars tells a similar story of the burning of a church in which the minster's wife "had her Ruffe and Linnen next her body, burnt off, and her body it self grievously scorched. One Mistresse Ditford, sitting in the seat with her, had her Gowne, two Wast-coats, and her linnen next her body also grievously scorched" (*Prodigies & Apparitions*, 33).

58. The fact that Stubbes's *exempla* features a Dutch woman (the "daughter of a rich Antwerp Merchant") might suggest an implicit critique of Elizabeth's own fashion excesses, including her 1562 importation of a Dutch woman—Gwillam Boone—to starch her own elaborate ruffs (on Boone, see Jones and Stallybrass, *Renaissance Clothing*, 68).

59. *A True Relation of the birth of three Monsters in the City of Namen in Flanders* (London, 1609). All references to this pamphlet will be cited parenthetically in the text.

60. Although, as Lawrence Stone argues, wider kinship systems were displaced by the patriarchal nuclear family in the seventeenth century, the wealthy sister does not neglect her sister for her own familial obligations: in the story, she has no husband, and her pursuits are neither domestic nor charitable (*Family, Sex and Marriage*, 93–146). See also Cressy, "Kinship and Kin Interaction"; and Chaytor, "Household and Kinship."

61. Stubbes, *Anatomie of Abuses*, 38. A prayer included in Henry Bull's collection, *Chris-*

tian Prayers and Holy Meditations, advises people when they are appareling themselves to pray thus: "O Christ, clothe me with thine own self, that I may be so far from making provision for my flesh to fulfil the lusts of it, that I may clean put off all my carnal desires, and crucify the kingdome of flesh in me. Be thou unto me a garment to keep me warm and to defend me from the cold of this world . . . Grant therefore, that as I compass this my body with this garment, so though wouldest clothe me wholly (but specially my soul) with thine own self" (63).

62. The *OED* defines bone-lace as "lace, usually of linen thread, made by knitting upon a pattern marked by pins, with bobbins originally made of bone; formerly called bone-work lace; now largely superseded by bobbin-net." See also Fairholt, *Costume in England*, 372. The headdress could also refer to the fan-shaped ruff (1570–1625) which was worn with a low-necked bodice and rose from the sides and back of the décolletage, spreading out fan-wise behind the head; or the rebato (1580–1635), "a shaped collar, wired to stand up round the back of the head from the edge of the low-necked bodice to which it was pinned, similarly to the fan-shaped ruff; or the wired head rail (1590–1620) which formed an arch over the head which might be bent into fanciful shapes, such as a trefoil, the center leaf curving over the head, or might be left merely as a high collar spreading round the back of the head," according to C. Willett Cunnington and Phillis Cunnington, *Handbook of English Costume in the Sixteenth Century*, 168, 170. For a similar pamphlet published in Germany in 1612, see Ewinkel, *De monstris Deutung und Funktion von Wundergeburten*, 74, 315 (Abb. 25).

TWO: "The mother of a monster, and not of an orderly birth"

1. Awdeley, *The forme and shape of a Monstrous Child borne at Maydstone in Kent*, 1568.

2. This was a term used in accusations of infidelity. In Winwick Lancashire in 1592, Thomas Grimsford claimed that his wife Margery "hath plaied the naughtie packe and dyd roune awaie with another man." She was excommunicated (Hair, *Before the Bawdy Court*, 40).

3. As R. W. Scribner argues, in the evolution of image-based popular texts, although the image remains central, the text ultimately plays a larger role (*For the Sake of Simple Folk*, 30–37).

4. William Harrison, *The Description of England, or a briefe rehersall of the nature and qualities of the people of England* (1587), 189–90.

5. Harrison's imagination of this history was undoubtedly informed by the "Sermon against whoredome and uncleanesse," which refers, among other things, to the ancient Egyptians who punished adulterous women by cutting of their noses, and to the "Arabyans who "hadd [adulterous women's] heades strucke from their bodies" *Certaine Sermons appointed by the Quenes Maiesty*, Hiv-v.

6. Gowing, *Domestic Dangers*, 80. In Stepney in 1618, Alice Squire scratched Katherine Berry's face and said she has given her a "whores marke" (103).

7. Ibid., 88.

8. I. R., *A most straunge, and true discourse, of the wonderfull iudgement of God*, 8. Subsequent references will be cited parenthetically in the text.

9. Gregory, "Witchcraft, Politics and 'Good Neighbourhood.'"

10. "It is credibly reported," I.R. writes, "that two of them lived incontinently with her" (4).

11. See *Certaine Sermons appointed by the Quenes Maiesty* (London, 1563), Vr.

12. The following précis of early modern social policing is based on Keith Wrightson's article, "Two Concepts of Order: Justices, Constables and Jurymen in Seventeenth-Century England," in Brewer and Styles, *An Ungovernable People*, 21–46.

13. Ibid., 24.

14. After the 1590s, Articles of Inquiry were issued by central governments as guides for the justices of the peace, but according to Wrightson, conformity was really only pursued during times of acute economic crisis or when magistrates were motivated by a peculiar zeal for social discipline and godly reformation (ibid., 38–39).

15. Ibid., 23.

16. Ingram, *Church Courts, Sex and Marriage*, 239, 243. "Before the Reformation such matters may have been dealt with by confessor; they had probably never been subject to public discipline, and the post-Reformation church courts did not commit the folly of trying to bring them into their orbit after the practice of compulsory auricular confession had been abolished" (ibid., 240). A tenth of the church courts cases pertained to marital or sexual offences: fornication, premarital sex, adultery, bearing or fathering a bastard, harbouring an illegitimately pregnant women, or running a bawdy house (Gowing, *Domestic Dangers*, 31).

17. Ingram, *Church Courts, Sex and Marriage*, 245. "Near the beginning of Elizabeth's reign the Church of England set forth its 'table of kindred and affinity' specifying which relations by blood or by marriage a person was prohibited from marrying. Every church had to display this table" (Bossy, *The Development of the Family and Marriage in Europe*, 173–78). On the placards, see Ingram, *Church Courts, Sex and Marriage*, 249, and Gowing, *Domestic Dangers*, 39–41.

18. Wrightson quotes the song of James Gyffon, Constable of Albury (1626):

The Justices will set us by the heels
If we do not as we should,
Which if we perform, the townsmen will storm,
some of them hang's if they could.

The lyrics point to the "conflict between concept of order of the governing magistracy of seventeenth-century England as embodied in legislation, and the somewhat broader area of behaviour permitted to themselves by a group of villagers" ("Two Concepts of Order," 21).

19. According to Keith Thomas, next to politics and religion, the most persistent source of cases of conscience was to be found in the domestic sphere, and usually concerning marital issues ("Cases of Conscience," 46).

20. The essential requisite for a legally binding union was not the formal solemnization of marriage in church but a contract—called, in popular usage, "spousals," "making sure," or "handfasting"—by which the couple took each other as husband and wife using the words of the present tense (*per verba de praesenti*). As long as marital law allowed an informal contract without banns or a church solemnization to create a binding union, moral ambiguities about the status of the affianced parties were inevitable.

21. Cressy, *Birth, Marriage, and Death*, 198.

22. The Puritan *Admonition to the Parliament* (1572), for example, argued that ministers used the wedding ring as a "sacramental sign, to which they attribute the virtue of wedlock," and that the ceremony forced the man "to make an idol of his wife, saying: with this ring I thee wed, with my body I thee worship" (Cressy, *Birth, Marriage, and Death*,

344). There were also many contingent early modern folk beliefs and superstitions around the power of the ring, including the belief that the ring could serve as a recipe against unkindness and discord as long as the bride continued to wear it (see O'Hara, "The Language of Tokens and the Making of Marriage," 27). Such beliefs, as Keith Thomas points out, showed how church sacraments—even former sacraments—generated "attendant sub-superstitions which endowed the spiritual formulae of the theologians with a crudely material efficacy" (*Religion and the Decline of Magic*, 39).

23. Philip Stubbes also criticizes the lax punishment of sexual immorality: "as light and as easie as this punishment is, it may be, and is daiely dispensed with-all for monie" (*Anatomie of Abuses*, 99).

24. Barnard recorded the baptism and the burial in the entries in the Colwall Parish Registers on January 6 and 9, 1600. The child's name is registered as "*Quod Deus Vult*," and is identified as the child of "Francis Browne." Robert Hole ("Incest, Consanguinity and a Monstrous Birth," 184) locates the story "on the eve of a scientific revolution" and sees it as giving insight into "the state of English provincial ideas." He seeks to relate the pamphlet to Francis Bacon's call for a cooperative program of scientific research "leading to a new interpretation of nature," and later explains the monstrous birth in scientific terms as a result of incest. Hole claims that the author was educated, "but not one well read in the latest international works on the subject" (199). Although Hole remarks on the reading materials I.R. proposes, he makes nothing of the story-telling aspects of the pamphlet, seeing it only in terms of its ignorance of scientific empiricism.

25. Although there is no hard evidence, it is these final claims that suggest to me that the author of the pamphlet, I.R., is none other than John Rainolds, the Puritan polemicist most famous for the contemporaneous treatise against theaters: *Th'Overthrow of Stage-Plays* (Middleburgh: Imprinted by Richard Schilders, 1600).

26. *Gods handy-worke in wonders*. All subsequent references to this pamphlet will be cited parenthetically in the text. Ingram records the following similar story: Mary Leighton was with child when she got married around 1630, but because the couple were very poor the parishioners of Great Bedwyn opposed their petition to the county justices for leave to erect a cottage. The husband had to remain as a household servant, while Mary was forced to "wander up and down" and for a long time could find shelter only in a barn (*Church Courts, Sex and Marriage*, 144–45). The second, beaked, monster featured in the woodcut is the subject of a separate story.

27. Given the nature of poverty and wage labor, women dominated the migration streams of early modern England (Ingram, *Church Courts*, 72, 74). See also Ezell, *The Patriarch's Wife*, 19; and Gowing, *Domestic Dangers*, 15.

28. The first of these acts gave justices the power to examine the circumstances of the birth of a bastard child left at the charge of the parish in order to punish the offenders and make an order for the maintenance of the child; the supplementary Jacobean act provided that the mothers of such bastards be sent to the house of correction for one year (Ingram, *Church Courts*, 152).

29. On the desire for physical sanctions, see Ingram, *Church Courts*, 151–54. On vagabonds, see Kinney, ed. *Rogues, Vagabonds and Sturdy Beggars*, 46–51.

30. Cited in Kinney, *Rogues, Vagabonds, and Sturdy Beggars*, 48. After the whipping, "the same person shall have a testimonial subscribed by the hand and sealed with the seal of the same Justice of the Peace, constable, headborough or tithing man and of the minister of the same parish, or any two of them, testifying that the same person that been pun-

ished according to this Act, and mentioning the day and place of his or her crime" (ibid., 48).

31. Beier, *Masterless Men*, 117.

32. Act of 14. Eliz c. 5: *Such a vagabond Rogue as shall be duely convicted of his Roguish and vagabond life, by the Oathes of two sufficient witnesses, or by inquest of office, shall be grievously whipped and burnt through the gristle of their right Eare with an hot Iron, of the compasse of one inch about, manifesting his Roguish kind of life and his punishment received for the same; which shall presently be executed on him, unlesse some Subsidie man or house-holder of honest condition; shall take him into service for one yeares space, and if hee depart from his service within that time without his Masters consent then the sayd penalty to be executed on him* (cited in William Prynne, *A New Discovery of the Prelates Tyranny* [1641]).

33. Gowing, "Secret Births and Infanticide," 87.

34. Ibid., 109, italics added.

35. J. A. Sharpe, *Crime in Seventeenth Century England*, 59.

36. Susan Dwyer Amussen tells the story of Mary Goodchild, a servant in East Dereham in 1676, to illustrate the difficulty women had in concealing their births. Mary "did so by disappearing: she asked her mistress for permission to see a doctor about her illness, but instead went to London where she bore her bastard, and the returned to service, leaving the baby in Shipdam where it has maintained by its father Edward Mason" (*An Ordered Society*, 113).

37. Cressy, *Birth, Marriage, and Death*, 74.

38. Sharpe, *Crime in Seventeenth Century England*, 166; Beier, *Masterless Men*, 25.

39. Ingram, *Church Courts*, 274.

40. Amussen, *An Ordered Society*, 159.

41. Cressy, "De la fiction dans les archives? Ou le monster de 1569," 1313. See also Cressy, *Travesties and Transgression*, esp. 13.

42. Cressy, *Birth, Marriage, and Death*, 76.

43. Cressy cites the case of a woman brought to bed in the house of Nicholas Matthews of St. Botolph, Aldgate, in 1627, who "having no certificate of her marriage," fled unchurched and unpunished after her baby was born (*Birth, Marriage, and Death*, 331–32). Church court records are in fact full of cases of women who gave birth and departed "without doing any penance for [their] offence[s]" (Hair, *Before the Bawdy Court*, 207).

44. D. Gardiner, ed. *The Oxinden and Peyton Letters 1642–1670* (London, 1937), 186, cited in Pollock, "Embarking on a Rough Passage," 53.

45. *Strange nevves out of Kent*. All references will be cited parenthetically in the text. On Barley, see Lievsay, "William Barley, Elizabethan Printer and Bookseller," 218–25. Barley claims that the monster's existence is "certified" by "iudiciall censurers," and men "of credite and substantiall reputation." Such creditable men were the same sort of "iudiciall censurers" who were expected to write and sign the criminal statements that vagabonds and sex offenders were forced to bear as testaments to their crimes. The pamphlet thus mimics the government's legal formulae of recording and signing a testament of the crime and punishment. As Peter Burke (*Popular Culture in Early Modern Europe)* has pointed out, popular genres often mocked or used official forms such as legal writs.

46. Ingram, *Church Courts, Sex and Marriage*, 282. There were prosecutions for helping to convey away pregnant women; allowing daughters or servants to escape without punishment; for receiving, harboring, and allowing them to depart unpunished or without naming the father of the child (286).

47. Melling, ed. *Kentish Sources IV. The Poor,* 49.

48. Bentwich, *History of Sandwich in Kent,* 39.

49. Ibid., 287.

50. *Strange Signes seene in the Aire, strange Monsters bebelde on the Land.* See also *Strange fearfull & true newes, which hapned at CARLSTADT, in the kingdome of CROATIA. Declaring how the Summer did shine like Bloude nine dayes together, and how two Armies were seene in the Ayre, the one encountering the other. And how also a Woman was delivered of three prodigious sonnes, which Prophesied many strange & fearefull thinges, which should shortly come to passe, All which happened the twelfth of June, last 1605.* Ingram records that the wife of one of the men who was indicted for harboring a pregnant wandering woman was the local midwife, which suggests that it was she who, like Goodwife Wattes, was the harborer, and that her husband was prosecuted for legal reasons (*Church Courts, Sex and Marriage,* 288).

51. There were men who were compassionate as well: "In Horsham Sussex 1626 Thomas Davy presented for harbouring a woman with child and suffering her to be brought to bed in his hows. And when he brought the child to church to be baptised, he would not confess the father's or the child nor the mother's name" (Hair, *Before the Bawdy Court,* 110).

52. Ingram, *Church courts, Sex and Marriage,* 289, emphasis added.

53. On working women, see Alice Clark, *The Working Life of Women in the Seventeenth Century,* and Margaret George, *Women in the First Capitalist Society.* On midwives, see Evenden, "Mothers and their Midwives in Seventeenth-century London." Evenden argues that midwives were better trained through an "unofficial" system of apprenticeship served under the supervision of senior midwives than has previously been assumed (9).

54. In one of the earliest preserved oaths made by a midwife prior to her receiving a license (26 August 1567), she agrees to help women, rich and poor: "Also I will not permit or suffer that women being in labour or travail shall name any other to be the father of her child, than only he who is the right and true father thereof; and that I will not suffer any other body's child to be set, brought or laid before any women delivered of child in the place of her natural child, so far forth as I can know and understand." She also agrees not to use sorcery or harm the child, and, in case of emergency, to baptize the child. The Visitation of the Commisary of St. Mary's, Salop, in 1584 asked: "Whether any mydwife within your parishe in tyme of weomens travill be knowne or suspected to use sorcerie, witchcrafte, charmes, unlockynge of chests and dores, . . . or to saye unlawful praiers of superstitious invocations" (McLaren, *Reproductive Rituals,* 51).

55. There was some concern about midwives' desires to collectivize as a society in the seventeenth century and about their ability to baptize the child according to the wrong form or even religion. Peter Chamberlen called on King James in 1616 to found a society of midwives, "[t]hat some order may be settled by the State for [their] instruction and civil government," but was soundly rejected. See Irving S. Cutter and Henry R. Viets, *A Short History of Midwifery* (Philadelphia: Saunders, 1964), 44–47, for the history of the Chamberlens.

56. The pamphlet features a woodcut of the monster on the frontispiece, perhaps ready to be taken off and posted in a public place, and an identical cut on the second page. In using the woodcut twice, Barley first solicits the eye of the bookstall consumer and then invites the already-hooked reader to compare the woodcut to the story's accompanying descriptions. Like almost all of the woodcuts of monstrous births, the woodcut's details

correlate with those reported in the pamphlet and were clearly designed specifically for its publication.

57. Peter Symon, M.A. was presented on 23 December and inducted on 24 December 1600. He died in December 1616 (Boys, *Collections for an History of Sandwich in Kent,* 29).

58. Ibid., 503.

59. Ibid., 502. His payment came from every housekeeper in town (505).

60. Ibid., 515.

61. Peter Clark, "The Migrant in Kentish Towns, 1580–1640," 117, 126.

62. Ibid., 145. In the 1590s the neighborliness of alms-giving had to give way to a compulsory rate (152).

63. Bentwich, *History of Sandwich in Kent,* 41.

64. Clark, "The Migrant in Kentish Towns," 153; idem, "Popular Protest and Disturbance in Kent, 1558–1640," 365–82.

65. Foucault, *Discipline and Punish,* 67.

66. Ibid., 67–68.

67. Laqueur, "Bodies, Details, and the Humanitarian Narrative," 176.

68. Ibid., 177.

69. See *Lamentable newes, shewing the wonderfull deliuerance of Maister Edmond Pet sayler, and maister of a ship, dwelling in Seething Lane in London, neere Barking church. With other strange things lately hapned concerning these great windes and tempestuous weather, both at sea and lande* (Imprinted at London: By T. C[reede] for William Barley, dwelling ouer against Cree-church, neere Algate, 1613), STC (2nd ed.) 19792; and *The brideling, sadling and ryding, of a rich churle in Hampshire, by the subtill practise of one Iudeth Philips, a professed cunning woman, or fortune teller* (Printed at London: By T[homas] C[reede] and are to be solde by William Barley, at his shop in New-gate Market, neare Christ-Church, 1595).

70. *The groundworke of conny-catching, the manner of their pedlers-French, and the meanes to vnderstand the same, with the cunning slights of the counterfeit cranke. [. . .] Done by a justice of peace of great authoritie, who hath had the examining of diuers of them.* (Printed at London: by Iohn Danter for William Barley, and are to be sold at his shop at the vpper end of Gratious streete, ouer against Leaden-hall, 1592), STC (2nd ed.), 12789.

71. Kinney, ed., *Rogues, Vagabonds and Sturdy Beggars,* 144, 139–42.

72. B.H., *The glasse of mans folly and meanes to amendment of life,* A3r-v.

T H R E E : Forms of Imperfect Union

1. *The Registers of the Parish Church of Standish in the County of Lancaster 1560–1653.*

2. "A Letter sent from the Preachers of Manchester to the Archbishop of York," *A Visitation of the Diocese of Chester,* 9.

3. The ministers point out that they have made many "pntmts of the papists amongst [them]" before both the ecclesiastical and civil authorities, and, as a result, many of the papists in their parishes are roused with "malice" against them (11). Having taken courage from the visitation and thinking their ministers without protection, these papists "make revenge of our former dutifull imploiments against them, by bringing us in question at the assises and sessions for these matters of inconformitie" (11)The charges of nonconformity leveled against them, that is, are simply the revenge of papists whom the ministers reported for recusancy.

4. "An Answere Unto Mr. Hopwood his L're (By the Archbishop of York)," *A Visitation of the Diocese of Chester.*

5. In his formal letter of response, the Archbishop wrote: "I can hardly be perswaded that the breaking of the orders of the church, the omitting of the dutie of the ministers can make for the peace of the same and the furtheraunce of the gospell" ("An Answere to my Lord of Chesters Letter Concerning the Premises [by the Archbishop of York]," 15).

6. "The smaller the matters are," he writes, "the sooner they are obeyed, and as small as they are *schisma est eadem sequentium separatio* in these externall thinges *Quare cum leuiora quae fingities fugitis, ipsu sacrilegiu schismatis, quod est gravius omnibus comisistis*" (ibid.).

7. Ferrell, "Kneeling and the Body Politic," 72.

8. Ibid., 74.

9. Ibid., 81.

10. Porteus, *A History of the Parish of Standish Lancashire*, 69. In his will, a thoroughly Puritan document, Leigh refuses traditional burial rites, decrying "superstition in praying for the dead" (15).

11. Standish Church was rebuilt in 1582 with a rood loft, suggesting that the parishioners hoped for a return of pre-Reformation practices (ibid., 17). Leigh's father-in-law, John Wrightington, was also a zealous Puritan involved in movement to secure better observation of the Sabbath.

12. Ibid., 9. Porteus points out the "dubious loyalty of many of the Lancashire justices of the peace" to Elizabethan settlement, suggesting that many were recusants (xvii).

13. See the *Dictionary of National Biography* entry on William Leigh.

14. James I, *Basilicon Doron*, in *Political Writings*, ed. Sommerville, 5; Porteus, *History of the Parish of Standish*, 67.

15. Bastardy cases animate the Lancashire quarter sessions; fathers and mothers were whipped and put in stocks, did public penance in church, appeared before the courts. See *Lancashire Quarter Sessions Records*, ed. James Tait, Vol. I. Quarter Sessions Rolls 1590–1606 (Printed for the Chetham Society, 1917), xxiii.

16. Ibid., 299. John Walmesley of Chipping said that "he cared not for the king nor his laws nor any of his subjects or officers, neither would he obey them," and John Ashton was accused of calling the king "an heretycke" (279, 283).

17. *The Dampe of Death*, "Dedicatory," A6v.

18. *Strange Newes of a prodigious Monster, borne in the Towneship of Adlington.* All subsequent references to this pamphlet will be cited parenthetically in the text.

19. *The true reporte of the forme and shape of a monstrous childe, borne at Muche Norkesleye.*

20. About one out of every forty babies was born out of wedlock. Bastardy rates varied, but the best available statistics point to an overall rate around 2 or 3 percent, rising to a peak of 4 percent around 1600, then falling in the early Stuart period. See Cressy, *Birth, Marriage, and Death*, 73.

21. Mellys, *The true description of two monsterous children, laufully begotten between George Steuens and Margerie his wyfe.*

22. Whitney, *A Choice of Emblemes, and other Devises*, 108. While Macrobius suggested that Janus was a figure of wisdom, pictured with two faces because of his ability to know the past and foresee the future, Janus was also a popular figure of hypocrisy: "two-faced" Iago swears by Janus as a sign of his moral duplicity. See Guibbory, "Sir Thomas Browne's Allusions to Janus," 270–71.

23. Foucault, *Discipline and Punish*, 93.

24. *Lancashire Quarter Sessions Records*, ed. James Tait. Vol. 1 *Quarter Session Rolls 1590–1606* (Printed for the Chetham Society, 1917), xix. For the details of their complaints, see Waik, *Elizabethan Recusancy in Cheshire*, 78–79.

25. James I, *Basilicon Doron*, in *Political Writings*, 31.

26. Ibid., 39, 43.

27. Ibid., 43.

28. *A wonder worth the reading*. Subsequent references will be cited parenthetically in the text.

29. In 1604 he informed against Richard Bancroft, Bishop of London, for harboring priests and permitting the publication of Roman Catholic books. King James ignored the charges and kept him in prison for months. See Curtis, "William Jones: Puritan Printer and Propagandist," 38–66.

30. Curtis, "William Jones: Puritan Printer and Propagandist," 38. The texts printed by Jones's secret press included *A Treatise of the Nature and Use of Things Indifferent* (1605); a tract entitled *English Puritanisme* (1605); and Henry Jacob's *A Christian and modest offer of a most indifferent conference, or disputation, about the maine and principall controversies betwixt the prelats, and the late silenced and deprived ministers in England: tendered by some of the said ministers to the archbishops, and bishops, and all their adherents* ([London]: Imprinted [by William Jones' secret press], 1606).

31. McKerrow, *A Dictionary of Printers and Booksellers*, 161.

32. James I commanded the Attorney "to finde a day, if it be possible this term, for the Puritan Printer to be in the Star Chamber" (Curtis, "William Jones," 38).

33. See Thomas Taylor's *The progresse of saints to full holinesse* (London: Printed by W[illiam] I[ones] for Iohn Bartlet, at the signe of the Guilded Cuppe in Cheapeside, in Goldsmiths Rowe, 1630) and John Preston's *The new covenant, or The saints portion. A treatise vnfolding the all-sufficiencie of God, mans vprightnes, and the covenant of grace* (London: Printed by I[ohn] D[awson], George Purslowe, and William Jones] for Nicolas Bourne, and are to be sold at the south entrance of the Royall Exchange, 1631). In 1624, Jones secretly published John Reynolds' *Vox coeli, or Newes from heauen* and Thomas Scott's *The second part of Vox populi*, two notorious Puritan texts that led directly to James's 1624 law against "seditious books."

34. Walsham, *Providence in Early Modern England*, 48.

35. These sinners "receive the word with no more reverence & attention, then a prophane Stageplay, or winter's tale: some sitting idly at their doores, gaping and gasing" (B). For the commonplace association of theater-going with immorality, see Barish, *Antitheatrical Prejudice*.

36. Collinson, *The Birthpangs of Protestant England*, 31.

37. *The drumme of devotion*. Arthur Johnson registered it (Arber, *Stationers*, 240). All subsequent references to the sermon will be cited parenthetically in the text.

38. The citation continues: "Have we not had within this one land of England, the hideous Heptarchie of seven heads at once? nay hath not the whole Iland of Britania, being a bodie perfectly shaped, rounded, and bounded with an inuironing sea, beene a long time thus disseuered, and dissfigured by that vnluckie dualitie the author of division?" (*A Comparative Discourse of the Bodies Natural and Politique*, 4). Forset explains his work through the claim that "Man is the fittest patterne to imitate in the forming of a civill state," and that it is easier to understand the government when "deduced from a more fa-

miliar example" (3a; 4b). The idea of the body politic with the king as the head was widely deployed as an ideology of governance, but it was also nuanced for parliamentarian ends. John Rous describes a sermon he heard at the March 8, 1630, assizes by one Mr. Ramsay, who had been selected by the high sheriff: "A similitude he had of the head receiving all the nourishment, and causing the other members to faile and the whole man to die, which he applied to the commonwealth, where all is sucked upwards and the commons left without nourishment" (Rous, *The Diary of John Rous*, 50).

39. Forset was a justice of the peace involved in the prosecution of the gunpowder plotters and the author of a text condemning the Gunpowder Plot. He also wrote *A Defence of the Right of Kings*, which justified the Oath of Allegiance and was dedicated to James I. Published in 1624, it was written ten or twelve years earlier. James granted Forset the manor of Tyburn in 1611.

40. Ashton, ed. *James I by His Contemporaries*, 169.

41. John Ponet, *A shorte treatise of politike pouuer and of the true obedience which subiectes owe to kynges and other ciuile gouernours*, Kii-v. "Ther was never great miserie, destruction, plage or visitacion of God, that came on any nacion, citie or countrey," Ponet writes, that was not "before prophecied and declared by the prophetes and ministers of Goddes worde, or by some revelaciones, wondres, monsters in the earthe, or tokens and signes in thelement [*sic*] (sig. Kii-v). In addition to Day's 1552 monster, he lists other monsters that he reads as signs of a disordered body politic, chief among them a child "with a great head, evil shaped, the armes with bagges hanging out at the Elbowes and heles, and fete lame" (Kiii). This child signifies that "the natural body of England shalbe weake, the chief membres (tharmes and legges) which is the nobilitie, so clogged with chaines of golde, and bagges of money, that the hande shall not be hable to drawe out the sworde, nor the heles to spurre the horde to helpe and defende the body, that is the commones. And as the head of it is the greatest part, and greater than it ought to be, with to muche superfluitie of that is should not have, wherfore it must pull from the other membres to confort it, and lacke of that good proporcion that it ought to have; so shall the governors and headdes of Englande sucke out the wealth and substaunce of the people (the politike body) and kepe it bare" (Kiiii-v).

42. Thomas Lanquet and Thomas Cooper, *Coopers chronicle contenynge the vvhole discourse of the histories as well of thys realme*, 356–57.

43. Equivocate: to use a word in more than one application or sense; to use words of double meaning; to deal in ambiguities. In a pejorative sense, to mean one thing and express another; to prevaricate (OED). On equivocation, see Sommerville, "The 'new art of lying,'" 160.

44. Ibid., 172. See also Keith Thomas, "Cases of Conscience," 32.

45. *Great Britaines Great Deliverance*, C2. Leigh dedicated the text to Prince Henry. In *Triplici nodo, triplex cuneous, or An Apologie for the Oath of Allegiance*, first published in 1608, James I also describes the plot as monstrous: "What a monstrous, rare, nay neuer heardof Treacherous attempt, was plotted within these few yeeres here in England, for the destruction of Mee, my bed-fellow, and our posteritie, the whole house of Parliament, and a great number of good Subjects of all sorts and degrees," *Political Writings* (85).

46. *The King's Booke* (1605), cited in Paul, *The Royal Play of Macbeth*.

47. Macduff says to Macbeth: "Then yield thee, coward, / And live to be the who and gaze o' th' time! / We'll have thee, as our rarer monsters are, / Painted upon a pole, and underwrit, 'Here you may see the tyrant'" (5.8.23–37).

48. On libels, see Fox, "Ballads, Libels and Popular Ridicule," 48.

49. Two days later the justice examined a man whose wife had kept the straw, and the story was soundly condemned as a false miracle by the Protestant press (Wills, *Witches and Jesuits*, 103).

50. Pricket wrote other texts, including *A souldiers wish vnto his soueraigne lord King Iames* (London, 1603), and *Times anotomie [sic]. Containing: the poore mans plaint, Brittons trouble, and her triumph. The Popes pride, Romes treasons, and her destruction* (London, 1606).

51. Although critics have drawn attention to the issues of equivocation in *Macbeth*, no one has noted the similarity between the crowned child of the "Jesuit's miracle" and the apparition of the crowned child in *Macbeth*. The third apparition, a "crowned child, with a branch in its hand," "rises like the issue of a king, / and weares upon his baby-brow the round / and top of sovereignty" (4.1.87–8). The crowned child, like the line of Banquo's (James's ancestor) descendents, portends the crown's continuation.

52. Despite rebellions against James, "By miracle God kept his maiestie / And gave to him great Brittans Monarchie" (E3).

53. E4. "Who dares not sweare allegiance to his king, / But vowes himself unto the Popes behest, / Will at the Popes command do any thing. / And such a one hides treason in his breast" (E).

54. Johann P. Sommerville, "Introduction," *Political Writings*, xxii.

55. James I, *Triplici nodo, triplex cuneus, or An Apologie for the Oath of Allegiance* (1608), in *Political Writings*, 86, emphasis added.

56. Ibid., 109.

57. See Kevin Sharpe, "Private Conscience and Public Duty in the Writings of James VI and I," 85.

58. James I, *A Meditation upon the Lords Prayer* (1619), 18, cited in ibid., 83.

59. James I, "A Speech in the Parliament House, November 9, 1605," in *Political Writings*, 153.

60. Lake, "Anti-popery: The Structure of a Prejudice," 88. James had secret dealings with the papacy and Catholic states even before he became king; in exchange for recognition of his succession, he offered to grant toleration to English Catholics and even hinted that his conversion was not to be despaired of (see Willson, *James VI and I*, 142). According to Willson, "James's cardinal error was his belief that he could be a champion of Protestantism and at the same time a friend of Spain (273).

61. *Triplici Nodo*, 92, 93. He wrote to the (Catholic) Earl of Northumberland: "As for the Catholics, I will neither persecute any that will be quiet and give *but an outward obedience to the law*, neither will I spare to advance any of them that will by good service worthily deserve it" (Willson, *James VI and I*, 148–49).

62. Weldon, *Court and Character of James I*, 32.

63. Kantorowicz, *The King's Two Bodies*, 331.

64. Sharpe, "Private Conscience and Public Duty," 85.

65. There was, as Roy Strong has argued, a "cult of a dynasty" around Prince Henry in the first decade of the seventeenth century. Henry himself was critical of James's Catholic-flirting; he maintained a separate court from which Catholics were barred, and he committed his life to militaristic Protestant and imperial projects. See Strong, "England and Italy: The Marriage of Henry Prince of Wales," 59–87.

66. Ibid., 87.

67. In *Basilicon Doron*, James tells his son that it is difficult to marry a bride of a differ-

ent religion because dissention "betwixt Preachers [. . .] wil breed and foster a dissention among your subjects, taking their example from your family" (*Political Writings*, 41).

68. Louis B. Wright, "Propaganda against James I's 'Appeasement' of Spain," 149–72.

69. Isaac Wake to Carleton, cited in Strong, *Henry, Prince of Wales*, 87, emphasis added.

70. "It is so common with report to rate the sicknese or death of princes at the prove of poyson," Frances Osborne wrote, that he would have ignored it had he "not heard by many, [Henry's] father did dread him." See Osborne, *Secret History of the Court* i, 259–69; cited in Robert Ashton, ed. *James I by His Contemporaries*, 99. Osborne wrote: "The palpable partiality that descended from the father to the Scots, did estate the whole love of the English upon his son Henry: whom they ingaged by so much expectation, as it may be doubted whether it ever lay in the power of any prince meerly humane to bring so much felicity into a nation" (98).

71. Louis B. Wright, "Propaganda," 156.

72. Ibid., 157

73. Gallagher, *Medusa's Gaze*, 11.

74. Keith Thomas, "Cases of Conscience," 42–43.

75. The date of the argument was April 3, Good Friday 1617 (Assheton, *Journal of Nicholas Assheton of Downham*, 82–83).

76. James I, *Political Works of James I*, ed. McIlwain, 140. For James's religious straddling, see Willson, *James VI and I*, 198–99.

77. James I, *Basilicon Doron*, in *Political Writings*, 6, emphasis added.

78. Ibid., 6, 7. It is interesting to note that James calls *Basilicon Doron* a "birth" "rightly proportioned in all the members, without any monstrous deformitie in any of them: and specially that since it was first written in secret and is now published, not of ambition, but of a kinde of necessitie; it must be taken of all men, for the trew image of my very minde, and forme of the rule, which I have prescribed to my selfe and mine" (11). He has brought his "secretest thoughts" forth, and they are not deformed.

79. Ibid., 27.

80. "To a large portion of the population, sermons were what the periodical press now is," writes Godfrey Davies ("English Political Sermons, 1603–1640"). "Even at the meager allowance of one sermon per parish per year, the total would be 360,000 sermons delivered [in the first forty years of the seventeenth century]" (1). The attempt to control the pulpit, under the early Stuarts, involved both the prescription of certain topics, and the prohibition of others (7).

81. Early in his reign, James I found cause to complain of the insatiable curiosity "an itching in the tongues and pens" of most of his subjects, reaching into "the deepest mysteries that belong to the persons or state of kings and princes" (ibid., 2). On Spanish policy, see Louis B. Wright, "Propaganda against James I."

82. James often complained against preachers: "We are told, for example, by the Venetian Ambassador, of James's anger that preachers dared to inveigh against the peace made with Spain in 1604" (Davies, "English Political Sermons," 8). In the same year, John Burges was imprisoned for preaching an offensive sermon before the king. He was called in for saying that some of the members hear mass in the morning, then attend Anglican service, sit in Council all the afternoon, and at night tell their wives all that had passed; the latter, being papists, would relate all again to their confessors, who would send it abroad (Birch, *Court and Times*, 1:210–11).

83. The rector's name was Edmund Peacham (Davies, "English Political Sermons," 8).

84. The campaign culminated in Thomas Scott's *Vox Populi* (1620), which inveighed against the Spanish Match, and James's resulting proclamation "against lavish and licentious speech about matters of state" (Davies, "English Political Sermons," 5). Like Leigh, Scott had formerly been intimately associated with the crown, listed in 1616 as one of the chaplains to King James (Louis B. Wright, "Propaganda," 150). James passed the law in 1624 (Davies, "English Political Sermons," 6).

85. Keith Thomas, "Cases of Conscience," 46.

FOUR: Heedless Women, Headless Monsters, and the Wars of Religion

1. *The Theater of Fine Devices*, B6. The full text reads:

Great monsters mentioned are in stories found,
As was *Chymera* of a shape most wondrous,
Girion, Pithon, Cerb'rus that hel-hound,
Hydra, Medusa, with their heads most hideous,
Satyres and Centaures; all these same were found
In bodies strange, deformed and prodigious:
    Yet none more marvellous in stories read,
    Then is a woman if she want a head.

2. *A myraculous, and Monstrous, but yet most true, and certayne discourse, of a Woman [. . .] in the midst of whose fore-head [. . .] there groweth out a crooked Horne.* All subsequent references to this pamphlet will be cited parenthetically in the text. The story is also recounted in T. I., *A World of wonders. A Masse of Murthers* (London, 1595).

3. However, as James Wood points out, no appearance before the Privy Council at that time is recorded in the published minutes of that body ("Woman with a Horn," 298).

4. The marginal note is a scriptural citation from Galatians 6.7: "God is not mocked: for whatsoever a man soweth, that shall he also reap." *A World of Wonders* also includes the story of a Piper, who said when his wife was pregnant: "[I]f it be a daughter the divell take my parte for me, for it is none of myne." In 1580 "it pleased God to send his wife to be with childe againe, and to be delivered of a monster, a male according to his desire, having the shape of two Children, from the shoulders upward it had two heads, having nature all proportions, saving that the one eare of each head was shapened like a horse eare, and the other like a swine" (E3). Again the monster is a literally embodiment of the sin (the baby is not a daughter, but it is not fully human either), and, in this case, punishment for a man who not only "murmured against his creator" but offered his part to the devil. The second quotation is from Keith Thomas, *Religion and the Decline of Magic*, 95–97.

5. T. I., *A World of wonders*, E2.

6. John Locke, *A strange and lamentable accident that happened lately at Mears-Ashby.* All subsequent references will be cited parenthetically in the text.

7. He gives biblical precedents to prove that God smites such sinners for their blasphemous errors: 2 Samuel 6.7. and Judges 18.27 (A3), and tells the story of a man who pissed on the Lord's table, "saying in scorne, that the Divine Providence tooke no care of outwarde ceremonies," and as punishment, suffered from an excruciating disease of the throat and mouth (A2v).

8. He points out that the year after "*Moore* and *Geofferey*, two of the divells agents, publisht their prodigious and hereticall tenents, to the allurement of many faithfull and con-

stant beleevers," many monstrous births appeared in England (A3v). Now, some eighty years later, another monstrous birth appears, again in response to divisions in religious belief and practice.

9. All citations from the title page. See also Bradshaw's *A Treatise of the Nature and use of Things Indifferent* (London, 1605). Godly or nonconforming ministers who resisted the established rites of the Church of England would omit using the cross in baptism "or any such needless ceremony" if they could get away with it, if they enjoyed sufficient community support, and if their ecclesiastical superiors left them alone. See *Certaine Questions by Way of Conference betwixt a Chauncelor and a Kinswoman of His Concerning Churching of Women* (Middleburg? 1601, STC 20557), 39; cited in Cressy, *Birth, Marriage, and Death*, 131. See also Milward, *Religious Controversies of the Jacobean Age*, viii–5.

10. See R. L. Greenall, *A History of Northamptonshire* (Phillimore, 1979), and Cater, *Northamptonshire Nonconformity 250 Years Ago*, 8. In 1604 a number of ministers were suspended "for not observing certain ceremonies," and fifty-seven Northamptonshire ministers refused to renew their subscription to the requirements of the church (Cater, *Northamptonshire Nonconformity*, 10).

11. Among other disobediences, "Noe man boweth at the pronouncing of the name of Jesus, and it is the greatest matter they sticke upon" (Cater, *Northhamptonshire Nonconformity*, 11). The rector of Courtenhall was attacked by his parishioners for using the sign of the cross in baptism (ibid., 10).

12. See *A certificate from Northampton-shire. 1. Of the pluralities. 2. Defect of maintenance. 3. Of not preaching. 4. Of scandalous ministers. As there is an order lately printed and published concerning ministers, by a committee of the high court of Parliament. Wherein every ingenuous person is desired to be very active to improve the present opportunitie, by giuing true information of all the parishes in their severall counties* (London: printed for William Sheares, 1641), Thomason E. 163[13]. According to the certificate, of the 326 livings in the county, 150 were scandalous (Cater, *Northhamptonshire Nonconformity*, 12). According to the *OED*, in the seventeenth century the term *scandalous* was applied to ministers of religion who were regarded as unfit for their office on the ground of heresy or unbecoming conduct. In January 1642, a group of Northampton Puritans sent a petition to Parliament laying out their expectations of "a certain reformation in religion," one frustrated by "the voting of Popish Lords and bishops in the house of Peers" (ibid., 11).

13. Even when the town and garrison of Northampton formally signed the "The Solemn League and Covenant" in March 1643, the Presbyterian system look little root in parts of the county where independents held sway (ibid., 11).

14. William Barnard earned his BA from Cambridge in 1602–3 and his MA in 1609. He was ordained deacon and priest March 8, 1603–4, and served as rector of Orwell from 1608 to 1644 (Longden, *Northampton and Rutland*, 1:195). John Locke was educated at Emmanuel College, Cambridge, where he earned his BA in 1627–28, his MA in 1630. He became deacon in June 1631 and priest in September 1631, and he died in 1661 (ibid., vol. 9).

15. Gerrard Winstanley, cited in Hill, *The World Turned Upside Down*, 148.

16. T. Case, *Spiritual Whordome discovered in a sermon before the House of Commons* (1647), 34, cited in Hill, *The World Turned Upside Down*, 100, emphasis added. Although Case's concern about "liberty of wives" refers to rampant adultery, that is to men sharing wives, it also invokes the freedom that women were claiming for themselves as petitioners, sectarians, and even soldiers.

17. The pamphlet also suggested that women's preaching was merely proud ambition: "What makes Artificers to be Preachers, by presuming on the assistance of the Spirit, if it is not the Spirit of pride?" (*The dolefull Lamentation of Cheap-side Crosse*, 3, 4). The threat was not only women's public speaking but the very idea that there were women's activities that the authorities did not know of and therefore could not monitor. Thomas Edwards, for example, castigated a man who denied the existence of a woman preacher in Kent: "M. Saltmarsh does not only assuredly know al things that al the women in the Parish do, but all what ever the whole Town of Brasteed knowes; for else how can he say so of all the women, and all the inhabitants of that place?" (*Gangraena*, 2:24–5).

18. Baillie and Edwards both mention one "she preacher" in particular: "*Attaway* the Mistresse of all the She-preachers in *Colemanstreet* was a disciple in *Lambs* Congregation, and made Antipaedobaptism oftentimes a part of her publicke exercises: the other feminine Preachers in *Kent, Norfolk*, and the rest of the Shires had their breeding, as I take it, in the same or the like school" (Baillie, *Anabaptisme, the true Fountaine of Independency*, 52, 53). Edwards mentions two women who preached in Colemanstreet "that now those dayes were come, and that was fulfilled which was spoken of in the Scriptures, that God would pour out of his Spirit upon the handmaidens, and they should prophecy" (*Gangraena*, 1:85).

19. The activities of the women preachers are derided both for their frivolity and for their threat. At the end of the pamphlet the author writes of returning the "female Academyes" to the University (Bedlam or Bridewell) and asks "Is it not sufficient that they may have the Gospell truly and sincerely Preached unto them, but that they must take their Ministers office from them?" (5).

20. *A Spirit Moving in the Women-Preachers* (London, 1646). Some of the women "preach in mixt congregations of men and women, in an insolent way, so usurping authority over men, and assuming a calling unwarranted by the word of God for women to use" (3).

21. Edwards, *Gangraena*, 1:66.

22. Foxe, *Actes and Monuments*, Vol. 1, 373.

23. The 1559 Act of Uniformity designated attendance at the Book of Common Prayer service as the means by which individuals were required to express obedience to the church established by law, and any resistance meant trouble.

24. Natalie Zemon Davis, "Women on Top," in *Society and Culture in Early Modern France*, 146.

25. McArthur, "Women Petitioners and the Long Parliament"; See also Laurence, "A Priesthood of She-Believers," 353. The petition was supposedly subscribed by 12,000 women who opposed Laudian innovations, bishops, stained glass, altars, surplices, and anthems.

26. On Dorothy Hazard, see Claire Cross, "He-goats before the Flocks"; and *The Records of a Church of Christ meeting in Broadmead, Bristol, 1640–87*, ed. E. B. Underhill (London, 1848).

27. Cressy, *Birth, Marriage, and Death*, 174.

28. Samuel Hieron, *A Help unto Devotion* (1612; STC 13407), 276–7, cited in Cressy, *Birth, Marriage, and Death*, 55. Thomas Edwards reported that in Holland, Lincolnshire, "there is a woman preacher who preaches, (its certain) and 'tis reported also she baptizeth, but thats not so certain" (Edwards, *Gangraena*, 1:84).

29. Keith Thomas, *Religion and the Decline of Magic*, 188, 205, 259. As Thomas points out, practices for safeguarding a woman in childbed included the invocation of Virgin

Mary and use of sanctified images, even after the Reformation. Furthermore, the idea of the efficacy of words and the role of the imagination in healing, although derided as popish, were often practiced by women and their midwives.

30. *The Pleasures of Matrimony* (1688), 127–28; cited in Cressy, *Birth, Death, and Marriage*, 85, italics added.

31. On petty treason and its relationship to female rebellion, see Dolan, *Dangerous Familiars*, especially chapter 1.

32. *Liturgical Services: Liturgies and Occasional Forms of Prayer Set Forth in the Reign of Queen Elizabeth*, 204, emphasis added.

33. Ibid.

34. Ibid., 169.

35. Thomas, *Religion and the Decline of Magic*, 39.

36. Bruno Ryves, ed. *Mercurius Rusticus, or The countries complaint of the murther, robbers, plundering and other outrages committed by the rebels of his Majesties faithfull subjects* (Oxford: s.n. 1643–44), Thomason 19:E.106 [12], 4, 10th June, 1643, 30.

37. Foxe, *Actes and Monuments*, Vol. 2, 1670.

38. Stapleton's preface to Bede's *The history of the church of Englande* (Antwerpe, 1565), fos. 8v–92, cited in Walsham, *Providence in Early Modern England*, 231.

39. Firth and Rait, eds., *Acts and Ordinances of the Interregnum*, 1:594–96.

40. George Thomason collected over 125 topics dealing with infant baptism between 1642 and 1660, for example, A. R., *A Treatise of the Vanity of Childish Baptism* (1642). See *The Thomason Tracts, 1640–1661: An Index to the Microfilm Edition of the Thomason Collection of the British Library* (Ann Arbor: University Microfilms International, 1981).

41. McGregor, "The Baptists: Fount of All Heresy," 25.

42. *Bloody Newes from Dover*, Av. All subsequent references will be cited parenthetically within the text.

43. Parents often debated whether or not to baptize their children. Lucy Hutchinson tells the story of a governor's wife who read arguments against infant baptism and "having perus'd them and compar'd them with the scriptures, found not what to say against the truths they asserted." Pregnant herself, she communicated her doubts to her husband, and when the infant was born in 1647, it was not baptized (*Memoirs of the Life of Colonel Hutchinson, with a Fragment of an Autobiography*, ed. N. H. Keeble [London: J.M. Dent, 1995], 210). Mary Champian, moreover, is identified as being from Feversham in Kent, a region popularly associated with radical women. *A discoverie of six women preachers, in Middlesex, Kent, Cambridgshire, and Salisbury* mentions the case of Joan Bauford, who "taught in Feversham, that husbands being such as crossed their wives wils might lawfully be forsaken" (4).

44. Baptists' critics frequently described them as false prophets who "creep into houses, and lead captive silly women laden with sins" (*Association Records of the Particular Baptists of England, Wales, and Ireland to 1660*, ed. B. R. White, 185; cited in McGregor, "The Baptists: Fount of All Heresy," 47). The quotation is from 2 Timothy 3.6. Although often condemned for allowing women to preach, the Baptists were actually conservative, ruling that women "may not speake as that their speaking shall shew a not acknowledging of the inferiority of their sexe and so be an usurping authority over the man" (ibid., 46–47).

45. 1647 began with the triumph of Presbyterians in Commons and city government,

and ended with army's entry into London and the triumph of the Independents. *Bloody News* thus seems to address a situation of hopeful Presbyterian triumph as much as sectarian resurgence.

46. Cope, *Handmaid of the Holy Spirit*, 41; cited in Mack, *Visionary Women*, 93.

47. Theophilus Philalethes Toxander, *Vox Coeli to England, or England's Forewarning from Heaven* (London, 1646), 3–11.

48. *Susanna's Apologie*, 14; cited in Mack, *Visionary Women*, 92.

49. *A declaration of a strange and wonderfull monster: born in Kirkham parish in Lancashire*. All subsequent references will be cited parenthetically within the text.

50. Bray, *Documents of the English Reformation*, 341. For example, the Parliamentarian *London Diurnall* reported that "three *Crucifixes*, one *Agnus Dei*, and a protection from the *Pope*" were found in the pocket of the Earle of Northampton. This is reported by the anti-Parliamentarian *Mercurius Aulicus* (April 2–9, 1643), which points out that the accusation is "a very fine, impudent slander," perhaps the most effective and readily available kind (Raymond, ed., *Making the News*, 96). The printer of Bernard Garter's *New yeares gifte* (1579) includes a large fold-out diagram of popish objects in order to help Protestant recognize a recusant (Watt, *Cheap Print and Popular Piety*, 179). Although the pamphlet putatively criticizes such symbols, it does provide a pull-out sheet representing them for readers. In 1638 the alehouse of Richard Brock of Bunbury was suppressed because Brock and "Joane his wife a recusant convict do keepe in their Alehouse (which is not fully five roodes distance from the chancell doore of the parish church) diverse pictures and other popish reliques" (Bennett and Dewhurst, eds. *Quarter Sessions records*, vol. 94, p. 93).

51. Stockden, *The Seven Women Confessors, or a Discovery of the Seven white Divels which lived at Queen-street in Coven-garden*, A3, emphasis added. For a comprehensive view of women, recusancy, and Catholicism in the seventeenth century, see Dolan, *Whores of Babylon*.

52. The secret burial is also intimately related to a famous case from New England, the subject of chapter 5.

53. See Rowlands, "Recusant women, 1560–1640," 162, 163.

54. Ibid., 150; 152. See especially the 1641 case of Jane Vaughan of Gloucestershire, who was imprisoned for harboring a priest and had a protracted battle with the law (159).

55. Ibid., 160. Recusants were often influential and powerful people in their local communities who were able to test the limits of state authority, and divisions in county communities over religious settlement often followed older established lines of rivalry between leading families (ibid., 150).

56. Leatherbarrow, *The Lancashire Elizabethan Recusants*, 103–4.

57. See Gregory, "Witchcraft, Politics and 'Good Neighbourhood,'" passim.

58. Patrick Collinson has argued that the social separation of the godly from the irreligious multitude, and a new concentration on the *friends of one's soul rather than neighbours*, "was more drastically divisive and stressful [. . .] than ecclesiastical separation itself" ("From Iconoclasm to Iconophobia," 281). As Collinson points out, Puritanism was not simply top-down social control of the disenfranchised; the religious and moral struggle was engaged *within* classes as well as between them.

59. J. C. Jeaffreson, *Middlesex Country Records*, III, 178, cited in Rollins, *Cavalier and Puritan*, 23. Viewing two sheep heads in a pot in 1643, a Westminster seamstress said that "she wished the kings' and Prince Rupert's heads were there instead of them" (Lindley,

Popular Politics and Religion in Civil War London, 234). It has been argued that public houses and other places of common resort associated with "good fellowship" were increasingly contested as respectable Protestants withdrew: "Protestant reformers directed their energies increasingly within a closed godly culture centred on the church and private household, rather than more public and 'popular' forms of recreation" (Watt, *Cheap Print and Popular Piety*, 70).

60. Kunzle, *The Early Comic Strip*, 3.

61. This story has interesting resonances with the exemplary hanging of the shorn and robed cat discussed in chapter 1.

62. For more information, see Lamont, *Marginal Prynn, 1600–69*, 11–84; Lake, "Anti-popery," 95.

63. In *A New Discovery of the Prelates Tyranny In their late prosecution of Mr William Prynne*, Prynne describes his ear cutting in great detail and calls "Laud's STAMPS" on his cheek "Stigmata Laudis." Prynne suggests that the three men's punishment "is such a prodigious Innovation, as neither Affrica nor England ever beheld the like, and never had beene brought forth into the World, had not a venomous Archprelate proved a Father to engender, a Mother to faster, a Midwife to produce and bring to its birth" (4).

64. Ibid., 108.

65. Vicars, *Jehovah-Jireh*, 430. In 1641 Vicars and Prynne wrote a book together against the use of images of Christ, *Sinfulness and Unlawfulness of Having or Making the Picture of Christ's Humanity* (London, 1641).

66. Ibid., 430–31.

67. Prynne, *A New Discovery of the Prelates Tyranny*, 116. If, Prynne asks, transient acts such as "[s]pitting in the face and smiting men on the cheek are reputed great reproaches and indignities in Scripture [. . .] what then is branding in the face and cheeks which is permanent?" (165).

68. The minister, Arthur Greenacres, was buried in September 1627; his wife Isabel died in February 1659 (Shaw and Shaw, *The Records of the Thirty Men of the Parish of Kirkham in Lancashire*, 148–54).

69. Broxap, *Great Civil War in Lancashire*, 9.

70. Shaw and Shaw, *Records of the Thirty Men*, 29.

71. Thomason's hand-written date on the title page.

72. Lancashire recusants petitioned the king to bear arms for his defense, and although not officially allowed, many made it into the ranks of the royalists. Parliament ordered these documents to be printed to arouse public opinion against the king, and the king gave orders to disarm popish recusants and sectaries (Broxap, *Great Civil War in Lancashire*, 10).

73. Ibid., 55. See such tracts as *Exceeding Joyful News out of Lancashire* (London: For Robert Wood, 1643), a Parliamentary account of a royalist defeat.

74. Edward Robinson's contemporaneous *A Discourse of the Warr in Lancashire* reports that Royalist forces quartered in Kirkham in 1643 "made grete enquiries to know the dwellings of the Roundheads from whom they plundered horses pewter brass bedding and what else they could carry," and the head of the reigning gentry family, the Earl of Derby, commanded the citizens of Kirkham to serve the king. Yet Royalists were not the only aggressors: "*For this very yeare 1643 began the Ordenance of Sequestration to be put in practice upon the Estaits of Delinquents and Papists*" (38, 44, italics added). On Alexander Rigby (1594–1650), see Greaves and Zaller, eds., *A Biographical Dictionary of British Rad-*

icals in the Seventeenth Century: "With John Moore and Ralph Asheton, his two closest Lancashire colleagues, Rigby reported to Parliament on 25 June 1642 that they had secured the power and match at Manchester, mustered and trained troops in Lancashire, negotiated a partial disengagement with the Royalist Lord Strange, and hindered other royalist maneuvers" (2:96).

75. Blackwood, *The Lancashire Gentry and the Great Rebellion*, 73.

76. Hoghton attended Charles in 1639 and 1640 and was appointed to the commission of array for his county, where he was also Commissioner of the Peace, a post he lost in 1642 with the rise of the Parliament (*Journals of the House of Commons*, 2:821, cited in Ormerod, ed., *Tracts Relating to Military Proceedings in Lancashire During the Great Civil War*, 60). See also Newman, *Royalist Officers in England and Wales, 1642–1660*. Hoghton was arrested in 1644 for stealing while sheriff in Lancashire. According to Newman, he died in 1644 or 1647 (*Royalist Officers*, 198).

There was a Parliamentarian garrison three miles from Hoghton's house, and in 1643 parliamentarian forces took possession of Hoghton Tower, a royalist symbol. Another family next to that of Hoghton of Hoghton Tower was Haughton of Park Hill (see Dugdale, *The Visitation of the County Palatine of Lancaster*, 154–55). William Haughton was a Catholic and a Lt. Colonel in the Horse regiment of Colonel Thomas Dalton of Park Hall Lancashire (a description very similar to Vicars's "Mistress *Haughton* wife to Master *William Haughton* of *Prickmarsh* within the parish of *Kirkham* in *Lefield* in *Lancashier*").

77. Omerod, *Tracts Relating to Military Proceedings in Lancashire*, 16, 29, 35. During the 1642 attack on Preston, a stronghold of Roman Catholicism, Gilbert Hoghton's brother Radcliffe Hoghton was killed, and his wife, Lady Hoghton, was taken prisoner (Broxap, *Great Civil War in Lancashire*, 62).

78. Lathom House was under siege from 1644–46 (Broxap, *Great Civil War in Lancashire*, 27).

79. Ormerod, *Tracts*, 176.

80. *A Briefe Journall of the Siege against Lathom*, 176, 177; cited in Broxap, *Great Civil War in Lancashire*, 108, italics added. See also the following verse:

Lathom House
Where they raised midst sap and siege
The banners of their rightful liege
At their she-captain's call,
Who, miracle of womankind,
Lent mettle to the meanest hind
That mann'd her castle wall! (Robinson, *A Discourse of the Warr in Lancashire*,
    xiii).

81. 4–11 July 1645 (Ormerod, *Tracts*, 210).

82. Broxap, *Great Civil War in Lancashire*, 140.

83. Blackwood, *The Lancashire Gentry and the Great Rebellion*, 113.

84. Ironically, in 1647, the year after the pamphlet was published, Alexander Rigby related: "I have had by the enemy all my mansion houses extremely plundered, defaced and left uninhabitable and even almost all my goods in them and upon my lands taken away" (Greaves and Zaller, eds., *A Biographical Dictionary*, 96).

85. *The severall votes and resolutions of both Houses of Parliament, concerning the Kings last message, sent from Huntington to both Houses, on Wednesday the 16. of March, 1641. With His*

Majesties message before to both Houses of Parliament, March 15. 1641 (Printed at London: for Rich. Harper and I.G., 1641) Thomason, E.140[8]; and John Flavel, *A briefe treatise of Gods mighty povver, and miraculous protection of his church and people, from the beginning of the world even to these our dayes* (Printed at London: for Rich: Harper, at the Bible and Harpe in Smithfield, 1642).

86. *A briefe and compendious narrative of the renowned Robert, Earle of Essex, his pedegree, and his valiant acts, performed when he was generall of the Parliaments army. With a summary chronicle of his life: and in what manner his buriall is appointed to be solemnized. Published according to order* (London: printed by Jane Coe, 1646), Thomason E.358[9]. The newsbooks were *The city-scout* (1645), *The moderate messenger* (1646), and *Perfect occurrences of both Houses of Parliament and martiall affairs* (Printed by Jane Coe, and published according to Order of Parliament, [1646]–1646 [i.e. 1647]).

87. *His Majesties declaration, directed to all persons of what degree and qualitie soever, in the Christian world. VVith a letter from divers godly ministers of the Church of England, to the assembly of the Kirk of Scotland; shewing the cause of these troubles. And a list of the popish vicker-generalls, Jesuites, priests and fryers, in England, and their names and places to them assigned, in the severall provinces of England, and Wales, to exstinguish the Protestant clergie, and religion, and bring in, and settle popery instead thereof* (London: Printed by Jane Coe, 1644); and *XXXVI. severall religions, held and maintained by the Cavaliers With a list of the names of the chief commanders in the squadron* (London: Printed by Jane Coe, 1645).

FIVE: *The ranters monster* and the "Children of God"

1. Foxe, *Actes and Monuments*, Vol. 2, 1764.

2. The child is initially retrieved from the fire, but the bailiff commands that the child—identified as a "faire man childe"—should be cast back. "And so the Infant baptised in his own blood, to fill up the number of Gods innocent saints, was both borne and died a martyr, leaving behind to the world, which it never sawe, a spectacle wherin the whole world may see the Herodian crueltie of this gracelesse generation of Catholic tormenters" (ibid., 1765). The martyred women are identified as Katherine Kawches and her two daughters, Guillemine Guilbert and Perotine Massey; the child was Perotine's. The women's crime is that they had been "disobedient to the commandements and ordinances of the church, in contemning and forsaking the masse, and the ordinances of the same" (1763).

3. Thomas Goodwin, *Childe of Light Walking in Darknes: or a Treatise Showing the Causes by which, The Cases wherein, The ends for which God leaves his children to distresse of conscience. Together with Directions how to walke, as to come forth of such a Condition* (1636), 116.

4. John Bale, *Workes*, 17.

5. *The ranters monster: being a true relation of one Mary Adams, living at Tillingham in Essex, who named her self the Virgin Mary*. All references will be cited parenthetically in the text.

6. Rublack, "Pregnancy, Childbirth," 86.

7. If women's childbirth prayers revealed their fears about the signs of election or reprobation being borne in their children's bodies (praying, for example, that their child be born without deformity, a privilege "far beyond" their sins), they also revealed their ability to bring forth a "sound and perfect creature after [God's] owne image." See the prayer of Elizabeth, Countess of Bridgewater, reproduced in a Crawford and Gowing, eds. *Women's Worlds in Seventeenth-Century England*, 20.

8. Edmund S. Morgan, *Visible Saints*, 66.

9. The essential reference on Protestant beliefs in the Holy Spirit is Geoffrey Nuttall, *The Holy Spirit in Puritan Faith and Experience* (1946). On the civil war and interregnum movements, see Cohn, *The Pursuit of the Millennium* (1970), and Knox, *Enthusiasm* (1961).

10. Nuttall, *Holy Spirit in Puritan Faith*, 1.

11. Ibid., 30.

12. Ibid., 50; R. Baxter, *Breviate of Life of M. Baxter*, ed. J. T. Wilkinson, p. 71, cited in Nuttall, *Holy Spirit in Puritan Faith*, 59.

13. R. Baxter, *Works* XII, 500, cited in Nuttall, *Holy Spirit in Puritan Faith*, 56–57.

14. *A Description of a Sect Called the Familie of Love* (1641) tells a similar story of a "vertuous and dutifull" woman who is driven mad by the Familists.

15. Rutherford, *A Survey of the Spirituall Antichrist*, 1:9–10; 171–72.

16. Antinomianism "was a caricature extension of the basic Protestant principle of the priesthood of all believers—the doctrine that God speaks directly to the individual conscience, dispensing with all mediators, whether the Virgin and the saints, or the hierarchy of the priesthood" (Hill, "Irreligion in the 'Puritan' Revolution," 199).

17. For good surveys of the controversy, see David D. Hall's introduction to *The Antinomian Controversy, 1636–1638*, and Edmund S. Morgan's introduction to *The Puritan Dilemma: The Story of John Winthrop.*

18. John Winthrop, *A Short Story of the Rise, reign, and ruine of the Antinomians, Familists & Libertines* (1644), cited in Hall, *Antinomian Controversy*, 222.

19. "A Report of the Trial of Mrs. Anne Hutchinson before the Church in Boston," in Hall, *Antinomian Controversy*, 372.

20. Ibid., 359.

21. "The Examination of Mrs. Anne Hutchinson at the Court at Newtown," in Hall, *Antinomian Controversy*, 337, 338.

22. Ibid., 337.

23. "A Report," 378–79.

24. The minister Thomas Shepherd claimed that she "never had any trew Grace in her hart," but only her own tenets (ibid., 383).

25. Winthrop feared that "for such bottomlesse revelations, as either came without any word, or without the sense of the word, which was framed to humane capacity, if they be allowed in one thing, must be admitted a rule in all things; for they being above reason and Scripture, they are not subject to controll" (*A Short Story*, 274).

26. Ibid., 214–15. The elders did catalogue Hutchinson's errors in their records of the case. Originally there were two main erroneous opinions: (1) that the person of the Holy Ghost dwells in a justified person, and (2) that no sanctification can help to evidence to us our justification. As the case went on, however, the list lengthened (Hall, *Antinomian Controversy*, 11).

27. "A Report," 380; and Winthrop, *A Short Story*, 215.

28. As Amy Schrager Lang puts it, "Revealed by the heavenly Father and interpreted by the earthly ones, the monsters, paradoxically, both signify Hutchinson's errors and denied her power" (*Prophetic Woman*, 57).

29. Winthrop dreamed of his wife in bed "with three or four of their children lying by her, with most sweet and smiling countenances, with crowns upon their heads," which he interpreted to mean "that God would take of her children to make them fellow heirs with Christ in his kingdom" (D. Hall, *Worlds of Wonder*, 87). Winthrop said he himself became like a "weaned child" when he had the assurance of salvation (E. S. Morgan, *The Puritan*

Dilemma, 72). John Cotton's child, Seaborn, was not baptized until the congregation was formed (ibid., 97).

30. Porterfield, *Female Piety in Puritan New England,* 115. For other texts that deal with Anne Hutchinson and the place of women in the colony, see Karlsen, *The Devil in the Shape of a Woman* (1987) and Koehler, *A Search for Power: The 'Weaker Sex' in Seventeenth Century New England* (1980).

31. Winthrop, *A Short Story,* 262, 266.

32. "A Report," 371, Lang, *Prophetic Woman,* 40–44.

33. Cotton Mather, *Magnalia Christi Americana* [1702] (New York: Russell and Russell, 1967), 2:516. As Lang writes, the court knew "that the force of the female heretic vastly exceeds her heresy" (*Prophetic Woman,* 65).

34. Cotton told her children: "[L]et me tell you from the Lord: though natural affection may leade you to speake in the Defense of your Mother and to take her part and to seeke to keepe up her Credit and respect, which may be lawfull and comendable in some cases and at some times, yet in the Cause of God you art nayther to know Father nor Mother, Sister nor Brother" ("A Report," 367).

35. Winthrop, *A Short Story,* 263.

36. "A Report," 373.

37. Ibid., 370.

38. Winthrop, *A Short Story,* 281–82.

39. [John Eliot], Letter to Reverend Thomas Brookes, Rector of St. Mary Magdalen, New Fish Street Hill, London, 19 May 1660. At Massachusetts Historical Society. For accounts of the monster, see Pagitt's *Heresiography,* 115; and Gataker, *Antinomianism Discovered and Confuted* (1652).

40. Schutte, "'Such Monstrous Births,'" 89. The best account of the Dyer controversy is Johann Winsser's "Mary Dyer and the 'Monster' Story." See also Plimpton, *Mary Dyer,* and Myles, "From Monster to Martyr," on Dyer's transition from Antinomian to Quaker.

41. Winthrop, *A Short Story,* 214–15.

42. Traister, "Anne Hutchinson's 'Monstrous Birth' and the Feminization of Antinomianism," 136.

43. For Thomas Weld, it was the antinomians' belief in a "faire and easie way to Heaven," a path which required nothing of an individual but the work of Christ within him or her, that made this doctrine so popular in London and "other parts of the Kingdom." "It pleaseth nature well," he wrote, "to have Heaven and their lusts too" (see the preface to Winthrop, *A Short Story,* 204). For the circulation of the story, see Hall, *Antinomian Controversy,* 21–22, 44, 200, 396. Weld's English version of Winthrop's account went through three different editions, and the story became a cautionary tale in the works of heresiographers, appearing in both Edwards' *Gangraena* (1646) and Pagitt's *Heresiography* (1647).

44. See Hall, *Antinomian Controversy,* 396.

45. Hall, *Antinomian Controversy,* 20.

46. See the appendix to Cohn, "The 'Free Spirit' in Cromwell's England" in *Pursuit of the Millennium.* It is interesting to note, however, that in 1652 Mary Dyer went to England with her husband on an embassy to Parliament, where she remained and became a Quaker (Myles, "From Monster to Martyr," 5 n. 12).

47. Muggleton, *The Acts of the Witnesses of the Spirit,* Epistle Dedicatory, A2, and Reeve, *A Transcendent Spiritual Treatise,* 4. His witnessing of the Spirit was, as Muggleton later

wrote, a reassuring answer to his fear that he "was none of the Redeem'd," but it was also an explicit challenge to both the ministry and the magistracy (26).

48. Muggleton, *Acts of the Witnesses,* 77. While they claimed that their status as witnesses of the Spirit was invisible to the eye (only Moses' commission was "manifested by natural signes visibly upon the bodies of men and women"), they contrasted their message with the "great lying signs and wonders" of one John Robins, who "shewed such signs as the Popes could never shew" (Reeves, *Transcendent Spiritual Treatise,* 7–8). Among Robins's many other lies was his claim that his wife, whom he renamed Eve, "should bring forth his son Jesus," a "fleshly" misinterpretation that Reeve uses to distinguish Robins's brand of Spirit-witnessing from his own.

49. Edwards tells the story of a man who called women "out of their bed to go a dipping in rivers, dipping many of them in the night, so that their husbands and Master could not keep them in their houses." After he had baptized a woman, "he bid her gape, and she gaped, and he did blow three times into her mouth, saying words to this purpose, either *receive the holy Ghost,* or *thou hast received the holy Ghost*" (Edwards, *Gangraena,* 2:147). One woman, when shown the Scriptures, "took the book and threw it out of her hand and said, that was not ordered by the holy Ghost to be printed, but it was the rogue Printer that did put it in" (ibid., 3:35).

50. Trapnel. *The Cry of a Stone* (1654), 66, cited in Keith Thomas, *Religion and the Decline of Magic,* 136.

51. The full title is *A Man-Child Born, or God Manifest in Flesh. Wherein is discovered, how God, or the eternal being, always dwels, inhabits, is revealed and brought forth in flesh, in ages and generations that ever were, are, or shall be, world without end. The mysterie of both father, mother, husband, and son, Of himself and us, of we the spouse of God and mother of Jesus, his being born of the Virgin Mary in flesh, a sign, his being born in us, the substance, also our being with child, and giving suck to any but Christ, and the woe that comes by it* (London, 1654), 6. Richard Coppin (fl. 1646–59) moved from Anglican to Presbyterian to Independent to Anabaptist before an inward experience like those of the Quakers led him to preaching. Associated with the Ranters, he was arrested for blasphemy and tried at the Worcester assizes on March 23, 1652. Among the charges against him was his declaration that God was as much in all men as in Christ (Greaves and Zaller, eds., *Biographical Dictionary,* 175).

52. Mack, *Visionary Women,* 39.

53. See *A Perfect Account,* No. 21., 28 May–4 June 1651, 496.021 [9.13], cited in Raymond, ed., *Making the News,* 27. The observation that she is "very big" appears in G.H., *The Declaration of John Robins, the False Prophet* (1651), 3.

54. In addition to the two publications cited in n. 53, the story is recounted in *The Faithful Scout,* which tells of a Ranter arrested in Shoreditch on May 24 who "said that she was the Virgin *Mary,* and (being with child) had conceiv'd a Son, to be the Saviour of the World, which was the onely and true *Christ*" (cited in Hopton, ed., *The Declaration of John Robins* [1992]). The proceedings of the trial are also recounted in *All the Proceedings at the Sessions of the Peace Holden at Westminster* (London: Printed by Thomas Harper, 1651), and in the *Middlesex County Records,* ed. J. C. Jeaffreson (London, 1888), Vol. 3. See also Friedman, *Blasphemy, Immorality, and Anarchy,* 121; and Greaves and Zaller, eds., *Biographical Dictionary,* 3:100–101.

55. On Franklin and Gadbury, see Mack, *Visionary Women,* 104; Hill, *The World Turned Upside Down,* 160: and Greaves and Zaller, eds., *Biographical Dictionary,* 1:304. Ellis tells

the story "so that it might be a special means to warn others to beware of these or the like deceits" (A2). Humphry Ellis, *Pseudochristus: or, A true and faithful relation of the grand impostures, horrid blasphemies, abominable practises gross deceits.* Thomason dates the pamphlet May 27. Subsequent references will be cited parenthetically in the text.

Ellis sees the story as evidence of "what a root of bitterness that unlimited, lawless, boundless Toleration is of all Religions, and of all things whatsoever under pretence of Religion, which some under liberty of conscience have contended for" (A2).

56. *A Vision: Wherein is Manifested the Disease and Cure of the Kingdome* (London, 1648), 1, both cited in Purkiss, "Producing the Voice, Consuming the Body," 153. See also Mack, *Visionary Women*, 39.

57. Ellis, *Pseudochristus*, 50. The text is peppered with accusations of whore and harlot, a common charge for dissenting women.

58. For an interesting discussion of the Franklin/Gadbury case, see Thomas H. Luxon "'Not I, But Christ': Allegory and the Puritan Self." Luxon talks about Ellis's references to Galatians 4.19: "My little children of whom I travail in birth again until Christ be formed in you," and argues that "for a woman to apply the same metaphors to herself [. . .] automatically threatens to reliteralize, and so re-gender, the very thing such metaphors sought to neutralize—the power and significance of material (particularly *mater*-ial) generation. Paul's argument in Galatians is precisely that fleshly birth counts for nothing in determining membership in God's true Israel; the true 'sons of Abraham' are born 'of the spirit,' not the flesh" (910). According to Ellis, says Luxon, a mother, "a carnal bearer of children, cannot speak this way without threatening to dissolve the ontological distinction between this world (fleshly bodies) and the next (spiritual bodies)" (911).

59. Magistrates were required to proceed against any who maintained "him or her self, or any meer Creature, to be very God, or to be Infinite or almighty, or in Honor, Excellency, Majesty, and Power to be equal, and the same with the true God, or that the true God, or the Eternal Majesty dwells in the Creature and no where else" (McGregor, "Seekers and Ranters," 132). Austin Woolrych points out that the Blasphemy Act of 2 May 1650 actually preceded by some months Parliament's publication of the Westminster Assembly's *Articles of the Christian Religion*, which delineated what, exactly, the orthodox doctrine they were defending from blasphemy was (*Britain in Revolution*, 407).

60. Unlike Franklin, neither Gadbury nor Margaret Woodward, the woman who testified to her "birth," ever admitted to any error. "[H]aving now suffered a little hardship, and tasted somewhat of the smart of the whip," Gadbury answered "all their Interrogatories concerning her name, her calling, her husband and children, her acquaintance with this man, and the occasion of their coming into this Country," but she never denied the truth of her spiritual knowledge (Ellis, *Pseudochristus*, 44). She claimed, to the end, that her visions and revelations were "not delusions, but of God" (48).

61. "The Examination," 341. Indeed, there is an interestingly equivocal moment in Ellis's narrative when he mentions that her examiners wondered if Mary Gadbury were "painted," her complexion being so fresh and beautiful. A candle is thus brought close to her face "where upon she stept forth presently and very boldly put her face very near to the candle and said, That she was glad the glory of God did shine so bright in her face, that they were forced to admire it" (Ellis, *Pseudochristus*, 40).

62. Raymond, *Making the News*, 159–60; 162.

63. Bunyan, *Works*, 3:613, cited in Hill, *The World Turned Upside Down*, 317.

64. Shepherd, *The joviall crew, or The devill turn'd Ranter*, B2.

65. Although the pamphlet is identified in both ESTC and EEBO as *Fire in the Bush*, the title on the pamphlet itself is *A Vindication of those Whose Endeavour is only to make the Earth a Common Treasure, called Diggers*.

66. Milward, *Religious Controversies of the Jacobean Age*, 84.

67. George Spinola, *Rules to get children by*. This pamphlet was published twice in the 1640s. The 1642 version is cited in the text.

68. It is interesting to note that one heresy cited by Edwards was the claim that all creatures are equal and loved; there is "no distance between the flesh of a Man, and the flesh of a Toad" (*Gangraena*, 1:20). It is tempting to argue that Mary Adams's toad-like monster illustrates the difference between men living in God's image and those who do not. God's image in man, the sectarians were said to claim, "is only our face and countenance; and every wicked man hath therefore Gods Image as well as good men" (24). Monsters seem to suggest that this is not so, that God is in some men and not in others; monsters belie the claim that "one man is no more spirituall then [*sic*] another" (24).

69. Leonard W. Levy, *Treason Against God*, 99.

70. In addition to Hadley, the list of witnesses includes James Townsworth, Andrew Farmer, Churchwardens; Richard Gittins, Constable; James Woodhouse, John Smith, John Walton, Collectors; William Jackson, Gilbert Pickering, Thomas Watson, Headboroughs.

71. T. W. Davis, *Annals of Evangelical Nonconformity*, 311.

72. Ibid., 312. They argued that a refusal to make public worship compulsory undermined the power of both civil magistrates and family governors: "For upon this *Agreement* no governor of any family may use any compulsion to his child or servant to cause him to attend upon the publique means of instruction, but must leave him free" (313).

73. Ibid.

74. Yule, *The Independents in the English Civil War*, passim.

75. On Trapnel, see *Severall Proceedings of State Affaires*, 12–19 January 1653, cited in Raymond, *Making the News*, 163.

76. Yule, *Independents in the English Civil War*, 41. Most Independents were allied with the Presbyterians until 1649 because they believed a parish church system was necessary for society. After Pride's Purge, it was more fashionable to be an Independent (ibid., 20–22). Woolrych (*Britain in Revolution*) argues that from 1649 onward, Independents and Presbyterians closed ranks against the threats from sectarians.

77. Yule, *Independents in the English Civil War*, 13.

78. Oliver Cromwell, cited in ibid., 17.

79. Ibid., 70.

80. Hall, *Antinomian Controversy*, 213 n.10.

81. Adams's story is recounted by a wide range of respected historians and literary scholars. Christopher Hill includes her in his list of radicals who claimed divinity (*World Turned Upside Down*, 249); Phyllis Mack includes her in her list of women visionaries (*Visionary Women*, 413); Keith Thomas mentions "the boast by the Ranter, Mary Adams, that she had conceived a child by the Holy Ghost" (*Religion and the Decline of Magic*, 137); and Christine Berg and Phillipa Berry identify Mary Adams as "probably the best known" of the women who proclaimed that they were pregnant with Christ ("'Spiritual Whoredom,'" 50–51). The survival of Mary Adams, a figure with no "historical" record, attests to the complicated ways in which popular and ephemeral literature participated in religious and political movements, and continues to inform "history."

82. The pamphlet was advertised in *The French Intelligencer*, 30 March 1652, and *The Faithful Scout*, 5–12 March 1652, records the same story (Raymond, ed., *Making the News*, 185). *A List of some of the Grand Blasphemers and Blasphemies* gives a list of thirty blasphemers, eleven of them women and one of them a woman named Mary Adams, who "said about 1652 *That she was conceived with childe by the Holy Ghost, and that all the Gospel that had been taught heretofore, was false; and that which was within her, was the true Messias.*" Many of the stories in the list are of women preachers and recusants, including that of Mrs. Gay, who said "*That she could serve God as well in her bed, or at work in her Garden on the Lords dayes, as at any Ordinances at any meeting place.*" As punishment for her blasphemy, she was deprived of the use of her limbs, bed-ridden for a year and then died.

83. Pagitt, *Heresiography*, 46.

84. See *Wonderful news, from the North: being a true and perfect relation, of severall strange and wonderful apparitions seen in the ayr, between Madely and Whitmore, in the county palatine of Chester* (London: Printed for George Horton, 1651); *The Worlds Wonder: Being a True Relation of the strange and dredful Apparitions seen in the Air, on Tuesday last was seven-night, at New-Market Heath and in the Western Parts. Brought by the Post, to the Ram-Inn, in West-Smithfield; and published for general satisfaction* (George Horton, 1659); and *The twelve Wonders of England Being a most strange and wonderful Relation of the Death of Mr. Parrey, an Inn-keeper, living at the sign of the Bell at Temple-bar; And the manner how twelve Serpents were voided from him a little before his Death on Thursday last, some having heads like Toads and Horses, and others like Neuts and Dogs, to the great admiration of all that shall read the ensuing subject. Together with a Narrative of his Life and Death, his Memento and Character to all Christians; and other memorable Examples of most strange and wonderful Prodigies* (London: Printed for G. Horton, 1655).

85. *The Worlds Wonder*, 3–4.

86. See *The tryall of Mr. Love* (London: printed by R.W. for George Horton, 1651); *The Black and terrible Warning Piece, or a Scourge to Englands Rebellion. Truly Representing The horrible Iniquity of the Times; the dangerous Proceedings of the Ranters, and the holding of no Resurrection by the Shakers, in Yorkshire and elsewhere*; and *The Quakers terrible Vision; or The Devil's Progresse to the City of London* (London: Printed for G. Horton, in the great year of Quaking 1655), 127:E 835 [10].

87. Friedman claims that the "G.H." who published *The Declaration of John Robins* may be George Horton, who published *Ranters Monster* and *The Black and Terrible Warning Piece* (November 28, 1653) (*Blasphemy*, 54). See also J. C. Davis, *Fear, Myth and History*, 108.

88. *The Quakers terrible Vision*, 3, 4, 6.

89. *A Declaration from the Children of Light* (1655), title page, 3.

90. The claim was made by Matthew Hammondner of Norfolk (see Stowe, *Annales of England* [1592], 1173–74, cited in Levy, *Treason Against God*, 181). In 1596 Robert Fisher was prosecuted for stating "That Christe was no saviour & the gospell a fable" (Nokes, *A History of the Crime of Blasphemy*, 11).

91. *A Routing of the Ranters*, 2, cited in Levy, *Treason Against God*, 237.

92. Foucault, *Discipline and Punish*, 113.

93. The *OED* defines a fable as a "fictitious narrative or statement; a story not founded on fact, esp. A fictitious story relating to supernatural or extraordinary persons or incidents, and more or less current in popular belief; a myth or legend [. . .] A foolish or ridiculous story; idle talk, nonsense [. . .] A fiction invented to deceive; a fabrication, false-

hood [. . .] A short story devised to convey some useful lesson; esp. one in which animals or inanimate things are the speakers or actors."

94. David Hall makes a similar argument about the ways in which these stories became "weapons in a complex game of politics" (*Worlds of Wonder*, 94); and Daston and Park suggest that competing portents led to their discrediting (*Wonders and the Order of Nature*, 176).

95. J. S., *Teratologia: Or, A Discovery of Gods Wonders*, 16.

96. In Horton's other pamphlets, the figures of authority are mocked: devils appear in the forms of lawyers; ghosts, in the forms of bishops; seditious witches are shown, at the bench and in front of witnesses, to have done no more than provide "healthy food" to their purported victims. Horton, unlike William Leigh, was no zealot; he was a publisher interested in promoting his own pro-Parliament newspapers (one 1652 pamphlet on the trial of a woman for witchcraft ends with a reference to *The Faithful Scout*, which, "(God willing) will be extant on Friday" (*Trial of Joan Peterson*, 8). His loyalty to both Cromwell and Independency stopped with the Restoration. In 1660 he published a mocking pamphlet of Hugh Peters, Cromwell's Independent preacher, including a story of how Cromwell had once fallen asleep in church when Peters was preaching. See *Hugh Peter's Figaries: Or, His Merry Tales* (London: Printed for George Horton, 1660), p. 7.

CONCLUSION

1. The best account of this shift and the ways in which it involved the discrediting of formerly conventional Puritan ideas of providentialism is provided by Michael Winship, *Seers of God* (1996). See also David Hall, *Worlds of Wonder*, 106–10. While Winship shows how royalists and Restoration theologians attacked Puritans' use of providentialism, calling it superstitious and enthusiastic, John Spurr argues that the Restoration church itself made use of providence to sustain virtue, religion, and government: "Anglican preachers dwelt in morbid detail upon the 'controversy' between a wrathful God and an incorrigible nation, and they strove to associate the stability, even the fate, of the country with the reformation of national manners" ("'Virtue, Religion and Government,'" 30).

2. Burke, *Popular Culture in Early Modern Europe* (1999); and Natalie Zemon Davis, *Society and Culture in Early Modern France* (1965), esp. chap. 8, "Proverbial Wisdom and Popular Errors." See also Daston and Park, *Wonders and the Order of Nature*, 305.

3. The pamphlet reports that one day in July 1649, workmen in Herefordshire "heard the Crying of an Infant or a young child" and pulled him to safety from the sheaves (3). After the mowers feed him milk and flowers, the child prophesies that after three more years of war the land will "Flourish againe: And in that Field where hee was found shall bee a great and bloody Battell fought, greater then any yet hath beene in this Kingdome, where the young King CHARLES *the Second* of that name, shall get the day, and win the Field" (4–5). At the end of his prophecy, the child warns his listeners to "meddle not with them that are given to change" (5). *Vox Infantis* is a royalist parable prophesying a reunion of workers, land, and harvest under the tillage of the rightful king. As revolutionary change upset the economic basis of the propertied, the restoration of the king seemed to promise the restoration of the lands to their proper owners and productivity. The royalist voice of *Vox Infantis*'s providential child provides a divinely mandated prophecy for the outcome of revolution: when the king rules again, the lands will flourish.

4. *The English Devil: or Cromwell and his Monstrous Witch Discover'd at White Hall* (London, 1660), A2. Subsequent references will be cited parenthetically in the text.

5. *The true and most miraculous narrative, of a child born with two tongues* (London, 1659). All subsequent references will be cited parenthetically in the text.

6. Rather than a sign of dissembling, the two-tongued child attests to the Spirit's ability "to speak with other tongues" (Acts 2.3–4).

7. See Burford and Shulman, *Of Bridles and Burnings*, 50–61.

8. Ibid., 56. See also Mack, *Visionary Women*, 248.

9. On these women's public prophesies, see Mack, *Visionary Women*, 99–101.

10. See, for example, Henry Neville, *A parliament of ladies: with their lawes newly enacted.* ([London, s.n.], Printed in the yeer 1647).

11. The story appears in the 19–26 August 1659 edition (Raymond, ed., *Making the News*, 439).

12. *The Age of Wonder, or Miracles are not Ceased Being*, 3. All subsequent references will be cited parenthetically in the text.

13. *Eniaytos terastios Mirabilis annus, or The year of prodigies and wonders* (1661), A4v. All subsequent references will be cited parenthetically in the text.

14. For example, "A Canonical and Conformable Parson who had uttered a false and lying Divination was smitten with a Cancerous distemper in his mouth and Throat whereby his Tongue Rotted in his Head" (74).

15. *Mirabilis annus secundus, or, The Second Year of Prodigies* (1662), 43, 49–50 and 84.

16. *Mirabilis annus secundus*, 61–62.

17. On the publishers of the *Mirabilis* tracts and royalist attempts to stop and discredit them, see Greaves, *Deliver Us From Evil*, 207–25; and Whiting, *Studies in English Puritanism*, 549–50. On the women arrested, see Greaves, 213–25. According to one Sergeant Morton, the "raising of Tumults is the more Masculine, and Printing and Dispersing Seditious books, is the Feminine part of every Rebellion" (Greaves, *Deliver Us From Evil*, 225).

18. See Durston, "Signs and Wonders and the English Civil War," 28.

19. *Mirabilis annus secundus*, A4.

20. Durston, "Signs and Wonders," 28.

21. John Gadbury, *Britains Royal Star or An Astrological Demonstration of Englands Future Felicity* (1661), 4, 3. Jeffey, *The Lords Loud Call to England* (1660) includes, among others, the story of a pregnant woman who, after cursing Roundheads, Anabaptists, and Quakers, gives birth to a child with blue spots on its body (30). See also John Gadbury, *Dies Novissimus, or, Dooms-day Not so Near as Dreaded:* "It hath been the subtil aims and endeavours of *Impostors, Incendiaries* and *Deluders*, in all Ages, first to coyn, and then to spread Stories and Fables incredible and miraculous, upon the Understandings and Beliefs of the Vulgar (which are always the most credulous) sport of Men" (1). Other texts attacking the "Fanaticks" stories include: *The Phanaticke's Plot Discovered* (London, 1660), Robert Clarke's *The Lying Wonders, or rather the Wonderful Lyes* (London, 1660), and *A Perfect Narrative of the Phanatick Wonders Seen in the West of England* (London, 1660).

22. According to Gadbury, *The Lords Loud Call* was pure propaganda, designed by "Fanaticks" to "make the ignorant Readers believe, that God doth own the Anabaptists for his peculiar dear children" and published during the same week as the Anabaptists' Confession of Faith. "It is a strange kind of prejudice," Gadbury writes, "that forceth men to write Fictions, and publish them to the world in the place of truths, hoping thereby to support their dying and perishing Opinions" (18).

23. Spencer, *A Discourse Concerning Prophecies* (Bv). Subsequent references will be cited

parenthetically in the text. On Spencer, see Daston and Park, *Wonders and the Order of Nature*, 321; Winship, *Seers of God*, 38; and Burns, "'[O]ur lot is fallen into an Age of Wonders.'"

24. According to Winship, Spencer's response to the *Mirabilis* tracts in 1663 did not deny signs and wonders, but sought to "define them in such a way as to make them inaccessible to political use" (*Seers of God*, 38). Spencer reprehends "the common vanity of receiving [natural prodigies] as a kinde of indication in bodies Politicke" and the use of prodigies as "mercenary soldiers" (*Discourse Concerning Prophecies*, 5). At this moment, Spencer says, prodigies are the tools of "loosers [*sic*]" who are "not pleasd' with what pleaseth God, of a great change of affairs, in state" (ibid., 105).

25. This way of thinking was due to the human vanity that reduces "all natural operations to a likeness with the acts of men" and assumes that God is "continually altering [. . .] nature and making [. . .] signs" for human edification (22, 37). Heaven and earth, Spencer writes, are not "concern'd in the standing or falling of [humans'] little interests and perswasions" (96).

26. There are better guidelines for determining the righteousness of a given cause than prodigies, including Scripture, state laws, "the councels of wise and good men," and reason (89). Spencer said that if he did believe that all strange accidents were the warnings of heaven, he would institute Colleges, as the Romans had, "which should profess themselves *Prodigiorum Interpretes* and should be ready to offer to the world the most trusty rules and Principles" (33). As it is, we cannot "receive them (without any *Interpreter* to explain their languages) as a kind of Divine messengers to bring us news from Heaven" (46).

27. Spencer, *A Discourse Concerning Vulgar Prophecies*, A2v. Subsequent references are cited parenthetically in the text. John Gadbury similarly condemned those who "pretend to believe they have a certain prescience of [. . .] things, either by Revelation from the Spirit, as they (sometimes blasphemously) word it: or else from the observation they seem to make of certain Apparitions or Prodigies" (*Dies Novissimus*, 18). Their "prodigies" are not the result of "supernatural cause"; they are the result of melancholy, or "villainy," the manipulative or deluded tools of "the Enthusiasts and Discontents of this Age" (19, 22). Henry More also claimed that the "strength of imagination" over Reason and Understanding, can make men think they are "*God the Father, the Messias, the Holy Ghost* [. . .] and the like" (*Enthusiasmus Triumphatus, or A Discourse of The Nature, Causes, Kinds and Cure of Enthusiasme*, 5). "Enthusiasme is nothing else but a misconceit of being inspired. Now to be inspired, is to be moved in an extraordinary manner by the power or spirit of God to act, speak, or think what is holy, just and true" (ibid., 2).

28. He made this claim on October 28, 1671; cited in Mack, *Visionary Women*, 279.

29. Gadbury singled out Hannah Trapnel (a Fifth Monarchist) and Dorcas Erbury (a Quaker) for attack (on both, see Mack, *Visionary Women*, 198). In *The Holy Sister's Conspiracy against their Husbands, and the City of London*, the Fifth Monarchist women claim to do everything at the urging of the Spirit, but their defense of the "liberty of Conscience" is simply a desire for sexual liberty ("We will not be Wives / And tye up our Love / To Villainous slaverie; / But couple in love and feare; / When mov'd by the spirit to't), and their "zeales" are enflamed by liquor (4). They threaten to "[c]ut the throats of such of our Husbands, as are Kinglings for the Man in Power, and Enemies to the Brethren" and who call them "Scismatick and Fanatick and Whore" (8).

30. Casaubon, *A Treatise Concerning Enthusiasm*, 9, 75, 157.

31. More, *Enthusiasmus Triumphatus*, 198, 99. More also named the Quakers "the most

Melancholy Sect that ever was yet in the world." Michael Heyd's *"So Sober and Reasonable"* (1995) reveals that the medical linking of inspiration, or "enthusiasm" to melancholy or mental illness was not in itself new. What was new was "the systematic employment of such arguments by ministers and divines, both in England and on the Continent" (7). Frustratingly, Heyd says nothing about the persistent gendering of enthusiasm.

32. Spencer, *A Discourse Concerning Prodigies*, A4. Subsequent references in the text.

33. It was precisely this debate over the role of maternal imagination that engaged Daniel Turner and James Blondel in the first two decades of the eighteenth century (Huet, *Monstrous Imagination*, 64–70). Belief in the maternal imagination was also the animating explanation for the famous case of Mary Toft, the woman who purportedly gave birth to seventeen rabbits and became a cause célèbre of both doctors and satirists in the 1720s. See Todd, *Imagining Monsters* (1995).

34. John Aubrey, *Three Prose Works*, 102. "Before printing, Old Wives's Tales were in-geniouse [. . .] Now a dayes, books are common, and most of the poor people understand letters; and the many good books and variety of turnes of affairs, have putt all the old Fa-bles out of doors" (102). "Old customes and old wives' fables are gross things: but yet ought not to be quite rejected: there may some truth and usefulness be elicited out of them: besides 'tis a pleasure to consider the Errours that enveloped former ages: as also the present." Under the definitions for fable, the *OED* includes: "A foolish or ridiculous story; idle talk, nonsense; esp. in phr. old wives' (women's) fables (arch.). Also to take (something) for fable, to hold at fable (transl. OF. tenir a fable). 1605 BACON Adv. Learn. I. iv. §9 After a . . time . . they [narrations of miracles] grew to be esteemed but as old wives' fables.

35. In his introduction to *Anecdotes and Traditions Illustrative of Early English History and Literature* (1839), to take but one example, William J. Thomas writes: "The fabulous history of every country is part of its history, and ought not to be omitted by later and more enlightened historians; because it has been believed at one time, and while it was believed it influenced the imagination, and there by, in some degree, the opinions and character of the people."

36. In *Wonders and the Order of Nature*, Daston and Park have convincingly both pro-posed and queried the historical narrative that took monsters from prodigies, to wonders, to the subjects of natural science; see especially p. 176.

37. Daston and Park argue that there were concerted efforts to emphasize "the de-lights of natural wonders at the expense of awe-inspiring divine interventions. Thus do-mesticated, wonder excited the contemplation and admiration of God's works rather than terror at his wrath" (336).

38. *Near Charing Cross, over against Northumberland (alias Suffolk) House, at a turners house, nigh the Golden Lyon Tavern, is to be seen the wonder of this present age* (1687). The au-thor of *Strange and Wonderful News of the Birth of a Monstrous Child With Two Heads and Three Arms* also refers to a surgeon's dissection.

39. The first broadsheet is *A Letter from an Eminent Merchant in Ostend, Containing an Account of a Strange and Monstrous Birth hapned there* (1682), and the second is *A True Re-lation of Two Prodigious Births, The like not hapning in many Generations, the signification whereof is left to the judicious to contemplate* (1680).

40. Spencer, *A Discourse Concerning Prodigies*, 34.

41. As David Hall writes: "Even though the wonder became fictive in the hands of printers, and though partisans of different causes shamelessly politicized the process of

interpretation, people never stopped believing that God signaled his intentions through extraordinary events" (*Worlds of Wonder,* 114).

42. The Folger copy of *The strange monster or, true news from Nottingham-shire* includes an image of the Middleton Stony monster cut and pasted from Lycosthenes. The narrative itself mentions several of the monster stories discussed in this book, including the Middleton Stony, Chichester, and Standish monsters. In addition the Folger Library owns an eighteenth-century bound compilation of a number of pamphlets, including *The strange monster* and STC 15428, STC 20863.5, STC 1791.2, Wing D602, Wing T2511.5, Wing B4610.2, Wing S5884.5, and an eighteenth-century title.

43. "One could not have absolute conviction regarding the mind of God" (Winship, *Seers of God,* 35). Walsham argues that people came to regard monsters "less as menacing tokens than [as] examples of the benevolence of the Creator and the fecundity of Nature, specimens suitable for anatomical and embryological analysis, objects of a complex curiosity largely divorced from pious apprehension" (*Providence in Early Modern England,* 222), yet as I hope I have shown, there was no comprehensive erasure of pious or politicized interpretations.

44. Foucault, *The Order of Things,* 40 n. 45.

45. Spencer, *A Discourse Concerning Prodigies,* 43. This view was not new. In his *Prodigies & Apparitions* (1643), Vicars writes that "some say with Naturalists and Philosophers" that a prodigious birth is "but a deficiencie and weaknesse of nature." This view, however, is the objection of "a meere naturalist and carnall man, who is willing only to look upon externall and secondary causes, not considering the wonders and operations of Gods hands" (23). Gadbury concurred: "[T]hings which seem strange are derived from natural causes, and also include God the chief and best cause of all things" (*Natura Prodigiorum,* 22).

46. Heywood, *The Rev. Oliver Heywood,* 2:278.

47. Winship argues that the dissenters' relationship to providence remained actively divinatory (*Seers of God,* 59–60).

48. *A Discourse Concerning Prophecies,* 4, 101. See also *A Compleat History of the most remarkable Providences* (1697), compiled by William Turner, the Vicar of Walberton in Sussex, which claims that compilations of prodigies are "one of the best methods that can be pursued against the abounding atheism of the age" (cited in Keith Thomas, *Religion and the Decline of Magic,* 95).

Bibliography

PRIMARY SOURCES

The age of vvonders, or miracles are not ceased. Being A true but strange relation of a child born at Burslem in Stafford-Shire, who, before it was three quarters old, spake and prophesied strange and wonderful things touching the King, three nights together, contained in the ensuring relation, as it was affirmed in a letter by Mr. Colclough, justice of the peace, to Colonel Pury, and attested upon oath by Elizabeth Locket and her husband, the childs nurse. With divers other remarkable predictions, signes and wonders, in relation to monarchy, and the child born with three crowns. London: Printed for Nehemiah Chamberlain, and are to be sold at the East end of St. Pauls, 1660.

Aristotle. *Generation of Animals.* Trans. A. L. Peck. Cambridge, MA: Harvard University Press, 1979.

Ashton, Robert, ed. *James I by His Contemporaries.* London: Hutchinson, 1969.

Assheton, Nicholas. *The Journal of Nicholas Assheton of Downham in the County of Lancaster for Part of the year 1617 and part of the year following.* Ed. Rev. F. R. Raines. Printed for the Chetham Society, 1854.

Aubrey, John. *Three Prose Works.* Ed. John Buchanan-Brown. Carbondale: Southern Illinois Press, 1972.

Awdeley, John. *The forme and shape of a Monstrous Child, borne at Maydstone in Kent, the xxiii of October 1568.* Imprinted at London: By John Awdeley, dwellyng in little Britain streete without Aldersgate, the xxiij of December, 1568. STC 2nd ed./ 17194.

Bale, John. *Select Works of John Bale: Containing the Examination of Lord Cobham, William Thorpe, and Anne Askew.* Edited for the Parker Society by the Rev. Henry Christmas. New York: Johnson Reprint Corp., 1968.

Barker, John. *The true description of a monsterous chylde borne in the Ile of Wight, in this present yeare of oure Lord God, M.D. LXIIII the month of October, after this forme with a cluster of longe heare about the nauell, the fathers name is James Johnsun, in the parys of Freswater.* Imprinted at London: In Fletestrete: at the sygne of Faucon, by Wylliam Gryffith, and are to be solde at his shope in saint Dunstons churchyarde, in the west of London, the .viii. daye of Nouember [1564]. STC 2nd ed., 1422.

Batman, Stephen. *The Doome Warning All Men to the Judgment.* 1581. Intro. by John R. McNair. Scholars' Facsimiles & Reprints, 1984.

Baillie, Robert. *Anabaptisme, the true Fountaine of Independency, Brownisme, Antinomy, Familisme, and most of the other errours which for the time doe trouble the Church of England.* London: Printed by M. F. for Samuel Gellibrand, at the Brazen serpent in Pauls Church-yard, 1647.

Beard, Thomas. *The Theatre of Gods Iudgements. Wherein is represented the admirable iustice of God against all notorious sinners, both great and small, but especially against the most eminent persons of the world, whose transcendent power breaketh though the barres of humane justice; deduced by the order of the Commaundements. Collected out of Sacred, Ecclesiasticall, and prophane Histories. Thomas Beard, Bachelor of Divinitie, and Preacher of the word of God in the Towne of Huntington.* London: Printed by Adam Islip, 1612. STC 1660.

Bedford, Thomas. *A True and Certaine Relation of a Strange Birth which was borne at Stonehouse in the Parish of Plinmouth, the 20 of October 1635. Together with the Notes of a Sermon, preached Octob. 22 1635 in the Church of Plinmouth, at the interring of the sayd Birth.* London: Printed by Anne Griffin for Anne Bowler dwelling at the Marigold in S. Pauls Church-yard. 1635. STC (2nd ed.) 1791.

Bennett, J. H. E., and J. C. Dewhurst, eds. *Quarter Sessions Records with Other Records of the Justices of the Peace for the County Palatine of Chester 1559–1760.* Record Society of Lancashire and Cheshire, 1940.

Bible. The Authorized King James Version. Ed. Robert Carroll and Stephen Prickett. Oxford: Oxford University Press, 1997.

Bloody News from Dover. Being a True Relation of the Great and Bloudy Murder, Committed by Mary Champion (an Anabaptist) Who Cut off Her Childs Head, being 7 weekes old, and held it to her husband to baptize. 1647. Thomason E.375[20].

The Book of Common Prayer. 1662 Version. With an introduction by Diarmaid MacCulloch. London: David Campbell, 1999.

Brathwait, Richard. *The English gentlewoman drawne out to the full body: expressing, what habiliments doe best attire her, what ornaments do best adorne her, what compliments doe best accomplish her.* London: Printed by B. Alsop and T. Fawcet, for Michael Sparke, dwelling in Green Harbor, 1631. STC 3565.5.

Bray, Gerald, ed. *Documents of the English Reformation.* Cambridge: James Clarke & Co, 1994.

Bull, Henry. *Christian Prayers and Holy Meditations. Collected by Henry Bull* (1566). Cambridge University Press, 1842.

Casaubon, Meric. *A Treatise Concerning Enthusiasm, as it is an effect of nature: but is mistaken by many for either divine inspiration, or diabolical possession.* London: R.D. for Tho. Johnson, 1655.

Certaine Sermons appointed by the Quenes Maiesty, to be declared and read, by al Parsons, Vicars, & Citrates, everi Sunday and holiday, in their Churche. Imprinted at London: In Powles Churcheyard, by Richard Jugge and Iohn Cawood, printers to the Quenes Maiestie, 1563, STC 13651 (from p 250 N. 11).

Certaine Sermons or Homilies appointed to be read in Churches, In the time of Late Queen Elizabeth of Famous Memory (London, 1623), at www.library.utoronto.ca/utel/elizhom .html, based on the textual facsimile in *Certaine Sermons,* ed. Mary Ellen Rickey and Thomas B. Stroup. Gainesville, FL: Scholars' Facsimiles, 1968.

Conjoined twins born in Middleton Stoney. Imprinted at London by Jhon Daye dwellinge over Aldersgate beneth S. Martyns, 1552.

Coppin, Richard. *A Man-Child Born, or God Manifest in Flesh. Wherein is discovered, how God, or the eternal being, always dwels, inhabits, is revealed and brought forth in flesh, in ages and generations that ever were, are, or shall be, world without end. The mysterie of both father, mother, husband, and son, Of himself and us, of we the spouse of God and mother of Jesus, his being born of the Virgin Mary in flesh, a sign, his being born in us, the substance, also our being with child, and giving suck to any but Christ, and the woe that comes by it.* London, 1654.

Crawford, Patricia and Laura Gowing, eds. *Women's Worlds in Seventeenth-Century England: A Sourcebook* New York: Routledge, 2000.

Crowley, Robert *A briefe discourse against the outwarde apparell and ministring garmentes of the popishe church* [Emden: Printed by Egidius van der Erve], 1566, STC (2nd ed.) 6079.

D., John. *A discription of a monstrous Chylde, borne at Chychester in Sussex, the xxiiii. daye of May. This being the very length, and bygnes of the same. MCCCCLXII.* Imprynted at London, by Leonard Orkel for Fraunces Godlys. In the yeare of oure Lorde, 1562. Huth 50 (33) STC 6177.

Davies, John. *A scourge for paper-persecutors. Or Papers complaint, compil'd in ruthful rimes, against the paper-spoylers of these times. By I.D. With a continu'd iust inquisition of the same subject, fit this season. Against paper-persecutors. By A.H.* Printed at London: for H. H[olland] and G. G[ibbs] and are to be sold at the Golden Flower Deluce in Popes-head Alley, 1625. STC (2nd ed.) 6340.

A Declaration from the Children of Light. London: Printed for Giles Calvert at the Black-Spread- Eagle at the West end of Pauls, 1655.

A declaration of a strange and wonderfull monster: born in Kirkham parish in Lancashire (the childe of Mrs. Haughton, a Popish gentlewoman) the face of it upon the breast, and without a head (after the mother had wished rather to bear a childe without a head then a Roundhead) and had curst the Parliamnet [sic]. Attested by Mr. Fleetwood, minister of the same parish, under his own hand; and Mrs. Gattaker the mid-wife, and divers other eye-witnesses: whose testimony was brought up by a member of the House of Commons. Appointed to be printed according to order: and desired to be published in all the counties, cities, townes, and parishes in England: being the same copies that were presented to the Parliament. London: Printed by Jane Coe, 1646. Thomason 53:E 325[20].

A Description of a Sect Called the Familie of Love: With Their Common Place of Residence. Being Discovered by Mrs. Susannah Snow of Pirford near Chersey in the County of Surrey, Who was Vainly Led Away for a Time through Their Base Allurements. London, 1641.

Diary of Walter Yonge, Justice of the Peace and MP for Honiton, 1604–1628, ed. George Roberts. London: Camden Society, 1848.

A discoverie of six women preachers, in Middlesex, Kent, Cambridgshire, and Salisbury. VVith a relation of their names, manners, life, and doctrine, pleasant to be read, but horrid to be judged of their names are these. Anne Hempstall. Mary Bilbrow. Ioane Bauford. Susan May. Elizab. Bancroft. Arabella Thomas. [London, s.n.], Printed, 1641.

Dod, John, and Robert Cleaver, *Seuen godlie and fruitful sermons. The six first preached by Master Iohn Kod: the last by Master Robert Cleauer. Whereunto is annexed, a brief discourse, touching, 1. Extinguishing of the spirit, 2. Murmuring in affliction.* At London: Imprinted by Felix Kyngston for William Wlby, and are to be sold at his shop in Pauls Churchyard, at the signe of the Swan, 1614, STC (2nd ed.) 6944.

———. *The dolefull Lamentation of Cheap-side Crosse: Or Old England sick of the Staggers.* London, 1642.

Duff, E. Gordon. *A century of the English book trade. Short notices of all printers, stationers, book-binders, and other connected with it from the issue of the first dated book in 1457 to the incorporation of the Company of stationers in 1557.* London: Bibliographical Society, 1948.

Dugdale, Sir William. *The Visitation of the County Palatine of Lancaster, Made in the year 1664–5.* Ed. Rev. F. R. Raines, Part II. Vol. 85. Printed for the Chetham Society, 1872.

Edwards, Thomas. *Gangraena*. Ed. M. M. Goldsmith and Ivan Roots. The Rota and the University of Exeter, 1977.

Elderton, William. *The true fourme and shape of a monsterous chyld, whiche was borne in Stony Stratforde, in North Hampton shire.* Imprinted at London: In Fletestrete beneath the Conduit: at the signe of S. Iohn Euangelist, by Thomas Colwell, 1565. STC (2nd ed.) 7565.

Ellis, Humphrey. *Pseudochristus: or, A true and faithful relation of the grand impostures, horrid blasphemies, abominable practises gross deceits; lately spread abroad and acted in the county of Southampton, by William Frankelin and Mary Gadbury, and their companions. The one most blasphemously professing and asserting himself to be the Christ, the Messiah, the Son of God who dyed and was crucified at Jerusalem for the sins of the people of God. The other as wickedly professing and asserting her self to be the Spouse of Christ, called, the Lady Mary, the Queen, and Bride, and Lambs Wife. Together with the visions and revelations, to which they did pretend their ways of deceiving, with the names and actions of sundry persons deceived by them. As also their examinations and confessions before the justices of the peace, their imprisonment, and their tryal before the judg of assize, at the last assize holden at Winchester, March 7. 1649. . . . By Humphry Ellis, minister of the word in the city of Winton.* London: printed by John Macock, for Luke Fawn, and are to be sold at his shop at the sign of the Parrot in Pauls Church-yard, 1650. Thomason, E.602[12].

The English devil: or, Cromwel and his monstrous witch discover'd at White-Hall. London: printed by Robert Wood, for George Horton; and are to be sold at the Royal Exchange in Cornhill, 1660.

Eyre, G. E. B., and C. R. Rivington, *A Transcript of the Registers of the Company of Stationers of London, 1640–1708.* 3 vols. London, 1915.

Fenton, Edward. *Certaine Secrete wonders of Nature, containing a description of sundry strange things, seming monstrous in our eyes and judgement, bicause we are not privie to the reasons of them. Gathered out of divers learned authors as well Greeke as Latine, sacred as prophane.* By E. Fenton. London, 1569. STC 10787.

Firth, Charles H., and R. S. Rait. *Acts and Ordinances of the Interregnum, 1642–1660.* 3 vols. London: His Majesty's Stationery Office, 1911.

Forset, Edward. *Comparative Discourse of the Bodies Natural and Politique Wherein out of the principles of Nature, is set forth the true forme of a Commonweale, with the dutie of Subjects, and the right of the Soveraigne: together with many good points of Politicall learning, mentioned in a Briefe after the Preface* London: Printed for John Bill, 1606, STC 11188.

Foxe, John. *Actes and monuments of matters most speciall and memorable, happening in the Church: with an vniuersall historie of the same: wherein is set forth in large the whole race and course of the Church from the primitiue age to these later times.* 2 vols. London, 1610.

Gadbury, John. *Britains royal star, Or An astrological demonstration of England's future felicity.* London: printed for Sam Speed, at the signe of the Printing-Press in St. Paul's Church-yard, 1661 [i.e., 1660].

———. *Dies Novissimus, or, Dooms-day Not so Near as Dreaded.* London: Printed by James Cottrel, 1664.

———. *Natura prodigiorum: or, A discourse touching the nature of prodigies. Together with the kinds, causes and effects, of comets, eclipses, and earthquakes. With an appendix touching the imposturism of the commonly-received doctrine of prophecies, spirits, images, sigils, lamens, the christal, &c. and the propugners of such opinions. By John Gadbury philoma theomatikos and publisher*. London: Printed by J. C. for Fr. Cossinet, at the Anchor and Mariner in Tower-street; and Tho. Basset in St. Dunstans-Church-yard in Fleetstreet, 1660.

Gataker, Thomas. *Antinomianism Discovered and Confuted: And Free-Grace As it is held forth in Gods Word*. London, 1652.

Gods handy-vvorke in vvonders. Miraculously shewen vpon two women, lately delivered of two monsters: with a most strange and terrible earth-quake, by which, fields and other grounds, were quite remoued to other places: the prodigious births, being at a place called Perre-farme, within a quarter of a mile of Feuersham in Kent, the 25. of Iuly last, being S. Iames his day. 1615. London: Printed for I. W., 1615. STC 11926.

Gosson, Stephen. *Pleasant quippes for vpstart newfangled gentlevvomen*. Imprinted at London: By Richard Ihones, at the signe of the Rose & Crowne, neere to S. Andrewes Church in Holborne, 1595. STC 12096.

Greg, W. W., C. P. Blagden, and I. G. Phillip, eds. *A Companion to Arber: Being a Calendar of Documents in Edward Arber's Transcript of the Registers of the Company of Stationers of London 1554–1640 with Text and Calendar of Supplementary Documents*. London: Oxford University Press, 1967.

H., B. *The glasse of mans folly and meanes to amendment of life. This glasse of our folly, is that we may knowe, the cause of the crueltie which among people flowe*. London: Printed by E. A[llde] for William Barley, and are to be solde at his shop in Gratious street, neere vnto Leaden Hall, 1595. STC (2nd ed.) 1256.

H., G. *The declaration of John Robins, the false prophet*. London: Printed by R. Wood, 1651. Thomason E.629 [13].

Harrison, William. *The Description of England: The Classic Contemporary Account of Tudor Social Life*. Ed. George Edelen. Washington: Folger Shakespeare Library, 1968.

Hayward, Sir John. *Annals of the first four years of the Reign of Queen Elizabeth*. Edited from a ms. in the Harleian Collection by John Bruce. Camden Society, ser. no. 1, 7; New York: Johnson Reprint Corp, 1968.

Heywood, Oliver. *The Rev. Oliver Heywood 1630–1702. His Autobiography, Diaries, Anecdote and Event Books; Illustrating the General and Family History of Yorkshire and Lancashire*. Ed. J. Horsfall Tuner. London, 1881.

Hilliard, John. *Fire from Heaven. Burning the body of one John Hitchell of Holne-hurst, within the parish of Christ-church, in the County of South-hampton the 26 of June last 1613 who by the same was consumed to ashes, and no fire seene, lying therein smoaking and smothering three dayes and three nights, not to bequenched by water, nor the help of mans hand. With the lamentable burning of his house and one childe, and the grievous scorching of his wife: with the birth of a Monster, and many other strange things hapning about the same time: the like was never seene nor heard of. Written by John Hilliard Preacher of the word of life in Sopley. Reade and tremble. With the fearefull burning of the towne of Corchester upon Friday the 6. Of August last 1613*. Printed at London for John Trundle, and are to be sold at his shop in Barbycan at the signe of Nobody. 1613. STC 13507.

The Holy Sister's Conspiracy against their Husbands, and the City of London, designed at their last Farewell of their Meeting-houses in Coleman-street; together with their Psalm of mercy. London: Printed by T.M. 1661.

Hopton, Andrew, ed. *The Declaration of John Robins and other writings*. London: Aporia Press, 1992.

Humphrey, Lawrence. *A View of the Romish Hydra and Monster, Traison, Against the Lords*

Annointed: Condemned by David, I. SAM,. 26. and Nowe confuted in seven Sermons: To Per-suade Obedience to Princes, Concord among our selves, and a generall Reformation and Re-pentance in all states. Oxford. Printed by Joseph Barnes and are to be solde in Paules Church-yearde at the signe of the Tygershead, 1588.

James I. *The Political Works of James I.* Ed. Charles Howard McIlwain. New York: Russell & Russell, 1965.

James VI and I. *Political Writings.* Ed. Johann P. Sommerville. Cambridge: Cambridge University Press, 1994.

Jeffey, Henry. *The Lords Loud Call to England: Being a True Relation of some late, Various, and Wonderful Judgements, or Handy-works of God.* London, 1660.

Jones, Sampson. *Vox Infantis, or The Propheticall Child. Being a true Relation of an Infant that was found in a Field, neere Lempster, in Herefordshire, July 16 1649. That did Declare and Fore-tell of many Strange things that Shall ensure in England and Ireland, within the space of three yeeres. Concerning the Crowning of Charles the second King of England, Scotland, and Ireland; His great Victories, with the Destruction of this present Parliament and Army; and many other passages touching the Death of our late King.* London: [s.n.], 1649. Thoma-son 87: E566 [27].

Kinney, Arthur F., ed. *Rogues, Vagabonds and Sturdy Beggars: A New Gallery of Tudor and Early Stuart Rogue Literature.* University of Massachusetts Press, 1990.

Lanquet, Thomas, and Thomas Cooper. *[Epitome of chronicles] Coopers chronicle contenynge the vvhole discourse of the histories as well of thys realme, as all other countreis. with the suc-cession of theyr kynges, the tyme of theyr raign, and what notable actes were done by the[m] newely enlarged and augmented as well in the first parte wyth diuers profitable historries. as in the latter ende wyth the whole summe of those thynges that Paulus Iouius and Sleigdane hath written of late yers that is, now lately ouersene and with great dilligence corrected and augmented vnto the. vii. yere of the raigne of our most gracious Quene Elizabeth that nowe is.* [London: s.n.], Anno. 1565. the first day of Auguste. STC (2nd ed.) 15220.

La Perrière, Guillaume de. *The Theater of Fine Devices, containing an hundred morall Em-blemes. First penned in French, and translated into English by Thomas Combe.* London, 1614. STC 15230.

Leigh, William. *Strange Newes of a prodigious Monster, borne in the Towneship of Adlington in the Parish of Standish in the Countie of Lancaster, the 17 day of Aprill last, 1613. Testi-fied by the Reverend Divine Mr. W. Leigh, Bachelor of Divinitie, and Preacher of Gods word at Standish aforesaid.* Printed by I. P. for S.M. and are to be sold at his Shop in Pauls Church-yard at the Signe of the Bull, 1613. STC 15428.

———. *The Dampe of Death: Beaten back with the glorious light & life of Jesus Christ in a Ser-mon Preached at Lancaster Assizes in Lent last.* London: Printed by Tho. Creede for Ar-thur Johnson, dwelling in Pauls Churchyard at the signe of the white horse, 1613.

———. *The drumme of devotion, striking out an allarum to prayer, by signes in heaven, and prodigies on earth. Together with the perfume of prayer. In two sermons, preached by William Leigh, Bachelor in Divinitie and pastor of Standish in Lancashire.* London: Printed by Tho: Creede, for Arthur Johnson, dwelling in Pauls Churchyard, at the signe of the white Horse, 1613. STC 15423.7.

A Letter from an Eminent Merchant in Ostend, Containing an Account of a Strange and Mon-strous Birth hapned there. London: Printed for J. Stans, and Sold by R. Janeway, 1682.

A List of some of the Grand Blasphemers and Blasphemies, Which was given in to The Commit-

tee for Religion. Very fit to be taken notice of, Upon the occasion of the day of Publicke Fasting and Humiliation. London: Printed by Robert Ibbitson, 1654. Thomason 669.f.17 [80].

Liturgical Services: Liturgies and Occasional Forms of Prayer Set Forth in the Reign of Queen Elizabeth. Ed. William Keatinge Clay. Cambridge: Parker Society, 1847.

Locke, John, Cleric. A strange and lamentable accident that happened lately at Mears-Ashby in Northamptonshire. 1642. Of one Mary Wilmore, wife to Iohn Wilmore rough mason, who was delivered of a childe without a head, and credibly reported to have a firme crosse on the brest, as this ensuing story shall relate. Printed at London: for Rich: Harper and Thomas Wine, and are to be sold at the Bible and Harpe in Smithfield, 1642. Thomason E.113[15].

Lycosthenes, Conrad. Prodigiorum ac ostentorum Chronicon. Bale, 1557.

Machyn, Henry. The Diary of Henry Machyn, citizen and merchant-tailor of London, from AD 1550 to AD 1563. Ed. John Gough Nichols. London: Printed for the Camden Society by J. B. Nichols and Son, 1848.

Mellys, John. The true description of two monsterous children, laufully begotten between George Steuens and Margerie his wyfe, and borne in the parish of Swanburne in Buckingham shyre, the. iiii. of Aprill. anno Domini. 1566. the two children hauing both their belies fast ioyned together, and imbracyng one another with their armes: which children wer both a lyue by the space of half an hower, and wer baptized, and named the one John, and the other Joan. Imprinted at London: by Alexander Lacy, for William Lewes: dwellyng in Cow lane aboue Holborne cundit, ouer against the signe of the Plough, 1566. STC (2nd ed.), 17803.

[Eniaytos terastios] Mirabilis annus, or The year of prodigies and wonders being a faithful and impartial collection of severall signs that have ben seen in the heavens, in the earth, and in the waters; together with many remarkable accidents, and judgements befalling divers persons, according as they have been testified by very credible hands: all of which have happened within the space of one year last past, and are now made publick for a seasonable warning to the people of these three kingdoms speedily to repent and turn to the Lord, whose hand is lifted up amongst us. [London: s.n.], 1661. Wing (CD-ROM, 1996) / E3127.

Mirabilis annus secundus or The second part of the second years prodigies being a true additional collection of many strange signs and apparitions which have this last year been seen in the heavens, and in the earth, and in the waters: together with many remarkable accidents and signal judgments which have befell divers persons who have apostatized from the truth, and have been persecutors of the Lord's faithful servants: published as a warning to all, speedily to repent, and to meet the Lord in the way of His judgments. [London?: s.n.], 1662. Wing / M2204.

Mirabilis annus secundus or the Second Part of the Second Years Prodigies. London 1662, Wing M2204.

The Miracle of Miracles Being a full and true account of Sarah Smith who lately was an inhabitant of Darken Parish in Essex, that brought to bed of a strange monster. London, 1715.

More, Henry. Enthusiasmus Triumphatus, or A Discourse of The Nature, Causes, Kinds and Cure of Enthusiasme. London: Printed by F. Flesher, and are to be sold by W. Morden, Bookseller in Cambridge, 1656.

The most strange and wounderfull apperation of blood in a poole at Garraton in Leicester-shire, which continued for the space of foure dayes, the rednesse of the colour for the space of those foure dayes every day increasing higher and higher, to the infinet amazement of many hundreds of beholders of all degrees and conditions, who have dipped their handketchers in this bloody *poole, . . . As also the true relation of a miraculous and prodigious birth in Shoo-lane, where one Mistris Browne a cuttlers wife was delivered of a monster without a head or feet, and in stead of a head had a hollow out of which a child did proceed, which was little but lovely, perfect in all but very spare and leane. As also the Kings sending to his Parliament for hostage for the security of his person to come unto London and to sit with his parliament for the composing the diffirences in the kingdome.* Printed at London, by I.H. [1645].

Muggleton, Lodowick. *The Acts of the Witnesses of the Spirit.* London, 1699.

A myraculous, and Monstrous, but yet most true, and certayne discourse, of a Woman (now to be seene in London) of the age of threescore yeares, or there abouts, in the midst Of whose forehead (by the wonderfull worke of God) there groweth out a crooked Horne, of foure ynches long. Imprinted at London by Thomas Orwin, and are to be sold by Edward White, dwelling at the little North dore of Paules Church, at the Signe of the Gun. 1588. STC 69107.

Near Charing Cross, over against Northumberland (alias Suffolk) House, at a turners house, nigh the Golden Lyon Tavern, is to be seen the wonder of this present age. London: Printed by T. James at the printing-press in Mincing-lane, 1687, Wing (2nd ed.) N362.

Ormerod, George, ed. *Tracts Relating to Military Proceedings in Lancashire During the Great Civil War.* Printed for the Chetham Society, 1844.

Pagitt, Ephraim. *Heresiography: or, a description of the heretickes and sectaries of these latter times. By E. P.* London, 1654. Wing P180.

Paré, Ambroise. *Des monstres et prodiges.* 1573. Ed. Jean Céard. Geneva: Librarie Droz, 1971.

———. *On Monsters and Marvels.* Translated with an Introduction and notes by Janis L. Pallister. Chicago: University of Chicago Press, 1982.

The Pepys Ballads. Ed. H. E. Rollins, 8 vols. Cambridge, MA: Harvard University Press, 1929–31.

Perkins, William. *The Works.* [Cambridge]: Printed by John Legate, printer to the Universitie of Cambridge, 1608.

Ponet, John. *A shorte treatise of politike pouuer and of the true obedience which subiectes owe to kynges and other ciuile gouernours, with an exhortacion to all true naturall Englishe men.* Strasbourg: Printed by the heirs of W. Köpfel, 1556. STC 20178.

Porta, John Baptista. *Natural Magick.* London, 1658.

Pricket, Robert. *The Iesuits Miracles, or new Popish Wonders. Containing the Straw, the Crowne, and the Wondrous Child, with the confutation of them and their follies.* Printed at London: [By Nicholas Okes] for C. P[urset] and R. I[ackson] and are to be sold at his shop in Fleetstreet neere the Conduit, 1607. STC 20340I.

Prynne, William. *A New Discovery of the Prelates Tyranny In their late prosecution of Mr William Prynne, and eminent Lawyer, Dr. John Bastwick, a leaned Physitian and M. Henry Burton a reverend Divine.* London, 1641.

The Quakers terrible Vision; or The Devil's Progresse to the City of London. London: Printed for G. Horton, in the great year of Quaking 1655. Thomason 127:E 835 [10].

R., I. *A most straunge, and true discourse, of the wonderfull iudgement of God. Of a monstrous, deformed infant, begotten by incestuous copulation, betweene the brothers sonne and the sisters daughter, being both vnmarried persons. Which childe was borne at Colwall, in the country and diocese of Hereford, vpon the sixt day of Ianuary last, being the feast of the Epiphany, commonly called Twelfth day. A notable and most terrible example against incest and whoredome.* Imprinted at London, By E. Allde for Richard Iones, 1600.

The ranters monster: being a true relation of one Mary Adams, living at Tillingham in Essex, who named her self the Virgin Mary, blasphemously affirming that she was conceived with child by the Holy Ghost; that from her should spring forth the savior of the world; and that all those that did not believe in him were damn'd: with the manner how she was deliver'd of the ugliest ill-shapen monster that ever eyes beheld, and afterwards rotted away in prison: to the great admiration of all those that shall read the ensuing subject; the like never before heard of. London, printed for Geoge [*sic*] Horton, 1652. Thomason E.658[6].

Raymond, Joad, ed. *Making the News: An Anthology of the Newsbooks of Revolutionary England, 1641–1660*. New York: St. Martin's Press, 1993.

Reeve, J. *A Transcendent Spiritual Treatise upon several heavenly doctrines*. London: Printed for the author, 1652.

The Registers of the Parish Church of Standish in the County of Lancaster, 1560–1653. Transcription by Henry Brierly. Cambridge: University Press for the Lancashire Parish Register Society, 1912.

Robinson, Edward (?). *A Discourse of the Warr in Lancashire*. Ed. William Beamont. Chetham Society, 1864.

Rollins, Hyder E., ed. *Cavalier and Puritan: Ballads and Broadsides Illustrating the Period of the Great Rebellion, 1640–1660*. New York: New York University Press, 1923.

———. *The Pack of Autolycus, or Strange and Terrible News of Ghosts, Apparitions . . . as Told in the Broadside Ballads of the Years 1624–1693*. 1927. Cambridge: Harvard University Press, 1969.

Rous, John. *The Diary of John Rous*. Ed. M. A. Everett Green. Camden 1st series lxvi. London, 1856.

Rueff, Jakob. *De conceptu et generatione hominis*. Frankfurt, 1580.

Rutherford, Samuel. *A survey of the spirituall Antichrist. Opening the secrets of Familisme and Antinomianisme*. London, 1648.

S., J. *Teratologia: Or, A Discovery of Gods Wonders*. London: Printed for Nath. Brooks at the Angell in Cornhill, 1650. Thomason E.612 [16].

Sadler, John. *The sicke womans private looking-glasse wherein methodically are handled all uterine affects, or diseases arising from the wombe; enabling women to informe the physician about the cause of their griefe*. London: Printed by Anne Griffin, for Philemon Stephens, and Christopher Meridith, at the Golden Lion in S. Pauls Church-yard, 1636. STC (2nd ed.) 21544.

The Seven Women Confessors, or a Discovery of the Seven white Divels which lived at Queen-street in Coven-garden. Viz. Katherine Wels, Susan Baker, Anne Parker, Katherine Smith, Elinor Hall, Mary Jones, Dorothy March Whose Articles are Herein Declared and their mad pranks presented to thei view of the World. Discovered by John Stockden, a Yeoman, Jan 22. 1641 London: Printed for John Smith. 1641.

The Shape of ii. Monsters. MDLxii. Imprinted at London at the Long Shop in the Pultry by John Alde. STC 11485

Sharp, Jane. *The Midwives Book or the Whole art of Midwifery Discovered*. Ed. Elaine Hoby. New York and Oxford: Oxford University Press, 1999.

Shepherd, Samuel. *The joviall crew, or The devill turn'd Ranter: being a character of the roaring Ranters of these times. / Represented in a comedie, containing a true discovery of the cursed conversations, prodigious pranks, monstrous meetings, private performances, rude revellings, garrulous greetings, impious and incorrigible deportments of a sect (lately sprung up amongst us) called Ranters. Their names sorted to their severall natures, and both lively presented in action*. London: Printed for W. Ley, 1651.

*Signes and wonders from heaven. With a true relation of a monster borne in Ratcliffe Highway,
at the signe of the three Arrows, Mistris Bullock the midwife delivering here thereof. Also shewing how a cat kitned a monster in Lombard street in London. Likewise a new discovery of
witches in Stepney parish. And how 20. witches more were executed in Suffoke this last assise.
Also how the divell came to Soffam to a farmers house in the habit of a gentlewoman on horse-
backe. With divers other strange remarkable passages.* Printed at London, By I.H. 1645.

*A speciall grace, appointed to haue been said after a banket at Yorke, vpo[n] the good nues and
Proclamacion thear, of the entraunce in to reign ouer vs, of Our Soueraign Lady Elizabeth by
the grace of God, Quene of England, Fraunce and Ireland, defendour of the faith, and in earth
the supreme hed of the church of England, and also of Ireland, in Nouember. 1558.* STC (2nd
ed.) 7599.

Speed, John. *Theatrum imperii Magnæ Britanniæ; exactam regnorum Angliæ Scotiæ Hiberniæ
et insularum adiacentium geographia[m] ob oculos ponens: vna cum comitatibus, centurijs, vr-
bibus et primarijs comitatum oppidis intra regnum Angliæ, divisis et descriptis. Opus, nuper
quidem à Iohanne Spédo cive Londinensi Anglicè conscriptum: nunc verò, à Philemone Hol-
lando, apud Coventrianos medicinæ doctore, Latinitate donatum.* Imprinted at London: Ex-
cusum [T. Snodham] apud Ioann: Sudbury a Georg: Humble, Anno cum privilegio
1616), STC 23044.

Spencer, John. *A Discourse Concerning Prophecies: Wherein the Vanity of Presages by them is
reprehended, and their true and proper Ends asserted and vindicated.* Printed by John Field
for Will Graces Bookseller, and are to be sold at his Shop over against Great S. Maries
Church in Cambridge, 1663.

———. *A Discourse Concerning Vulgar Prophecies. Wherein The Vanity of receiving them as
the certain Indications of any future Event is discovered; And some Characters of Distinction
between true and pretending Prophets are laid down.* London: Printed by F. Field for Timothy Garthwait at the Kings head in S. Pauls Church-yard, 1665.

Spinola, George. *Rules to get children by vvith handsome-faces: or, Precepts for the papists, that
get children by book; and for the extemporary sectaries, that get children without book, to consider what they have to doe, and look well before they leape. That so the children of the papists
may not have such prodigious ill-boding faces as their fathers, who became so ill physiognomied,
not only being crossed over the face in baptisme, nor the children of the sectaries, by outfacing
men that they had any originall sinne at all, but also by their ignorance in these precepts, for
the begetting of children with handsome ingenious features, and symmetrious limbes. Composed by George Spinola.* Published according to order. London: printed for T.S., 1646.

———. *Rules to get children by with handsome faces: or, Precepts for the extemporary sectaries
which preach, and pray, and get children without book to consider and look on, before they leape.
That so, their children may not have such strange, prodigious, ill-bodeing faces as their fathers,
who (unhappily) became so ill-phisnomied themselves, not only by being born before their conversion, by originall sin, and by being crost over the face in baptisme; but by the lineall ignorance of their parents too in these presepts, for begetting children of ingenuous features and symmetrious limbes. Composed by George Spinola.* London: printed for R. H., 1642. E.238[11]

*A Spirit Moving in the Women-Preachers: or, Certaine Quaeres, Vented and put forth unto this
affronted, brazen-faced, strange, new Feminine Brood. Wherein they are proved to be rash,
ignorant, ambitious, weake, vaine-glorious, prophane and proud, moved onely by the spirit of
errour.* London, 1646.

Stow, John. *The Annales of a generall chronicle of England.* Londini: impensis Thomae Adams,
1615.

———. *The Chronicles of England, from Brute vnto this present yeare of Christ. 1580. Collected by John Stow citizen of London.* Printed at London: By [Henry Bynneman for] Ralphe Newberie at the assignment of Henrie Bynneman. 1580. STC 23333.

Strange and Wonderful News of the Birth of a Monstrous Child With Two Heads and Three Arms, Which was lately Born at Attentree in the County of Meath, in Ireland. Dublin, January the 31th, 1684 London: Printed for John Smith, 1685.

The strange monster or, true news from Nottingham-shire of a strange monster born at Grasly in Nottingham-shire, three miles from Nottingham with a relation of his strange and wonderful shape, the time his mother was in travail with him, with several other things of note. Together with a brief relation of several monstrous and prodigious births which happened heretofore in this our nation. Licensed according to order. [London]: Printed by Peter Lillierap [*sic*] living in Clerkenwell-Close, 1668. STC 20863.5 10/23/47.8. All leaves cut and inlaid. Also bound with: STC 15428, STC 1791.2, Wing D602, Wing T2511.5, Wing B4610.2, and an 18th-century title.

Strange Newes. At London printed for G. Vincent and W. Blackwal and are to be sold at Guildhall gate, 1605. STC 4658.

Strange newes from Scotland, or; A Strange relation of a terrible and prodigious monster, borne to the amazement of all those that were spectators, in the kingdome of Scotland, in a village neere Edenborough, call'd Hadensworth, Septem. 14. 1647. and the words the said monster spake at its birth. Printed according the originall relation sent over to a great divine hereafter mentioned. Printed at London: By E.P. for W. Lee, 1647.

Strange newes out of Kent, of a monstrous and misshapen child, borne in Olde Sandwitch, vpon the 10. of Iulie, last, the like (for strangenes) hath neuer beene seene. Imprinted at London, By T. C[reede]. for W. Barley, and are to be sold at his shop in Gratious-street, 1609. STC 14935.

Strange Signes seene in the Aire, strange Monsters behelde on the Land, and wonderfull Prodigies both by land and sea, over, in, and about the Citie of Rosenberge in high Germany the nineteenth of Ianuarie last past. Truly translated out of the high Dutch Copie printed at Rosenberge in Germany. London: Printed by Iohn Danter, and are to bee solde by William Barley at his shop in Gratious-street neere Leaden Hall, 1594. STC 21321.

Strype, John. *Annals of the Reformation and establishment of religion and other various occurrences in the Church of England during Queen Elizabeth's happy reign, together with an appendix of original papers of state, records, and letters.* 4 v. ser. New York: Burt Franklin, 1968.

Stubbes, Phillip. *The Anatomie of Abuses.* 1583. Preface by Arthur Freeman. New York: Garland Publishing, 1973.

T. I. *A World of wonders. A Masse of Murthers. A Covie of Cosonages. Containing many of the moste notablest Wonders, horrible Murthers and detestable Cosonages that haue beene within this Land.* Imprinted at London: [By Abel Jeffes] for William Barley, to be sold at his shop in Gratiousstreat neere unto Leadenhallgate, 1595.

Trapnel, Hannah. *The cry of a stone. Or A relation of something spoken in Whitehall, by Anna Trapnel, being in the visions of God. Relating to the governors, Army, churches, ministry, universities: and the whole nation. Uttered in prayers and spiritual songs, by an inspiration extraordinary, and full of wonder. In the eleventh moneth, called January. 1653.* London Printed: [s.n.], 1654.

The true and most miraculous narrative, of a child born with two tongues, At the lower end of East-Smithfeild, in the Suburbs of London, &c. Who three dayes after his Birth, was heard plainly, and expresly to cry out, A King, a King, a King, Which it hath ever since continued, to the admiration of all that hear it. As also its being sent for by divers Personages of the Greatest Dignity, and many Honorable Ladies in the Cities of London and Westminster, who not contented to behold, and but one time to hear it, have sent their Coaches for it again, and again. Together with the many various interpretations and Constructions that every where are made of it.* Printed for R. Harper neer the Hospital Gate in Smithfield, 1659. WING T2511.5.

The true discription of a Childe with Ruffes borne in the parish of Micheham in the Countie of Surrey in the yeere of our Lord. MDLXVI . . . Imprinted at London by *John Allde and Richarde Johnes* and are to be solde at the Long Shop adioining unto S. Mildreds Churche in the Pultrie and at the litle shop adjoining to the Northwest doore of Paules Churche. Anno domini. MDLXVI the xx. of August, 1566. STC 1033.

The true discription of two monsterous Chyldren Borne at Herne in Kent. The xxvii daie of Auguste in the yere our of [sic] Lorde, MCCCCCLX. They were booth women Chyldren and were Chrystened, and lyved halfe a daye. The one departed afore the other almoste an howre. Imprinted at London in Fletestreat by Thomas Colwell: for Owen Rogers dwelling at S. Sepulchers Churchdoore [1565]. STC 6774.

A True Relation of the birth of three Monsters in the City of Namen in Flanders: As also Gods Judgement upon an unnaturall sister of the poore womans, mother of these abortive children, whose house was consumed with fire from heaven, and her selfe swallowed into the earth. All which hepned the 16. of December last. 1608. [London: Printed by Simon Stafford, for Richard Bunnian, and are to be sold at the signe of the red Lion upon London Bridge, 1609.] STC 18347.5.

A True Relation of Two Prodigious Births, The like not hapning in many Generations, the signification whereof is left to the judicious to contemplate. London: Printed by T.D. 1680.

The true reporte of the forme and shape of a monstrous childe, borne at Muche Norkesleye, a willage three myles from Colchester, in the Countye of Essex, the xxi daye of Apryll in this yeare 1562. Imprinted at London in Fletestreate nere to S. Dunstons church by Thomas Marshe, 1562. STC 12207.

Of two Woonderful Popish Monsters, to wyt, Of a Popish Asse which was found at Rome in the river of Tyber, and of a Moonkish Calfe, calved at Friberge in Misne. Which are the very foreshewings and tokens of Gods wrath, against blinde, obstinate, and monstrous Papists. Witnessed, and declared, the one by Philip Melancthon, the other by Martyn Luther. Translated out of French into English by John Brooke of Assh, next Sandwich. These bookes are to be sould in Powles Churchyard at the signe of the Parat, 1579. STC 17797.

Vicars, John. *Jehovah-Jireh. God in the Mount.* By T. Paine and M. Simmon for J. Rothwell and T. Underhill, London: 1644.

———. *Prodigies & Apparitions or Englands Warning Pieces Being a Seasonable Description by lively figures & apt illustrations of many remarkable & prodigious fore-runners apparents Predictions of God Wrath against England, if not timely prevented by true Repentence.* [London?]: 1643. Wing (2nd ed.) P3651.

———. *The Sinfulness and Unlawfulness of having or Making the Picture of Christ's Humanity. Set forth in a succint and plain discourse, and the main and most vulgar reasons and objections against this Truth clearly evinced and refuted by John Vicars. Whereunto is annexed a sweet and solid Essay or Epigram in verse, against Crucifixes and pictures of christ, by that most eminently pious and faithfull servant of christ M. William Prinne, Gentleman.* Printed at London by M.F. for John Bartlet, at the signe of the Gilt-cup in Pauls Church-yard, near S. Austin's Gate 1641.

A Vindication of those Whose Endeavour is only to make the Earth a Common Treasure, called Diggers. Or, Some Reasons given by them against the immoderate use of creatures, of the excessive community of women, called Ranting, or rather Renting. London: Printed for Giles Calvert, and are to be sold at the Black-Spread-Eagle, at the West end of Pauls, 1650. Wing 2nd ed. W3043.

A Visitation of the Diocese of Chester by John Archbishop of York, Held in the Chapter House of the Collegiate and Parish Church of Manchester 1590, with the Archbishop's Correspondence with the Clergy, ed. Rev. F. R. Raines. Printed for the Chetham Society, 1875, rept. in *Remains, Historical and Literary connected with the Palatine Counties of Lancaster and Chester,* Vol. 96. Published by the Chetham Society, Manchester: Charles Sinns and Co., 1875.

Vitry, Jacques de. *The Exempla or Illustrative Stories form the Sermones Vulgares of Jacques de Vitry.* Ed. Thomas F. Crane. New York: Burt Franklin, 1971.

Whitney, Geoffrey. *A Choice of Emblemes, and other Devises.* London: 1586. STC 25438.

Winthrop, John. *A Short Story of the Rise, reign, and ruine of the Antinomians, Familists & Libertines.* Preface by Thomas Weld (1644) in David D. Hall, ed. *The Antinomian Controversy, 1636–1638: A Documentary History.* Durham: Duke University Press, 1990.

A wonder worth the reading, or, A true and faithfull relation of a woman, now dwelling in Kentstreet, who, vpon Thursday, being the 21 of August last, was deliuered of a prodigious and monstrous child, in the presence of diuers honest, and religious women to their wonderfull feare and astonishment. London: Imprinted by William Jones, dwelling in Red-crosse-streete, 1617. STC 14935.

The Zurich Letters: comprising the correspondence of several English bishops and others. Trans. and ed. Hastings Robinson. Cambridge: Printed at the University Press, 1842.

SECONDARY SOURCES

Achinstein, Sharon. "Audiences and Authors: Ballads and the Making of English Renaissance Literary Culture." *Journal of Medieval and Renaissance Studies* 22(3) (1992): 311–26.

Amussen, Susan Dwyer. *An Ordered Society: Gender and Class in Early Modern England.* New York: Oxford University Press, 1988.

Andersen, Flemming G. "From Tradition to Print: Ballads on Broadsides." In *The Ballad as Narrative: Studies in the Ballad Traditions of England, Scotland, Germany and Denmark,* ed. Flemming G. Andersen, Otto Holzapfel, and Thomas Pettit, 39–58. Odense University Press, 1982.

Andersson, Christiane. "Popular Imagery in German Reformation Broadsheets." In *Print and Culture in the Renaissance: Essays on the Advent of Printing in Europe,* ed. Gerald P. Tyson and Sylvia S. Wagonheim, 120–50. Newark: University of Delaware Press, 1986.

Arber, E., ed. *A Transcript of the Registers of the Company of Stationers of London 1554–1640,* 5 vols. London, 1875–94.

Aston, M. *England's Iconoclasts.* Oxford: Oxford University Press, 1988.

Baldwin, F. E. *Sumptuary Legislation and Personal Regulation in England.* Baltimore: Johns Hopkins Press, 1926.

Ballantyne, J. W. *Teratogenesis: An Inquiry into the Causes of Monstrosities. History of the Theories of the Past.* Edinburgh: Oliver and Boyd, Tweeddale Court, 1897.

Barish, Jonas. *The Antitheatrical Prejudice.* Berkeley: University of California Press, 1981.

Beier, A. L. *Masterless Men: The Vagrancy Problem in England 1560–1640*. London: Methuen, 1985.

Bentwich, Helen Caroline. *History of Sandwich in Kent*. 3rd ed. [Sandwich]: H. C. Bentwich, 1980.

Berg, Christine, and Philippa Berry. "'Spiritual Whoredom': An Essay on Female Prophets in the Seventeenth Century." In *1642: Literature and Power in the Seventeenth Century*, ed. Francis Barker, et al., 37–54. Colchester: University of Essex, 1981.

Birch, Thomas, ed. *The Court and Times of James the First: Illustrated by authentic and confidential letters, from various public and private collections*. 2 vols. London: Henry Colburn, 1848.

Blackwood, R. G. *The Lancashire Gentry and the Great Rebellion 1640–60*. Manchester: Printed for the Chetham Society, 1978.

Blagden, Cyprian. "Notes on the Ballad Market in the Second Half of the Seventeenth Century." *Studies in Bibliography* 6 (1954): 161–80.

———. *The Stationers' Company: A History, 1403–1959*. Cambridge, MA: Harvard University Press, 1960.

Bossy, John. *The Development of the Family and Marriage in Europe*. Cambridge: Cambridge University Press, 1983.

Boys, William. *Collections for an History of Sandwich in Kent*. Canterbury, 1892.

Brewer, John, and John Styles, eds. *An Ungovernable People: The English and Their Law in the Seventeenth and Eighteenth Centuries*. New Brunswick, NJ: Rutgers University Press, 1980.

Brigden, Susan. *London and the Reformation*. Oxford: Clarendon, 1989.

Briggs, John, Christopher Harrison, Angus McInnes, and David Vincent. *Crime and Punishment in England: An Introductory History*. London: UCL Press, 1996.

Broxap, Ernest. *The Great Civil War in Lancashire (1642–1651)*, 2nd ed. Manchester: Manchester University Press, 1973.

Burford, E. J., and Sandra Shulman. *Of Bridles and Burnings: The Punishment of Women*. New York: St. Martin's Press, 1992.

Burke, Peter. *Popular Culture in Early Modern Europe*. New York: Harper, 1978.

Burns, William E. "'Our lot is fallen into an age of Wonders': John Spencer and the Controversy Over Prodigies in the Early Restoration." *Albion* 27(2) (Summer 1995): 237–52.

Burnett, Mark Thornton. "'Strange and Woonderfull Syghts': *The Tempest* and the Discourses of Monstrosity." *Shakespeare Survey* 50 (1997): 187–99.

Bynum, Caroline Walker. *Metamorphosis and Identity*. New York: Zone Books, 2001.

Capp, Bernard. *The Fifth Monarchy Men: A Study in Seventeenth-Century English Millenarianism*. London: Faber and Faber, 1972.

———. "Popular Culture and the English Civil War." *Journal of European Ideas* 10(1) (1989): 31–41.

Catalogue of the Thomason Tracts in the British Museum, 1640–1661. London, 1908.

Cater, F. Ives. *Northamptonshire Nonconformity 250 Years Ago*. Northampton: Archer and Goodman, 1912.

Céard, Jean. *La Nature et les prodiges: l'insolite au 16c siècle, en France*. Travaux d' Humanisme et Renaissance, 1977. Genève: Librairie Droz, 1996.

———. "The Crisis of the Science of Monsters." In *Humanism in Crisis: The Decline of the French Renaissance*, ed. Philippe Desan, 181–205. Ann Arbor: University of Michigan Press, 1991.

Charnes, Linda. *Notorious Identity: Materializing the Subject in Shakespeare.* Cambridge, MA: Harvard University Press, 1993.

Chartier, Roger. "Leisure and Sociability: Reading Aloud in Early Modern Europe." In *Urban Life in the Renaissance*, ed. Susan Zimmerman and Ronald F. E. Weissman, 103–20. Newark: University of Delaware Press, 1989.

Chaytor, Miranda. "Household and Kinship: Ryston in the Late 16th and 17th Centuries." *History Workshop Journal* 10 (1980): 25–60.

Clark, Alice. *The Working Life of Women in the Seventeenth Century.* 1919; rept. New York: A. M. Kelley, 1968.

Clark, Peter. "The Migrant in Kentish towns, 1580–1640." In *Crisis and Order in English Towns 1500–1700*, ed. Peter Clark and Paul Slack, 117–63. London: Routledge, 1972.

———. "Popular Protest and Disturbance in Kent, 1558–1640." *Economic History Review*, 2nd ser., 29(3) (1976): 365–82.

Clark, Sandra. *The Elizabethan Pamphleteers: Popular Moralistic Pamphlets 1580–1640.* London: Athlone Press, 1983.

Cohn, Norman. *The Pursuit of the Millennium: Revolutionary Millenarians and Mystical Anarchists of the Middle Ages.* 3rd ed. London: Temple Smith, 1970.

Cole, Richard G. "The Use of Reformation Woodcuts by Sixteenth-Century Printers as a Mediator Between the Elite and Popular Cultures." *Journal of Popular Culture* 21(3) (1987): 111–30.

———. "Pamphlet Woodcuts in the Communication Process of Reformation Germany." In *Pietas et Societas: New Trends in Reformation Social History*, ed. Kyle C. Sessions and Philip N. Bebb, 103–21. Kirksville, MO: Sixteenth Century Journal Publisher, 1985.

Collinson, Patrick. *The Birthpangs of Protestant England: Religious and Cultural Change in the Sixteenth and Seventeenth Centuries.* New York: Macmillan, 1988.

———. "The Elizabethan Church and the New Religion." In *The Reign of Elizabeth*, ed. Christopher Haigh. London: Macmillan, 1987.

———. *The Elizabethan Puritan Movement.* London: Jonathan Cape, 1967.

———. "From Iconoclasm to Iconophobia: The Cultural Impact of the Second English Reformation." In *The Impact of the English Reformation, 1500–1640*, ed. Peter Marshall, 278–308. London: Arnold, 1997.

Cope, Esther S. *The Handmaid of the Holy Spirit: Dame Eleanor Davies, Never Soe Mad a Ladie.* Ann Arbor: University of Michigan Press, 1992.

Coupe, William A. *The German Illustrated Broadsheet in the Seventeenth Century: Historical and Iconographical Studies*, Vol. 1. Baden-Baden: Verlag Librairie Heitz-GMBH, 1966.

Crawford, Patricia. "The Construction and Experience of Maternity in Seventeenth-century England." In *Women as Mothers in Pre-Industrial England. Essays in Memory of Dorothy McLaren*, ed. Valerie Fildes, 3–38. New York: Routledge, 1996.

Cressy, David. *Birth, Marriage, and Death: Ritual, Religion and the Life-Cycle in Tudor and Stuart England.* New York: Oxford University Press, 1997.

———. "De la Fiction dans les Archives? Ou le Monstre de 1569." *Annales E.S.C* 48 (1993): 1309–29.

———. "Kinship and Kin Interaction in Early Modern England." *Past and Present* 113 (1986): 38–69.

———. *Travesties and Transgression in Tudor and Stuart England: Tales of Discord and Dissension.* New York: Oxford University Press, 2000.

Cross, Claire. "'He-goats before the Flocks': A Note on the Part Played by Women in the

Founding of Some Civil War Churches." In *Popular Belief and Practice*, ed. G. J. Cuming and Derek Baker, 195–202. Cambridge: Cambridge University Press, 1972.

Cunnington, C. Willett, and Phillis Cunnington. *Handbook of English Costume in the Sixteenth Century*. Boston: Plays Inc., 1970.

Curtis, Mark H. "William Jones: Puritan Printer and Propagandist." *The Library* 5th sr. XIX (1964): 38–66.

Cust, Richard. "News and Politics in Early Seventeenth-Century England." *Past and Present* 112 (1986): 60–90.

Cust, Richard, and Ann Hughes, eds. "Introduction: After Revisionism." In *Conflict in Early Stuart England: Studies in Religion and Politics, 1603–1642*. London: Longman, 1989.

Daston, Lorraine. "Marvelous Facts and Miraculous Evidence in Early Modern Europe," *Critical Inquiry* 18 (Autumn 1991): 93–124.

Daston, Lorraine, and Katherine Park. "Unnatural Conceptions: The Study of Monsters in France and England." *Past and Present* 92 (1981): 20–54.

———. *Wonders and the Order of Nature 1150–1750*. New York: Zone Books, 1998.

Davenport-Hines, Richard. *Sex, Death and Punishment: Attitudes to Sex and Sexuality in Britain since the Renaissance*. London: Collins, 1990.

Davies, Godfrey. "English Political Sermons, 1603–1640." *Huntington Library Quarterly* 1 (October 1939): 1–22.

Davis, J. C. *Fear, Myth and History: The Ranters and the Historians*. Cambridge: Cambridge University Press, 1986.

Davis, Lennard. *Factual Fictions: The Origins of the English Novel*. New York: Columbia University Press, 1983.

Davis, Natalie Zemon. *Society and Culture in Early Modern France*. Stanford: Stanford University Press, 1975.

———. *Fiction in the Archives: Pardon Tales and their Tellers in Sixteenth-Century France*. Stanford, CA: Stanford University Press, 1987.

———. "The Historian and Popular Culture." In *The World and the Lamb: Popular Culture in France from the Old Regime to the Twentieth Century*, ed. Jacques Beauroy, Marc Bertrans, and Edward T. Gagan, 9–16. Anma Libri, 1977.

Davis, T. W. *Annals of Evangelical Nonconformity in the County of Essex*. London: Jackson, Walford and Hodder, 1863.

Diehl, Huston. *Staging Reform, Reforming the State Protestantism and Popular Theater in Early Modern England*. Ithaca, NY: Cornell University Press, 1997.

Dolan, Frances E. *Dangerous Familiars: Representations of Domestic Crime in England 1550–1700*. Ithaca, NY: Cornell University Press, 1994.

———. *Whores of Babylon: Catholicism, Gender, and Seventeenth-Century Print Culture*. Ithaca, NY: Cornell University Press, 1999.

Duffy, Eamon. *The Stripping of the Altars: Traditional Religion in England, 1400–1580*. New Haven, CT: Yale University Press, 1992.

Durston, Chris. "Signs and Wonders and the English Civil War." *History Today* (October 1987): 22–8.

Eire, Carlos M. N. *The War Against the Idols: The Reformation of Worship from Erasmus to Calvin*. Cambridge: Cambridge University Press, 1986.

Erickson, Amy Louise. *Women & Property in Early Modern England*. London: Routledge, 1993.

Esdaile, Arundell. "Autolycus' Pack: The Ballad Journalism of the Sixteenth Century." *The Quarterly Review* 218 (1913): 372–91.

Evenden, Doreen. "Mothers and Their Midwives in Seventeenth-century London." In *The Art of Midwifery: Early Modern Midwives in Europe*, ed. Hilary Marland, 9–26. London: Routledge, 1993.

Ewinkel, Irene. *De monstris: Deutung und Funktion von Wundergeburten auf Flugblättern im Deutschland des 16. Jahrhunderts.* Tübingen: Max Niemeyer Verlag, 1995.

Ezell, Margaret J. M. *The Patriarch's Wife: Literary Evidence and the History of the Family.* Chapel Hill: University of North Carolina Press, 1987.

Fairholt, F. W. *Costume in England: A History of Dress from the Earliest Period Until the Close of the Eighteenth Century.* 2nd ed. London: Chapman and Hall, 1860.

Ferrell, Lori Anne. "Kneeling and the Body Politic." In *Religion, Literature, and Politics in Post- Reformation England 1540–1688*, eds. Diane Hamilton and Richard Strier, 70–92. New York: Cambridge University Press, 1996.

Fildes, Valerie. *Women as Mothers in Pre-Industrial England. Essays in Memory of Dorothy McLaren.* London: Routledge, 1996.

Fishwick, Henry C. *The History of the Parish of Kirkham, in the County of Lancaster.* Printed for the Chetham Society, 1874.

Foucault, Michel. *Discipline and Punish: The Birth of the Prison.* Trans. Alan Sheridan. New York: Vintage, 1977.

———. *The Order of Things.* New York: Pantheon, 1970.

Fox, Adam. "Ballads, Libels and Popular Ridicule in Jacobean England." *Past and Present* 145 (November 1994): 47–83.

Frank, J. *The Beginnings of the English Newspaper, 1620–1660.* Cambridge, MA: Harvard University Press, 1961.

Freedberg, David. *The Power of Images: Studies in the History and Theory of Response.* Chicago: University of Chicago Press, 1989.

Friedman, Jerome. *Blasphemy, Immorality, and Anarchy: The Ranters and the English Revolution.* Athens: Ohio University Press, 1987.

Friedman, John Block. *The Monstrous Races in Medieval Art and Thought.* Cambridge, MA: Harvard University Press, 1981.

Gallagher, Lowell. *Medusa's Gaze: Casuistry and Conscience in the Renaissance.* Stanford, CA: Stanford University Press, 1991.

George, Margaret. *Women in the First Capitalist Society: Experiences in Seventeenth Century England.* Urbana: University of Illinois Press, 1988.

Gowing, Laura. "Secret Births and Infanticide in Seventeenth-Century England." *Past and Present* 156 (August 1997): 87–115.

———. *Domestic Dangers: Women, Words, and Sex in Early Modern London.* Oxford: Clarendon, 1996.

Gramsci, Antonio. *Selections from the Prison Notebooks.* Ed. Quintin Hoare and Geoffrey Nowell-Smith. New York: International Publishers, 1971.

Greaves, Richard L. *Deliver Us From Evil: The Radical Underground in Britain, 1660–1663.* New York: Oxford University Press, 1986.

Greaves, Richard L., and Robert Zaller, eds. *A Biographical Dictionary of British Radicals in the Seventeenth Century*, 3 vols. Brighton: Harvester Press, 1982–84.

Greenall, R. L. *A History of Northamptonshire.* London: Phillimore, 1979.

Greenblatt, Stephen. *Marvelous Possessions: The Wonder of the New World.* Chicago: University of Chicago Press, 1991.

Gregory, Annabel. "Witchcraft, Politics and 'Good Neighbourhood' in Early Seventeenth-Century Rye." *Past and Present* 133 (1991): 31–66.

Grundy, Isobel, and Susan Wiseman, eds. *Women, Writing, History 1640–1740.* Athens: University of Georgia Press, 1992.

Guibbory, Achsah. "Sir Thomas Browne's Allusions to Janus." *English Language Notes* 12 (1975): 269–73.

Haigh, Christopher. "The English Reformation: A Premature Birth, a Difficult Labour and a Sickly Child." *Historical Journal* 33 (1990): 449–59.

Hair, Paul, ed. *Before the Bawdy Court: Selections from Church Court and Other Records Relating to the Correction of Moral Offences in England, Scotland and New England, 1300–1800.* London: Elek, 1972.

Halasz, Alexandra. *The Marketplace of Print: Pamphlets and the Public Sphere in Early Modern England.* Cambridge: Cambridge University Press, 1997.

Hall, David. "Introduction." *Understanding Popular Culture: Europe from the Middle Ages to the Nineteenth Century,* ed. Stephen L. Kaplan. Berlin: Mouton, 1984.

Hall, David D. *Worlds of Wonder, Days of Judgement: Popular Religious Belief in Early New England.* Cambridge, MA: Harvard University Press, 1989.

———, ed. *The Antinomian Controversy, 1636–1638: A Documentary History.* Durham, NC: Duke University Press, 1990.

Hall, Stuart. "Notes on Deconstructing 'the Popular.'" *Cultural Theory and Popular Culture,* ed. John Storey, 2nd ed., 442–53. Athens: University of Georgia Press, 1998.

Hanafi, Zakiya. *The Monster in the Machine: Magic, Medicine, and the Marvelous in the Time of the Scientific Revolution.* Durham, NC: Duke University Press, 2000.

Harkness, Georgia. *John Calvin: The Man and His Ethics.* New York: Henry Holt and Co., 1931.

Harraway, Donna. "The Promises of Monsters: A Regenerative Politics for Inappropriate/d Others." In *The Cultural Studies Reader,* ed. Lawrence Grossberg, Cary Nelson, and Paula A. Treichler. New York: Routledge, 1992.

Harris, Tim, ed. *Popular Culture in England, c. 1500–1850.* New York: St. Martin's Press, 1995.

Haugaard, William P. *Elizabeth and the English Reformation: The Struggle for a Stable Settlement of Religion.* Cambridge: Cambridge University Press, 1968.

Heyd, Michael. *"So Sober and Reasonable": The Critique of Enthusiasm in the Seventeenth and Early Eighteenth Centuries.* Leiden: E. J. Brill, 1995.

Higgins, Patricia. "The Reaction of Women, with Special Reference to Petitioners." In *Politics, Religion, and the English Civil War,* ed. Brian Manning, 178–222. London: Edward Arnold Press, 1973.

Hill, Christopher. "Irreligion in the 'Puritan' Revolution." In *Radical Religion in the English Revolution,* ed. J. F. McGregor and B. Reay, 191–211. London and New York: Oxford University Press, 1984.

———. *The World Turned Upside Down: Radical Ideas During the English Revolution.* Harmondsworth: Penguin, 1972.

Hind, Arthur M. *An Introduction to a History of Woodcut With a Detailed Survey of Work Done in the Fifteenth Century.* 2 Vols. New York: Dover, 1963.

Hinds, Hilary. *God's Englishwomen: Seventeenth-Century Radical Sectarian Writing and Feminist Criticism.* Manchester: Manchester University Press, 1996.

Hobby, Elaine. "'Discourse so unsavoury': Women's Published Writings of the 1650s." In *Women, Writing, History 1640–1740,* ed. Isobel Grundy and Susan Wiseman, 16–32. Athens: University of Georgia Press, 1992.

Hodgen, Margaret. *Early Anthropology in the 16th and 17th Centuries.* Philadelphia: University of Pennsylvania Press, 1971.

Hole, Robert. "Incest, Consanguinity and a Monstrous Birth in Rural England, January 1600," *Social History* 25(2) (2000): 183–99.

Holstun, James, ed. *Pamphlet Wars: Prose in the English Revolution.* London: Frank Cass, 1992.

Holtgen, Karl Josef, "The Reformation of Images and Some Jacobean Writers on Art." In *Functions of Literature: Essays Presented to Erwin Wolff on his Sixtieth Birthday,* ed. Ulrich Broich, Theo Stemmler, and Gerd Stratmann, 119–46. Tübingen: Max Niemeyer Verlag, 1984.

Hopton, Andrew, ed. *The Declaration of John Robins and Other Writings.* London: Aporia Press, 1992.

Huet, Marie-Hélène. "Living Images: Monstrosity and Representation." *Representations* 4 (1983): 73–87.

———. *The Monstrous Imagination.* Cambridge, MA: Harvard University Press, 1993.

Ingram, Martin. *Church Courts, Sex and Marriage in England, 1570–1640.* Cambridge: Cambridge University Press, 1987.

———. "The Reformation of Manners in Early Modern England." In *The Experience of Authority in Early Modern England,* ed. Paul Griffiths, Adam Fox, and Steve Hindle, 47–88. London: St. Martin's Press, 1996.

Jackson, Mark. *New-born Child Murder: Women, Illegitimacy and the Courts in Eighteenth-century England.* Manchester: Manchester University Press, 1996.

Jackson, William A. *Records of the Court of the Stationers' Company, 1602–1640.* London: Bibliographical Society, 1957.

Jardine, Lisa. *Still Harping on Daughters: Women and Drama in the Age of Shakespeare,* 2nd ed. New York: Columbia University Press, 1989.

Jones, Ann Rosalind, and Peter Stallybrass. *Renaissance Clothing and the Materials of Memory.* Cambridge: Cambridge University Press, 2000.

Jones, Norman. *The Birth of the Elizabethan Age: England in the 1560s.* London: Blackwell, 1993.

Kantorowicz, Ernst H. *The King's Two Bodies: A Study in Mediaeval Political Theology.* Princeton, NJ: Princeton University Press, 1957.

Karlsen, Carol. *The Devil in the Shape of a Woman.* New York: Vintage, 1987.

Keeble, N. H. *Richard Baxter: Puritan Man of Letters.* Oxford: Clarendon Press, 1982.

Kenseth, Joy, ed. *The Age of the Marvelous.* Hanover, NH: Hood Museum of Art, Dartmouth College, 1991.

Knox, Ronald A. *Enthusiasm: A Chapter in the History of Religion With Special Reference to the XVII and XVIII Centuries.* New York: Oxford University Press, 1961.

Koehler, Lyle. *A Search for Power: The 'Weaker Sex' in Seventeenth-Century New England.* Urbana: University of Illinois Press, 1980.

Kunzle, David. "World Upside Down: The Iconography of a European Broadsheet Type." In *The Reversible World: Symbolic Inversion in Art and Society,* ed. Barbara A. Babcock. Ithaca, NY: Cornell University Press, 1978.

————. *The Early Comic Strip: Narrative Strips and Picture Stories in the European Broadsheet from c.1450 to 1825*. Berkeley: University of California Press, 1973.

Lake, Peter. "Defining Puritanism—Again?" In *Puritanism: Transatlantic Perspectives on a Seventeenth-Century Anglo-American Faith*, ed. Francis J. Brener, 3–29. Boston: Massachusetts Historical Society, 1993.

————. "Popular Form, Puritan Content? Two Puritan Appropriations of the Murder Pamphlet from Mid-Seventeenth-Century London." In *Religion, Culture and Society in Early Modern Britain: Essays in Honour of Patrick Collinson*, ed. Anthony Fletcher and Peter Roberts, 313–34. Cambridge: Cambridge, 1994.

————. "Anti-popery: The Structure of a Prejudice." In *Conflict in Early Stuart England: Studies in Religion and Politics, 1603–1642*, ed. Richard Cust and Ann Hughes. London: Longman, 1989.

————. "Deeds against Nature: Cheap Print, Protestantism and Murder in Early Seventeenth-Century England." *Culture and Politics in Early Stuart England*, ed. Kevin Sharpe and Peter Lake, 257–83. Stanford, CA: Stanford University Press, 1993.

Lamont, William M. *Marginal Prynne, 1600–1669*. London: Routledge & K. Paul, 1963.

Lang, Amy Schrager. *Prophetic Woman: Anne Hutchinson and the Problem of Dissent in the Literature of New England*. Berkeley: University of California Press, 1987.

Laqueur, Thomas W. "Bodies, Details, and the Humanitarian Narrative." In *The New Cultural History*, ed. Lynn Hunt, 176–204. Berkeley: University of California Press, 1989.

Laurence, Anne. "A Priesthood of She-Believers: Women and Congregations in Mid-Seventeenth-Century England." In *Women in the Church*, ed. W. J. Sheils and Diana Wood, 345–63. London: Basil Blackwell, 1990.

Leatherbarrow, Joseph Stanley. *The Lancashire Elizabethan Recusants*. Manchester: Chetham Society, 1947.

Leites, Edmund, ed. *Conscience and Casuistry in Early Modern Europe*. Cambridge: Cambridge University Press, 1988.

Levy, F. J. "How Information Spread Among the Gentry, 1550–1640." *Journal of British Studies* 21(2) (1982): 11–34.

Levy, Leonard W. *Treason Against God: A History of the Offense of Blasphemy*. New York: Schocken Books, 1981.

Lievsay, John L. "William Barley, Elizabethan Printer and Bookseller." *Studies in Bibliography* VIII (1956): 218–25.

————. "Newgate Penitents: Further Aspects of Elizabethan Pamphlet Sensationalism." *Huntington Library Quarterly* 7(1) (1943): 47–69.

Lindley, Keith. *Popular Politics and Religion in Civil War London*. Brookfield, VT: Scolar Press, 1997.

Livingston, Carole Rose, ed. *British Broadside Ballads of the Sixteenth Century: A Catalogue of the Extant Sheets and an Essay*. New York: Garland Publishing, 1991.

Llewellyn, Nigel. *The Art of Death: Visual Culture in the English Death Ritual c. 1500–1800*. London: Published in Association with the Victoria and Albert Museum by Reaktion Books, 1991.

Longden, H. I. *Northampton and Rutland Clergy from 1500*. 16 vols. Northampton, 1939–52.

Luborsky, Ruth Samson, and Elizabeth Morely Ingram. *A Guide to English Illustrated Books 1536–1603*. Tempe, AZ: Medieval and Renaissance Texts and Studies, 1998.

Luxon, Thomas H. "'Not I, but Christ': Allegory and the Puritan Self." *English Literary History* 60 (1993): 899–937.

Luther, Martin. *Luther's Works*. Ed. Jarslav Pelikan. St. Louis: Concordia, 1960.

Mack, Phyllis. *Visionary Women: Ecstatic Prophecy in Seventeenth-Century England*. Berkeley: University of California Press, 1992.

Maclean, Ian. *The Renaissance Notion of Woman*. Cambridge: Cambridge University Press, 1980.

Manning, Roger B. *Religion and Society in Elizabethan Sussex*. Leicester: Leicester University Press, 1969.

Marcus, Leah S. *Puzzling Shakespeare: Local Reading and Its Discontents*. Berkeley: University of California Press, 1988.

Marland, Hilary, ed. *The Art of Midwifery: Early Modern Midwives in Europe*. London: Routledge, 1993.

Marrus, Michael. "Folklore as an Ethnographic Source: A 'Mise au Point.'" In *The World and the Lamb: Popular Culture in France from the Old Regime to the Twentieth Century*, ed. Jacques Beauroy, Marc Bertrans, and Edward T. Gagan, 109–26. Anma Libri, 1977.

Maxwell-Stuart, P. G., ed. *The Occult in Early Modern Europe: A Documentary History*. New York: St. Martin's Press, 1999.

McArthur, E. A. "Women Petitioners and the Long Parliament." *English Historical Review* 24 (1909): 698–709.

McGregor, J. F. "The Baptists: Fount of All Heresy." In *Radical Religion in the English Revolution*, ed. J. F. McGregor and B. Reay, 24–63. London and New York: Oxford University Press, 1984.

———. "Seekers and Ranters." In *Radical Religion in the English Revolution*, ed. J. F. McGregor and B. Reay, 121–39. London and New York: Oxford University Press, 1984.

McGregor, J. F., and B. Reay, eds. *Radical Religion in the English Revolution*. Oxford: Oxford University Press, 1984.

McKerrow, R. B., ed. *A Dictionary of Printers and Booksellers in England, Scotland and Ireland, and of Foreign Printers of English Books, 1557–1640*. London: Blades, East, and Blades, 1910.

McLaren, Angus. *Reproductive Rituals: The Perception of Fertility in England from the Sixteenth Century to the Nineteenth Century*. London: Methuen, 1984.

Melling, Elizabeth, ed. *Kentish Sources IV. The Poor*. Maidstone: Kent County Council, 1964.

Miller, John. *Religion in the Popular Prints 1600–1832*. Cambridge: Chadwyck-Healey, 1986.

Milward, Peter. *Religious Controversies of the Elizabethan Age: A Survey of Printed Sources*. Lincoln: University of Nebraska Press, 1977.

———. *Religious Controversies of the Jacobean Age: A Survey of Printed Sources*. London: Scholar Press, 1978.

Morgan, Edmund S. *Visible Saints: The History of a Puritan Idea*. New York: New York University Press, 1963.

———. *The Puritan Dilemma: The Story of John Winthrop*, 2nd ed. London: Longman, 1999.

———. "The Case Against Anne Hutchinson." *New England Quarterly* 10 (December 1937): 635–49.

Morgan, John. *Godly Learning: Puritan Attitudes Toward Reason, Learning and Education 1560–1640*. Cambridge: Cambridge University Press, 1986.

Morrill, John, Paul Slack, and Daniel Woolf, eds. *Public Duty and Private Conscience in Seventeenth-Century England: Essays Presented to G. E. Aylmer.* Oxford: Clarendon Press, 1993.

Muchembled, Robert. *Popular Culture and Elite Culture in France 1400–1750.* Trans. Lydia Cochrane. 1978; Baton Rouge: Louisiana State University Press, 1985.

Myles, Anne G. "From Monster to Martyr: Re-Presenting Mary Dyer." *Early American Literature* 36(1) (2001): 1–30.

Newman, Karen. *Fashioning Femininity and English Renaissance Drama.* Chicago: University of Chicago Press, 1991.

Newman, P. R. *Royalist Officers in England and Wales, 1642–1660. A Biographical Dictionary.* New York: Garland, 1981.

Niccoli, Ottavia. *Prophecy and People in Renaissance Italy.* Trans. Lydia G. Cochrane. 1987; Princeton, NJ: Princeton University Press, 1990.

Nokes, G. D. *A History of the Crime of Blasphemy.* London: Sweet and Maxwell, 1928.

Nuttall, Geoffrey. *The Holy Spirit in Puritan Faith and Experience.* Oxford: Basil Blackwell, 1946.

O'Connell, Sheila. *The Popular Print in England 1550–1850.* London: British Museum Press, 1999.

O'Hara, Diana. "The Language of Tokens and the Making of Marriage." *Rural History* 3(1) (1992): 1–40.

Otten, Charlotte F. "Women's Prayers in Childbirth in Sixteenth Century England." *Women and Language* 16(1) (Spring 1993): 18–21.

Owst, G. R. *Literature and Pulpit in Medieval England.* Oxford: Basil Blackwell, 1961.

Paster, Gail Kern. *The Body Embarrassed: Drama and the Disciplines of Shame in Early Modern England.* Ithaca, NY: Cornell University Press, 1993.

Pateman, Carole. "Conclusion: Women's Writing, Women's Standing: Theory and Politics in the Early Modern Period." In *Women Writers and the Early Modern British Political Tradition,* ed. Hilda Smith, 363–82. Cambridge: Cambridge University Press, 1998.

Paul, Henry N. *The Royal Play of Macbeth.* New York: Macmillan, 1950.

Phillips, John. *The Reformation of Images: Destruction of Art in England 1535–1660.* Berkeley: University of California Press, 1973.

Platt, Peter, ed. *Wonders, Marvels, and Monsters in Early Modern Culture.* Newark: University of Delaware Press, 1999.

Plimpton, Ruth Talbot. *Mary Dyer: Biography of a Rebel Quaker.* Boston: Branden, 1994.

Plomer, Henry R., ed. *A Dictionary of the Booksellers and Printers Who Were at Work in England, Scotland and Ireland from 1641–1667.* London: Bibliographical Society, 1907.

Plowden, Alison. *Women All on Fire: The Women of the English Civil War.* Phoenix Mill: Sutton, 1998.

Pollard, A. W., and G. R. Redgrave, comps. *A Short-Title Catalogue of Books Printed in England, Scotland, and Ireland and of English Books Printed Abroad, 1475–1640.* London: Bibliographical Society, 1926.

Pollock, Linda A. "Embarking on a Rough Passage: The Experience of Pregnancy in Early-Modern Society." In *Women as Mothers in Pre-Industrial England: Essays in Memory of Dorothy McLaren,* ed. Valerie Fildes, 39–67. London and New York: Routledge, 1996.

Porteus, Thomas Cruddas. *A History of the Parish of Standish Lancashire.* Wigan: J. Starr & Sons, 1927.

Porterfield, Amanda. *Female Piety in Puritan New England: The Emergence of Religious Humanism.* New York: Oxford University Press, 1992.

Prior, Mary, ed. *Women in English Society, 1500–1800.* London: Methuen, 1985.

Purkiss, Diane. "Producing the Voice, Consuming the Body: Women Prophets of the Seventeenth Century." In *Women, Writing, History 1640–1740,* ed. Isobel Grundy and Susan Wiseman, 139–58. Athens: University of Georgia Press, 1992.

Razovsky, Helaine. "Popular Hermeneutics: Monstrous Children in English Renaissance Broadside Ballads." *Early Modern Literary Studies* 2(3) (1996):1–34. Available at http://purl.oclc.org/emIs/)2–3/razoball.html.

Robin, Percy Ansell. *Animal Lore in English Literature.* London: J. Murray, 1932.

Rollins, Hyder Edward. *An Analytical Index to the Ballad-Entries (1557–1709) in the Registers of the Company of Stationers in London.* Hatboro, PA: Tradition Press, 1967.

———, ed. *The Pack of Autolycus.* Cambridge, MA: Harvard University Press, 1927

———, ed. *A Pepysian Garland: Black-letter Broadside Ballads of the Years 1595–1639, Chiefly from the Collection of Samuel Pepys.* Cambridge: Cambridge University Press, 1922.

———. "The Black-Letter Broadside Ballad." *PMLA* 34 (1919): 258–339.

———. "Martin Parker, Ballad Monger." *Modern Philology* 16(9) (January 1919): 113–38.

———. "William Elderton: Elizabethan Actor and Ballad-Writer." *Studies in Philology* 17 (1920): 199–245.

Roper, Lyndal. *Oedipus and the Devil: Witchcraft, Sexuality and Religion in Early Modern Europe.* New York: Routledge, 1994.

———. *The Holy Household: Women and Morals in Reformation Augsburg.* Oxford: Clarendon, 1989.

Rowlands, Marie B. "Recusant Women, 1560–1640." In *Women in English Society 1500–1800,* ed. Mary Prior, 149–80. London: Methuen, 1985.

Rublack, Ulinka. "Pregnancy, Childbirth and the Female Body in Early Modern Germany." *Past and Present* 150 (February 1996): 84–110.

Schiesari, Juliana. "The Face of Domestication: Physiognomy, Gender Politics, and Humanism's Others." In *Women, 'Race' and Writing in the Early Modern Period,* ed. Margo Hendricks and Patricia Parker, 55–70. London: Routledge, 1994.

Schutte, Anne Jacobson. "'Such Monstrous Births': A Neglected Aspect of the Antinomian Controversy." *Renaissance Quarterly* 38(1) (1985): 85–106.

Scribner, Robert W. "The Reformation, Popular Magic and the 'Disenchantment of the World." *Journal of Interdisciplinary History* 23 (1993): 475–94.

———. *For the Sake of Simple Folk: Popular Propaganda for the German Reformation.* Cambridge: Cambridge University Press, 1981.

Seaver, P. S. *Wallington's World: A Puritan Artisan in Seventeenth Century London.* Stanford, CA: Stanford University Press, 1985.

Semonin, Paul. "Monsters in the Marketplace: The Exhibition of Human Oddities in Early Modern England." In *Freakery: The Cultural Spectacle of the Extraordinary Body,* ed. Rosemarie Garland Thomson, 69–81. New York: New York University Press, 1996.

Shaaber, M. A. *Some Forerunners of the Newspaper in England 1476–1622.* Philadelphia: University of Pennsylvania Press, 1929.

Sharpe, J. A. *Crime in Seventeenth Century England: A County Study.* Cambridge: Cambridge University Press, 1983.

Sharpe, Kevin. "Private Conscience and Public Duty in the Writings of James VI and I."

In *Public Duty and Private Conscience in Seventeenth-Century England, Essays Presented to G. E. Aylmer,* ed. John Morrill, Paul Slack, and Daniel Woolf, 77–100. Oxford: Clarendon Press, 1993.

Shaw, R. Cunliffe, and Helen G. Shaw, *The Records of the Thirty Men of the Parish of Kirkham in Lancashire.* Kendal: Titus Wilson and Son, 1930.

Sheils, W. J., and Diana Wood, eds. *Women in the Church.* Published for the Ecclesiastical History Society. London: Basil Blackwell, 1990.

Sillar, Frederick Cameron, and Ruth Mary Meylower. *Cats: Ancient and Modern.* London: Studio Vista, 1966.

Smith, Norman R. "Portent Lore and Medieval Popular Culture." *Journal of Popular Culture* 14 (1980): 47–59.

Sommerville, Johann R. "The 'New Art of Lying': Equivocation, Mental Reservation, and Casuistry." In *Public Duty and Private Conscience in Seventeenth-Century England,* ed. Morrill, Slack, and Woolf, 159–84. Oxford: Clarendon Press, 1993.

Spufford, Margaret. *Small Books and Pleasant Histories: Popular Fiction and Its Readership in Seventeenth Century England.* Cambridge: Cambridge University Press, 1981.

———. "Puritanism and Social Control?" In *Order and Disorder in Early Modern England,* ed. A Fletcher and I. Stevenson, 4–57. Cambridge: Cambridge University Press, 1985.

Spurr, John. "'Virtue, Religion and Government': The Anglican Uses of Providence." In *The Politics of Religion in Restoration England,* ed. Tim Harris, Paul Seaward, and Mark Goldie, 29–47. London: Basil Blackwell, 1990.

Starr, George. *Defoe and Casuistry.* Princeton, NJ: Princeton University Press, 1971.

———. *The Family, Sex and Marriage in England 1500–1800,* abr. ed. New York: Harper & Row, 1979.

Strong, Roy. *Henry, Prince of Wales and England's Lost Renaissance.* London: Thames and Hudson, 1986.

———. "England and Italy: The Marriage of Henry Prince of Wales." In *For Veronica Wedgwood These: Studies in 17th-Century History,* ed. R. Ollard and P. Tudor-Craig, 59–87. London: Collins, 1986.

———. *Portraits of Queen Elizabeth.* Oxford: Clarendon Press, 1963.

Thomas, Keith. *Religion and the Decline of Magic: Studies in Popular Beliefs in Sixteenth and Seventeenth Century England.* New York: Oxford University Press, 1971.

———. "Women and the Civil War Sects." *Past and Present* 13 (1958): 42–62.

———. "Cases of Conscience in Seventeenth-Century England." In *Public Duty and Private Conscience in Seventeenth-Century England,* ed. John Morrill, Paul Slack and Daniel Woolf. Oxford: Clarendon Press, 1993, 29–56.

Thomas, William J., ed. *Anecdotes and Traditions Illustrative of Early English History and Literature.* London: Printed for the Camden Society, 1839.

Thompson. C. J. S. *The Mystery and Lore of Monsters: With Accounts of some Giants, Dwarfs and Prodigies.* London: Williams & Norgate, 1930.

Todd, Dennis. *Imagining Monsters: Miscreations of the Self in Eighteenth-Century England.* Chicago: University of Chicago Press, 1995.

Torey, Michael. "'The plain devil and dissembling looks': Ambivalent Physiognomy and Shakespeare's Richard III," *English Literary Renaissance* 30(2) (2000): 123–53.

Traister, Bryce. "Anne Hutchinson's 'Monstrous Birth' and the Feminization of Antinomianism." *Canadian Review of American Studies* 27(2) (1997): 133–58.

Underdown, David. *Pride's Purge: Politics in the Puritan Revolution.* Oxford: Clarendon, 1971.

Vieira, Yara Frateschi. "Emblematic Monsters in Portuguese Pamphlets of the Eighteenth Century." *Portuguese Studies* 4 (1988): 84–99.

Waik, K. R. *Elizabethan Recusancy in Cheshire.* Printed for the Chetham Society, 1971.

Walsham, Alexandra. *Providence in Early Modern England.* Oxford: Oxford University Press, 1999.

Walton, Michael T., Robert F. Fineman, and Phyllis J. Walton, "Of Monsters and Prodigies: The Interpretation of Birth Defects in the Sixteenth Century." *American Journal of Medical Genetics* 47 (1993): 7–13.

Ward, Benedicta. *Miracles and the Medieval Mind: Theory, Record, and Event, 1000–1215.* Philadelphia: University of Pennsylvania Press, 1982.

Watt, Tessa. *Cheap Print and Popular Piety, 1550–1640.* Cambridge: Cambridge University Press, 1991.

Wear, Andrew. "Puritan Perceptions of Illness in Seventeenth Century England." In *Patients and Practitioners Lay Perceptions of Medicine in Pre-industrial Society,* ed. Roy Porter, 55–99. Cambridge: Cambridge University Press, 1985.

Weldon, Anthony. *The Court and Character of James I.* London: G. Smeetin, 1817.

Whiting, C. E. *Studies in English Puritanism from the Restoration to the Revolution, 1660–1688.* New York: Macmillan, 1931.

Williams, Ethyn Morgan. "Women Preachers in the Civil War." *Journal of Modern History* 1 (1929): 561–69.

Wills, Gary. *Witches and Jesuits: Shakespeare's Macbeth.* New York: Oxford University Press, 1995.

Willson, David Harris. *James VI and I.* London: Jonathan Cape, 1959.

Wilson, Dudley. *Signs and Portents Monstrous Births from the Middle Ages to the Enlightenment.* New York: Routledge, 1993.

Wiltenburg, Joy. *Disorderly Women and Female Power in the Street Literature of Early Modern England and Germany.* Charlottesville: University Press of Virginia, 1992.

Winship, Michael. *Seers of God: Puritan Providentialism in the Restoration and Early Enlightenment.* Baltimore: John Hopkins University Press, 1996.

Winsser, Johann. "Mary Dyer and the 'Monster' Story." *Quaker History* 79(1) (1990): 20–34.

Wittkower, Rudolf. "Marvels of the East: A Study in the History of Monsters." *Journal of the Warburg and Courtauld Institute* 5 (1942): 159–97.

Wood, James O. "Woman with a Horn." *Huntington Library Quarterly* 29 (1966): 295–300.

Wood, Thomas. *English Casuistical Divinity During the Seventeenth Century.* London: Billing and Sons, 1952.

Woolrych, Austin. *Britain in Revolution, 1625–1660.* Oxford: Oxford University Press, 2002.

Worden, Blair. "Providence and Politics in Cromwellian England." *Past and Present* 101 (1985): 55–99.

Wright, Louis B. *Middle-Class Culture in Elizabethan England.* Chapel Hill: University of North Carolina Press, 1935.

———. "Propaganda against James I's 'Appeasement' of Spain." *Huntington Library Quarterly* 6(2) (1943): 149–72.

———. "William Perkins: Elizabethan Apostle of 'Practical Divinity.'" *Huntington Library Quarterly* 3(2) (1940): 171–96.

Wright, Thomas. *A History of Caricature and Grotesque in Literature and Art.* London: Virtue Brothers, 1865.

Wrightson, Keith. *English Society 1580–1680*. New Brunswick, NJ: Rutgers University Press, 1984.

———. "Two Concepts of Order: Justices, Constables and Jurymen in Seventeenth-Century England." In *An Ungovernable People: The English and Their Law in the Seventeenth and Eighteenth Centuries*, ed. John Brewer and John Styles, 21–46. New Brunswick, NJ: Rutgers University Press, 1980.

Würzbach, Natascha. *The Rise of the English Street Ballad, 1550–1650*. Trans. Gayna Walls. Cambridge: Cambridge University Press, 1990.

Yonge, Walter. *The Diary of Walter Yonge, Justice of the Peace and MP for Honiton, 1604–1628*, ed. George Roberts. London: Camden Society, 1848.

Yule, George. *The Independents in the English Civil War*. Cambridge: Cambridge University Press, 1958.

Index

Page numbers in *italics* refer to figures and illustrations.